PATTERN-ORIENTED SOFTWARE ARCHITECTURE

PATTERN-ORIENTED SOFTWARE ARCHITECTURE

A Pattern Language for Distributed Computing

Volume 4

Frank Buschmann,
Siemens, Munich, Germany

Kevlin Henney,
Curbralan, Bristol, UK

Douglas C. Schmidt,
Vanderbilt University, Tennessee, USA

BICENTENNIAL
1807
WILEY
2007
BICENTENNIAL

John Wiley & Sons, Ltd

Other Wiley Editorial Offices

John Wiley & Sons Inc., 111 River Street, Hoboken, NJ 07030, USA

Jossey-Bass, 989 Market Street, San Francisco, CA 94103-1741, USA

Wiley-VCH Verlag GmbH, Boschstr. 12, D-69469 Weinheim, Germany

John Wiley & Sons Australia Ltd, 42 McDougall Street, Milton, Queensland 4064, Australia

John Wiley & Sons (Asia) Pte Ltd, 2 Clementi Loop #02-01, Jin Xing Distripark, Singapore 129809

John Wiley & Sons Canada Ltd, 6045 Freemont Blvd, Mississauga, Ontario, L5R 4J3, Canada

Wiley also publishes its books in a variety of electronic formats. Some content that appears
in print may not be available in electronic books.

British Library Cataloguing in Publication Data

A catalogue record for this book is available from the British Library

ISBN-13: 978-0-470-05902-9 (hbk)

Typeset in 10/13 Bookman-Light by Laserwords Private Limited, Chennai, India

Printed in the UK

For Anna, Bebé[†], and Martina

Frank Buschmann

For Carolyn, Stefan, and Yannick

Kevlin Henney

For Lori, Bronson, Mom, and Dad

Douglas C. Schmidt

---

† Bebé, July 3, 1999

Table of Contents

Foreword

The patterns movement has been around for over a decade now, and has gone through the usual cycle of inflated expectations, backlash, and quiet acceptance. Frank, Doug, and Kevlin have been there the whole time, lauded and scoffed at, but above all quietly collecting good ideas from the field and describing them. The POSA series of books is rightly regarded as one of the most solid elements in the patterns literature, and every volume has a space in my library.

Earlier POSA volumes were traditional patterns books, describing patterns in a range of specific areas, mostly with patterns that hadn't been written up before. This book is different. Distributed Computing is a very wide topic and even the patterns we've captured so far is far more than would fit in a single volume. Indeed they are spread over multiple books, both within and outside the POSA series. This book's mission is to pull these patterns together. As a result you've got many more patterns here than you'd usually find, and consequentially a much terser description. Some of the patterns described here aren't primarily about distribution, but have some relevance for distributed system work. As a result the descriptions in this book highlight that usage, summarizing a pattern in a distributed systems context.

This book is also about more than the individual patterns—it's also about how they relate. Any system contains multiple patterns used together, but I for one find it harder to talk about inter-relationships than the individual patterns. A book like this cannot dodge this question, so here you'll find a lot of advice on how to combine patterns with distribution.

Distribution is a hard problem and often causes trouble. Indeed I'm often quoted for my tongue-in-cheek First Law of Distributed Object Design: 'Don't distribute your objects.' I wrote my first law for a good reason—distribution makes software harder, and as a result I always recommend avoiding it when you can. But however great my desire to question every distribution boundary, the reality is that distribution is an essential part of many software systems. And since distribution is hard, it's particularly important to take care over its design—which is why this book is also an important addition to a developer's library.

Martin Fowler

About This Book

Distributed computing is connecting the world and leveling playing fields [Fri06]. The ubiquity of the Web and e-commerce today exemplify a common motivation for distributed computing: the ability to connect to and access vast quantities of geographically dispersed information and services. The popularity of instant messaging and chat rooms on the Internet underscores another common motivation: staying connected to family, friends, colleagues, and customers. Other motivators for distributed computing include enhancing performance, scalability, and fault tolerance, as well as reducing costs by sharing expensive hardware and peripherals.

Given the importance of distributed computing in our professional and personal lives, many patterns in the software literature focus on this topic [POSA1] [POSA2] [POSA3] [Lea99] [VSW02] [VKZ04] [HoWo03] [PLoPD1] [PLoPD2] [PLoPD3] [PLoPD4] [PLoPD5]. Unfortunately, many of these patterns are described in relative isolation, referencing few other patterns, most of which are in the same publication. Despite the utility of each individual pattern, there is no holistic view of distributed computing that emphasizes how relevant patterns complete and complement each other. Building complex distributed systems therefore remains largely a dark art mastered only by a few wizards and gurus.

To provide a more holistic view, this book—the fourth volume of the *Pattern-Oriented Software Architecture* (POSA) series—describes a single pattern language that links many patterns relevant to distributed computing. Each pattern in this language either deals directly with distributed computing, or plays an important supporting role in that context. Our pattern language thus provides a guide to—and a communication vehicle for—the best practices in key areas of distributed computing.

Intended Audience

Our focus is on the design and implementation of software for distributed computing systems. The main audience for this book is therefore professional software architects or advanced students who are involved in developing software for distributed computing systems, both designing new applications and improving and refactoring existing ones. Our pattern language presents a rich set of patterns aimed at helping architects to create sustainable designs for distributed systems, and which address their requirements thoughtfully and professionally.

A secondary audience for this book is application developers who use component and communication middleware in their professional work. Our pattern language provides developers with an overview of the current state-of-the-practice in designing distributed systems, so that they can better understand how to use middleware effectively. A third group who can benefit from our pattern language is project and product managers. The language can give managers a deeper understanding of the essential capabilities of systems whose development they are leading, and provide a useful vocabulary for communicating with software architects and developers.

We do not however intend end-users or customers to use our pattern language directly. While judicious use of real-world metaphors might make the material accessible to this audience, it would require an alternative presentation of the language. Moreover, the book is not intended as a general tutorial on distributed computing. Although we discuss many aspects of this subject, and include an extensive glossary, readers need prior familiarity with core distributed computing concepts and mechanisms such as deadlock, transactions, synchronization, scheduling, and consensus. Additional information on topics related to distributed computing, such as the design of networking protocols and operating systems, can be found in the references.

Structure and Content

This book is arranged in three parts: some concepts, a story, and the pattern language itself.

Part I, *Some Concepts*, introduces the context of the book: the core pattern concepts necessary for an understanding of the book, an overview of the benefits and challenges of distributed computing, a summary of technologies for supporting distribution, and an introduction to our pattern language.

Part II, *A Story*, describes how a real-world process control system for warehouse management was designed using our pattern language for distributed computing. The story focuses on three areas of this software system: its baseline architecture, its communication middleware, and its warehouse topology representation.

Part III, *The Language*, forms the main part of the book. It contains a pattern language for distributed computing that addresses the following technical topics relevant to the construction of distributed systems:

- Specifying an initial software baseline architecture
- Understanding communication middleware
- Event demultiplexing and dispatching
- Interface partitioning
- Component partitioning
- Application control
- Concurrency
- Synchronization
- Object interaction
- Adaptation and extension
- Modal behavior
- Resource management
- Database access.

Each chapter introduces the topic area it addresses, summarizes key challenges, and then presents a set of patterns that help master these challenges. In total, our pattern language for distributed computing contains 114 patterns and connects to more than 150 patterns presented in other publications. It is thus one of the largest—if not *the* largest—software pattern language documented to date.

Although distributed computing is the language's focus, many parts of it have broader applicability. For example, most applications must be adaptable and extensible in some way, and each software system needs well-designed interfaces and components. For selected technical areas, our pattern language can therefore serve as a general guide to the best practices in modern software development, and is therefore not limited to distributed computing.

The book ends with a short reflection on our pattern language for distributed computing, a glossary of frequently used terms, an extensive list of references to work in the field, a pattern index, a general subject index, and an index that lists everyone who helped us shape the book.

There are undoubtedly properties and patterns of distributed systems that we have omitted, or which will emerge over time through the application and extension of the pattern language in practice. If you have comments, constructive criticism, or suggestions for improving the style and content of this book, please send them to us via electronic mail to siemens-patterns@cs.uiuc.edu. Guidelines for subscription can be found on the patterns home page at http://hillside.net/patterns/. This link also provides an important source of information on many aspects of patterns, such as available and forthcoming books, conferences on patterns, papers on patterns, and so on.

Acknowledgments

It is a pleasure for us to thank the many people who supported us in creating this book, either by sharing their knowledge with us or by reviewing earlier drafts of its various parts.

Champion review honors go to Michael Kircher, our shepherd, who reviewed all our material in depth, focusing on its correctness, completeness, consistency, and quality. Michael's feedback significantly increased the quality of the material in this book.

In addition, we presented parts of the language at three EuroPLoP pattern conferences, and also to several distribution and pattern experts. Ademar Aguimar, Steve Berczuk, Alan O'Callaghan, Ekatarina Chtcherbina, Jens Coldewey, Richard Gabriel, Ian Graham, Prashant Jain, Nora Koch, Doug Lea, Klaus Marquardt, Andrey Nechypurenko, Kristian Sørensen, James Siddle, Michael Stal, Steve Vinoski, Markus Völter, Oliver Vogel, and Uwe Zdun provided us with extensive feedback, which led to many minor—and also some major—revisions of the language and its presentation.

Many thanks go to Mai Skou Nielsen, who took the photos of Kevlin and Frank when they met at the JAOO 2006 conference in Aarhus, Denmark. Anton Brøgger helped locate details about the photo we present in the chapter on interface partitioning patterns. Publicis Kommunikationsagentur GmbH and Lutz Buschmann permitted us to use photos from their collections in this book.

Special thanks go to Lothar Borrmann and Reinhold Achatz for their managerial support and backing at the software engineering labs of Corporate Technology of Siemens AG, Munich, Germany.

Very special thanks go to our editor, Sally Tickner, our former editor Gaynor Redvers-Mutton, and everyone else at John Wiley & Sons who made it possible to publish this book. It was Gaynor who convinced us to write this POSA volume despite heavy loads in our daily work as software professionals. Sally, in turn, had an enormous amount of patience with us during the years we spent completing the manuscript. Very special thanks also go to Steve Rickaby, of

WordMongers Ltd, our copy editor, for enhancing our written material. This is the fourth POSA book fostered by Steve, and we look forward to working with him on forthcoming volumes.

Last but not least, we thank our families for their patience and support during the writing of this book!

About The Authors

Frank Buschmann

Frank Buschmann is Senior Principal Engineer at Siemens Corporate Technology in Munich, Germany. His research interests include object technology, software architecture, product lines, model-driven software development, and patterns. He has published widely in all these areas, most visibly in his co-authorship of the first two POSA volumes [POSA1] [POSA2], and the last two POSA volumes, this book and [POSA5]. Frank was a member of the ANSI C++ standardization committee X3J16 from 1992 to 1996, initiated the first EuroPLoP conference in 1996, co-edited several books on patterns [PLoPD3] [SFHBS06], and serves as an editor of the Wiley Series in Software Design Patterns. In his development work at Siemens, Frank has led architecture and implementation efforts for several large-scale industrial software projects, including business information, industrial automation, and telecommunication systems.

When not at work Frank spends most of his time enjoying life with his wife Martina and daughter Anna, having fun riding his horse Eddi, watching the time go by in Munich beer gardens, getting excited when watching his favorite soccer team Borussia Dortmund, dreaming when listening to a performance at the Munich opera, and relaxing with rare Scotch single malts before bedtime.

Kevlin Henney

Kevlin Henney is an independent consultant based in Bristol, UK. His work involves teaching, mentoring, and practicing across his areas of interest, which include programming languages and techniques, software architecture, patterns, and agile development. His clients range from global firms to smaller start-ups that are involved in the worlds of systems software, telecommunications, embedded systems, middleware development, business information, and finance.

Kevlin is a regular speaker at software conferences, and has also been involved with the organization of many conferences, including EuroPLoP. He has been involved with the C++ standard through the BSI and ISO, as well other language standardization efforts. Kevlin is also known for his writing, which has included conference papers and regular (and irregular) columns for many publications, including *C++ Report, C/C++ Users Journal, Java Report, JavaSpektrum, Application Development Advisor, The Register, EXE,* and *Overload.*

In what passes for spare time, Kevlin enjoys spending time with Carolyn, his wife, and Stefan and Yannick, their two sons. This takes in Lego, toy fixing, reading, and the odd beer or glass of wine.

Douglas C. Schmidt

Doug Schmidt is a Professor of Computer Science and Associate Chair of the Computer Science and Engineering program at Vanderbilt University, Nashville, Tennessee, USA. His research focuses on patterns and pattern languages, optimization principles, and empirical analysis of techniques that facilitate the development of quality of service (QoS)-enabled component middleware and model-driven engineering tools that support distributed real-time and embedded systems.

Doug is an internationally recognized expert on patterns, object-oriented frameworks, real-time middleware, modeling tools, and open-source development. He has published over 300 papers in top technical journals and conferences, has co-authored books on patterns [POSA2] and C++ network programming [SH02] [SH03], and has also co-edited several popular books on patterns [PLoPD1] and frameworks [FJS99a] [FJS99b]. In addition to his academic research, Doug has led the development of ACE, TAO, CIAO, and CoSMIC, which are widely used open-source middleware frameworks and model-driven engineering tools that contain a rich set of reusable components, implemented using the patterns presented in this book.

In his rare spare time, Doug enjoys spending time with his wife Lori and their son Bronson, as well as weight-lifting, guitar playing, debating world history and politics, and driving Chevy Corvettes.

Guide To The Reader

You can have it all. You just can't have it all at once.

Oprah Winfrey

This book is structured so that you can read it in various ways. The most straightforward way is to read it from cover-to-cover. If you know where you want to go, however, you can choose your own route through the book. In this case, the following hints can help you decide which topics to focus on and the order in which to read them.

Introduction to Patterns and Pattern Languages

This book presents a distributed computing *pattern language*, which is a family of interrelated patterns that define a process for systematically resolving problems that arise when developing software for distributed systems. We designed the book to help you use these patterns in your daily software development activities, to create working, sustainable software architectures for distributed systems. It is not a comprehensive tutorial *about* patterns and pattern languages in general, however, since we assume that you are familiar with both concepts.

If this book is your initial exposure to patterns, we suggest you first read the introduction to patterns in *A System of Patterns* [POSA1] and *Design Patterns* [GoF95]. Both books explore the fundamental concepts and terminology related to patterns for software architectures and designs. If you are familiar with patterns, but not with pattern languages, we recommend you read Chapter 1, *On Patterns and Pattern Languages*, and the white paper on *Software Patterns* by James O. Coplien [Cope96], which outline the concept of pattern languages in enough detail to allow you to benefit from the distributed computing pattern language this book. Both the above briefly also explore advanced aspects of the pattern concept that go beyond the fundamental ideas presented in [POSA1] and [GoF95].

Introduction to Distributed Computing

This book assumes that you are familiar with the key concepts and mechanisms of distributed computing. Chapter 2, *On Distributed Systems*, describes briefly the benefits and challenges of distributed computing and summarizes technologies for supporting distribution, but does not discuss distributed computing and distributed systems in detail. The chapter is intended to provide the overall theme of the book: to achieve the benefits of distributed computing, you must explicitly and thoughtfully address the challenges associated with it, guided by patterns in our language.

If you need more background information on distributed computing, we recommend *Distributed Systems: Principles and Paradigms* by Andrew S. Tanenbaum and Maarten van Steen [TaSte02] and *Reliable Distributed Systems* by Ken Birman [Bir05].

Introduction to the Pattern Language for Distributed Computing

Before you start reading all or selected patterns in our pattern language, we suggest you read Chapter 3, *On the Pattern Language*. This chapter introduces you to our language as a whole, focusing on:

- Its intent, scope, and audience.

- The general structure of the language, the key topics and challenges in distributed computing it addresses, and the concrete patterns it contains.

- The pattern form and notation we use to describe and illustrate the patterns in the language.

The chapter also serves as a general map to the pattern language, so that you will know where you are when reading a particular pattern or set of patterns. This map helps to keep you from losing the forest for the trees when reading specific details on each pattern.

The Pattern Language in Action

Part II of this book, *A Story*, presents a concrete example of how our pattern language for distributed computing can be applied in practice on a warehouse management process control system. Through the story of the construction of a real-world system we illustrate how our pattern language for distributed computing can inform the architectures and developers of high-quality software systems. If you learn best by example, we recommend you to read the story before you read the pattern language in depth, although the story also works well when read after the language. The story demonstrates how our pattern language can support the creation and understanding of:

- *Baseline architectures* for distributed systems that effectively partition their functional and infrastructure responsibilities, and enable the systems to meet their quality of service requirements.

- *Communication middleware* that allows the components of a distributed system to interact with one another efficiently, robustly, and portably.

- The detailed design of concrete components in a distributed system that support their assigned responsibilities and meet their requirements.

Although the story is self-contained, the best way to digest it is to read a specific section until the fundamental solution statement for the problem addressed in that section is described. At this point, we recommend you read the pattern synopsis in Part III if you are not familiar with it. Once you are comfortable with your understanding of the pattern, continue reading the story to see how the chosen pattern is applied in the warehouse management system, and consider which alternative patterns were not selected, and why.

The Pattern Language in Detail

Part III of the book, *The Language*, contains the pattern language for distributed computing that addresses key technical topics relevant to the construction of distributed systems. Here are some ways to read this material:

- *Start-to-finish.* The technical topics covered by the language and the patterns that address them are (roughly) presented in their order of relevance and application when building distributed systems.

- *Topic-wise.* If you are interested in a specific technical topic, such as the partitioning of components, you can read the corresponding chapter of the language. An introduction lists and discusses the challenges associated with the technical concerns, introduces the patterns that help master these challenges, and contrasts and compares them regarding their commonalities and differences. The condensed summaries of the patterns themselves, the main part of the chapter, follows this introduction.

- *Pattern-wise.* Finally, if you are interested in a specific pattern, you can use the inner front cover or the index to locate it in the language and read it directly.

The pattern summaries do not address detailed implementation issues, such as how a pattern is realized in a specific programming language or on a specific middleware platform. Each pattern summary presents and discusses the essential problem and the forces the pattern addresses, the key solution it embodies, and the consequences it introduces. In addition, each pattern is linked with all other patterns of the language that help implement it, as well as with other patterns whose implementation it can support. Throughout this book, where a pattern from the language is mentioned, it is followed by its page reference in parentheses. If you are interested in specific realization details, we recommend that you consult the pattern's original source(s), which we reference for each pattern. Throughout this book, where a pattern from the language is mentioned, it is followed by its page reference in parentheses.

Patterns described in this book

From Mud To Structure: DOMAIN MODEL (182), LAYERS (185), MODEL-VIEW-CONTROLLER (188), PRESENTATION-ABSTRACTION-CONTROL (191), MICROKERNEL (194), REFLECTION (197), PIPES AND FILTERS (200), SHARED REPOSITORY (202), BLACKBOARD (205), and DOMAIN OBJECT (208).

Distribution Infrastructure: MESSAGING (221), MESSAGE CHANNEL (224), MESSAGE ENDPOINT (227), MESSAGE TRANSLATOR (229), MESSAGE ROUTER (231), BROKER (237), CLIENT PROXY (240), REQUESTOR (242), INVOKER (244), CLIENT REQUEST HANDLER (246), SERVER REQUEST HANDLER (249), and PUBLISHER-SUBSCRIBER (234).

Event Demultiplexing and Dispatching: REACTOR (259), PROACTOR (262), ACCEPTOR-CONNECTOR (265), and ASYNCHRONOUS COMPLETION TOKEN (268).

Interface Partitioning: EXPLICIT INTERFACE (281), EXTENSION INTERFACE (284), INTROSPECTIVE INTERFACE (286), DYNAMIC INVOCATION INTERFACE (288), PROXY (290), BUSINESS DELEGATE (292), FACADE (294), COMBINED METHOD (296), ITERATOR (298), ENUMERATION METHOD (300), and BATCH METHOD (302).

Component Partitioning: ENCAPSULATED IMPLEMENTATION (313), WHOLE-PART (317), COMPOSITE (319), MASTER-SLAVE (321), HALF-OBJECT PLUS PROTOCOL (324), and REPLICATED COMPONENT GROUP (326).

Application Control: PAGE CONTROLLER (337), FRONT CONTROLLER (339), APPLICATION CONTROLLER (341), COMMAND PROCESSOR (343), TEMPLATE VIEW (345), TRANSFORM VIEW (347), FIREWALL PROXY (349), and AUTHORIZATION (351).

Concurrency: HALF-SYNC/HALF-ASYNC (359), LEADER/FOLLOWERS (362), ACTIVE OBJECT (365), MONITOR OBJECT (368).

Synchronization: GUARDED SUSPENSION (380), FUTURE (382), THREAD-SAFE INTERFACE (384), DOUBLE-CHECKED LOCKING (386), STRATEGIZED LOCKING (388), SCOPED LOCKING (390), THREAD-SPECIFIC STORAGE (392), COPIED VALUE (394), and IMMUTABLE VALUE (396).

Object Interaction: OBSERVER (405), DOUBLE DISPATCH (408), MEDIATOR (410), MEMENTO (414), CONTEXT OBJECT (416), DATA TRANSFER OBJECT (418), COMMAND (412), and MESSAGE (420).

Adaptation and Extension: BRIDGE (436), OBJECT ADAPTER (438), INTERCEPTOR (444), CHAIN OF RESPONSIBILITY (440), INTERPRETER (442), VISITOR (447), DECORATOR (449), TEMPLATE METHOD (453), STRATEGY (455), NULL OBJECT (457), WRAPPER FACADE (459), EXECUTE-AROUND OBJECT (451), and DECLARATIVE COMPONENT CONFIGURATION (461).

Object Behavior: OBJECTS FOR STATES (467), METHODS FOR STATES (469), and COLLECTIONS FOR STATES (471).

Resource Management: OBJECT MANAGER (492), CONTAINER (488), COMPONENT CONFIGURATOR (490), LOOKUP (495), VIRTUAL PROXY (497), LIFECYCLE CALLBACK (499), TASK COORDINATOR (501), RESOURCE POOL (503), RESOURCE CACHE (505), LAZY ACQUISITION (507), EAGER ACQUISITION (509), PARTIAL ACQUISITION (511), ACTIVATOR (513), EVICTOR (515), LEASING (517), AUTOMATED GARBAGE COLLECTION (519), COUNTING HANDLE (522), ABSTRACT FACTORY (525), BUILDER (527), FACTORY METHOD (529), and DISPOSAL METHOD (531).

Database Access: DATABASE ACCESS LAYER (538), DATA MAPPER (540), ROW DATA GATEWAY (542), TABLE DATA GATEWAY (544), and ACTIVE RECORD (546).

I Some Concepts

*Language is a city to the building of which
every human being brought a stone.*

Ralph Waldo Emerson

The first part of this book provides the context for our pattern language for distributed computing. We outline the concepts of patterns and pattern languages briefly, introduce the benefits and challenges of distributed computing, and provide an overview of, and introduction to, the pattern language itself.

This book focuses on patterns and a pattern language for distributed computing. To understand these patterns and the language, and to apply it successfully when building production distributed systems, knowledge of the relevant concepts in patterns and distributed computing, as well as of available distribution technologies, is both helpful and necessary. In addition, using the pattern language effectively in development projects requires you to understand its general scope, structure, content, and presentation.

The first part of the book therefore provides an overview of these concepts, and also provides an overview of our pattern language for distributed computing.

- Chapter 1, *On Patterns and Pattern Languages*, outlines all aspects of the pattern and pattern language concepts that are relevant for understanding our pattern language for distributed computing. We introduce the fundamental concept of patterns, discuss core properties of this concept, and show how patterns can be connected to form *pattern languages*, networks of patterns that work together systematically to address a set of related and interdependent software development concerns.

- Chapter 2, *On Distributed Systems*, provides an overview of the key benefits and challenges of building distributed systems, and outlines which of those challenges are addressed by various generations of distribution technologies, how the technologies address the challenges, and which remain unresolved and must be addressed by the architectures of applications in distributed systems.

- Chapter 3, *On the Pattern Language*, introduces our pattern language for distributed computing. We address the language's intent and scope to define its general applicability. An overview of the thirteen problem areas and 114 patterns illustrates the concrete structure and scope of the language. Information is given about the language's presentation, such as the pattern form and notations used, along with hints about its use to support applications in production development projects.

The three chapters in this part set the context for the entire book: the pattern story about a process control system for warehouse management that we tell in Part II, *A Story*, and the pattern language itself, in Part III, *The Language*.

1 On Patterns and Pattern Languages

Neither can embellishment of language be found without arrangement and expression of thoughts, nor can thoughts be made to shine without the light of language.

Marcus Tullius Cicero, Roman stateman, orator, and philosopher, 106–43 BC

In this chapter we introduce patterns briefly, including their history, along with a number of pattern concepts. We examine the anatomy of a pattern, what it offers, and what drives it. We explore the relationships we often find between patterns. We conclude with a discussion of pattern languages, what they are, and how they can be presented and used.

1.1   Patterns Introduced

From a design perspective, software is often thought of in terms of its parts: functions, source files, modules, objects, methods, classes, packages, libraries, components, services, subsystems, and so on. These all represent valid views of the different kinds and scales of units of composition with which developers work directly. These views focus on the parts, however, and de-emphasize the broader relationships and the reasoning that make a design what it is. In contrast, patterns have become a popular and complementary way of describing and evolving software designs, capturing and naming proven and common techniques. They emphasize the *why*, *where*, and *how* of designs, not just the *what*.

A pattern documents a recurring problem–solution pairing within a given context. A pattern, however, is more than either just the problem or just the solution structure: it includes both the problem and the solution, along with the rationale that binds them together. A problem is considered with respect to conflicting forces, detailing why the problem *is* a problem. A proposed solution is described in terms of its structure, and includes a clear presentation of the consequences—both benefits and liabilities—of applying the solution.

The recurrence of patterns is important—hence the term *pattern*—as is the empirical support for their designation as patterns. Capturing the commonality that exists in designs found in different applications allows developers to take advantage of knowledge they already possess, applying familiar techniques in unfamiliar applications. Of course, by any other name this is simply 'experience.' What takes patterns beyond personal experience is that patterns are named and documented, intended for distilling, communicating, and sharing architectural knowledge.

From Building Architecture to Software Architecture

Although patterns are now popular and relatively widespread in the world of software development, they originated in the physical world of building rather than the virtual world of software. Throughout the 1960s and 1970s the architect Christopher Alexander and his colleagues identified the concept of patterns for capturing architectural decisions and arrangements [Ale79] [AIS77]. In particular, they wanted to focus on patterns that were 'whole'—proven solutions drawn from experience that helped to improve the quality of life for people whose environment could be shaped by such patterns. Identifying architectural patterns was a response to the perceived dysfunctionality of many popular but unsuccessful trends and practices in contemporary building architecture.

The patterns they documented were combined as a coherent set, a *pattern language* that embraced different levels of scale—the city, the neighborhood, the home—with a connected view of how to apply one pattern in the presence of another. This approach first made its way into software in the form of a handful of user-interface design patterns by Kent Beck and Ward Cunningham [BeCu87], which included suggestions of a larger pattern language for object-oriented programming. Related ideas emerged over the following years, from Jim Coplien's book on C++ idioms and styles [Cope92] to Erich Gamma's thesis on framework design [Gam92], and Bruce Andersen's vision of a *Handbook of Software Architecture*. Following this groundswell of interest and convergence of thinking, the Gang-of-Four's[1] seminal *Design Patterns* book [GoF95] was published.

In addition to the widespread interest in software patterns, a whole community has sprung up focusing on collecting and documenting patterns, improving them through shepherding and writer's workshops. Many patterns have been published online, in journals, and in books following the early work. One series of books has been the *Pattern Language of Program Design* series [PLoPD1] [PLoPD2] [PLoPD3] [PLoPD4] [PLoPD5], which are distillations from the PLoP conferences held around the world. Another is the *Pattern-Oriented Software Architecture* volumes. The first volume, *A System of Patterns* [POSA1], was complementary to *Design Patterns* in that some of its patterns built on or extended the Gang-of-Four patterns. It was also complementary in the sense that it focused more explicitly on different levels of scale in software architecture, with an emphasis on large-scale systems. The second volume in the series, *Patterns for Concurrent and Networked Objects* [POSA2], and the third, *Patterns for Resource Management*

---

1 The 'Gang of Four,' as they and their book have become known, are Erich Gamma, Richard Helm, Ralph Johnson, and the late John Vlissides.

[POSA3], explored specific topics of architecture—particularly concurrency and networked applications—in greater detail. The fourth volume, *A Pattern Language for Distributed Computing*, is in your hands.

1.2 Inside Patterns

Consider the following situation. You check the cupboard: it's bare. You check the refrigerator: the only thing going on is the light. It is therefore time to go shopping—you need milk, juice, coffee, pizza, fruit, and many of the other major food types. You go to the supermarket, enter, find the milk, pick some up, pay for the it, return home, and put the milk in the fridge. You then go back to the supermarket, enter, find the juice, pick some up, pay for it, return home, and put the juice in the fridge. Repeat as necessary, until you have everything you need.

Although shopping in this way is possible, it is not a particularly effective approach—even if the supermarket is next door to you. There are wiser ways to spend your time. Significant performance improvements will not come about from tweaks and micro-optimizations, such as leaving the front door unlocked, leaving the fridge door open, using cash rather than card. Instead, a fundamentally different approach to shopping is needed.

Take 2: you make out a shopping list, go to the supermarket, enter, collect a shopping cart, find each of the items on the shopping list and place them in your cart (less the ones that are out of stock, plus some impulse buys), pay for the items in the cart, return home, unpack, and put the items away.

A Problem in a Context

The domain of groceries may at first seem far removed from the domain of software development, but what we have just described is essentially a distributed programming problem and its resolution. The programming task is that of *iteration*: traversing a collection to fulfill a particular objective. When the code performing the iteration is collocated in the same process as the collection object being accessed, the cost of access is minimal to the point of irrelevant. A change of situation can invalidate this assumption, however, along with any solution that relies on it. A distributed system introduces a significant overhead for any access—any design that does not take this context into account is likely to be inefficient, inflexible, and inadequate. This observation is generally true of patterns and design: context helps to frame and motivate a particular problem, and any solution must be sensitive to this.

Forces: The Heart of Every Pattern

Where the context sets the scene for a problem, the forces are what characterize it in detail. Forces determine what an effective solution must take into account. For any significant design decision, forces inevitably find themselves in conflict.

Returning to the context of distributed computing and the problem of traversing a collection, we are presented with a number of issues that must be considered. There is a significant time overhead in communicating over a network (or going out of the house to visit the supermarket), so a time-efficient solution cannot assume that the overhead is negligible. A further space and time overhead is involved in communication, because values (or groceries) must be marshaled and unmarshaled (packed and unpacked). We must also, however, consider convenience: picking up a carton of milk, paying for it, and putting it in the fridge involves much less ceremony than taking a shopping cart around the supermarket and packing and unpacking bags. Fine-grained iteration is more familiar to programmers, better supported by libraries and languages, and leads to less apparent blocking. We must also consider partial failure (or partial success): networks can become 'notworks.'

Solutions and Consequences

An effective solution needs to balance the forces that make the problem a problem. It should also be described clearly. In this particular case, our solution involves preparing and sending a bulk request (the shopping list) from one address space to another, implemented with respect to the appropriate protocol (driving, walking, cycling, and so on), performing all the traversal locally in a single batch (walking around the supermarket with the shopping cart), marshaling the results back to the caller and unmarshaling them into the local address space (paying, packing, and returning home), and then traversing the batch result locally (unpacking and putting everything away).

Another feature of any design decision is that it may not be perfect, in the sense that every design decision has consequences, some of which are benefits and some liabilities. An effective application of a pattern is therefore one in which the benefits clearly outweigh the liabilities, or one in which the liabilities do not even appear to come into play.

In this case, perhaps the overriding consideration is the communication-to-computation ratio, which has led to a design that minimizes the amount of communication involved (once out, once back) for the amount of work done (accessing multiple items) and ensures that partial failure does not result in partial state—all results are returned, or none at all. There is no 'free lunch,' however. Instead of a single iteration, there are many: a local iteration to prepare the call (compile the shopping list), a remote iteration to perform the computation and collect the results for each item in the request (walking round the supermarket), a local iteration to process each result (unpacking and putting away the groceries). The design style is rather idiomatic for distributed systems, but not necessarily for the more common programming experience of iteration over collections collocated in the same address space.

The Naming of Names

A pattern contributes to the software design vocabulary, which means that it must have a name. The name is the shorthand we use in conversation and the way we index and refer to the pattern elsewhere. Without a name, we find ourselves having to redescribe the essential elements of the pattern in order to communicate it to others.

The most effective names for patterns are those that identify some key aspect of the solution, which means that names are often noun phrases. In the example examined here the name of the pattern is BATCH METHOD (302). This name helps to differentiate the pattern from other iteration patterns that are appropriate for different contexts or slightly different problems, such as ITERATOR (298)—the pattern applied in the first shopping attempt—and ENUMERATION METHOD (300)—a pattern that inverts the sense of iteration, encapsulating the loop within the collection and calling out to a piece of code for each element.

Brief Notes on the Synthesis of Pattern Form

Patterns are often recognized and used informally, acquiring a name based on a particular implementation, with the implication that any use of the key characteristics of a particular design follows that pattern. For software architects and developers to apply patterns more generally and broadly, however, a more concrete description is often needed. We have detailed the anatomy of a pattern in terms of concepts such as *context* and *forces*, but how are we to present the pattern in writing?

It turns out that there is more than one answer to this question. There are many pattern forms in common use, each with different emphases, and each with a different audience or reading style in mind. For example, full documentation of a single pattern that is focused on a pattern common to a particular programming language is often high on technical detail, including sample code. It may best be motivated through one or more examples. For long patterns, dividing the pattern into clearly titled subsections may make it more accessible to readers and potential users. Conversely, a pattern presented alongside many other patterns that are intended as general development-process guidelines is not as well served by length, detail, and code. A more summarized and less elaborate form may thus be appropriate in this case.

Whichever form is adopted for a pattern or catalog of patterns, the form should state the essential problem and solution clearly, emphasize forces and consequences, and include as much structure, diagramming, and technical detail as is considered appropriate for the target audience.

1.3   Between Patterns

Patterns can be used in isolation with some degree of success. They represent foci for discussion, point solutions, or localized design ideas. Patterns are generally gregarious, however, in that they are rather fond of the company of other patterns. Any given application or library will thus make use of many patterns.

Patterns can be collected into catalogs, which may be organized according to different criteria—patterns for object-oriented frameworks, patterns for enterprise computing, patterns for security, patterns for working with a particular programming language, and so on. In these cases what is perhaps most interesting is how the patterns relate. An alphabetical listing is good for finding patterns by name, but it does not describe their relationships.

Software architecture involves an interlocking network of many different decisions, each of which springs from, contradicts, suggests, or otherwise relates to other decisions. To make practical sense as an architectural concept, therefore, where they compete and cooperate, patterns inevitably enlist other patterns for their expression and variation.

Pattern Complements

It is all too easy to get stuck in a design rut, always applying a particular pattern for a general class of problem. Although this strategy can often be successful, there are situations in which not only is a habitual pattern-of-choice not the most effective approach, it can actually be the least effective. To paraphrase Émile-Auguste Chartier, 'nothing is more dangerous than a design idea when you have but one design idea.'

In a design vocabulary, as with any vocabulary, part of effective expression is based on breadth of vocabulary, particularly synonyms, each of which has slightly different qualities and implications. Two or more patterns may appear to solve the same or similar problems—ITERATOR and BATCH METHOD, for example. Deciding between them involves a proper appreciation of the context, goal of the problem, forces, and solution trade-offs. In this sense the patterns are perceived as complementary because together they present the choices involved in a design decision.

Patterns can also cooperate, so that one pattern can provide the missing ingredient needed by another. The goal of this cooperation is to make the resulting design better balanced and more complete. In this sense patterns are complementary because they coexist and reinforce one another in the same design. Moreover, many patterns that might be characterized as alternatives that are in competition with each other, such as ITERATOR and BATCH METHOD, can also complement one another through cooperation.

Consider again the distributed iteration problem. By accessing a single element each time around the loop, ITERATOR on its own offers an overly fine-grained approach that is inefficient for remote collection access. BATCH METHOD, in contrast, replaces loop repetition across the network with repetition of data—passing and/or receiving collections. This works well in many cases, but for large collections, or for clients that need responsive replies, the time spent marshaling, sending, receiving, and unmarshaling can lead to unacceptably long periods of time when the client is just blocked. An alternative approach is to combine both patterns: use the basic concept of an ITERATOR as a traversal position, but instead of stepping a single element at a time, use a BATCH METHOD to take larger strides.

Pattern Compounds

Pattern compounds capture recurring subcommunities of patterns. They are common and identifiable enough to allow them to be treated as a single decision in response to a recurring problem. In distributed computing, the technique of combining ITERATOR and BATCH METHOD, for example, is one such example, to which the names BATCH ITERATOR and CHUNKY ITERATOR are often applied.

Pattern compounds are also known as *compound patterns*, and were originally known as *composite patterns*. In conversation, however, there is obvious scope for confusion between 'a composite pattern' and 'the COMPOSITE (319) pattern,' which is one of the widely known Gang-of-Four patterns.

In truth, most patterns are compound at one level or other, or from one viewpoint or other, so the concept is essentially relative to the design granularity of interest.

Pattern Stories

The development of a system can be considered a single narrative example, in which design questions are asked and answered, structures assembled for specific reasons, and so on. We can view the emergence and refinement of many designs as the progressive application of particular patterns. The design emerges from a narrative—a pattern story—that builds one pattern on another, responding to the design issues introduced or left outstanding by the previous pattern.

As with many stories, they capture the spirit, although not necessarily the truth, of the detail of what happens. Sequential ordering matters more in presenting a design and its evolution than it does in the actual evolution of a design. It is rare that our design thinking fits into a tidy, linear arrangement, so there is a certain amount of retrospection, revisionism, and rearrangement involved in retelling how a design played out over time.

These stories, then, may be of systems already built, forecasts of systems to be built, or simply hypothetical illustrations of how systems could be built. They may be recovered whole or idealized from the development of real systems, a guide to the architecture and its design rationale. They may be used as storyboarding technique for envisioning and exploring future design decisions and paths for a system. They may be speculative and idealized, intended to teach or explore design thinking, but not an actual system.

Pattern Sequences

Pattern sequences are related to pattern stories in the same way that individual patterns are related to examples that illustrate or motivate those patterns: they generalize the progression of patterns and the way a design can be established, without necessarily being a specific design. In this sense, a given pattern sequence can be considered a highly specific development process. Predecessor patterns form part of the context of each successive pattern.

For example, BATCH ITERATOR as the application of ITERATOR and BATCH METHOD can also be seen as a (very) short sequence, in which first ITERATOR is applied to provide the notion of a traversal position, then BATCH METHOD is applied to define the style of access.

1.4   Into Pattern Languages

While patterns represent a design vocabulary, pattern languages are somewhat like grammar and style. Through the use of patterns, a pattern language offers guidance on how to create a particular kind of system, or how to implement a certain kind of class, or how to fulfill a particular kind of cross-cutting requirement, or how to approach the design of a particular family of products. Whether we are interested in building a distributed system for managing a warehouse, writing exception-safe code in C++, or developing a Java-based Web application, if there is experience in the domain of interest, it is likely that this experience can be distilled into patterns and organized as a pattern language.

From Sequences to Languages

While pattern stories are concrete and linear, pattern sequences are more abstract but still essentially linear. Feedback should inform the designer how to apply the next pattern in a sequence, or whether to revisit an earlier application. Pattern languages are more abstract still, and typically more richly interconnected.

A pattern language defines a network of patterns that build on one another, typically a tree or directed graph, so that one pattern can optionally or necessarily draw on another, elaborating a design in a particular way, responding to specific forces, taking different paths as appropriate. The relationships explored in the previous section, *Between Patterns*, are those that can be found in various forms within a pattern language. For example, a pattern sequence defines a path through a language, taking in some or all of its patterns, and a pattern story recalls a route along one path.

Presenting and Using Pattern Languages

A pattern language includes its sequences, and the knowledge of how to handle feedback should be considered part of the scope and responsibility of a language. A given pattern sequence can be used as a guide to the reader about one way that a language has been, can be, or is to be used. When taken together, a number of sequences can be seen to provide guidance on the use of a given pattern language—or, alternatively, when taken together, a number of sequences can be used as the basis of a pattern language.

Pattern sequences therefore have the potential to play a number of roles. Other than in the form of pattern stories, however, they are normally not made explicit as part of the presentation of a language. As a result there is generally more discussion in the patterns community about pattern sequences than actual cataloging or specific description of them. Given that different pattern sequences give rise to different common design fragments with different properties that are useful in different situations, it seems worthwhile to document some of these, even if briefly. Of course, enumerating all the reasonable sequences for anything but a small or simply structured language is likely to be a Sisyphean task that will overwhelm both its author and any readers who try to use it for guidance.

The common vehicle for illustrating pattern languages in action is stories. Of course, there is the risk that stories may be taken too literally. In the way that a motivating example in a pattern is sometimes mistaken for the pattern itself, a pattern story may end up stealing the limelight from the language it represents. Although readers are free to generalize, they may be drawn to the specifics of an example to the exclusion of its general themes and structure.

It is therefore crucial to strike the right balance between the specific and the general to ensure that the patterns within a language are also documented in a sufficiently complete form individually, but with obvious emphasis on their interconnections. A single pattern can often be used in a variety of situations and a variety of different pattern languages. To keep its role within a language focused, it makes sense to concentrate on documenting the aspects that are relevant to the language, and reducing or omitting aspects that are only relevant in other situations. The context for a given pattern can also be narrowed to predecessor patterns in the language. This overall mix of specific examples, in-context patterns, and relationships between patterns offers a practical approach to presentation and usage of pattern languages.

1.5   Patterns Connected

The value that individual patterns have should not be underrated, but the tremendous value that they have when brought together as a community should not be underestimated. Patterns are outgoing, fond of company, and community spirited.

It is this networking on the part of patterns that reflects the nature both of design and of designs. The notions of synthesis, overlap, reinforcement, and balance across different design elements according to the roles that they play reinforces what to some appears an initially counterintuitive view of design: that the code-based units of composition found in a given design are not themselves necessarily the best representation of the design's history, rationale, or future.

2 On Distributed Systems

*A distributed system is one in which the failure
of a computer you didn't even know existed
can render your own computer unusable.*

Leslie Lamport

A distributed system is a computing system in which a number of components cooperate by communicating over a network. The explosive growth of the Internet and the World Wide Web in the mid-1990s moved distributed systems beyond their traditional application areas, such as industrial automation, defense, and telecommunication, and into nearly all domains, including e-commerce, financial services, health care, government, and entertainment. This chapter describes the key characteristics and challenges of developing distributed systems and presents several key software technologies that have emerged to resolve these challenges.

2.1 Benefits of Distribution

Most computer software traditionally ran in *stand-alone systems*, in which the user interface, application 'business' processing, and persistent data resided in one computer, with peripherals attached to it by buses or cables. Few interesting systems, however, are still designed in this way. Instead, most computer software today runs in *distributed systems,* in which the interactive presentation, application business processing, and data resources reside on loosely coupled computing nodes and service tiers connected together by networks.

The following diagram illustrates a three-tier distribution architecture for a warehouse management process control system, whose pattern-based design we discuss in depth in Part II, *A Story.* The three tiers in this example are connected by a BROKER architecture (237).

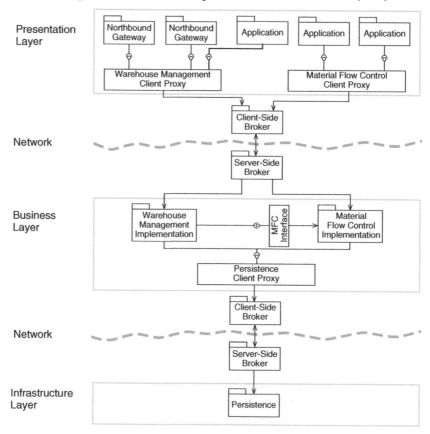

The following properties of distributed systems make them increasingly essential as the foundation of information and control systems [Tan92]:

- *Collaboration and connectivity.* An important motivation for distributed systems is their ability to connect us to vast quantities of geographically distributed information and services, such as maps, e-commerce sites, multimedia content, and encyclopedias. The popularity of instant messaging and chat rooms on the Internet highlights another motivation for distributed systems: keeping in touch with family, friends, co-workers, and customers.

- *Economics.* Computer networks that incorporate PDAs, laptops, PCs, and servers often offer a better price/performance ratio than centralized mainframe computers. For example, they support decentralized and modular applications that can share expensive peripherals, such as high-capacity file servers and high-resolution printers. Similarly, selected application components and services can be delegated to run on nodes with specialized processing attributes, such as high-performance disk controllers, large amounts of memory, or enhanced floating-point performance. Conversely, small simple applications can run on inexpensive commodity hardware.

- *Performance and scalability.* Successful software typically collects more users and requirements over time, so it is essential that the performance of distributed systems can scale up to handle the increased load and capabilities. Significant performance increases can be gained by using the combined computing power of networked computing nodes. In addition—at least in theory—multiprocessors and networks can scale easily. For example, multiple computation and communication service processing tasks can be run in parallel on different nodes in a server farm or in different virtual machines on the same server.

- *Failure tolerance.* A key goal of distributed computing is to tolerate partial system failures. For example, although all the nodes in a network may be live, the network itself may fail. Similarly, an end-system in a network, or a CPU in a multiprocessor system, may crash. Such failures should be handled gracefully without affecting all—or unrelated—parts of the system. A common way to implement fault tolerance is to replicate services across multiple nodes and/or networks. Replication helps minimize single points of failure, which can improve system reliability in the face of partial failures.

- *Inherent distribution.* Some applications are inherently distributed, including telecommunication management network (TMN) systems, enterprise business systems that span multiple company divisions in different regions of the world, peer-to-peer (P2P) content sharing systems, and business-to-business (B2B) supply chain management systems. Distribution is not optional in these types of systems—it is essential to meet customer needs.

2.2   Challenges of Distribution

Despite the increasing ubiquity and importance of distributed systems, developers of software for distributed systems face a number of tough challenges [POSA2], including:

- *Inherent complexities*, which arise from fundamental domain challenges. For example, components of a distributed system often reside in separate address spaces on separate nodes, so inter-node communication needs different mechanisms, policies, and protocols than those used for intra-node communication in stand-alone systems. Similarly, synchronization and coordination is more complicated in a distributed system, as components may run in parallel and network communication can be asynchronous and non-deterministic. The networks that connect components in distributed systems introduce additional forces, such as latency, jitter, transient failures, and overload, with corresponding impact on system efficiency, predictability, and availability [VKZ04].

- *Accidental complexities*, which arise from limitations of software tools and development techniques, such as non-portable programming APIs and poor distributed debuggers. Ironically, many accidental complexities stem from deliberate choices made by developers favoring low-level languages and platforms such as C and C-based operating system APIs and libraries, which scale up poorly when applied to distributed systems. As the complexity of application requirements increases, new layers of distributed infrastructure are conceived and released, not all of which are equally mature or capable, which complicates the development, integration, and evolution of working systems.

- *Inadequate methods and techniques.* Popular software analysis methods and design techniques [Fow03b] [DWT04] [SDL05] have focused on constructing single-process, single-threaded applications with 'best-effort' QoS requirements. The development of high-quality distributed systems—particularly those with stringent performance requirements, such as video-conferencing or air traffic control systems—has been left to the expertise of skilled software architects and engineers. Moreover, it has been hard to gain experience with software techniques for distributed systems without spending a lot of time wrestling with platform-specific details and fixing mistakes by costly trial and error.

- *Continuous re-invention and re-discovery* of core concepts and techniques. The software industry has a long history of recreating incompatible solutions to problems that have already been solved. There are dozens of general-purpose and real-time operating systems that manage the same hardware resources. Similarly, there are dozens of incompatible operating system encapsulation libraries, virtual machines, and middleware that provide slightly different APIs that implement essentially the same features and services. If effort had instead been focused on enhancing a smaller number of solutions, developers of distributed system software would be able to innovate more rapidly by reusing common tools and standard platforms and components.

2.3   Technologies for Supporting Distribution

To address the challenges described above, therefore, three levels of *support* for distributed computing were developed: *ad hoc network programming*, *structured communication*, and *middleware* [Lea02]. At the *ad hoc network programming* level reside interprocess communication (IPC) mechanisms, such as shared memory, pipes, and sockets [StRa05], that allow distributed components to connect and exchange information. These IPC mechanisms help address a key challenge of distributed computing: enabling components in different address spaces to cooperate with one another.

Certain drawbacks arise, however, when developing distributed systems using only ad hoc network programming support. For example, using sockets directly within application code tightly couples the code to the socket API. Porting this code to another IPC mechanism, or redeploying components to different nodes in a network, thus becomes a costly manual programming effort. Even porting the code to another version of the same operating system can require code changes if each platform has slightly different APIs for the IPC mechanisms [POSA2] [SH02]. Programming directly to an IPC mechanism can also cause a paradigm mismatch: for example, local communication uses object-oriented classes and method invocations, whereas remote communication uses the function-oriented socket API and message passing.

Some applications and their developers can tolerate the deficiencies of ad hoc network programming. For example, traditional embedded systems, such as controllers for automobile engines or power grids, run in a homogeneous distributed environment whose initial functional requirements, component configuration, and choice of IPC mechanism rarely changes. Most other types of applications cannot tolerate these deficiencies, however, because they run in a heterogeneous computing environment and/or face continuous requirement changes.

The next level of support for distributed computing is *structured communication*, which overcomes limitations with ad hoc network programming by not coupling application code to low-level IPC mechanisms, but instead offering higher-level communication mechanisms to distributed systems. Structured communication encapsulates machine-level details, such as bits and bytes and binary reads and writes. Application developers are therefore presented with a programming model that embodies data types and a communication style closer to their application domain.

Historically significant examples of structured communication are Remote Procedure Call (RPC) platforms, such as Sun RPC [Sun88] and the Distributed Computing Environment (DCE) [RKF92]. RPC platforms allow distributed applications to cooperate with one another much as they would in a local environment: they invoke functions on each other, pass parameters along with each invocation, and receive results from the functions they call. The RPC platform shields them from the details of specific IPC mechanisms and low-level operating system APIs. Other examples of structured communication include PROFInet [WK01], which provides a runtime model for industrial automation that defines several message-oriented communication protocols, and ACE [SH02] [SH03], which provides reusable C++ wrapper facades and frameworks that perform common structured communication tasks across a range of OS platforms.

Despite its improvements over ad hoc network programming, structured communication does not fully resolve the challenges described above. In particular, components in a distributed system that communicate via structured communication are still aware of their peers' remoteness—and sometimes even their location in the network. While location awareness may suffice for certain types of distributed systems, such as statically configured embedded systems whose component deployment rarely changes, structured communication does not fulfill the following properties needed for more complex distributed systems:

- *Location-independence of components*. Ideally, clients in a distributed system should communicate with collocated or remote services using the same programming model. Providing this degree of location-independence requires the separation of code that deals with remoting or location-specific details from client and service application code. Even then, of course, distributed systems have failure modes that local systems do not have [WWWK96].

- *Flexible component (re)deployment.* The original deployment of an application's services to network nodes could become suboptimal as hardware is upgraded, new nodes are incorporated, and/or new requirements are added. A redeployment of distributed system services may therefore be needed, ideally without breaking code and/or shutting down the entire system.

- *Integration of legacy code.* Few complex distributed systems are developed from scratch. Instead, they are constructed from existing elements or applications that may not originally have been designed to integrate into a distributed environment—in fact, the source code may not even be available. Reasons for integrating legacy code include leveraging existing software components, minimizing software certification costs, or reducing time-to-market.

- *Heterogeneous components.* Distributed system integrators are faced increasingly with the task of combining heterogeneous enterprise distributed systems built using different off-the-shelf technologies, rather than just integrating proprietary software developed in-house. Moreover, with the advent of enterprise application integration (EAI) [HoWo03], it has become necessary to integrate components and applications written in different programming languages into a single, coherent distributed system. Once integrated, these heterogeneous components should perform a common set of tasks properly.

Mastering these challenges requires more than structured communication support for distributed systems. Instead it requires dedicated *middleware* [ScSc01], which is distribution infrastructure software that resides between an application and the operating system, network, or database underneath it. Middleware provides the properties described above so that application developers can focus on their primary responsibility: implementing their domain-specific functionality.

Realizing the need for middleware has motivated companies such as Microsoft, IBM, and Sun, and consortia such as the Object Management Group (OMG) and the World Wide Web Consortium (W3C), to develop technologies for distributed computing. Below, we describe a number of popular middleware technologies, including distributed object computing, component middleware, publish/subscribe middleware, service-oriented architectures, and Web Services [Vin04a].

Distributed Object Computing Middleware

The emergence of *distributed object computing (DOC) middleware* in the late 1980s and early 1990s was a key contribution to distributed system development. DOC middleware represented the confluence of two major information technologies: RPC-based distributed computing systems and object-oriented design and programming. Techniques for developing RPC-based distributed systems, such as DCE [OG94], focused on integrating multiple computers to act as a unified scalable computational resource. Likewise, techniques for developing object-oriented systems focused on reducing complexity by creating reusable frameworks and components that reify successful patterns and software architectures. DOC middleware therefore used object-oriented techniques to distribute reusable services and applications efficiently, flexibly, and robustly over multiple, often heterogeneous, computing and networking elements.

CORBA 2.x [OMG03a] [OMG04a] and Java RMI [Sun04c] are examples of DOC middleware technologies for building applications for distributed systems. These technologies focus on interfaces, which are contracts between clients and servers that define a location-independent means for clients to view and access object services provided by a server. Standard DOC middleware technologies like CORBA also define communication protocols and object information models, to enable interoperability between heterogeneous applications written in various languages and running on various platforms [HV99].

Despite its maturity, performance, and advanced capabilities, however, DOC middleware has various limitations, including:

- *Lack of functional boundaries.* The CORBA 2.x and Java RMI object models treat all interfaces as client/server contracts. These object models do not, however, provide standard assembly mechanisms to decouple dependencies among collaborating object implementations. For example, objects whose implementations depend on other objects need to discover and connect to those objects explicitly. To build complex distributed applications, therefore, application developers must program the connections among interdependent services and object interfaces explicitly, which is extra work that can yield brittle and non-reusable implementations.

- *Lack of software deployment and configuration standards.* There is no standard way to distribute and start up object implementations remotely in DOC middleware. Application administrators must therefore resort to in-house scripts and procedures to deliver software implementations to target machines, configure the target machine and software implementations for execution, and then instantiate software implementations to make them ready for clients. Moreover, software implementations are often modified to accommodate such *ad hoc* deployment mechanisms. The need for most reusable software implementations to interact with other software implementations and services further aggravates the problem. The lack of higher-level software management standards results in systems that are harder to maintain and software component implementations that are much harder to reuse.

Component Middleware

Starting in the mid to late 1990s, *component middleware* evolved to address the limitations of DOC middleware described above. In particular, to address the lack of functional boundaries, component middleware allows a group of cohesive component objects to interact with each other through multiple provided and required interfaces, and defines the standard runtime mechanisms needed to execute these component objects in generic applications servers. To address the lack of standard deployment and configuration mechanisms, component middleware often also specifies the infrastructure to package, customize, assemble, and disseminate components throughout a distributed system.

Enterprise JavaBeans [Sun03] [Sun04a] and the CORBA Component Model (CCM) [OMG02] [OMG04b] are examples of component middleware that define the following general roles and relationships:

- *A component* is an implementation entity that exposes a set of named interfaces and connection points that components can use to collaborate with each other. Named interfaces are service method invocations that other components call synchronously. Connection points are joined with named interfaces provided by other components to associate clients with their servers. Some component models also offer event sources and event sinks, which can be connected to support asynchronous message passing.

- *A container* provides the server runtime environment for component implementations. It contains various predefined hooks and operations that give components access to strategies and services, such as persistence, event notification, transaction, replication, load balancing, and security. Each container defines a collection of runtime policies, such as transaction, persistence, security, and event delivery strategies, and is responsible for initializing and providing runtime contexts for the managed components. Component implementations often have associated metadata written in XML that specifies the required container policies [OMG03b].

In addition to the building blocks outlined above, component middleware also typically automates aspects of various stages in the application development lifecycle, notably component implementation, packaging, assembly, and deployment, in which each stage of the lifecycle adds information pertaining to these aspects via declarative metadata [DBOSG05]. These capabilities enable component middleware to create applications more rapidly and robustly than their DOC middleware predecessors.

Well-defined relationships exist between components and objects in a component architecture [Szy02]. In general, components are created at build time, may be loaded at runtime, and define the implementation details for runtime behavior. Likewise, objects are created at runtime, their type is packaged within a component, and their run-time actions are what drives program behavior. Thus, components get written, built and loaded, whereas objects get created and interact.

Publish/Subscribe and Message-Oriented Middleware

RPC platforms, DOC middleware, and component middleware are all based on a request/response communication model, in which requests flow from client to server and responses flow back from server to client. However, certain types of distributed applications, particularly those that react to external stimuli and events, such as control systems and online stock trading systems, are not well-suited to specific aspects of the request/response communication model. These aspects include *synchronous communication* between the client and server, which can underutilize the parallelism available in the network and endsystems, *designated communication*, in which the client must know the identity of the server, which tightly couples it to a particular recipient, and *point-to-point communication*, in which a client communicates with just one server at a time, which can limit its ability to convey its information to all interested recipients.

An alternative approach to structuring communication in some types of distributed systems is therefore to use *message-oriented middleware*, which is supported by IBM's MQ Series [IBM99], BEA's MessageQ [BEA06] and TIBCO's Rendezvous, or *publish/subscribe middleware*, which is supported by the Java Messaging Service (JMS) [Sun04b], the Data Distribution Service (DDS) [OMG05b], and WS-NOTIFICATION [OASIS06c] [OASIS06c]. The main benefits of message-oriented middleware include its support for *asynchronous communication*, in which senders transmit data to receivers without blocking to wait for a response. Many message-oriented middleware platforms provide transactional properties, in which messages are reliably queued and/or persisted until consumers can pick them up. Publish/subscribe middleware augments this capability with *anonymous communication*, in which publishers and subscribers are loosely coupled and thus do not know about each other's existence, as the address of the receiver is not conveyed with the event data, and *group communication*, in which there can be multiple subscribers that receive events sent by a publisher.

Publish/subscribe middleware typically allows applications to run on separate nodes and write/read events to/from a global data space in a distributed system. Applications can share information with others by using this global data space to declare their intent to produce events, which is often categorized into one or more topics of interest to participants. Applications that want to access topics of interest—or simply handle all messages on a particular queue—can declare their intent to consume the events.

The elements of publish/subscribe middleware are separated into the following roles:

- *Publishers* are sources of events, that is, they produce events on specific topics that are then propagated through the system. Depending on the architecture implementation, publishers may need to describe the type of events they generate *a priori.*

- *Subscribers* are the event sinks of the system, that is, they consume data on topics of interest to them. Some architecture implementations require subscribers to declare filtering information for the events they require.

- *Event channels* are components in the system that propagate events from publishers to subscribers. These channels can propagate events across distribution domains to remote subscribers. Event channels can perform various services, such as filtering and routing, QoS enforcement, and fault management.

The events passed from publishers to consumers can be represented in various ways, ranging from simple text messages to richly typed data structures. Likewise, the interfaces used to publish and subscribe the events can be generic, such as `send` and `recv` methods that exchange arbitrary dynamically typed XML messages in WS-NOTIFICATION, or specialized, such as a data writer and data readers that exchange statically typed event data in DDS.

Service-Oriented Architectures and Web Services

Service-Oriented Architecture (SOA) is a style of organizing and using distributed capabilities that may be controlled by different organizations or owners. It therefore provides a uniform means to offer, discover, interact with and use the capabilities of loosely coupled [Kaye03] and interoperable software services to support the requirements of business processes and application users [OASIS06a]. The term 'SOA' was originally coined in the mid-1990s [SN96] as a generalization of the interoperability middleware standards available at the time, including RPC-, ORB-, and messaging-based platforms.

The ubiquity of the World Wide Web (WWW) and the lessons learned from earlier forms of middleware were leveraged to form the initial version of SOAP [W3C03]. SOAP is a protocol for exchanging XML-based [W3C06b] messages over a computer network, normally using HTTP [FGMFB97]. Initially SOAP was intended as a platform-agnostic protocol that could be used over the Web to allow interoperability with various types of middleware, including CORBA, EJB, JMS, and proprietary message-oriented middleware systems, such as IBM's MQ Series and TIBCO Rendezvous.

The introduction of SOAP spawned a popular new variant of SOA called *Web Services* that is being standardized by the World Wide Web Consortium (W3C). Web Services allow developers to package application logic into services whose interfaces are described with the Web Service Description Language (WSDL) [W3C06a]. WSDL-based services are often accessed using standard higher-level Internet protocols, such as SOAP over HTTP. Web Services can be used to build an Enterprise Service Bus (ESB), which is a distributed computing architecture that simplifies interworking between disparate systems. Mule [Mule06] and Celtix [Celtix06] are open-source examples of the ESB approach to melding groups of heterogeneous systems into a unified distributed application.

Despite some highly publicized drawbacks [Bell06] [Vin04b], Web Services have established themselves as the technology of choice for most enterprise business applications. This does not mean, however, that Web Services will completely displace earlier middleware technologies such as EJB and CORBA. Rather, Web Services complement these earlier successful middleware technologies and provides standard mechanisms for interoperability. For example, the Microsoft Windows Communication Foundation (WCF) platform [MMW06] and the Service Component Architecture (SCA) [SCA05] currently being defined by IBM, BEA, IONA, and others combine aspects of component-based development and Web technologies. Like components, WCF and SCA platforms provide black-box functionality that can be described and reused without concern over how a service is implemented. Unlike traditional component technologies, however, WCF and SCA are not accessed using the object model-specific protocols defined by DCOM [Box97] [Thai99], Java RMI, or CORBA. Instead, Web services are accessed using Web protocols and data formats, such as HTTP and XML respectively.

Since initial Web Services developments provided an RPC model that exchanged XML messages over HTTP, they were touted as replacements for more complicated EJB components or CORBA objects. When used for fine-grained distributed resource access, however, the performance of Web Services is often several orders of magnitude slower than DOC middleware, due to its their use of plain-text protocols such as XML over HTTP [EPL02]. As a result, the use of Web Services for performance-critical applications, such as distributed real-time and embedded systems in aerospace, military, financial services, and process control domains, is now considered much less significant than using them for loosely coupled document-oriented applications such as supply-chain management.

Rather than trying to replace older approaches, today's Web Services technologies are instead focusing on middleware integration, thereby adding value to existing middleware platforms. WSDL allows developers to describe Web Service interfaces abstractly, while also defining concrete bindings such as the protocols and transports required at runtime to access the services. By providing these common communication mechanisms between diverse middleware platforms, Web Services allow component reuse across an organization's entire application set, regardless of their implementation technologies. For example, projects such as the Apache Web Services Invocation Framework (WSIF) [Apache06], Mule, and CeltiXfire, aim to allow applications to access Web Services transparently via EJB, JMS, or the SCA. This move towards integration allows services implemented in these different technologies to be integrated into an ESB and made available to a variety of client applications. Middleware integration is thus a key focus of Web Services applications for the foreseeable future [Vin03]. By focusing on integration, Web Services increases reuse and reduces middleware lock-in, allowing developers to use the right middleware to meet their needs without precluding interoperability with existing systems.

2.4   Limitations of Middleware

Despite the many benefits of middleware described in this chapter, it is not a panacea for distributed systems. All the middleware technologies described above are primarily just 'messengers' between elements in distributed applications, and sometimes the messages just cannot be delivered despite heroic efforts from the middleware. As a result, distributed applications must be prepared to handle network failures and server crashes. Likewise, middleware cannot magically solve problems resulting from poor deployment decisions, which can significantly degrade system stability, predictability, and scalability.

In other words, middleware is an important part of a distributed system, but it cannot handle responsibilities that are application-specific and thus beyond its scope. Distributed systems must therefore be designed and validated carefully, even when middleware allows them to be independent of the concrete location of other components.

3 On the Pattern Language

The limits of my language are the limits of my world.

Ludwig Wittgenstein

This chapter introduces our pattern language for distributed computing, outlining its intent, scope, audience, origin, genesis, structure, content, presentation, and use. The chapter thus presents the general context for the language, defining how it relates to common software engineering practice, as well as the existing body of pattern literature.

3.1 Intent, Scope, and Audience

The main intent of our pattern language for distributed computing is to serve as an overview about, introduction to, guide through, and communication vehicle for, the best practices and state-of-the-art in key areas of the construction of distributed software systems. Topics covered by the language range from fundamental and strategic concerns regarding application decomposition, component deployment, and communication middleware, to supplementary and tactical aspects that address the detailed design of components in a distributed system and the management of system resources.

To achieve our intent, the pattern language connects patterns from a variety of different sources into a single, coherent pattern network that provides a holistic and consistent view of the construction of distributed software. The language captures our production experience to date with building distributed software systems—hence our confidence in presenting it—but it is not the final word on distributed architecture. We have chosen not to speculate how the discipline will evolve in future, because it is the empirically supported patterns we wish to present.

Software architects, developers, and advanced students can use our pattern language for distributed computing to create, communicate, and refactor the architectures of distributed systems, as well as to understand the paradigms and baseline architectures of common middleware platforms and products. In addition, product and project managers can get deeper understanding of the essential capabilities of distributed systems whose development they are leading, which simplifies communication with their software architects and developers. We do not, however, intend end-users or customers to use our pattern language directly. While real-world metaphors might make the material accessible to this audience, it would require an alternative presentation of the language.

Our pattern language is not a comprehensive tutorial on distributed computing in general. Its clear focus is on the *design* of distributed software systems. We therefore assume readers have some familiarity with core distributed computing concepts and mechanisms, such as deadlock, transactions, synchronization, remoting, and scheduling.

3.2   Origins and Genesis

The patterns in our pattern language originate from many software experts, including Deepak Alur, Bruce Anderson, Kent Beck, Roy Campbell, Jens Coldewey, John Crupi, Eduardo Fernandez-Buglioni, Martin Fowler, Erich Gamma, Richard Helm, Michi Henning, Gregor Hohpe, Duane Hybertson, Prashant Jain, Ralph Johnson, Wolfgang Keller, Michael Kircher, Doug Lea, Silvano Maffeis, Dan Malks, Gerard Meszaros, Regine Meunier, Hans Rohnert, Alexander Schmid, Markus Schumacher, Peter Sommerlad, Michael Stal, Steve Vinoski, John Vlissides, Markus Völter, Eberhard Wolff, Bobby Woolf, Uwe Zdun, and ourselves. You can therefore consider this language as a compressed expression of collective expertise about building distributed software systems.

Although most patterns in our language—and some of their relationships—were readily available, it was hard to connect the patterns to form a coherent, consistent, and larger pattern language. We therefore had to recast and rewrite all the patterns, to both highlight their essence more explicitly and situate them in their proper context. For example, we had to identify which problems in distributed computing the patterns address, how they resolve these challenges, why they resolve the challenges the way they do, and how the patterns relate to each other. This information was present in many of the original pattern descriptions, so we had only to extract it. For other patterns, however, we had to dig deeper and mine the context from our own and others' experience. Only a few patterns are 'new' in the language: they mainly close holes not covered by existing patterns, or serve as an 'umbrella' that integrates a set of existing patterns under a common theme.

We enhanced many patterns with additional rationales for significant solution decisions that specifically apply within the context of distributed computing. We also supplemented the discussions of forces and consequences to embrace this context more closely. We added many new relationships between the patterns, so that they connect more strongly than they did in their original descriptions. To avoid distracting readers from the big picture of how all the patterns fit together, however, we intentionally omitted some details found in the original pattern descriptions, choosing a more lightweight and narrative form. For example, we omitted CRC cards for core roles, fine-grained structure and interaction diagrams, implementation hints and activities, variants, examples and known uses, and consequences of minor importance. If you are interested in these details, you can refer to them in the original pattern sources, which we list for all patterns included in our language.

3.3   Structure and Content

Our pattern language for distributed computing includes 114 patterns, which are grouped into thirteen problem areas. Each problem area addresses a specific technical topic related to building distributed systems, and contains all the patterns in our language that address the challenges associated with that technical topic. The main intent of the problem areas is to make the language and its patterns more tangible and comprehensible: patterns that address related problems are presented and discussed within a common and clearly scoped context. The problem areas are presented (roughly) in their order of relevance and applicability when building distributed systems, and include the following:

1. *From Mud to Structure* (167). This problem area includes the root patterns of our pattern language for distributed computing. They help transform the mud of requirements and constraints with which we usually start into a coarse-grained software structure with clearly separated, tangible parts that comprise the system being developed. In addition, the patterns in this chapter address several key concerns of sustainable software architectures, ranging from operational

aspects such as performance and availability to developmental qualities like extensibility and maintainability.

2. *Distribution Infrastructure* (211). This problem area describes patterns pertaining to *middleware*, which is distribution infrastructure software that helps to simplify applications in distributed systems. The patterns in this problem area help developers to understand the fundamental communication paradigms supported by common middleware products and platforms, as well as key aspects of their software architectures.

3. *Event Demultiplexing and Dispatching* (253). At its core, distributed computing involves the handling of and response to events received from the network, even if applications use a more sophisticated communication model, such as synchronous request–response, asynchronous messaging, or publish/subscribe dissemination. Due to its pivotal role, this event-driven core must not become a performance bottleneck.

4. *Interface Partitioning* (271). Interfaces are the 'business card' of a component that inform clients about the component's responsibilities and usage protocols. They should also make it easy for clients to collaborate with the component effectively and correctly. Designing and specifying usable and meaningful component interfaces is therefore essential for successful software development. Yet specifying useful component interfaces is hard, as they should reflect component responsibilities clearly, be meaningful for clients, and hide clients from the cost of change and evolution of component implementations.

5. *Component Partitioning* (305). Components are the implementation building blocks that provide well-defined services to their clients. Though clients are generally not interested in the internal design of a component, this partitioning has a significant impact on the component's visible quality properties, such as performance, scalability, flexibility, availability, and fault-tolerance.

6. *Application Control* (329). Transforming user input for an application into concrete service requests on its functionality, executing these requests, and transforming any results back into output that is meaningful for users can be hard. All these aspects are even harder if the application's user interface is decoupled from the realization

of its functionality. This decoupling is typically done to simplify the evolution of user interfaces and application functionality, gracefully handle changes in their underlying technologies, or enable the deployment of different component configurations on a variety of platforms.

7. *Concurrency* (353). Software for distributed systems often benefits from concurrency, particularly servers and server-side applications that handle requests from multiple clients simultaneously. In addition, an increasing number of multi-core CPUs and multi-CPU computers are designed to run multiple threads of control in parallel to compensate for the stall in Moore's Law [Sut05a]. Developers of distributed system software therefore must become proficient with process and thread management mechanisms. No single software concurrency architecture, however, is suitable for all workload conditions and platforms.

8. *Synchronization* (371). Synchronizing access to shared components, objects, and resources in a manner that avoids deadlocks, race conditions, and other concurrency hazards is one of the hard tasks in building distributed systems. Moreover, synchronization can incur significant overhead, so applications should be designed to minimize or avoid unnecessary synchronization.

9. *Object Interaction* (399). Most collaboration between objects in standalone programs involves calling methods and services on each other, passing parameters with the calls, and waiting synchronously for the invoked objects to return their results. Interactions between objects in a distributed systems, however, are often much more complex, due to the need to balance competing forces such as latency, scalability, and reliability.

10. *Adaptation and Extension* (423). Some applications are specifically developed for a single customer, whereas others are developed as products for a mass market. Even applications targeted at a single customer may benefit from a common architectural base, to simplify repeat business for the customer, or to simplify customization for similar applications sought by new customers. Even if multiple customers can benefit from a particular software infrastructure, however, each often has unique and specific requirements that are not supported by default. Consequently, components in long-lived distributed systems should be configurable, adaptable, and evolvable.

11. *Modal Behavior* (463). Some objects in a system are inherently state-driven: entire methods—or significant portions of them—behave differently depending on their current state. There are many ways to implement state-driven lifecycles for an object. Sometimes simple flags and conditional statements within the object's method control flow are enough. Other times, however, many or all methods of an object can behave entirely differently in different object states. Such a lifecycle is often modeled as a state machine, but many design choices face developers of state machines, and some choices yield unnecessarily complex implementations.

12. *Resource Management* (473). Management of resources is crucial for the success of distributed systems. For example, the performance of a server can degrade if it keeps too many unused objects in memory. It is hard, however, to manage resources correctly and efficiently. Many application qualities of service properties, such as performance, scalability, flexibility, stability, reliability, portability, and security, depend on how efficiently resources are created or acquired, accessed and used, disposed of or released, and managed in general. What makes resource management particularly hard is trying to balance trade-offs among these requirements, since satisfying one of them often conflicts with others.

13. *Database Access* (533). Many distributed systems use databases to store their persistent data, and increasingly these systems use the relational database model in conjunction with object-oriented techniques. The object model and the relational model, however, do not map perfectly to one another. Mapping from an object-oriented application design to a relational database schema efficiently and flexibly is often more challenging than it should be.

All thirteen problem areas outlined above complement and complete each other in terms of various technical aspects related to building distributed systems. The major relationships that connect the problem areas are illustrated in the following diagram.

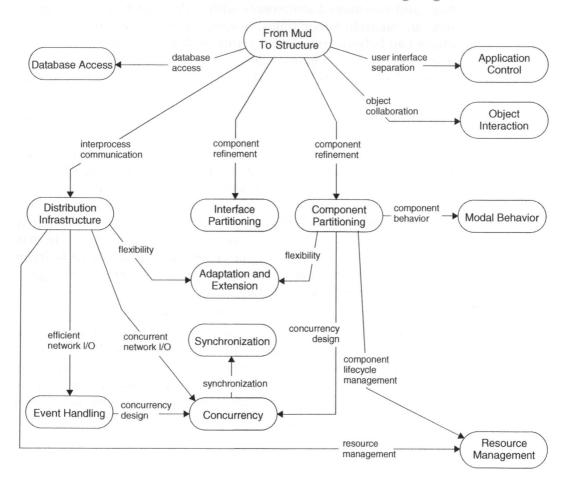

There are other relationships between problem areas that are not outlined in the diagram. For example, some patterns that address adaptation and extension concerns reference patterns related to interface partitioning, as they define explicit and stable interfaces that hide the details of a varying implementation. Nevertheless, the omitted relationships between problem areas are not as significant as the relationships that are shown.

The patterns in our pattern language for distributed computing are interconnected in more ways than just problem areas. We therefore present them in a top-down fashion, starting with the language's root patterns, followed by patterns that complete the root patterns, and likewise for the patterns that complete those patterns, and so on. We finally arrive at the 'leaves' of the network: patterns that complete many other patterns, but which themselves are not refined by finer-grained patterns within the language.

Our pattern language thus defines a yo-yo-like process for designing distributed systems: starting with the definition of their baseline architectures, moving on to specifying their components, and ending with addressing topics of component-internal design, but also supporting refactoring from the bottom of a specific design. Since the flow of text in this book is constrained to be sequential, however, the presentation of the language is not properly hierarchical. Some patterns are presented later in the sequence than their position in the language's network hierarchy would suggest.

The 114 patterns of our pattern language that we explicitly describe in this book are:

- *From Mud To Structure*: DOMAIN MODEL (182), LAYERS (185), MODEL-VIEW-CONTROLLER (188), PRESENTATION-ABSTRACTION-CONTROL (191), MICROKERNEL (194), REFLECTION (197), PIPES AND FILTERS (200), SHARED REPOSITORY (202), BLACKBOARD (205), and DOMAIN OBJECT (208).

- *Distribution Infrastructure*: MESSAGING (221), MESSAGE CHANNEL (224), MESSAGE ENDPOINT (227), MESSAGE TRANSLATOR (229), MESSAGE ROUTER (231), BROKER (237), CLIENT PROXY (240), REQUESTOR (242), INVOKER (244), CLIENT REQUEST HANDLER (246), SERVER REQUEST HANDLER (249), and PUBLISHER-SUBSCRIBER (234).

- *Event Demultiplexing and Dispatching*: REACTOR (259), PROACTOR (262), ACCEPTOR-CONNECTOR (265), and ASYNCHRONOUS COMPLETION TOKEN (268).

- *Interface Partitioning*: EXPLICIT INTERFACE (281), EXTENSION INTERFACE (284), INTROSPECTIVE INTERFACE (286), DYNAMIC INVOCATION INTERFACE (288), PROXY (290), BUSINESS DELEGATE (292), FACADE (294), COMBINED METHOD (296), ITERATOR (298), ENUMERATION METHOD (300), and BATCH METHOD (302).

- *Component Partitioning*: Encapsulated Implementation (313), Whole-Part (317), Composite (319), Master-Slave (321), Half-object plus Protocol (324), and Replicated Component Group (326).

- *Application Control*: Page Controller (337), Front Controller (339), Application Controller (341), Command Processor (343), Template View (345), Transform View (347), Firewall Proxy (349), and Authorization (351).

- *Concurrency*: Half-Sync/Half-Async (359), Leader/Followers (362), Active Object (365), Monitor Object (368).

- *Synchronization*: Guarded Suspension (380), Future (382), Thread-Safe Interface (384), Double-Checked Locking (386), Strategized Locking (388), Scoped Locking (390), Thread-Specific Storage (392), Copied Value (394), and Immutable Value (396).

- *Object Interaction*: Observer (405), Double Dispatch (408), Mediator (410), Memento (414), Context Object (416), Data Transfer Object (418), Command (412), and Message (420).

- *Adaptation and Extension*: Bridge (436), Object Adapter (438), Interceptor (444), Chain of Responsibility (440), Interpreter (442), Visitor (447), Decorator (449), Template Method (453), Strategy (455), Null Object (457), Wrapper Facade (459), Execute-Around Object (451), and Declarative Component Implementation (461).

- *Object Behavior*: Objects for States (467), Methods for States (469), and Collections for States (471).

- *Resource Management*: Object Manager (492), Container (488), Component Configurator (490), Lookup (495), Virtual Proxy (497), Lifecycle Callback (499), Task Coordinator (501), Resource Pool (503), Resource Cache (505), Lazy Acquisition (507), Eager Acquisition (509), Partial Acquisition (511), Activator (513), Evictor (515), Leasing (517), Automated Garbage Collection (519), Counting Handle (522), Abstract Factory (525), Builder (527), Factory Method (529), and Disposal Method (531).

- *Database Access*: Database Access Layer (538), Data Mapper (540), Row Data Gateway (542), Table Data Gateway (544), and Active Record (546).

For several problem areas more patterns are documented than we describe explicitly. For example, whole pattern languages exist in the area of remoting [VKZ04] and messaging [HoWo03], which complement the patterns in the distribution infrastructure problem area. Our pattern language for distributed computing therefore integrates other pattern sources that refine and complement the patterns we present. In particular, it connects to:

- A pattern language for designing server components [VSW02]
- A pattern language for remoting [VKZ04]
- A pattern language for messaging [HoWo03]
- A pattern collection for designing enterprise application architectures [Fow03a]
- A pattern collection for security [SFHBS06]
- Four pattern collections and languages for accessing relational and object-relational databases [BW95] [KC97] [Kel99] [Fow03a]
- A pattern language for reference counting in C++ [Hen01b]
- Two collections of patterns for designing applications using specific middleware platforms [ACM01] [MS03].

In other words, our pattern language for distributed computing is not standalone and isolated, but tightly integrated with major parts of the known pattern universe. These relationships integrate approximately a further 150 patterns into our pattern language, which makes it one of the largest pattern languages in software documented to date. Although we do not describe all these patterns explicitly in this book, they are an integral part of our pattern language for distributed computing. Please refer to the sources referenced above to learn about those patterns for which we do not have room to present explicitly.

It is important to note that we do not consider our pattern language as complete—it is *work in progress*. We have not covered all relevant topics, such as security, in full depth, and with growing experience in building distributed systems, new patterns need integration with the language, and existing patterns need refactoring.

3.4   Presentation

To support your reading, comprehension, and digestion of our pattern language for distributed computing, as well as to help you extract useful advice and suggestions to build your own systems from it, all problem area descriptions and pattern descriptions follow a common, structured format. Each problem area description provides an overview of the problem and solution spaces of a specific technical topic in the construction of distributed systems. This description also summarizes issues to consider when resolving specific problems with the help of the associated patterns. A problem area description is structured into four parts:

- An *introduction* to the general scope and major challenges of the problem area, which is the general context for its constituent patterns.

- The *abstracts* of the patterns that address the challenges arising in the problem area, as well as diagrams that show how selected patterns in that area are integrated into our pattern language.

- A *discussion* that compares and contrasts the patterns, and also outlines application scenarios outside the scope of our pattern language, if there are any.

- The *pattern description* that explains each pattern in more depth, focusing on its application context, the problem and forces it addresses, the solution, its consequences, key implementation hints, and relationships to other patterns in our pattern language.

The following diagram illustrates the structure of an introduction to a problem area:

Name
of the
problem area

Scope
of the
problem area

List of
challenges
to be resolved
by the patterns
that 'belong' to
the problem area

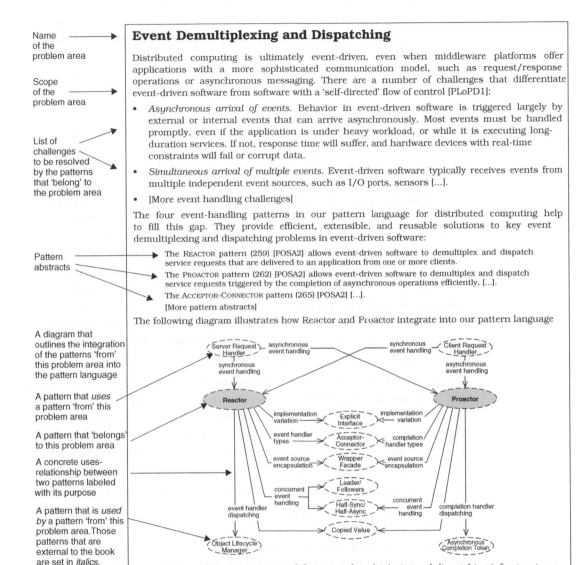

Event Demultiplexing and Dispatching

Distributed computing is ultimately event-driven, even when middleware platforms offer applications with a more sophisticated communication model, such as request/response operations or asynchronous messaging. There are a number of challenges that differentiate event-driven software from software with a 'self-directed' flow of control [PLoPD1]:

- *Asynchronous arrival of events.* Behavior in event-driven software is triggered largely by external or internal events that can arrive asynchronously. Most events must be handled promptly, even if the application is under heavy workload, or while it is executing long-duration services. If not, response time will suffer, and hardware devices with real-time constraints will fail or corrupt data.

- *Simultaneous arrival of multiple events.* Event-driven software typically receives events from multiple independent event sources, such as I/O ports, sensors [...].

- [More event handling challenges]

The four event-handling patterns in our pattern language for distributed computing help to fill this gap. They provide efficient, extensible, and reusable solutions to key event demultiplexing and dispatching problems in event-driven software:

Pattern
abstracts

The REACTOR pattern (259) [POSA2] allows event-driven software to demultiplex and dispatch service requests that are delivered to an application from one or more clients.

The PROACTOR pattern (262) [POSA2] allows event-driven software to demultiplex and dispatch service requests triggered by the completion of asynchronous operations efficiently, [...].

The ACCEPTOR-CONNECTOR pattern (265) [POSA2] [...].

[More pattern abstracts]

The following diagram illustrates how Reactor and Proactor integrate into our pattern language

A diagram that
outlines the integration
of the patterns 'from'
this problem area into
the pattern language

A pattern that *uses*
a pattern 'from' this
problem area

A pattern that 'belongs'
to this problem area

A concrete uses-
relationship between
two patterns labeled
with its purpose

A pattern that is *used
by* a pattern 'from' this
problem area.Those
patterns that are
external to the book
are set in *italics*.

A discussion
on the patterns
from this
problem area

The Reactor and Proactor patterns define event demultiplexing and dispatching infrastructures that can be used by event-driven applications to detect, demultiplex, dispatch, and process events they receive from the network. Although both patterns resolve essentially the same problem in a similar context, and also use similar patterns to implement their solutions, the concrete event-handling infrastructures they suggest are distinct, due to the to orthongonal which each pattern is exposed. [More discussion].

Our pattern form is designed to present the essence of each pattern quickly and easily so that you know what it is about, how it addresses the problem and forces, what consequences to consider when applying it, and how to implement it using other patterns in our language. Our goal is to provide enough detail to make each pattern comprehensible, without losing sight of how it fits into the overall pattern language. The pattern form we find most suitable for meeting this objective is based closely on the form used by Christopher Alexander [AIS77].

The form begins with the name of the pattern, which is labeled with either no stars, one star, or two stars. The number of stars denote our level of confidence in the pattern's maturity. Two stars mean that we are confident the pattern addresses a genuine problem in its respective problem area and that it is essential to implement the proposed solution in one of its possible variants to resolve this problem effectively. One star means that we think that the pattern addresses a genuine problem and that its solution is a good one, but know that pattern needs to mature. No stars means that we observed the problem addressed by the pattern every now and then, and also found its proposed solution to be useful, but the pattern needs significant revision to reach the quality of a one-star or two-star pattern. A no star pattern description may also indicate there are alternative, better patterns to take its place.

After the pattern's name comes the context of the pattern. It specifies one or more development activities in which we can potentially apply the pattern, together with the names and page references of all patterns in our language in whose implementations we are performing the respective activities. These references thus connect the pattern to those 'higher-level' patterns in our language that can benefit from it.

The main part of the pattern follows after the context. We separate this main part from its preceding 'introduction' by three diamonds, '◆◆◆.' The first paragraph of the pattern's main part contains the essential problem statement, so we set this paragraph in bold face. Next come the forces associated with the problem: what are the requirements for, and desired properties of, its solution, or the constraints to consider when resolving it? Each force typically corresponds to a (part of a) particular challenge outlined in the introduction of the pattern's enclosing problem area.

The word 'therefore' introduces the next section: the core of the solution that the pattern proposes to resolve the problem and its associated forces. Within one or more boldface paragraphs, this solution core is stated as an instruction, so that we can consider it as a 'mini-process' for implementing the pattern. The first one or two sentences of this instruction emphasize the general solution principle. After this comes a stepwise description of the concrete structure to create and an outline of the behavior that executes in this structure. A diagram illustrates the structure and its behavior. The notation that we use intentionally does *not* follow any of the popular modeling formats for software systems.

One reason we do not use popular modeling notations is to avoid the fallacy of 'false concreteness,' which often leads readers to think that what is in the diagram is the *only* way to implement a pattern. Instead, we provide a solution sketch, not a concrete specification with classes, objects, and relationships between them. Our notation therefore mixes many aspects: role specification, role organization, role collaboration, pseudo-interfaces, and pseudo-code, whatever appears appropriate to show a particular pattern.

Another '♦♦♦' indicates the end of the pattern's main part. All subsequent paragraphs explain its solution part in more depth. For example, they describe the pattern's proposed structure and behavior, justify why this structure and behavior resolves the problem and its forces, and list important consequences of this structure and behavior. This part of the description connects the pattern to other patterns in our language. If another pattern can help with the current pattern's implementation, we reference the other pattern by its name and the page where you can find it, and also present a short summary of its contribution to the implementation.

Naturally, the use of other patterns is a suggestion, because it is the concrete context of the application under development that determines whether or not it is helpful to apply them. The use of another pattern may or may not be essential to the solution and character of the enclosing pattern. In our pattern descriptions, we make this difference explicit: where the application of a pattern is mandatory, its use is phrased imperatively, otherwise we offer a recommendation rather than a rule.

The following diagram illustrates the pattern form and notation we use:

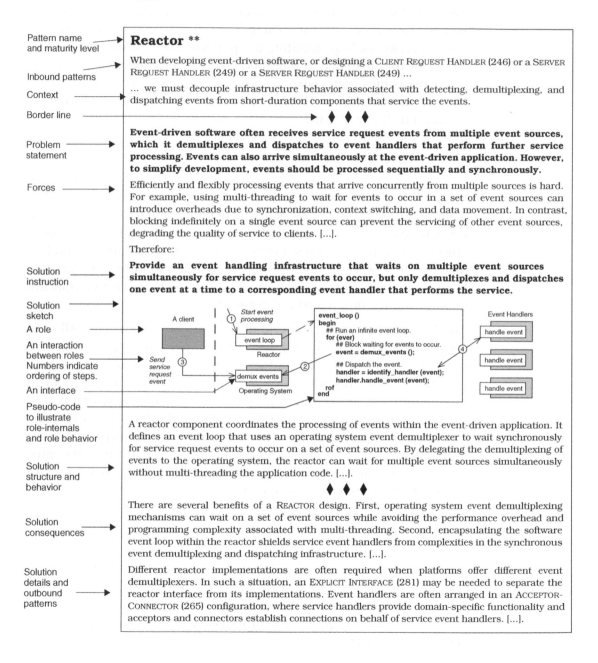

Pattern name and maturity level

Reactor **

Inbound patterns

When developing event-driven software, or designing a CLIENT REQUEST HANDLER (246) or a SERVER REQUEST HANDLER (249) or a SERVER REQUEST HANDLER (249) …

Context

… we must decouple infrastructure behavior associated with detecting, demultiplexing, and dispatching events from short-duration components that service the events.

Border line

♦ ♦ ♦

Problem statement

Event-driven software often receives service request events from multiple event sources, which it demultiplexes and dispatches to event handlers that perform further service processing. Events can also arrive simultaneously at the event-driven application. However, to simplify development, events should be processed sequentially and synchronously.

Forces

Efficiently and flexibly processing events that arrive concurrently from multiple sources is hard. For example, using multi-threading to wait for events to occur in a set of event sources can introduce overheads due to synchronization, context switching, and data movement. In contrast, blocking indefinitely on a single event source can prevent the servicing of other event sources, degrading the quality of service to clients. [...].

Therefore:

Solution instruction

Provide an event handling infrastructure that waits on multiple event sources simultaneously for service request events to occur, but only demultiplexes and dispatches one event at a time to a corresponding event handler that performs the service.

Solution sketch
A role

An interaction between roles
Numbers indicate ordering of steps.

An interface

Pseudo-code to illustrate role-internals and role behavior

A client

Start event processing

event loop

Reactor

Send service request event

demux events

Operating System

event_loop ()
begin
  ## Run an infinite event loop.
  for (ever)
    ## Block waiting for events to occur.
    event = demux_events ();

    ## Dispatch the event.
    handler = identify_handler (event);
    handler.handle_event (event);
  rof
end

Event Handlers

handle event

handle event

handle event

Solution structure and behavior

A reactor component coordinates the processing of events within the event-driven application. It defines an event loop that uses an operating system event demultiplexer to wait synchronously for service request events to occur on a set of event sources. By delegating the demultiplexing of events to the operating system, the reactor can wait for multiple event sources simultaneously without multi-threading the application code. [...].

♦ ♦ ♦

Solution consequences

There are several benefits of a REACTOR design. First, operating system event demultiplexing mechanisms can wait on a set of event sources while avoiding the performance overhead and programming complexity associated with multi-threading. Second, encapsulating the software event loop within the reactor shields service event handlers from complexities in the synchronous event demultiplexing and dispatching infrastructure. [...].

Solution details and outbound patterns

Different reactor implementations are often required when platforms offer different event demultiplexers. In such a situation, an EXPLICIT INTERFACE (281) may be needed to separate the reactor interface from its implementations. Event handlers are often arranged in an ACCEPTOR-CONNECTOR (265) configuration, where service handlers provide domain-specific functionality and acceptors and connectors establish connections on behalf of service event handlers. [...].

Each pattern description can be read in one of three ways:

- If you are only interested in a brief overview, just read the bold faced paragraphs that capture the essence of the pattern.
- If you are also interested in knowing about the forces associated with the main problem statement, as well as in structural and behavioral details of the fundamental solution idea, read all parts of the pattern up to the second '◆◆.'
- Finally, if you are interested in how a pattern integrates into the pattern language, read its entire description.

Since we are focusing on the forest more than the trees, describing the details of each pattern implementation is not within the focus of our pattern language. If you are interested in these aspects, please refer to the original source of the respective pattern.

3.5 Practical Use

Our pattern language aims to cover the best practices in distributed computing and to present these practices in a way that can benefit the development of new systems, as well as the refactoring of existing systems. Using the language in actual software projects is therefore straightforward. When developing a new distributed application you can enter the language through its root pattern: DOMAIN MODEL (182). This pattern supports the fundamental partitioning of your application domain by separating the various problem domains and technical infrastructure concerns in development. Following the implementation hints in DOMAIN MODEL that are applicable to the system you are developing will lead you—one by one—to other patterns in our language, such as LAYERS (185), DOMAIN OBJECT (208), BROKER (237), and MODEL-VIEW-CONTROLLER (188). These other patterns help resolve subproblems, such as distribution infrastructure, application and component partitioning, and internal component design, that arise within the context of realizing a DOMAIN MODEL as a distributed system.

The referenced patterns are applied typically in the sequence they are presented, unless they represent alternatives to one another. Similarly, when realizing the referenced patterns, you are guided to yet other patterns that provide even more detail to the existing design. This linear but recursive process of unfolding continues until you arrive at a pattern whose implementation process does not reference other patterns, or one where you decide to not follow such references. The presentation order of the language therefore follows closely what might be considered the principal *pattern sequences* within the language.

You can take a particular path through the pattern language either with a breadth-first or a depth-first approach to traverse the outgoing references from DOMAIN MODEL, or even a mixture of both approaches. The result will be a sequence of patterns that guides the design of the distributed application being developed. The software architecture that results from applying this sequence thus exposes a high density of tightly integrated patterns that complete and complement one another consistently and coherently. Similarly, when refactoring the design of an existing distributed application, you enter the language via the particular pattern that addresses the problem whose current design is subject to refactoring, and continue from there.

Using our pattern language allows you to create a near infinite variety of distinct software architectures for distributed systems. Different requirements, design objectives, or constraints for the application being developed or refactored probably require you to select other pattern alternatives that are suggested by the patterns of our language, or to follow or not follow a particular pattern reference. Each individual decision will create a different path through the language—and thus a different pattern sequence—which can yield a different software architecture. Our pattern language acknowledges and supports the fact that there is no one-size-fits-all software architecture for distributed systems. Nevertheless, the concrete software architectures you can create with our pattern language will share a similar philosophy and style with successful distributed systems.

To show how our pattern language for distributed computing can be used in production software, Part II, *A Pattern Story*, discusses in depth how pattern sequences from the language informed the architecture of a warehouse management process control system. The story introduces the domain of warehouse management and outlines a corresponding DOMAIN MODEL, which in its subsequent chapters is transformed iteratively into a concrete software architecture. We start with the system's baseline architecture, then look inside its communication middleware, and end by describing the subsystem that represents the warehouse storage topology. Each section discusses the problem addressed in the design of the warehouse management process control system, as well as its associated forces, presents a pattern from our language that helps to address the problem and forces, and discusses how that pattern is realized in the system's software architecture. For cases in which we considered alternative patterns, we briefly discuss what patterns they were and why we did not chose them.

For example, the pattern sequence presented in Part II, *A Story*, resulted in the design of a product-line architecture for warehouse management process controls systems, as shown below.

Layering and core Domain Objects of the
Warehouse Management Process Control
product-line architecture

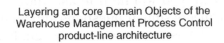

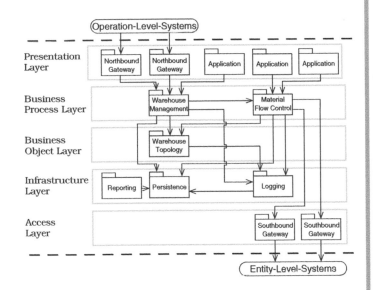

Pattern sequence that informed
the product-line architecture

Pattern	Challenge
DOMAIN MODEL	Separation of functional concerns
LAYERS	Separation of abstraction levels
DOMAIN OBJECT	Encapsulation of functionality
EXPLICIT INTERFACE	Domain Object realization
ENCAPSULATED IMPLEMENTATION	Domain Object realization
BROKER	Distribution Infrastructure
MODEL-VIEW-CONTROLLER	User Interface Separation
HALF OBJECT PLUS PROTOCOL	Component Distribution
ACTIVE OBJECT	Concurrency Infrastructure
LEADER/FOLLOWERS	Concurrency Infrastructure
DATABASE ACCESS LAYER	Database Separation
COMPONENT CONFIGURATOR	System Configuration

Another pattern sequence presented in Part II helped in creating a product-line architecture for highly efficient and flexible communication middleware, which also forms the basis of several BROKER (237) implementations, including the *Component-Integrated ACE ORB (CIAO)* [WSG+03], *The ACE ORB (TAO)* [SNG+02], and *ZEN* [KSK04].

Although the software architecture for the warehouse management process control system shares a range of properties with the architectures of many other distributed systems, it is *not* a reference architecture for distributed systems in general. Since the specific requirements and constraints of the system being developed informed the software architecture of the system, different requirements and constraints could have yielded a different architecture. Nevertheless, the story exemplifies the dialog to have when developing distributed systems using our pattern language, and the aspects to consider when applying its patterns in production settings. When using the language in your own context, you will need to ask your architects, developers, and system engineers similar questions and address similar design considerations, whose answers can be guided by our pattern language.

II   A Story

> *Don't be too timid and squeamish about your actions. All life*
> *is an experiment. The more experiments you make the better.*
>
> *Ralph Waldo Emerson*

The second part of this book tells a pattern story: we describe how a real-world process control system for warehouse management was designed with our pattern language for distributed computing. The story focuses on three areas of this software system: its baseline architecture, its communication middleware, and the representation of warehouse topology.

Using an example from the real world, we illustrate how a software architecture can be designed systematically with help of patterns. Step by step we unfold the vision of this architecture. We start with the fundamental baseline architecture, then look inside the system's communication middleware, and end by detailing the subsystem that represents the warehouse storage topology.

Our goal with this part is, however, not only to present an illustrative example of the use of the pattern language for distributed systems that we present in Part III. We also want to demonstrate that patterns and pattern languages in general are a powerful tool for developing software architectures on the basis of thoughtful and explicit design decisions and considerations, so that the resulting software systems can fulfill their required functional, operational, and developmental qualities.

The chapters in this part are structured as follows:

- Chapter 4, *Warehouse Management Process Control*, briefly introduces the domain and context of warehouse management process control systems.

- Chapter 5, *Baseline Architecture*, describes the architecture vision of the warehouse management process control system: its partitioning into subsystems, their relationships and interactions, and key design principles that guide the refinement of this baseline.

- Chapter 6, *Communication Middleware*, presents the core design of the communication infrastructure for the warehouse management process control system. This infrastructure is a realization of the CORBA Component Model reference architecture [OMG02] [OMG04a].

- Chapter 7, *Warehouse Topology*, outlines how the physical storage structure of a warehouse is represented.

- Chapter 8, *The Story Behind The Pattern Story*, finishes our pattern story by reflecting retrospectively on its plot and conceptual highlights in relation to the pattern language concept.

Using a real-world story to illustrate our pattern language for distributed systems has several pros and cons. A key strength of the story is that it really happened—it therefore reflects and compresses the concrete discussions led, and design decisions made, during the development of a real-world warehouse management process software system.

As a consequence of documenting reality, however, the story is also colored with aspects and considerations that are individual to the specific system that was developed, and not necessarily general for the domain. One such aspect is the choice of programming language. Some portions of our warehouse management process control system were written in C++, others in Java. Although the pattern sequences discussed in the ensuing chapters are largely language-independent, there are some aspects that differ depending on the choice of language and the features available in standard libraries and frameworks. We discuss these differences at the appropriate points in the chapters.

The key message we want to convey with this pattern story is not affected by such system-specific aspects, however: patterns are an important tool to support the creation of sustainable, high-quality software architectures and implementations.

4 Warehouse Management Process Control

Warehouse Management Systems (WMS) are a key part of the supply chain and provide directed stock rotation, intelligent picking directives, automatic consolidation and cross-docking to maximize the use of valuable warehouse space. The systems also direct and optimize stock put-away based on real-time information about the status of bin utilization. Having a WMS in place means you don't depend any more on people's experience, the system has the intelligence.

Wikipedia

This chapter introduces the key concepts and requirements of warehouse management process control systems. We outline core functional responsibilities, operational requirements, and developmental considerations, and illustrate how warehouse management process control systems can be integrated with other software systems and environments.

4.1 System Scope

Warehouse management process control systems provide logistics support to manage the flow of items and assets in, and across, warehouse storage facilities. Users of such control systems include couriers, such as UPS, FedEx, and DHL, and large trading and manufacturing companies, such as Wal-Mart and BMW. To understand the responsibilities of warehouse management process control systems—and also the key factors that influence their software architecture—it helps first to define their concrete scope and relationships to other, surrounding systems.

Warehouse management process control systems belong to the broad category of industrial automation systems, which can be further classified into three layers that together form the so-called automation pyramid:

- At the top level, the *operation* level, we find systems that manage end-to-end industrial business processes, such as enterprise resource planning (ERP), manufacturing execution (ME), and supply chain process management (SCPM) systems. SAP is a widely known example of such a system, which can be used for all the three activities above. In the context of warehouse management, operation-level systems are responsible for planning, scheduling, and supervising the progress of all business-level operations within a warehouse.

- At the intermediate level, the *process control* level, reside the systems that are responsible for the correct and timely execution of all activities planned and scheduled at the operation level. In the warehouse management domain this includes administrative tasks such as stock management, order management, receiving and shipping, and the management of storage and transportation facilities in the warehouse, as well as operational tasks such as the execution of concrete transportation orders. The system that is the subject of our pattern story lives at this level in the pyramid.

- At the bottom level, the *entity* level, there are the field devices and network elements that are used by the systems at the process control level to execute concrete operations in the physical world. In the context of warehouse management these are the systems that represent and control the underlying automation hardware, such as conveyor belts, stacker cranes, or the devices for human-computer interaction on manually operated transportation facilities, such as fork-lift trucks.

The diagram below outlines the three levels of the automation pyramid:

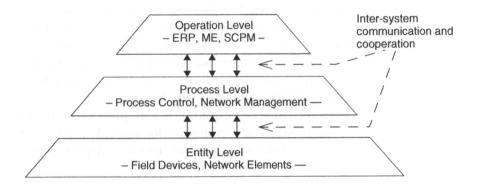

The automation pyramid also raises two fundamental and system-wide requirements for process control systems:

- A process control system resides in the middle of the pyramid: it receives orders from the operation level and reports back to it any and all progress in executing these orders, as well as controlling and supervising the underlying entity level to execute a specific order. Ultimately, all automation processes are end-to-end, beginning and ending at the operation level and involving the systems at the process control and entity level in their control flow. The different software systems in an industrial automation environment are often provided by different vendors, however, which in turn requires appropriate application integration measures to support end-to-end operations seamlessly across multiple systems.

- The entire IT infrastructure outlined by the automation pyramid is inherently distributed. The architectures of all software systems must therefore take into account that their partner systems are remote and only accessible via some form of IPC.

4.2   Warehouse Management Process Control

As we identified in the previous section, a warehouse management process control system resides at the intermediate level of
the automation pyramid. It is generally responsible for executing
and supervising administrative and operational tasks in a warehouse, including communication with the systems at the operation
and entity level. The following list of responsibilities provides a brief
overview of core functionality of a warehouse management process
control system—thus forming its fundamental DOMAIN MODEL (182).
Note that we neither list all responsibilities of a warehouse management process control system, nor specify the listed responsibilities
in full detail. Our objective is to give readers a rough idea of the
scope of warehouse management process control systems, enough
to understand the rationale for specific design decisions and pattern selections in the subsequent chapters of this pattern story. The
relevant responsibilities include:

- *Stock management.* For each type of item, the warehouse management process control system maintains relevant master data, such
  as the item's name, its description, and the available stock. For each
  individual item, the system maintains data necessary for correct
  and efficient order management, such as its sell-by date, its current
  storage time, and, most importantly, where in the warehouse the
  actual item is stored.

- *Order management.* From the systems at the operation level the
  warehouse management process control system receives different
  types of orders that must be executed: shipping orders for a specific
  customer, replenishment orders from a manufacturing or production line, receipt of orders from the receiving department, and
  announcements of future receipts and shippings.

  For orders, the system must first check if the ordered types of
  item are available in the ordered quantity. If they are, the second step is to decide from where in the warehouse to fetch the
  item. This decision typically is based on the information the system
  maintains about each item, such as its sell-by date. Finally, the
  order management functionality generates specific transportation
  orders to fetch each item from the warehouse and transport it to a

designated shipping destination for further handling. The progress and status of each order is reported back to the appropriate system at the operation level of the automation pyramid. For shipping and receiving announcements, the order management functionality prepares the corresponding transportation orders, for example by reserving appropriate amount of physical storage and transportation facilities, and schedules them for execution at the designated time.

- *Shipping.* Items fetched from the warehouse must be collected and prepared for shipping, which includes tasks such as quality and quantity checking, updating all master and individual data for the items to be shipped, packing, and printing packing slips. A special task in the context of shipping is *picking*: a certain quantity of an item is picked manually or automatically from a box or container that contains more items than needed. This task includes the selection of the box or container from the warehouse, its transportation to the picking station, all updates of the master and individual data of the relevant items, and the transportation of the box or container with all remaining items back into its correct location in the warehouse.

- *Receiving.* Items that arrive at the warehouse must be prepared before being stored, which involves unpacking, quality and quantity checking, and entering or updating all master and individual data for the items received. Once prepared, transportation orders are created to store the items in the warehouse.

- *Material Flow Control.* A transportation order for a specific quantity of items created by the order management functionality only specifies the target storage, destination storage, the transportation unit containing the items, and information about the items themselves. However, moving the transportation unit from the target storage to the destination storage can involve multiple legs, each of which can be executed by different transportation facilities. For example, a pallet of boxes could be fetched from the warehouse gates by a forklift truck and transported to a transfer bin, from where a stacker crane picks it up to store on a high rack. Decomposing transportation orders into legs, assigning appropriate transportation facilities to each leg, and monitoring the execution of all legs is one responsibility of the material flow control functionality. Optimizing the entire material flow within the warehouse to achieve an optimal throughput is the other. The material flow control functionality sends concrete transportation instructions to the respective automation hardware, and receives acknowledgements and status messages in response. Any progress in executing transportation orders is reported back to the order management functionality.

- *Topology management.* A warehouse process control system is also responsible for managing the warehouse topology, as well as providing a representation of that topology to the order management and material flow control. All physical storage in a warehouse, such as different types of bin and high rack, as well as the available transportation facilities such as forklifts, conveyor belts, and stacker cranes, is arranged in a warehouse topology to ensure proper and effective warehouse operation. For example, high racks are organized with respect to aisles and sides in an aisle, and each aisle is associated with one or more stacker cranes and transfer bins from which the stacker cranes can pick up transportation units. The storage in a warehouse is also partitioned according to various storage organization criteria, such as storage for hazardous items, or items that require a certain storage temperature.

In addition to functional requirements, a warehouse management process control system must also support several operational and developmental properties. Again, brevity demands that we focus on only a few of the many relevant operational and developmental requirements, so that readers can better understand the pattern story told in the following chapters:

- *Distribution.* A warehouse management process control system is inherently distributed. Its functionality must therefore be accessible from many different, distributed clients, such as PCs at the picking stations and mobile clients on forklifts.

- *Performance.* Although a warehouse management process control system is not a 'hard' real-time system—that is, a system in which operations must meet defined deadlines—performance is business-critical. There is a required throughput for the system as a whole, so the system must ensure that all transportation orders are executed in a timely and efficient manner without any visible interruption or stop-and-go behavior.

- *Scalability.* Warehouses can differ significantly in their size. A warehouse management process control system must therefore be able to support small warehouses with just a few thousand bins, as well as large warehouses with well over a million bins. Warehouses can also vary in the functionality they need. For example, depending on the capabilities of the partner systems at the operation and entity level of the automation pyramid, a warehouse management process control system must provide more or less powerful administrative and operational functionality. Finally, the number of devices participating in a warehouse management process control can vary: small installations involve only a few dozen computational devices, whereas large installations can include thousands.

- *Availability.* Many warehouses operate in 24/7 mode with three shifts per day. Availability is therefore crucial for supporting the business case for a warehouse management process control system. Any downtime disrupts supply chains, the state and operation of other systems, people, and so on, which ultimately means loss of business and money. Industrial automation systems in general, and process control systems specifically, therefore, typically demand a minimum availability of 99.999%—a maximum downtime of just over five minutes per year!

- *Persistence.* Most state maintained by the warehouse management process control system, for example the warehouse topology, the available stock, and all orders under processing, must be maintained persistently. It is important that the system can always rely on consistent, up-to-date data, be it for book-keeping purposes or for system restart in the event of intentional or unexpected shutdowns.

- *Portability.* The system must run on multiple hardware and operating system platforms. Windows is typically the prime choice for user devices, while UNIX or Linux is the most likely for machines hosting core functionality. Similarly, the system must be able to use different databases, for instance, Oracle and SQL Server.

- *Dynamic configuration.* There is a strong need for runtime (re)configuration and (re)deployment of a warehouse management process control system. For example the warehouse capacity may be temporarily extended to handle seasonal peaks. Similarly, depending on the contents of a warehouse, strategies for fetching and storing items can change. However, stringent business constraints on availability require that the system cannot be shut down for (re)configuration and (re)deployment activities.

- *Human-computer interaction.*   Users communicate with a warehouse management process control system through a wide variety of user interfaces. Examples include form-based interfaces served by keyboards and scanners, hand-held terminals with just a few buttons to press, and fully fledged graphical user interfaces served by mice, keyboards, touch screens, and so on.

- *Component integration.*   Wherever useful or necessary, a warehouse management process control system integrates third-party products such as databases, or existing legacy software such as that for accessing the entity level in the automation pyramid.

- *Generality.*   The business intent of our warehouse management process control system is to provide a general solution for this domain, one whose architecture and implementation is configurable and adaptable to meet the needs of a specific real-world warehouse. For example, the scalability requirement distinguishes different warehouse sizes, the portability requirement lists several operating systems and database management systems to be supported, and the human-computer interaction requirement outlines a wide range of different user interface types to be offered. Depending on customer needs, concrete instances of the warehouse management process control system can also vary in the domain functionality they offer. For example, some customers do not need the functionality for stock and order management, because it is already provided by systems at the operation level of the automation pyramid. Or, as another example, they use warehouse management process control systems from other vendors that cover all functions except material flow control.

In summary, warehouse management process control systems must meet many challenging requirements, operational and developmental as well as functional. It is the job of the system's software architecture to balance the requirements such that the demands of specific warehouses can be met appropriately.

5 Baseline Architecture

There is at the back of every artist's mind,
a pattern or type of architecture.

G.K. Chesterton, lone quote at the beginning of the
Father Brown Mysteries Series of books.

This chapter tells the beginning of the pattern story: the specification of the baseline architecture for our warehouse management process control system. We outline how patterns helped to partition the system's core domain and infrastructure functionality, address distribution and concurrency concerns, and support users and other applications to access, or integrate with, its functionality. The result is the foundation for a product-line architecture: a structural backbone that captures the high-level aspects common to all configurations of the warehouse management process control system, and which also provides infrastructure and architectural measures for defining and handling the variations in specific instances of the system.

5.1   Architecture Context

Chapter 4, *Warehouse Management Process Control*, showed that warehouse management process control systems must provide a large set of integrated and effective administrative and operational domain functionality. The characteristics of this functionality, as well as the functionality set provided, can also differ between different instances of the system, depending on the capabilities of the IT environment into which these instances must be integrated. Realizing the domain functionality further requires an appropriate infrastructure, for example for interprocess communication, persistence, and logging. Finally, the system's functionality must be easily accessible by both users and systems that reside at the operation level of the automation pyramid: the warehouse management process control system itself needs well-defined access to all entity-level systems it supervises.

With such a diverse and potentially conflicting set of requirements to fulfill, an approach that can respond to any conflicts and balance such diversity is needed to define the baseline architecture for the system. One such approach is a product line [Bosch00] [ClNo01]—which, at the level of software design, is typically achieved via a product-line architecture. A product-line architecture is a software architecture that serves as a common basis for all envisioned members of a product line. It defines which structural and behavioral aspects are common and invariant for all system instances and which structural and behavioral aspects can vary, explicitly separates the invariant from the variant aspects, and supports handling the variant aspects in a well-defined and controlled manner [Bus03].

Designing a quality product-line architecture is non-trivial. Thoughtful design decisions and explicit use of known architectural principles—ranging from separation of concerns, through loose coupling, to strict encapsulation—are needed at all levels of abstraction granularity and from all points of view. At the baseline level of a product-line architecture this means providing a proper and loosely coupled partitioning and modularization of the system's main responsibilities, an infrastructure to handle its required variabilities, and support for its integration into envisioned IT environments.

5.2   Partitioning the Big Ball of Mud

The basis for a sustainable product-line architecture is a clear separation and encapsulation of different system concerns, be they functional in nature or infrastructure-related. Otherwise, the implementation of these concerns will likely be tangled rather than loosely coupled, which complicates their independent development, configuration for a specific instance of the product line, and deployment in a computer network. Another motivation for a clear separation of concerns in a product-line architecture is that different system aspects can change at different rates. For example, user interfaces typically evolve faster than the system's core functionality, which itself evolves faster than database schemas. Yet modifications should affect only the parts that need to change, but no more—any ripple effect should be avoided.

How can we organize the system's functionality into coherent groups such that each group can be developed and modified independently?

Partition the system into multiple interacting LAYERS *(185), with each layer representing a specific responsibility or concern of relevance and comprising all functionality that addresses that concern.*

For the warehouse management process control system, we can identify five different layers:

- *Presentation.*   This layer contains the interfaces to systems at the operation level of the automation pyramid, the so-called 'northbound gateways,' as well as user-level applications that access the system's functionality directly, such as for picking and warehouse topology management.

- *Business process.*   This layer provides the administrative and operational functionality the system must support, such as stock management, order management, shipping, receiving, and material flow control.

- *Business objects.*   This layer comprises representations of domain-specific physical and logical entities on which the functionality in the business process layer operates. The main responsibility of this layer is to maintain and provide access to the warehouse topology.

- *Infrastructure.* This layer provides all domain-independent infrastructure functionality, such as persistence and logging, that is necessary to implement the business object and business process layers.

- *Access.* This layer provides the interfaces to systems residing at the entity level of the automation pyramid, the so-called 'southbound gateways.'

The LAYERS pattern supports a strict separation of concerns in our warehouse management process control system. In particular, it helps to partition a 'big ball of mud' of functionality into tangible levels of abstraction, each of which groups elements that share a common stability and can be developed and modified independently without unanticipated effects on other parts.

5.3   Decomposing the Layers

Layers are an important step toward providing a product-line architecture for the warehouse management process control system. Yet layers alone are still too coarse-grained to support truly modular software development, because they only separate concerns between functionality at different levels of abstraction, and not between different functionality at the same level of abstraction. For example, it is still possible in our system to develop overly interwoven warehouse management and material flow control functionality in the business process layer, although both functionalities address distinct concerns that are only loosely coupled.

How can we refine a LAYERS (185) architecture into smaller, strictly separated modular parts with each part having a clearly defined and scoped responsibility?

Provide a DOMAIN OBJECT (208) for each self-contained, coherent functionally related responsibility within a LAYERS design to strictly separate, encapsulate, and modularize different functional responsibilities at the same level of abstraction.

In the presentation layer of our system we can distinguish the different northbound gateways and client applications we must support. In the business process layer we can separate the warehouse management functionality, comprising all administrative tasks, from the material flow control functionality that controls the systems at the entity level. In the infrastructure layer, each different functionality, such as logging, reporting, and persistence, can also be separated, and the access layer can comprise a separate southbound gateway for each supported entity-level-system.[2] The following diagram illustrates this layering.

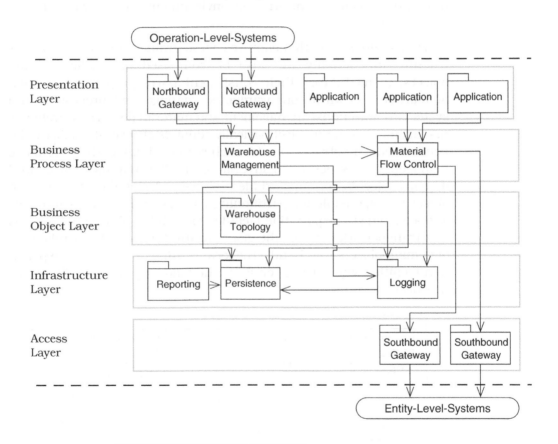

---

2 Note that this diagram only shows functionality that plays a role in our pattern story. In the real world the business process, business object, and infrastructure layers of a warehouse management process control system include much more functionality, for example for alarm management, monitoring and control, and security. In addition, we bend UML notation to our needs and use the package symbol to denote a domain object. The package symbol allows us to denote that a domain object can—like a service—consist of more than one component or class.

Using DOMAIN OBJECT to partition application functionality is ideal for modular software development and the design of product-line architectures. Domain objects provide the right level of granularity, separation of concerns, and inner cohesion so that each domain object can be developed and evolved independently. Domain objects are also appropriate units of functional configuration for different system instances. Several well-established technologies are available for realizing domain objects, whether fine-grained object-oriented frameworks, component-oriented environments, or service-oriented infrastructures.

Large domain objects that capture coarse-grained business or infrastructure functionality can also be composed of smaller domain objects, to modularize their constituent parts properly. Two such domain objects within our warehouse management process control system are warehouse management and material flow. The warehouse management domain object basically consists of several smaller independent domain objects, one for each responsibility of the warehouse management, as described in Chapter 4. The material flow-control domain object is decomposed hierarchically. A global routing domain object is responsible for partitioning transportation orders into legs and assigning transportation facilities to each leg. To execute the legs of a transportation order, the global routing uses and controls a set of domain objects that handle the local routing of specific transportation facilities within the given legs. The following diagram illustrates this decomposition:

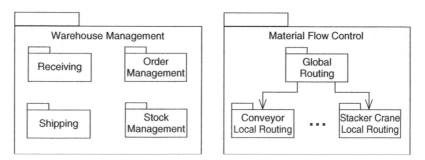

The decomposition of the warehouse topology domain object is illustrated in Chapter 7, *Warehouse Topology*.

5.4 Accessing Domain Object Functionality

The partitioning of the warehouse management process control system into layers containing domain objects provides a sustainable foundation for modular software development, from loose coupling during development to simple deployment of the system's functionality in a computer network. If we analyze the first diagram from the previous section, however, we see that in spite of the clear separation of different responsibilities, the domain objects are still tightly connected: each domain object accesses the implementations of the domain object it uses directly. Direct access increases the coupling of both layers and domain objects, because changes in the implementation of any domain object can affect all layers and domain objects using it.

How can we ensure that DOMAIN OBJECT *(208) do not depend on implementations of other* DOMAIN OBJECT?

Split each DOMAIN OBJECT *into an* EXPLICIT INTERFACE *(281) with a corresponding* ENCAPSULATED IMPLEMENTATION *(313) to separate the object's public contract from its realization.*

Let clients of a domain object access its functionality only through explicit interfaces, regardless of whether the object resides inside another or within the same layer as its clients. The explicit interface of the domain object publishes the possible set of client requests, notionally forwarding these requests, via polymorphism, to the associated encapsulated implementation for execution. Results are returned correspondingly to the client.

EXPLICIT INTERFACE and ENCAPSULATED IMPLEMENTATION separate the access to a domain object from its concrete implementation. Changes to the encapsulated Implementation of a domain object do not affect its clients as long as its explicit interface remains stable. This decoupling further supports modular software development and product-line architectures: other domain objects—and thus their development teams—can rely on stable and well-defined contracts for used domain objects, and need not bother about their realization.

The diagram below outlines the use of EXPLICIT INTERFACE and ENCAPSU-
LATED IMPLEMENTATION for the business process layer in our warehouse
management process control system:

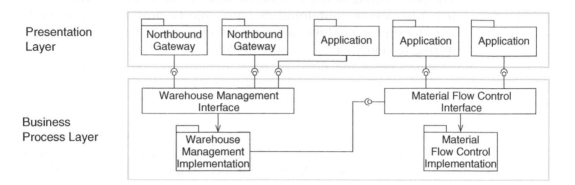

Domain objects from other layers define and use their explicit interfaces and encapsulated implementations correspondingly.

5.5 Bridging the Network

Most installations of the warehouse management process control
system are deployed across a computer network to meet their performance, scalability, and availability requirements. As a result there
could be a process or machine boundary between any two layers in
the system, and also between any two domain objects of a layer.

The introduction of a network, however, forces us to address several
challenges in the baseline architecture of the system. First and foremost, access to local domain objects differs from access to remote
domain objects. In a local deployment clients can invoke operations
on domain objects directly, while in a remote deployment they must
interact with them through a network. However, clients should not
have to distinguish whether the domain objects with which they
interact are local or remote, otherwise they are either dependent on
a specific system configuration, or their code is bloated with zillions

of special cases for local and remote system deployments. Ideally, a client simply invokes an operation on an explicit interface regardless of whether the called domain object is local or remote. In addition, before two remote domain objects in a distributed system can interact, they must first find one another and establish a network connection between them using an appropriate on-the-wire protocol—a procedure domain objects should not have to be bothered with.

How can we shield DOMAIN OBJECTS *(208) in the warehouse management process control system from dealing with networking issues directly and support a location-independent interaction between them?*

Introduce a BROKER *(237) to allow distributed* DOMAIN OBJECT *to find, access, and communicate with one another in the same way as if both parties were collocated.*

Local brokers on each network node negotiate and perform all interprocess communication on behalf of the system's domain objects. Explicit interfaces of remote domain objects are implemented as CLIENT PROXY (240) in the address spaces of their clients and handle all interaction with the brokers. In addition, the brokers offer functionality for domain objects to register their location in the network together with their published explicit interfaces, as well as functionality that allows them to retrieve explicit interfaces of any other registered domain object, be it local or remote.

The two key advantages of a BROKER architecture are *encapsulation* and *location independence*. Encapsulation enables application developers to focus on providing useful domain functionality: they do not need to bother with low-level networking issues. Location independence allows clients to access remote domain objects in the same manner as domain objects collocated in the same address space, which supports their flexible deployment in a computer network. Location independence also has a positive impact on the system's scalability and availably, because it can take advantage of the collective computing power that is available in the network, for example by means of replication and federation of domain objects. All three properties of location independence are especially important in the context of product-line architectures, because different product-line instances have different concrete functional and operational requirements.

The following diagram illustrates the use of the BROKER-based communication infrastructure for the presentation and business process layers of the warehouse management process control system. In this diagram we also assume that domain objects within a layer are collocated. Remote interaction between other layers of the system, or between domain objects of the same layer, is organized correspondingly.

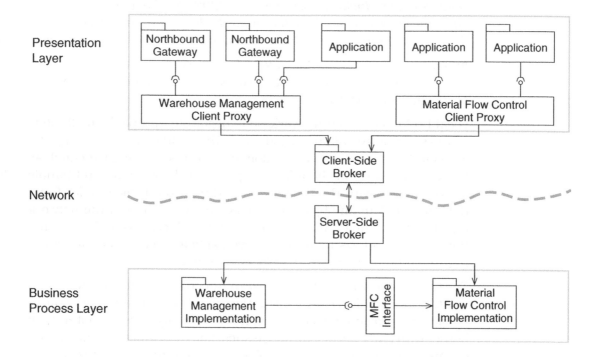

In the specific use of BROKER for our warehouse management process control system, all inter-process communication is asynchronous and message-oriented. Invoking a method on a client proxy initiates asynchronous sending of a typed message—which in the automation domain is called a 'request telegram.' Similarly, the result of a remote invocation is returned asynchronously via a 'response telegram.' Asynchronous messaging is used because otherwise it would be hard to achieve the performance and throughput that is typically required to operate large warehouses.

However, a purely asynchronous communication mechanism is often hard to understand, and even more so to use correctly and effectively in the implementation of application services. It is the job of the client proxies to encapsulate all asynchronous communication, and to offer client domain objects the specific communication and invocation model they need. This encapsulation supports the ability for application developers to use the asynchronous communication facilities in a straightforward, easy to understand, and convenient manner.

Using a Broker approach for the communication middleware also yields an advantage especially applicable to product-line development of the warehouse management process control system: several (de facto) standards for distributed computing middleware are based on a Broker architecture, for example the CORBA Component Model (CCM), Enterprise JavaBeans (EJB), and Microsoft's COM and. NET, This makes it possible to consider the use of an off-the-shelf product for the system's communication infrastructure, rather than a home-made custom implementation. Using a widely accepted communication middleware standard also supports the interoperation of the warehouse management process control system with its surrounding systems, most notably with applications residing in the operation and entity levels of the automation pyramid.

At the time this system was developed, however, no suitable off-the-shelf middleware was available that could meet the stringent requirements of the warehouse management process control system. We therefore had to design and implement our own communication middleware. We realized this in line with the CORBA standard [OMG04a], to support its later replacement with a suitable off-the-shelf product.

Chapter 6, *Communication Middleware*, describes how we 'zoom in' on the Broker pattern to implement key elements of the communication middleware for the system.

5.6   Separating User Interfaces

According to our current architecture, the presentation layer of the warehouse management process control system contains the gateways and interfaces to other systems, as well as user-level applications that access the system's functionality. In other words, the main responsibility of this layer is to publish functionality to external parties, be they human users or software systems, and to provide them with information about the system's current computational state. Domain objects in the presentation layer neither implement any business logic nor maintain any business state—both responsibilities are assigned to other layers that are accessed by the presentation layer.

The information that is presented should of course be up-to-date. We cannot afford users or clients of the warehouse management process control system to be misinformed or to make incorrect decisions on the basis of outdated information. Changes in the state of the system therefore must be immediately reflected by the domain objects of the presentation layer. However, the strict top-down access model in a LAYERS architecture makes it hard for domain objects in the presentation layer to ensure that the information they present is up-to-date at any time. They must poll the explicit interfaces of lower-level domain objects regularly to access this information. Consequently, state changes are not propagated directly when they occur, but only when a domain object in the presentation layer explicitly polls for updated information. As a result of the polling approach, the information held in the presentation layer can be stale. In addition, if there are no state changes, each poll also consumes resources and bandwidth just to discover that there is no need for an update of already-displayed information.

How can we ensure that the DOMAIN OBJECT *(208) in the presentation layer always provide fresh and timely state information to their clients without breaking the coupling rules of a* LAYERS *(185) architecture, but avoid unnecessary updating overhead?*

Use a MODEL-VIEW-CONTROLLER *(188) design to minimize the coupling between* DOMAIN OBJECTS *in the presentation layer and* DOMAIN OBJECTS *in the business layers, and ensure their efficient cooperation and mutual consistency.*

Domain objects in the business layers embody the role of models that provide information to applications and gateways in the presentation layer. Application and gateway domain objects, in turn, play the role of views if they present information to their clients, or they play the role of controllers if they trigger or use the functionality provided by the business layers. A change propagation mechanism between the three roles notifies views and controllers about all changes or updates of the state maintained by the model. The notified views and controllers can then call back the model to retrieve and display the updated information.

The main benefit of MODEL-VIEW-CONTROLLER is that it supports an immediate propagation of modified state and data to users and clients of the system with minimal use of computing resources. It also strengthens the loose coupling of the system's layers—as long as the interfaces of the business layers remain stable, the presentation layer can evolve independently towards customer needs or the use of new UI technologies. This property is especially important in the context of product-line architectures.

An alternative to a MODEL-VIEW-CONTROLLER arrangement is a PRESENTATION-ABSTRACTION-CONTROL (191) structure, which, at its bottom line, introduces specialized and independent user interfaces for each distinct subsystem of an application. For example, the warehouse management domain object could provide a form-based user interface and the material flow control domain object a command-line interface, with both interfaces being completely decoupled from one another. In the context of the warehouse management process control system, however, PRESENTATION-ABSTRACTION-CONTROL does not provide additional value over MODEL-VIEW-CONTROLLER, but it is much more complicated to implement. The simplest feasible design for separating user interface from application functionality is MODEL-VIEW-CONTROLLER, thus this pattern is used in the design.

The following diagram illustrates the Model-View-Controller configuration in our warehouse management process control system. The
views and controllers are provided by the domain objects in the presentation layer, while the model is represented by the domain objects
in the business process layer.

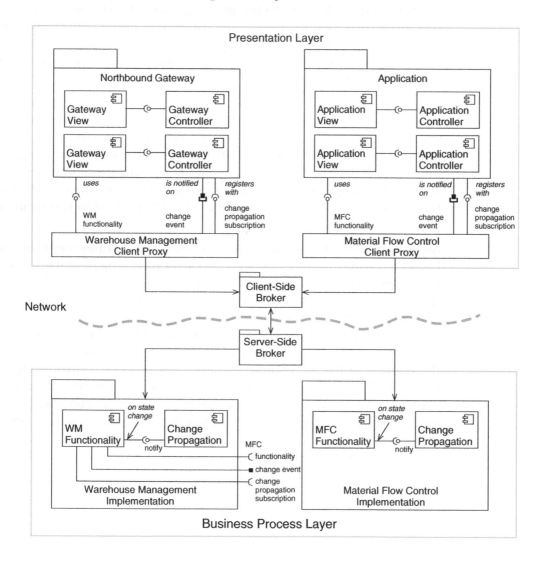

5.7   Distributing Functionality

The diagram shown in Section 5.5 gives the impression that the encapsulated implementation of a remote domain object in our system is always monolithic, hosted at a single network node, and accessible only through explicit interfaces realized as REMOTE PROXY (310) in the address spaces of its clients. While this is the simplest possible distribution model—it is both easy to implement and comprehend—it may, however, be insufficient for domain objects to meet their performance and scalability requirements.

For example, if a domain object is accessed frequently by clients from many different address spaces, this simple distribution model yields additional network traffic, latency, and jitter. Even worse, if requests arrive at domain objects faster than they can be handled, the domain objects can become overloaded and ultimately drive a system into saturation. If the domain objects do not maintain state, providing replication to all client address spaces would resolve this problem, because all replicas can execute independently. But what if the domain objects maintain modifiable, system-global state, such as the warehouse topology in our process control system, which maintains a warehouse's configuration of physical storage and associated transportation facilities? Replication would not be an effective solution to our problem, because all the overhead saved by having local copies could be reintroduced through the need to keep all distributed replicas consistent with one another whenever state is modified.

The overhead of keeping replicas consistent is particularly expensive if the use of the state maintained by a domain object can be partitioned with respect to location, time, and subset of the total state. In the case of a multi-site configuration of the warehouse management process control system, for example, there is no need to (fully) replicate the detailed topology of each site at other locations, because most warehouse operations are local to a specific site. Only a few warehouse operations affect multiple sites and thus need to access the entire warehouse topology, for example shipping and receiving orders of large quantities of items, and callbacks of whole item batches due to quality problems.

How can we provide efficient access to a Domain Object *(208) that maintains global state and whose clients reside in multiple address spaces?*

Realize the Domain Object *as a* Half-Object plus Protocol *(324) that splits its functionality into a set of self-coordinating half-objects, with one half-object collocated in each client address space.*

Each half-object implements only the specific functionality of a domain object that is required by its local clients. Equally, it maintains only the specific data accessed by these clients. A communication protocol between the half-objects coordinates all activities that involve more than one address-space and keeps the state of the half-objects consistent.

In the case of the warehouse topology domain object, we can let each half-object be responsible for representing only a specific part of the entire warehouse. For example, if the system manages a multi-site warehouse, half-objects could be hosted on site-local servers and represent only the specific topology of their respective site. In such a configuration, most shipping and receiving orders initiated by any site could execute locally, and thus efficiently. There is no need to use the network or to coordinate with other half-objects, even in case of state changes of the local topology. Multiple half-objects would participate in the computation only if multiple sites must be involved to serve a request. For example, if a site initiates an order whose quantity of items is not available at that site, multiple half-objects would coordinate themselves transparently through their protocols on behalf of their clients.

The following diagram briefly illustrates the use of Half-Object plus Protocol in the design of the topology management domain object. In this particular configuration two half-objects are involved, but more half-objects can be added by connecting them to the Broker (237) communication infrastructure. The protocol implemented between the half-objects ensures their correct cooperation both automatically and transparently to clients, using the communication infrastructure provided by the client proxies and the Broker.

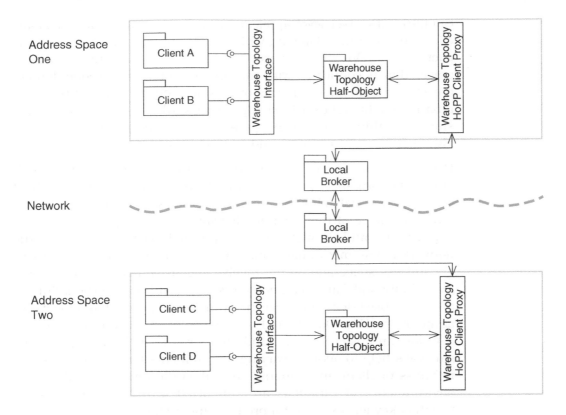

Two other types of domain object are also designed as HALF-OBJECT PLUS PROTOCOL arrangements in our warehouse management process control system. The northbound and southbound gateways that connect the warehouse management process control system with its environment are partitioned into half-objects that provide external applications with a 'standard' API for the system's functionality, and several half-objects that map from the required interface of a specific external application to this 'standard' API. The half-objects that interface with the external applications are located in these applications' address spaces, while the half-object that provides the standard gateway API resides in the address space of the warehouse management process control system.

Similarly, if a user-level application is designed as a rich or smart client, its core functionality, which plays the role of a model in the client's MODEL-VIEW-CONTROLLER (188) design, is implemented as a half-object that is connected with the corresponding server-side domain object of the business process or business object layer. This design guarantees that all user-level applications, whether designed as rich, smart, or thin clients, can operate in a coordinated fashion and always on top of a common and consistent system state.

HALF-OBJECT PLUS PROTOCOL designs contribute significantly to the scalability, performance, throughput, fault tolerance, and availability of our system. Scalability is supported because domain objects can take advantage of the available distributed hardware in a network. Performance and throughput are supported because the use of the network is minimized: most operations can run locally within a single address space and do not involve expensive network operations. Availability and fault tolerance are supported because the failure of any half-object does not affect the availability of other half-objects. In addition, the HALF-OBJECT PLUS PROTOCOL design of the warehouse topology domain object, the rich and smart client applications, and the gateways help to address varying requirements for warehouse sizes, richness of client applications, and integration with the existing IT environment. All variations are supported with a common design, which is key for a successful product-line architecture.

5.8   Supporting Concurrent Domain Object Access

Realizing domain objects of the warehouse management process control system as half-objects plus protocols yields notable performance, scalability, and throughput gains. However, half-objects plus protocols only address the situation in which clients are *distributed* across the network. If a domain object has many concurrent *local* clients, it can still become a throughput bottleneck, because at any one time it is accessible by only one client. Other clients are either blocked until it is their turn, or asked to wait and try again later. While this behavior can sometimes be tolerated for small system installations, it is generally unacceptable for large installations with high performance, throughput, and scalability requirements.

Within such installations, core domain objects in the system such as the warehouse topology must always be accessible. Also, concurrent clients should never block if a core domain object cannot serve them immediately. Neither should these clients be denied issuing their requests: this is especially important for high-priority requests, such as an emergency stop for (parts of) the transportation facilities. In addition, if the system is installed on, or upgraded to, hardware with better computational power—for example multiple processors—it should require no modifications in the system implementation to use these additional resources.

How can we provide concurrent access to a shared DOMAIN OBJECT *(208) such that clients can always issue their requests without blocking, but allow the* DOMAIN OBJECT *to process these requests in any order that assures a high throughput?*

Realize the DOMAIN OBJECT *as an* ACTIVE OBJECT *(365) that separates request invocation from request execution in both space and time.*

The encapsulated implementation of the domain object runs in a separate pool of threads, while its explicit interfaces are offered in the threads of its clients. Clients can issue requests to the explicit interfaces without blocking, proceed with other tasks while the requests are processed, and access results when they need them. The explicit interfaces objectify all requests they receive so that the encapsulated implementation of the domain object can schedule their execution in any order that is appropriate under a given set of constraints.

In the HALF-OBJECT PLUS PROTOCOL (324) design of the warehouse topology domain object, for example, each involved half-object is implemented as an active object. Any specific active object in this arrangement that is executed on a multi-processor machine can thus handle multiple requests in parallel. To use the available processing power most effectively, the assignment of warehouse topology to half-objects and their active object implementations mirrors the physical world: parts of the warehouse that can operate independently and in parallel of one another, such as different warehouse buildings, are assigned to different active objects, or threads within an active object, so that they can also operate independently and in parallel of one another within the software. Parts that cannot operate independently or in parallel, such as all high racks served by the same stacker crane, are assigned to the same active object, or even the same thread within an active object. Capturing the real-world parallelism of the warehouse topology within a set of half-objects implemented as active objects can therefore significantly improve the throughout of the domain object.

The diagram below illustrates the Active Object arrangement for one specific half-object in the Half-Object plus Protocol design of the warehouse topology domain object.[3]

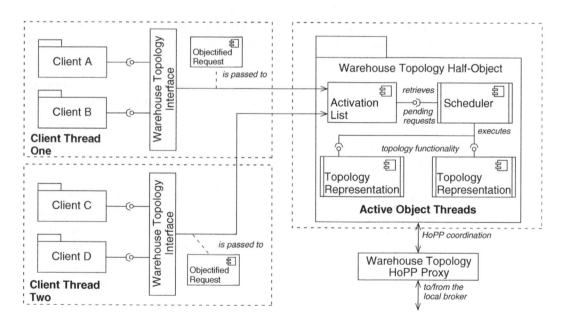

---

3 Again we bend UML notation to our needs. UML does not support a convenient way of expressing an active component that runs in its own thread of control. To be as close to UML standard notation as possible, we denote active components similarly to active objects, and active classes using parallel lines in the component symbol.

5.9 Achieving Scalable Concurrency

To support the execution of domain functionality, the warehouse management process control system implements a set of different infrastructure services. One such service is logging: various types of information records that the system's domain objects can generate, such as errors and traces, are stored persistently for later evaluation. Using the logging functionality should only have a minimal impact on the system's operational qualities, in particular performance: domain objects should not block because the logging domain object cannot process the received logging records in a timely manner. Yet many events may need to be logged, depending on the current computational state, resulting in a correspondingly high volume of logging records to store. Distributed logging can alleviate this problem by providing separate logging domain objects for each network node that store logging records in distributed persistent storage, but this does not help if a specific node in the network produces many logging records.

How can we avoid logging becoming a performance penalty even in the case in which a high volume of logging records must be processed?

Implement the logging Domain Object *(208) using the* Leader/Followers *(384) concurrency model, which uses a pre-allocated pool of threads to avoid dynamic threading overhead.*

Logging records that arrive at the logging domain object on a specific network node are read, processed, and stored into a node-local instance of a distributed persistent storage by a self-coordinating pool of threads. While the leader thread is listening for a logging record to arrive, the other threads are waiting as followers until it is their turn to listen for logging records. When the leader thread receives the logging record it converts to the role of a processing thread, promotes one of the waiting follower threads to become the new leader thread, and then processes and stores the received logging record. Multiple processing threads can therefore operate simultaneously to deal with high-volume logging traffic. Once a logging record is stored in persistent storage, a processing thread converts itself to a follower thread to wait until it becomes the leader thread again.

The key benefit of a LEADER/FOLLOWERS arrangement is performance: for executing small, repetitive, and atomic actions, such as processing logging records, it provides an efficient and resource-conserving concurrency model. As shown in the figure below, an ever-rotating 'wheel' of threads is handling all incoming logging records. Ideally, the size of the thread pool should be able to handle the heaviest expected load, so that logging records arriving at the logging DOMAIN OBJECT are received and processed immediately.

An alternative to a LEADER/FOLLOWERS design is a HALF-SYNC/HALF-ASYNC (359) structure that uses an appropriately sized queue to buffer logging records that arrive faster than they can be processed. This solution, however, is less straightforward and also less elegant than a LEADER/FOLLOWERS design, so LEADER/FOLLOWERS was preferred over HALF-SYNC/HALF-ASYNC in the design of the system.

The following diagram outlines the LEADER/FOLLOWERS design for the logging domain object using a pool of five threads. The thread that receives a logging record from the logging interface plays the role of the leader thread, the two threads that write logging records to the persistence interface embody the role of processing threads, and the two remaining threads represent follower threads waiting to become the new leader thread.

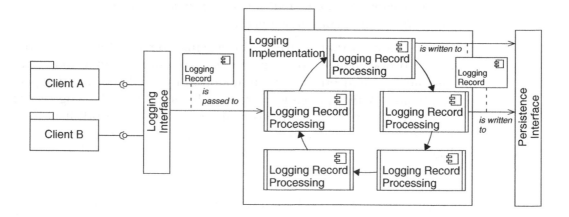

A backend-reporting domain object generates various reports from the logging records stored in distributed persistent storage. The correct ordering of logging records stored at different network nodes is possible because they contain a time-stamp created by a distributed time-domain object that ensures accurate clock synchronization for computers collaborating in the network.

5.10   Crossing the Object-Oriented/Relational Divide

All data created and maintained by the warehouse management process control system must be stored persistently, and changed transactionally, to ensure that the system can always operate with consistent, up-to-date information about a warehouse's current state. The infrastructure layer, therefore, provides a persistence domain object that allows other domain objects to store their business objects in, and retrieve them from, a database.

For typically non-technical reasons this database is often from one of the major database vendors, which means that it usually follows the relational paradigm. However, exposing the relational nature of the database directly to the warehouse management process control system—which is designed and implemented in terms of behavioral objects—introduces a paradigm mismatch. Business objects, such as shipping orders, elements of the warehouse topology, and logging records, must first be converted into an appropriate table structure before they can be passed to the persistence domain object. Conversely, data organized in tables must first be converted into properly formed business objects before they can be used and processed by domain objects. In other words, the application-level code of the warehouse management process control system becomes polluted with, and dependent on, table-oriented data structures and SQL queries. If we need to port the system to another database, the situation gets even worse: it is very likely that the new database offers different interfaces, which require corresponding modifications in all code that deals with persistence.

How can we bridge the chasm between the object-oriented view of business objects used within the warehouse management process control system and the relational view of business objects required by the database without exposing each view to the other side?

Introduce a DATABASE ACCESS LAYER *(538) between the warehouse man-agement process control system and the relational database that separates the logical, domain-specific representation of application data from the physical representation of this data in tables.*

The explicit interface of the persistence domain object provides the system's expected view of persistent storage, allowing it to pass and receive business objects as they are modeled in the object-oriented world. The encapsulated implementation of the persistence domain object realizes a bidirectional mapping between the object-oriented structure of the business objects and the table structure required by the interfaces the relational database provides. All effort necessary to port the persistence domain object to another database is localized in this DATABASE ACCESS LAYER design. The encapsulation of database variation behind a stable interface thus contributes significantly to the product-line character of the baseline architecture for our system.

The following diagram illustrates this design:

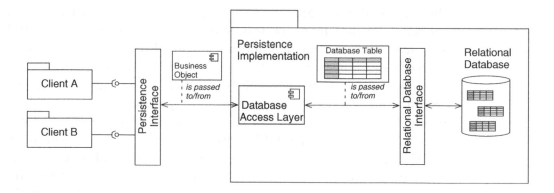

5.11   Configuring Domain Objects at Runtime

The requirements for our warehouse management process control system specify an availability of 99.999%, which means a total downtime of no more than five minutes fifteen seconds per year! However, there are many things that can change in the system while it is in operation. Changes in the physical warehouse structure, for example, could trigger a system reconfiguration with different algorithms for specific domain objects, or even with different domain object implementations. Changes in the computer network running the system, such as the addition of a new server, may suggest a redeployment of domain objects to best utilize the new hardware. The warehouse management process control system must be able to respond to such reconfiguration and redeployment needs both flexibly and on demand, but without degrading its availability.

How can we support flexible (re)configuration and (re)deployment of the warehouse management process control system without the need to shut it down?

Provide a Component Configurator *(490) infrastructure that supports dynamic, runtime (re)configurations and (re)deployments of* Domain Object *(208) without effects on the availability of system parts that are not involved in these activities.*

The Component Configurator infrastructure enables dynamic loading of new domain object implementations or configurations into the running system, and acts as a system-central control instance that orchestrates the runtime exchange, (re)configuration, and (re) deployment of these implementations and configurations. To be reconfigurable and redeployable, the explicit interfaces of domain objects must implement lifecycle functionality that is accessible by the component configurator, to control and manage their (re)configuration or (re)deployment correctly, efficiently, and without causing inconsistencies in the system's overall state. A Component Configurator infrastructure thus balances the conflict raised by the need for high availability and the need to support system evolution.

5.12   Baseline Architecture Summary

In the previous sections we described how the patterns from the pattern language in Part II of this book helped to create the baseline architecture for a warehouse management process control system. In this section we reflect on the applied pattern sequence as a whole, outlining some of the general properties that made it suitable for designing the baseline architecture of the warehouse management process control system.

The first two patterns in the sequence are LAYERS (185) and DOMAIN OBJECT (208). Both patterns help us to comprehend the warehouse management process control system, allowing us to partition a big ball of mud into bite-sized chunks of tangible parts residing at different layers of abstraction. The partitioning is two-dimensional. LAYERS provide a fundamental, horizontal decomposition into separate concerns with a different focus from each another, for example separating presentational aspects from business and infrastructure logic. DOMAIN OBJECT supports an additional, vertical decomposition to partition different responsibilities within each layer, for example warehouse management functionality from material flow control functionality. The result of applying LAYERS and DOMAIN OBJECT is a clear identification and modular separation of all baseline architecture elements in both their responsibilities and core usage relationships. As such, a horizontal and vertical decomposition of an application's functionality is the basis for almost every software architecture: LAYERS and DOMAIN OBJECT are often the very first patterns applied in an intentionally pattern-based software development process, regardless of the application under development.

The next two patterns, EXPLICIT INTERFACE (281) and ENCAPSULATED IMPLEMENTATION (313) decouple the technical realization of a domain object from its provided functionality. Changes in the encapsulated implementation of a domain object do not affect its clients: they can program against a stable contract. Both patterns allow the partitioning defined by LAYERS and DOMAIN OBJECT to be implemented by suitable modular software technologies, such as components or services. Consequently, both patterns are not only applicable within the context of the warehouse management process control system, but can help to define the architecture of many other applications that must enforce modular software development.

The fifth pattern, BROKER (237), orchestrates the distributed nature of the warehouse management process control system, by defining clear networking boundaries between domain objects that can potentially be remote from each other. But BROKER introduces more than just the recognition that two domain objects can reside in different address spaces, and even on different network nodes: it actually defines a whole interprocess communication *philosophy*, beginning with how domain objects can announce their availability in the system, through how two or more domain objects can establish communication channels between one another, to how these domain objects communicate and interact using the communication channels.

The distribution philosophy advocated by BROKER addresses the remoting requirements of many distributed systems, not only those of our warehouse management process control system. Most middleware, such as CORBA,. NET, and J2EE, has adopted BROKER as the core architecture for interprocess communication functionality. Chapter 6, *Communication Middleware*, therefore unfolds the BROKER design in more detail.

The sixth pattern in the pattern sequence, MODEL-VIEW-CONTROLLER (188), organizes the cooperation between domain objects in the user interface layer of the warehouse management process control system and domain objects in its business process and business object layers. According to the LAYERS pattern, higher-level domain objects can call the explicit interfaces of lower-level domain objects, but not vice versa. This rule raises a problem for layered systems in which control flows cannot always begin at the user interface and 'fall down' to the runtime infrastructure. For example, in event-driven systems control flow is often instigated at the bottom of the layering and 'climbs up' to its top. In systems accessed by multiple user interface clients, state changes require coordinated update of all these clients to display the correct information.

MODEL-VIEW-CONTROLLER addresses such situations by inverting the control flow in an application according to the *Hollywood Principle*: 'Don't call us, we'll call you' [Vlis98a]. Views and controllers do not maintain application data and state, but changes in the model, which is responsible for maintaining this information, are propagated to views and controllers via notifications, which in turn can call the explicit interfaces of the model back 'at will' to update their own state. Control flow can ping-pong between layers, but without introducing undesirable dependencies from lower-level layers to higher-level layers. Like the other patterns applied so far, MODEL-VIEW-CONTROLLER is therefore not specific to warehouse management process control systems, but rather is a common structure for applications that provide interactive user interfaces.

The next three patterns in the pattern sequence aim at providing an appropriate operational quality for various domain objects. HALF-OBJECT PLUS PROTOCOL (324) introduces federation, to support performance, scalability, and availability of stateful domain objects that are accessed from multiple address spaces. ACTIVE OBJECT (365) and LEADER/FOLLOWERS (362) use defined *concurrency models* to enable a high throughput for domain object implementations that reside in a single address space. All three patterns provide generally applicable distribution and concurrency models, and are applied in many systems outside the warehouse management domain.

A DATABASE ACCESS LAYER (538) is a common approach to shielding the architecture of a software system from paradigm impedance mismatches and implementation details introduced by third-party database products. Replacing one database product by another requires only local modifications in the database access layer—though perhaps significant ones. Clients of the database, however, remain unaffected: changes do not ripple through to them. Last but not least, the introduction of a COMPONENT CONFIGURATOR (523) completes the loose coupling of domain objects in this baseline architecture by adding an infrastructure that supports their dynamic and flexible (re)configuration and (re)deployment in the event of software updates and environmental changes.

The table below summarizes the pattern sequence that helped create the baseline architecture for the warehouse management process control system, as well as the design challenges addressed by each pattern in the sequence.

Pattern	Challenges
LAYERS	Partitioning application functionality according to different levels of abstraction.
DOMAIN OBJECT	Partitioning and modularizing application functionality within the same level of abstraction.
EXPLICIT INTERFACE	Providing a well-defined access to DOMAIN OBJECT functionality.
ENCAPSULATED IMPLEMENTATION	Providing and encapsulating the realization of a DOMAIN OBJECT.
BROKER	Defining the baseline architecture for the communication middleware.
MODEL-VIEW-CONTROLLER	Separating application functionality from its presentation and control.
HALF-OBJECT PLUS PROTOCOL	Supporting federated DOMAIN OBJECTS across distribution boundaries.
ACTIVE OBJECT	Providing concurrency for DOMAIN OBJECTS that must support request scheduling.
LEADER/FOLLOWERS	Providing concurrency for DOMAIN OBJECTS that must support high-volume throughput.
DATABASE ACCESS LAYER	Shielding application functionality from database specifics.
COMPONENT CONFIGURATOR	Enabling dynamic configuration of applications from reusable components.

Analyzing the pattern sequence reveals nothing that couples it tightly to the domain of warehouse management. Rather, it is a fairly general sequence, applicable to the development of many distributed systems. This 'generality' indicates that, regardless of their application domain, distributed systems share many properties and requirements at their baseline level. It is thus quite natural that this sequence is supported by our pattern language for distributed computing, described in Part III of this book.

Most patterns in the sequence also contribute to the design of a product-line architecture for the warehouse management process control system. LAYERS, DOMAIN OBJECT, EXPLICIT INTERFACE, ENCAPSULATED IMPLEMENTATION, and COMPONENT CONFIGURATOR support an appropriate granularity of decomposition as well as loose coupling: BROKER enables the distribution of DOMAIN OBJECT in a computer network, ACTIVE OBJECT and LEADER/FOLLOWERS support flexible concurrency models, and MODEL-VIEW-CONTROLLER and DATABASE ACCESS LAYER encapsulate structural variation behind a common design and stable interface. The latter is of key importance for product-line architectures: if each potential variation in a domain were to be handled differently, it would be hard—if not impossible—to define a stable architecture for the common core shared by all product-line instances. Capturing variability with a common design avoids this problem, thereby supporting all product variants, as it is more concise to use the same baseline architecture.

This 'built-in' support for product-line architectures in the pattern sequence above is also independent of the warehouse management domain. Patterns in general capture many best practices of framework, platform, and product-line design [John97], therefore these practices are also supported by our pattern language for distributed computing.

6 Communication Middleware

*Good communication is as stimulating as black coffee
and just as hard to sleep after.*

Anne Morrow Lindbergh

This chapter illustrates the application of a key pattern sequence from the pattern language for distributed computing in Part II of this book. It describes the development of the communication middleware that is used for our warehouse management process control system, as well as a wide range of other distributed applications in the warehouse management domain and beyond. This middleware allows clients to invoke operations on distributed objects without concern for object location, programming language, operating system platform, communication protocols or interconnects, and hardware.

A novel aspect of our communication middleware is its highly configurable, scalable, and portable design and implementation, which can be tailored to meet specific application requirements and network/end-system characteristics more easily than crafting the code by hand, or using conventional middleware implementations that are hard-coded to a single set of strategies.

6.1   A Middleware Architecture for Distributed Systems

Concrete deployments of our warehouse management process control system typically involve different hardware and software platforms. For example, client applications and user interfaces are often deployed on Windows PCs, sensor and actuators are usually deployed on embedded devices running VxWorks, and DOMAIN OBJECTS (208) that represent business logic and infrastructure functionality are commonly deployed on servers running Solaris or Linux. Devices are connected via different types of network, such as wireless and wired LANs and WANs, using a variety of communication protocols such as TCP/IP, PROFIbus, or VME. Each system installation must also integrate with existing legacy and third-party software, particularly software that resides at the operational and entity level of the automation pyramid, which is often written in a variety of different programming languages such as C, C++, Java, and C#. The resulting heterogeneity presents development and integration challenges throughout the system's lifetime, particularly as software components are removed or replaced by components from other vendors.

Communication middleware, such as the *Common Object Request Broker Architecture* (CORBA) [OMG04a] and *Enterprise Java Beans* (EJB) [Sun03] [Sun04a], resides between clients and servers in a distributed system. The goal of communication middleware is to simplify application development and integration by providing a uniform view of lower-level—often heterogeneous—network and operating system services. Moreover, this middleware helps to transfer complex distributed system infrastructure tasks from application developers to middleware developers [ScSc01], who implement common network programming mechanisms such as connection management, data transfer, event and request demultiplexing, (de)marshaling, and concurrency control.

To simplify inter-process communication between the distributed domain objects of our system, and to shield their implementations from the heterogeneity of its computational environment, the system's baseline architecture uses BROKER-based (237) communication middleware. A broker allows distributed domain objects to find, access, and communicate with each other as if they were collocated, and decouples them within a distributed system so that they can be developed and integrated using diverse technologies in a heterogeneous environment.

The following diagram illustrates the use of the BROKER-based communication middleware for the presentation and business process layers of the system. This diagram assumes that domain objects within a layer are collocated. The remote interaction between other layers of the system or between domain objects of the same layer is organized correspondingly.

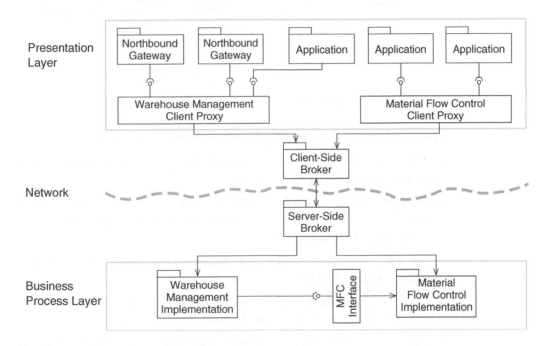

We implement the BROKER-based communication middleware for the system using the *CORBA Component Model* (CCM) [OMG02]. The CCM is communication middleware that allows applications to invoke operations on component instances without concern for their location, programming language, hosting platform, or networking protocol.

CCM is essentially a language and platform-independent variant of EJB that also includes specific capabilities found in Microsoft COM and .NET. At the heart of the CCM reference model is the broker, whose elements are shown in the following figure.

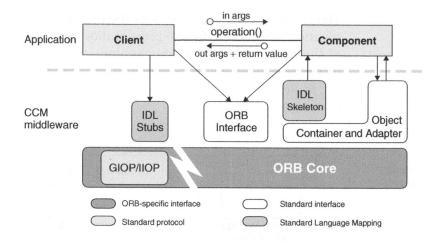

The CCM reference model defines the following key entities:

- *Clients* and *Components* implement the applications running above the communication middleware.

- An *Object Request Broker (ORB) Core*[4] is responsible for delivering an operation request from a client to a component instance and returning a response, if any.

- The *ORB Interface* decouples applications from implementation details of the ORB Core.

- *IDL Stubs and Skeletons* serve as a 'glue' between the client and server components respectively, and the ORB itself.

- A *Container* and *Object Adapte*r associate a component instance with an ORB by providing a runtime environment for managing component lifecycle properties, demultiplexing incoming requests to the component instance, and dispatching the appropriate upcall method on that instance.

---

4 The OMG CCM specification uses the term *Object* Request Broker for backwards compatibility with earlier versions of the CORBA specification, even though application developers who use CCM typically program and interact with *Component instances*.

The CCM reference model, however, intentionally just specifies the fundamental roles that must be present in an ORB, but does *not* define a concrete software architecture to use as the basis for a specific CCM implementation. We therefore used the BROKER pattern to define the actual components, their relationships, and the collaborations needed to implement CCM-compliant communication middleware, as shown in the following figure.

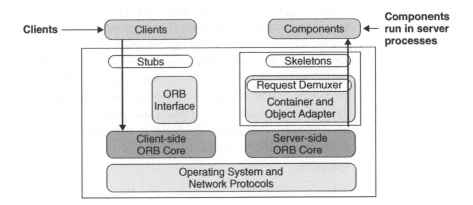

The client and remote component roles in the BROKER pattern represent the application-level clients and components in the OMG CCM reference model. The CLIENT PROXY (240) role is implemented by the ORB's stubs, which provide access to the services offered by remote components. Stubs also shield clients and servers from the location and implementation details of their remote communication partners, as well as from the specifics of the ORB implementation.

The Client-side ORB Core plays the REQUESTOR (242) role in the BROKER pattern, and the Server-side ORB Core plays the play the role of the INVOKER (244). The Container and Object Adapter plays the role of a CONTAINER (488) or an OBJECT ADAPTER (438). All these roles are responsible for the location-transparent transmission of requests from clients to servers, as well as the transmission of responses and exceptions from servers back to clients. The Server- and Client-side ORB Cores offer APIs to servers and clients for registering component instances and invoking methods on instances respectively. These APIs represent the ORB Interface of the CCM reference model and are often implemented as a FACADE (294).

Applying the BROKER pattern to implement a CCM-based ORB requires the resolution of a number of design challenges. Chief among these include structuring the ORB's internal design to separate concerns, encapsulating low-level system functions to enhance portability, demultiplexing ORB Core events and managing ORB connections efficiently and flexibly, enhancing ORB scalability by processing requests concurrently and using an efficient synchronized request queue, enabling interchangeable internal ORB mechanisms and consolidating these mechanisms into groups of semantically compatible strategies, and configuring these consolidated ORB strategies dynamically. The remainder of this chapter describes the pattern sequence we use to resolve these challenges. The resulting communication middleware provides the broker platform for our system, as well as other parts of the warehouse management domain. This middleware can also be applied to many other distributed systems in different domains, including telecommunications, e-commerce, aerospace, online financial services, and electronic medical imaging systems.

6.2   Structuring the Internal Design of the Middleware

CCM-based communication middleware has a number of important responsibilities, such as providing APIs to clients and components, routing requests from clients to local or remote component instances and their responses back to the clients, and initiating the transmission of such requests and responses over the network. The architecture defined by the BROKER (237) pattern separates application logic from communication middleware functionality. A CCM-based ORB itself, however, is far too complex to implement as a single monolithic component. Moreover, its responsibilities cover different types of capabilities that can be organized hierarchically. For example, APIs are at the application level, component policy management is at the container level, request routing and concurrency control at the object adapter and ORB core levels, and request (re)transmission at operating system and network protocol levels.

We therefore need to decompose our CCM-based ORB architecture further so that it meets the following requirements:

- *Changeability.* Enhancements and changes to one part of the ORB should be confined to a small number of components and not ripple through to affect unrelated components.

- *Stability.* External interfaces should be stable, and may even be prescribed by standards, such as the ORB Interface and the various mapping rules for the Interface Definition Language (IDL) defined by the OMG CCM specification.

- *Portability.* Porting the ORB to new operating system and compiler platforms should affect as little of the ORB as possible. For example, the ORB's transport mechanisms must run on conventional platforms such as Windows and Linux, as well as small embedded devices such as sensors and actuators running VxWorks or LynxOS.

How can we decompose the ORB to satisfy the changeability, stability, and portability requirements above, and partition its functionality into coherent groups with related responsibilities?

Use LAYERS *(185) to separate different responsibilities in the ORB by decomposing it into groups of classes that each handle particular types of capabilities.*

We divide our CCM-based ORB into four layers. The top layer provides the standard CCM ORB interface defined by the OMG, and represents the 'application view' of the entire ORB. The second layer provides the container and object adapter, which manage component policies, as well as demultiplexing and dispatching client requests to component instances. The third layer includes the ORB core, which implements the middleware's connection management, data transfer, event demultiplexing, and concurrency control logic. The bottom layer shields the rest of the ORB from the implementation details of the underlying operating system and network protocols.

The diagram below illustrates the layered design for our CCM-based ORB:

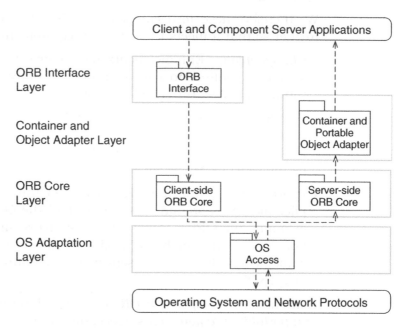

Using the LAYERS pattern to implement our CCM broker enables transparent changes to implementations in one layer without affecting other layers. For example, changing search structures in the object adapters from dynamic hashing to active demultiplexing [PRS+00] does not affect any other layers. LAYERS also enhances stability, because multiple higher-layer client and server applications have a well-defined interface to the lower-layer network programming services that the ORB provides. Moreover, LAYERS simplifies porting the ORB to new operating systems, if requested by customers, without affecting application code or even the bulk of the ORB implementation.

6.3 Encapsulating Low-level System Mechanisms

One role of communication middleware is to shield applications from operating system and networking characteristics, which are both varied and dense in their detail. CCM-based ORB middleware developers—as opposed to application developers—are therefore responsible for handing lower-level details such as demultiplexing events, sending and receiving requests across one or more network interfaces, and spawning threads to execute requests concurrently. It can be hard, however, to develop this layer of middleware, especially when using low-level system APIs written in C. Common problems faced by ORB developers working at this level include:

- *A requirement for an intimate knowledge of many operating system platforms.* Implementing an ORB using system-level C APIs forces middleware developers to deal with the non-portable, tedious, and error-prone operating system idiosyncrasies, such as using weakly typed socket handles to identify communication endpoints. In addition, such APIs are not portable across operating system platforms. For example, Windows, Linux, and VxWorks all have different threading APIs, as well as subtly different semantics for sockets and event demultiplexing.

- *Increased maintenance effort.* One way to build an ORB is to handle portability variations via explicit conditional compilation directives in the ORB source code. Using conditional compilation to address platform-specific variations *at all points of use*, however, increases the complexity of the source code. In particular, it is hard to maintain and extend conditionally compiled code, because platform-specific details are scattered throughout the ORB implementation files.

- *Inconsistent programming paradigms.* System mechanisms are accessed through C-style function calls, which cause an 'impedance mismatch' with the programming style supported by object-oriented languages such as Java, C++, and C#.

How can we avoid accessing low-level system mechanisms directly when implementing ORB middleware?

Structure the OS Adaptation layer of the ORB using WRAPPER FACADES *(482), to encapsulate system programming APIs and mechanisms within concise and cohesive object-oriented class interfaces.*

WRAPPER FACADE provides type-safe, modular, and portable class interfaces that encapsulate lower-level system and network programming mechanisms such as sockets, event demultiplexing, synchronization, and threading. In general, WRAPPER FACADE should be applied when existing system-level APIs are non-portable and non-type-safe.

To improve the robustness and portability of our ORB implementation, it accesses all system mechanisms via WRAPPER FACADES provided either by the Java Virtual Machine (JVM) [LY99], or by the ACE C++ network programming toolkit [SH02]. ACE encapsulate native OS concurrency, communication, memory management, event demultiplexing, and dynamic linking mechanisms with type-safe object-oriented interfaces, as illustrated in the following diagram.

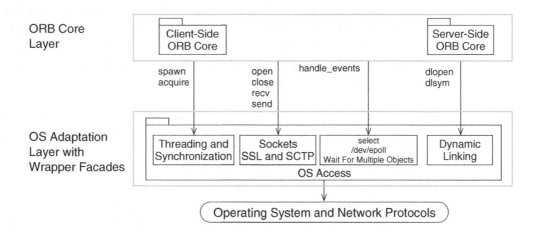

The encapsulation of the JVM and ACE wrapper facades provides a consistent object-oriented programming style, and alleviates the need for the ORB to access the weakly typed C system programming APIs directly. Standard compilers and language processing tools can therefore detect type system violations at compile-time rather than at runtime. As a result, we need much less effort to maintain the ORB, as well as to port it to new operating system and compiler platforms.

6.4 Demultiplexing ORB Core Events

One responsibility of an ORB core is to demultiplex I/O events from multiple clients and dispatch them to their associated event handlers. For example, a server-side ORB core listens for new client connections, reads General Inter-ORB Protocol (GIOP) `request` messages from connected clients, and writes GIOP `reply` messages back to the clients. To ensure responsiveness to multiple clients, an ORB core waits for connection, read, and write events to occur on multiple socket handles, via operating system event demultiplexing mechanisms such as `select`, `/dev/epoll`, `WaitForMultipleObjects`, and threads. The following problems make it hard to develop this layer of middleware:

- *Hard-coded event demultiplexers.* One way to develop an ORB is to hard-code it to use a single event demultiplexing mechanism such as `select`. Relying on one event demultiplexing mechanism is undesirable, however, because no single mechanism is the most efficient for all platforms and application requirements. For example, `WaitForMultipleObjects` is more efficient than `select` on Windows, whereas `/dev/epoll` is a more efficient demultiplexing mechanism than `select` on Linux.

- *Tightly coupled event demultiplexing and event handling code.* Another way to develop an ORB core is to tightly couple its event demultiplexing code with the code that handles the events, such as the GIOP protocol processing code. However, this prevents the demultiplexing code from being reused as a black box component by other applications that use communication middleware, including Web servers [HPS97] or video-on-demand applications [MSS00]. In addition, if new ORB strategies for threading or request scheduling algorithms are introduced, substantial portions of the ORB core must be rewritten.

How can an ORB implementation decouple itself from a single event demultiplexing mechanism, and decouple its demultiplexing code from its event handling code?

Use a REACTOR *(259) to reduce coupling and increase the extensibility of an ORB core by supporting demultiplexing and dispatching of multiple event handlers that are triggered by events that can arrive concurrently from multiple clients.*

The REACTOR pattern simplifies event-driven applications in general, and communication middleware in particular, by integrating the event demultiplexing and dispatch of the corresponding event handlers. In general, REACTOR should be introduced when applications or middleware components must handle events from multiple clients concurrently, without becoming tightly coupled to a single low-level mechanism such as select.

One way to implement an ORB is to use a reactor to drive the main event loop within its ORB Core, as part of the SERVER REQUEST HANDLER (249) within the INVOKER (244) of a BROKER (237) architecture, as shown in the following diagram of the server-side ORB.

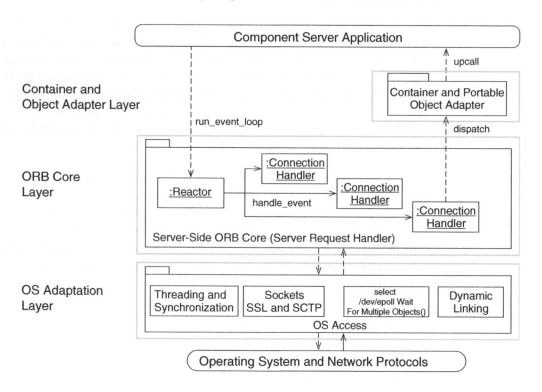

In this design a component server process initiates an event loop in the ORB core's Reactor instance, where it remains blocked on whichever event demultiplexing mechanism is configured until I/O events occur on one or more of the available endpoints. When a GIOP request event occurs, the Reactor demultiplexes the request to the appropriate event handler, which is an instance of the GIOP `ConnectionHandler` class that is associated with each connected socket. The `Reactor` then calls the `handle_event` method on the `ConnectionHandler`, which reads the request and passes it to the ORB's Container and Object Adapter layer. This layer then demultiplexes the request to the appropriate upcall method on the component instance, and dispatches the upcall method.

Using the REACTOR pattern enhances the extensibility of the ORB by decoupling the event handling portions of its ORB core from the underlying operating system event demultiplexing mechanisms. For example, the `WaitForMultipleObjects` event demultiplexing system function can be used on Windows, while the `select or/dev/epoll` mechanism can be used on UNIX and Linux platforms. Likewise, the REACTOR pattern can be implemented in Java using a `Selector` on `SelectableChannels`. REACTOR also simplifies the integration of new event handlers. For example, adding a new connection handler that uses the PROFIbus protocol to communicate with non-CCM portions of our warehouse management system does not affect the interface of the `Reactor class`.

Reactive event demultiplexing may not be the most scalable way to implement an ORB on operating systems that support efficient asynchronous I/O. In particular, highly efficient ORBs can be implemented on some platforms via the PROACTOR pattern (262), which structures event-driven concurrent applications that receive and process requests from multiple clients asynchronously. For example, the PROACTOR pattern can be implemented on Windows by using the `AcceptEx`, `ReadFile`, and `WriteFile` system functions to process TCP connections and GIOP requests asynchronously. When these asynchronous operations complete, Windows delivers their results to the ORB, which performs the appropriate actions before returning to its event loop.

The main benefit of PROACTOR is its scalability on platforms that implement efficient asynchronous I/O. The drawback is that relatively few platforms today provide this support correctly and efficiently. Our goal was to design a portable ORB, so we chose to use the REACTOR pattern as the basis for event demultiplexing.

6.5 Managing ORB Connections

Connection management is another key responsibility of an ORB core. For example, an ORB core that implements GIOP must establish TCP connections and initialize the protocol handlers for each TCP server endpoint. By localizing connection management logic in the ORB core, application components can focus solely on processing application-specific requests and replies, rather than dealing with low-level operating system and network programming tasks.

An ORB core is not limited, however, to running only over GIOP and TCP transports [OKS+00]. For example, although TCP transfers GIOP requests reliably, its flow control and congestion control algorithms preclude its use for warehouse management sensors and actuators with stringent timing requirements, whereas Streaming Control Transmission Protocol (SCTP) or Real-Time Protocol (RTP) may be more appropriate. Equally, it may be more efficient to use a shared memory transport mechanism when clients and component instances are collocated on the same endsystem whose operating system supports shared memory. Moreover, to protect the integrity and confidentiality of the data, it may be necessary to exchange requests and responses over an encrypted Secure Socket Layer (SSL) connection. An ORB core should therefore be flexible enough to support multiple transport mechanisms.

The CCM reference architecture decouples the connection management tasks performed by an ORB core from the request processing performed by application components explicitly. A common way to implement an ORB's *internal* connection management, however, is to use low-level network APIs such as sockets. Similarly, the ORB's connection establishment protocol is often tightly coupled to its communication protocol.

Unfortunately, this design hard-codes the ORB's connection management implementation with the socket network programming API, and the TCP/IP connection establishment protocol with the GIOP message format, leading to the following two problems:

- *Inflexibility.* If an ORB's connection management data structures and algorithms are too closely intertwined, substantial effort is required to modify the ORB core. It can therefore be time consuming to port a tightly coupled ORB core to new networking protocols and programming APIs, such as SSL, SCTP, RTP, shared memory, or Windows Named Pipes. For example, tightly coupling the ORB core to use the socket API makes it hard to modify the underlying transport mechanism to use shared memory or SSL rather than sockets.

- *Inefficiency.* Many internal ORB strategies can be optimized by allowing ORB and application developers to choose appropriate implementations late in a product's development, such as after extensive runtime performance profiling. For example, a multithreaded real-time client may need to store transport endpoints using THREAD-SPECIFIC STORAGE (392). Similarly, the concurrency strategy for a CCM component server might require that each connection run in its own thread to eliminate per-request locking overhead. If the connection management mechanism is hard-coded and tightly bound with other internal ORB strategies, however, it is hard to accommodate efficient new mechanisms without significant effort and rework.

How can an ORB core's connection management mechanisms support multiple transports and allow connection-related behaviors to be (re)configured flexibly at any point in the development cycle?

Use an ACCEPTOR-CONNECTOR *(265) arrangement to increase the flexibility of ORB core connection management and initialization, by decoupling connection establishment and service initialization from the tasks performed once these activities have completed.*

The acceptor component in the ACCEPTOR-CONNECTOR pattern is responsible for *passive* connection establishment and service initialization, which is performed by the server side of the ORB core. Conversely, the connector component in the pattern is responsible for *active* connection establishment and service initialization, which is performed by the client side of the ORB core. We use the Acceptor-Connector pattern in conjunction with the Reactor pattern (259) to create a pluggable protocols framework [OKS+00] for our ORB. This framework performs connection establishment and connection handler initialization for the various networking protocols supported in the ORB, as follows:

- *Client-side ORB core.* In response to an operation invocation or an explicit binding to a remote component instance, the client-side ORB core uses a `Connector` to initiate a connection to the designated server ORB for the desired type of protocol, then initializes the appropriate type of `ConnectionHandler` to service this connection when it completes.

- *Server-side ORB Core.* When a connection arrives from a client, the server-side ORB Core uses an `Acceptor` to create the appropriate type of `ConnectionHandler` to service each new client connection.

`Acceptors` and `Connectors` are both event handlers that can be dispatched automatically by the ORB's reactor when events become ready for processing, as shown by the following figure.

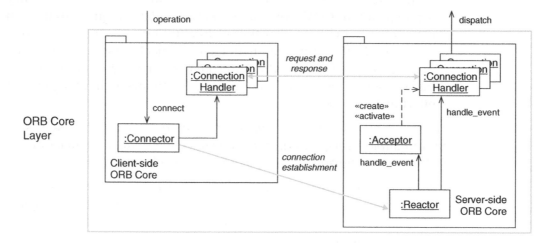

This figure shows that when a client invokes a remote `operation`, it makes a `connect` call via its `Connector` to obtain a connection and initialize a `ConnectionHandler` that corresponds to the desired networking protocol. In the server-side ORB core, the `Reactor` notifies an `Acceptor`, via its `handle_event` method, to accept the newly connected client and create the corresponding `ConnectionHandler`. After the `ConnectionHandler` is activated within the ORB core, it performs the requisite protocol processing on a connection, and ultimately dispatches the request to the appropriate component instance via the ORB's container and object adapter.

The combined use of ACCEPTOR-CONNECTOR and REACTOR in our CCM-based ORB increases its flexibility by decoupling event demultiplexing from connection management and protocol processing. This design also simplifies the integration of the networking protocols and network programming APIs that are most suitable for particular configurations of our warehouse management process control system.

6.6   Enhancing ORB Scalability

Achieving scalable end-to-end performance is important for handling the heavy traffic loads that arise as the number of clients increases. By default, GIOP runs over TCP, which uses flow control to ensure that senders do not produce data more rapidly than slow receivers or congested networks can buffer and process [Ste93]. If a CCM sender transmits a large amount of data over TCP faster than a receiver can process it, therefore, the connection will flow control and block the sender until the receiver can catch up.

Our initial REACTOR-based design, outlined in Section 6.4, *Demultiplexing ORB Core Events*, processed all requests within a single thread of control. Although this design is straightforward to implement, it suffers from the following problems:

- *Non-scalable.* Processing long-duration client requests reactively within a single-threaded reactive ORB server process scales poorly, because only one client request can be handled at a time.

- *Starvation.* The entire ORB server process can block indefinitely while waiting for flow control on a connection to clear when sending a reply to a client, thereby starving other clients from having their requests processed.

Conversely, however, multithreading all ORB processing may also be inefficient for short-duration processing, because threads can incur significant concurrency control overhead in terms of synchronization, context switching, and data movement [PSC+01].

How can an ORB manage concurrent processing efficiently, so that long-running requests can execute simultaneously on one or more CPUs without impeding the progress of other requests, while short-duration processing is handled efficiently without incurring unnecessary concurrency control overhead?

Use a HALF-SYNC/HALF-ASYNC (359) concurrency model to separate the short- and long-duration processing in the ORB, thereby enhancing scalability without incurring excessive concurrency control overhead.

The HALF-SYNC/HALF-ASYNC concurrency model for our CCM-based ORB uses a pool of `RequestHandlers` to process long-duration client requests and replies concurrently in separate threads of control. Conversely, short-duration `Acceptor` connection establishment and REQUEST event handling is processed *reactively* in `ConnectionHandlers` by borrowing the `Reactor`'s thread of control.

The following figure illustrates the HALF-SYNC/HALF-ASYNC-based design of our ORB. It shows how `Acceptor` connection establishment is driven entirely by the `Reactor` when it dispatches the `Acceptor`'s `handle_event` method. REQUEST event handling is driven partially by the `Reactor`, which dispatches the `ConnectionHandler`'s `handle_event` method to read the request message into a buffer. This buffer is then placed on a synchronized `RequestQueue`, which is used to pass requests to a pool of `RequestHandlers` that process the requests concurrently in separate threads of control.

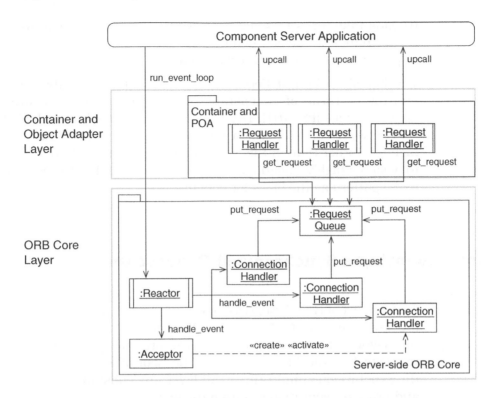

The use of HALF-SYNC/HALF-ASYNC in our ORB improves its scalability compared with the use of a purely REACTOR-based design, by allowing multiple client requests/replies to run concurrently in separate threads. Similarly, because each thread can block independently, the entire server ORB process need not wait for flow control to clear on a connection when sending a reply to a client. Some subsystems in our warehouse management process control system are better suited by a REACTOR-based design, however, so our ORB supports both approaches.

The HALF-SYNC/HALF-ASYNC model is not always the most efficient design for an ORB, however, because passing a request between a `Reactor` thread and a `RequestHandler` thread incurs dynamic memory allocation, multiple synchronization operations, a context switch, and cache updates. This overhead can make the ORB's latency unnecessarily high, particularly for short-duration requests. An alternative is to apply the LEADER/FOLLOWERS *pattern* (362), which provides a more efficient and predictable concurrency model in which multiple threads take turns to share event sources, such as a passive-mode socket handle to detect, demultiplex, dispatch, and process service requests that occur on the event sources.

The benefit of LEADER/FOLLOWERS is that it eliminates the need for, and the overhead of, a separate `Reactor` thread and synchronized `RequestQueue` [PSC+01]. The drawback is that it is less scalable than HALF-SYNC/HALF-ASYNC, which queues requests in the ORB's virtual memory rather than in the operating system kernel. As our goal was to design a highly scalable ORB, we chose to use the HALF-SYNC/HALF-ASYNC pattern as the basis for concurrency.

6.7 Implementing a Synchronized Request Queue

At the heart of HALF-SYNC/HALF-ASYNC (359) is a `RequestQueue` queueing layer. In our CCM-based ORB, the `ConnectionHandlers` in the asynchronous (reactive) layer are 'producers' that insert client requests into the `RequestQueue`. The pool of `RequestHandlers` in the synchronous (multi-threaded) layer are 'consumers' that remove and process client requests from the queue.

A naive implementation of a `RequestQueue` can cause several problems:

- Multiple producer and consumer ORB threads in the different layers of the HALF-SYNC/HALF-ASYNC pattern can corrupt the `RequestQueue`'s internal state if concurrent access is not serialized to protect against race conditions.

- If a simple mutual exclusion (mutex) lock is used, the producer and consumer threads can 'busy wait' when the queue is empty or full, which wastes CPU cycles unnecessarily.

How can the `RequestQueue` avoid race conditions or busy waiting when threads in different layers put and get client requests simultaneously?

Implement the RequestQueue *as a* MONITOR OBJECT *(368) to serialize concurrent method calls, so that only one method runs at a time, and allow its* put_request *and* get_request *methods to schedule their execution sequences cooperatively, to prevent producer and consumer threads from busy waiting when the* RequestQueue *is full or empty respectively.*

The synchronized RequestQueue uses a monitor lock to serialize access to the monitor object, and condition variables from POSIX Pthreads or java.util.concurrent.locks to implement the queue's not-empty and not-full monitor conditions. This synchronized RequestQueue can be integrated into the HALF-SYNC/HALF-ASYNC implementation in the ORB as shown in the following figure.

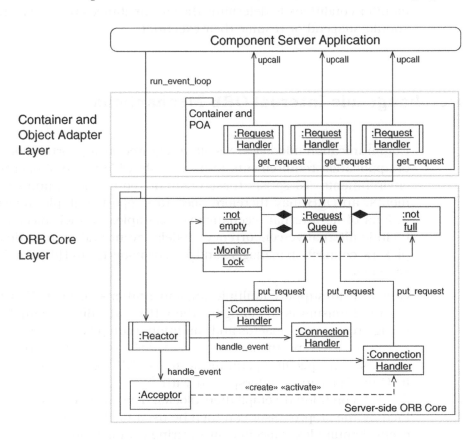

When a consumer thread running in the pool of `RequestHandlers` attempts to get a client request from an empty `RequestQueue`, the queue's `get_request` method atomically releases the monitor lock and the thread suspends itself on the not-empty monitor condition. It remains suspended until the `RequestQueue` is no longer empty, which happens when a `ConnectionHandler` running in the producer thread puts a client request into the queue.

MONITOR OBJECT simplifies our ORB's HALF-SYNC/HALF-ASYNC concurrency design by providing a concise programming model for sharing the `RequestQueue` among cooperating threads in which object synchronization corresponds to method invocation. The synchronized `put_request` and `get_request` methods use the `RequestQueue`'s monitor conditions to determine the circumstances under which they should suspend or resume their execution.

6.8   Interchangeable Internal ORB Mechanisms

Communication middleware is often required to support a wide range of application requirements in an equally wide range of operational environments. To satisfy these different requirements and environments, an ORB may therefore need to support multiple implementations of its internal mechanisms. Examples of such mechanisms include alternative concurrency models, event and request demultiplexers, connection managers and data transports, and (de)marshaling schemes.

One way to support multiple implementations of an ORB's internal mechanisms is to configure the ORB statically at compile time using preprocessor macros and conditional compilation. For example, `as/dev/epoll` and the `WaitForMultipleObjects` function are only available on specific operating systems, ORB source code written in C or C++ can be interspersed with `#if ... #elif ... #else ... #endif` conditional compilation blocks. The value of macros examined by the preprocessor can then be used to choose the appropriate event demultiplexer mechanisms during compilation.

Although many C/C++ ORBs use this approach, it suffers from the following problems:

- *Inflexibility.* Preprocessor macros can only configure mechanisms known statically at compile time, which makes it hard to configure an ORB to support mechanisms selected based on knowledge available dynamically during start-up or at runtime. For example, an ORB might want to configure itself to use different concurrency models or transport mechanisms depending on dynamically discoverable factors such as the number of CPUs, current workload, or the availability of specific networking protocols.

- *Error-proneness.* Using preprocessor macros and condition compilation makes it hard to understand and validate the ORB. In particular, changes to the behavior and state of the ORB tend to permeate through its source code, making it hard to compile and test all paths through the code [MPY+04].

How can an ORB permit replacement of its internal mechanisms in a more flexible manner, and encapsulate the state and behavior of each mechanism so that changes to one do not permeate throughout an ORB haphazardly?

Use STRATEGY *(455) configurations to support multiple transparently 'pluggable' ORB mechanisms by factoring out commonality among alternatives and associating the name of a strategy explicitly with its behavior and state.*

Our CCM-based ORB uses a variety of STRATEGIES to factor out internal mechanisms that are often hard-coded in conventional ORBs. The figure below illustrates where our ORB provides strategy hooks that use runtime polymorphism to simplify the dynamic (re)configuration of different mechanisms for (de)marshaling, request and event demuxing, connection management and client/server data transport, and concurrency.

Compile-time polymorphism can also be implemented using specialization techniques such as partial evaluation and aspect weaving, which are less extensible than runtime polymorphism, but often much more efficient [KGS+05].

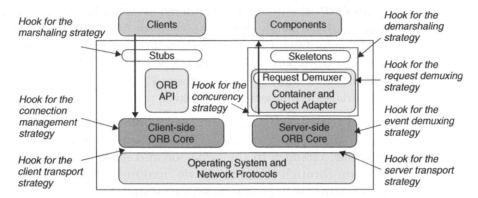

Using STRATEGY in our CCM-based ORB removes lexical dependencies on the ORB's internal mechanism implementations, because the configured mechanisms are only accessed via common base class interfaces. Moreover, STRATEGY simplifies the customization of ORB behavior using mechanisms that can be configured dynamically, either during start-up time or later during runtime, rather than only statically at compile time.

An alternative to STRATEGY would be the TEMPLATE METHOD pattern (453), which can also be used to support multiple transparently 'pluggable' ORB mechanisms. We chose STRATEGY because its use of delegation enables the selection and/or replacement of alternative ORB mechanisms dynamically, for example, during ORB initialization at runtime. In contrast, TEMPLATE METHOD uses inheritance, so the selection of alternative ORB mechanisms would be bound at compile time, which is too restrictive for our use cases.

6.9 Consolidating ORB Strategies

Our CCM-based ORB supports a wide range of strategies in its various layers:

- The stubs and skeletons support various *(de)marshaling strategies*, such as Common Data Representation (CDR), eXternal Data Representation (XDR), and other proprietary strategies suitable for ORBs that communicate specifically across homogeneous hardware, OS, and compilers.

- The Container and Object Adapter layer supports multiple *request demultiplexing strategies*, such as dynamic hashing, perfect hashing, or active demultiplexing [GS97a], and *lifecycle strategies*, such as session containers or entity containers.

- The ORB Core layer supports a variety of *event demultiplexing strategies*, such as reactors implemented with `select`, `/dev/epoll`, `WaitForMultipleObjects`, or VME-specific demuxers, *connection management strategies*, such as process-wide cached connections versus thread-specific cached connections, `ConnectionHandler` *concurrency strategies*, such as single-threaded reactive or multi-threaded half-sync/half-async, and different *transport strategies*, such as TCP/IP, SSL, SCTP, VME, and shared memory.

The table below illustrates the strategies used to create two configurations of the ORB for different subsystems in the warehouse management process control system:

- One for sensor and actuators deployed on embedded devices running VxWorks

- The other for warehouse business logic and infrastructure functionality deployed on servers running Solaris or Linux.

Application	Concurrency Strategy	Marshaling & Demarshaling Strategy	Request Demuxing Strategy	Protocol	Event Demuxing Strategy
Sensors and Actuators	Reactive	Proprietary	Perfect hashing	VME backplane	VME-specific demuxer
Warehouse business logic	HALF-SYNC/HALF-ASYNC	CDR	Active demuxing	TCP/IP	select-based demuxer

Using STRATEGY so extensively in our ORB, however, can cause the following problems:

- *Complicated maintenance and configuration.* ORB source code can become littered with hard-coded references to strategy classes, which make it hard to maintain and configure. For example, within a particular subsystem, such as sensors and actuators, or business logic, many independent strategies must act in harmony. Identifying these strategies individually by name, however, requires tedious replacement of selected strategies in one domain with a potentially different set of strategies in another domain.

- *Semantic incompatibilities.* It is not always possible for specific strategies to interact in semantically compatible ways. For example, the VME-specific event demultiplexing strategy will not work properly with the TCP/IP protocol. Moreover, some strategies are only useful when specific preconditions are met. For example, perfect hashing demultiplexing is only applicable to systems that statically register all their component instances off-line [GS97b].

How can a highly configurable ORB reduce the complexities required to manage its myriad of strategies, as well as ensure semantic compatibility when combining groups of strategies?

Introduce ABSTRACT FACTORIES *(525) to consolidate multiple ORB strategies into a manageable number of semantically compatible configurations.*

All our ORB strategies are consolidated into abstract factories that encapsulate all the client- and server-specific strategies described above. By using the ABSTRACT FACTORY pattern, application developers and end users can configure the internal mechanisms that comprise different types of ORBs with semantic consistency, by providing a single access point that integrates all strategies used to configure an ORB. Concrete subclasses then aggregate semantically compatible application-specific or domain-specific strategies, which can be replaced *en masse* in meaningful ways.

The following figure illustrates two abstract factory instances used to configure ORBs for applications running in the business logic or sensor and actuator subsystems of the system.

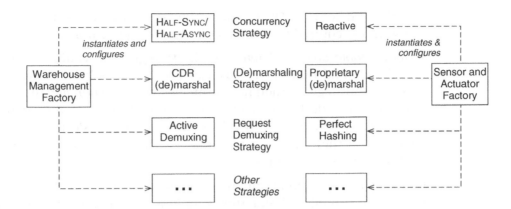

Our use of ABSTRACT FACTORY simplifies ORB maintenance and configuration by consolidating groups of ORB strategies with multiple alternative implementations that must vary together to ensure semantic compatibility for different warehouse management process control system subsystems.

6.10   Dynamic Configuration of ORBs

The cost of many computing resources such as memory and CPUs continues to decrease. However, ORBs still must often avoid excessive consumption of such finite system resources, particularly for real-time and embedded systems that require small memory footprints and predictable CPU processing overhead [GS98]. Similarly, many applications can benefit from an ability to extend ORBs dynamically by allowing the configuration of their strategies at runtime.

Although STRATEGY (455) and ABSTRACT FACTORY (525) make it easier to customize ORBs for specific application requirements and system characteristics in semantically compatible configurations, these patterns can still cause the following problems:

- *Excessive resource consumption.* Widespread use of STRATEGY can substantially increase the number of internal mechanisms configured into an ORB, which can in turn increase the system resources required to run the ORB and its applications.

- *Unavoidable system downtime.* If strategies are configured statically at build time using ABSTRACT FACTORY, it is hard to enhance existing strategies or add new strategies without *changing* the existing source code for the consumer of the strategy or the abstract factory, *recompiling* and *relinking* an ORB, and *restarting* running ORBs and their application component instances to update them with the new capabilities.

In general, static configuration is only feasible for a small and fixed number of strategies. Using this technique to configure more sophisticated, extensible ORBs complicates maintenance, increases system resource consumption, and requires system downtime to add or change existing component instances.

How can an ORB implementation reduce the 'overly large, overly static' side-effect of pervasive use of STRATEGY *and* ABSTRACT FACTORY?

Introduce a COMPONENT CONFIGURATOR *(490) to dynamically link/unlink custom strategy and abstract factory objects into an ORB at start-up or runtime.*

We use a component configurator in our CCM-based ORB to configure abstract factories at runtime that contain the desired group of semantically compatible strategies. The ORB's initialization code uses the dynamic configuration mechanisms provided by the operating system platform and/or encapsulated by the wrapper facades in the ORB's OS adaptation layer to link in the appropriate factory for a particular use case. Commonly used dynamic configuration mechanisms include the `dlopen/dlsym/dlclose` system functions in UNIX, the `LoadLibrary/GetProcAddress` system functions in Windows, and the Applet facilities in Java. By using COMPONENT CONFIGURATOR in conjunction with these system functions, the *behavior* of the ORB can be decoupled from *when* implementations of its internal mechanisms are configured into the ORB as semantically compatible strategies.

ORB strategies can be linked into an ORB from dynamic link libraries (DLLs) at compile time, start-up time, or even later during runtime.

Moreover, SMALL CAPS:Component Configurator can reduce the memory footprint of an ORB by allowing application developers to link dynamically only those strategies that they need to configure the ORB for their particular use cases. The figure below shows two factories tuned for either the business logic or the sensor and actuator subsystems of our warehouse management process control system.

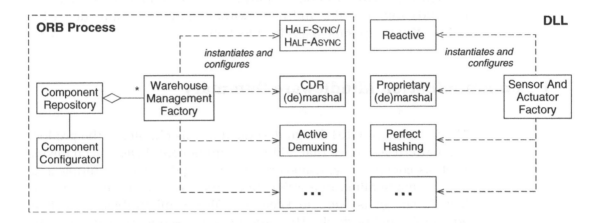

In this particular configuration the `WarehouseBusinessLogicFactory` is currently installed in the ORB's process. Applications using this ORB configuration will therefore be processed with the designated set of ORB concurrency, (de)marshaling, and request demultiplexing strategies, among others. In contrast, the `SensorAndActuatorFactory` resides in a DLL outside the current ORB process. By using COMPONENT CONFIGURATOR, this factory could be installed dynamically when the ORB process starts to run.

Within the ORB process, the `SensorAndActuatorFactory` is maintained by a `ComponentRepository` that manages all currently loaded configurable component instances in the ORB. The `Component-Configurator` uses the `ComponentRepository` to coordinate the (re)configuration of component instances, for example, by linking an optimized version of the `SensorAndActuatorFactory` and unlinking the current version.

COMPONENT CONFIGURATOR allows application developers to configure the behavior of our ORB dynamically, to tailor the ORB to meet their specific operational environments and application requirements. In addition to enhancing flexibility, this also ensures that the ORB does not incur the time and space overhead for strategies it does not use. Moreover, COMPONENT CONFIGURATOR allows application developers to configure the ORB without requiring access to, or modifications of, the ORB source code, and often without having to shut down the entire ORB to upgrade aspects of its behavior.

6.11   Communication Middleware Summary

The CCM-based ORB design described in this chapter is the product of a pattern sequence that addresses fundamental ORB mechanisms such as concurrency, transports, request and event demultiplexing, and (de)marshaling, in a well-defined and time-proven manner. Our key design goals were to keep the ORB configurable, extensible, adaptable, and portable. The patterns in the sequence used to create this design were selected, integrated, and implemented to achieve these goals based on extensive experience of the application of these patterns in other *standard middleware*, such as Web servers [POSA2][5] [HMS97], *object-oriented network programming frameworks*, such as ACE [SH03], and *networked applications*, such as application-level gateways [Sch00], electronic medical imaging systems [PHS96], and avionics mission computing systems [SGS01]. The first two patterns in the sequence, BROKER (237) and LAYERS (197), define the core structure for our CCM-based ORB. BROKER separates application functionality from communication middleware functionality, while LAYERS separates different communication middleware services according to their level of abstraction.

The third pattern in the sequence, WRAPPER FACADE (459) helps to structure the lowest layer in the ORB's design, the OS Abstraction

---

5 Chapter 1 in [POSA2] describes a pattern sequence for Web servers that includes many of the patterns described in this chapter.

Layer, into modular and independently usable building blocks. Each wrapper facade provides a meaningful abstraction for a specific responsibility and/or group of functionalities supported by an operating system, and encapsulates the corresponding API functions into a type-safe, modular, and portable class. Higher layers of the ORB can therefore be implemented without having explicit dependencies on a specific platform.

The next set of patterns in the sequence focus on the server-side ORB Core layer. In terms of the BROKER architecture, the server-side ORB core plays the role of the INVOKER (244), which uses a SERVER REQUEST HANDLER (249) to receive messages and requests from the network and dispatch these messages and requests to their intended component instance for further processing. REACTOR (259) provides a demultiplexing and dispatching infrastructure for the SERVER REQUEST HANDLER that can be extended to handle different event handling strategies, and which is independent from low-level demultiplexing mechanisms such as `select` and `WaitForMultipleObjects`. ACCEPTOR-CONNECTOR (265) leverages REACTOR by introducing specialized event handlers for initiating and accepting network connection events, thus separating connection establishment from communication in an ORB core. HALF-SYNC/HALF-ASYNC (359) and MONITOR OBJECT (368) augment REACTOR, so that client requests can be processed concurrently, thereby improving server-side ORB scalability.

The final three patterns in the sequence address configurability. STRATEGY (549) is used wherever variability is possible for the ORB's mechanisms, such as its connection management, concurrency, and event/request demultiplexing mechanisms. To configure the ORB with a specific set of semantically compatible strategies, the client- and server-side ORB implementations use an ABSTRACT FACTORY (549). These two patterns work together to make it easier to create variants of the ORB that are customized to meet the needs of particular users and application scenarios. COMPONENT CONFIGURATOR (523) is used to orchestrate updating of the strategies and abstract factories in the ORB without modifying existing code, recompiling or statically relinking existing code, or terminating and restarting an existing ORB and its application component instances.

The following table summarizes the mapping between specific ORB design challenges and the pattern sequence we used to resolve these challenges.

Pattern	Challenges
BROKER	Defining the ORB's baseline architecture
LAYERS	Structuring ORB internal design to enable reuse and clean separation of concerns
WRAPPER FACADE	Encapsulating low-level system functions to enhance portability
REACTOR	Demultiplexing ORB Core events effectively
ACCEPTOR-CONNECTOR	Managing ORB connections effectively
HALF-SYNC/HALF-ASYNC	Enhancing ORB scalability by processing requests concurrently
MONITOR OBJECT	Efficiently synchronizing the HALF-SYNC/HALF-ASYNC request queue
STRATEGY	Interchanging internal ORB mechanisms transparently
ABSTRACT FACTORY	Consolidating ORB mechanisms into groups of semantically compatible strategies
COMPONENT CONFIGURATOR	Configuring consolidated ORB strategies dynamically

Analyzing this pattern sequence reveals that it helps to design ORBs that not only meet the requirements of our warehouse management process control system, but are also configurable to meet the requirements of distributed systems in many other domains. In particular, we have used our pattern sequence to create a product-line architecture for a specific set of technological concerns—communication middleware—within a larger product-line architecture for an application domain—warehouse management process control. The architecture and implementation of ORBs based on our pattern sequence are thus extensible and reusable assets that not only meet our immediate needs, but can also be applied productively well beyond the domain of warehouse management.

Consequently it is no surprise that the pattern sequence described in this chapter forms the basis of several ORBs, including the *Component-Integrated ACE ORB (CIAO)* [WSG+03], *The ACE ORB (TAO)* [SNG+02], and *ZEN* [KSK04]. CIAO and TAO create a standards-based C++ communication middleware platform by combining *Lightweight CCM* [OMG04b] features, such as standard mechanisms for specifying, implementing, packaging, assembling, and deploying component instances, with *Real-Time CORBA* [OMG03a] [OMG05a] features, such as thread pools, portable priorities, synchronizers, priority preservation policies, and explicit binding mechanisms. ZEN is an implementation of Real-Time CORBA that uses Real-Time Java [BGB+00] features such as scoped memory and real-time threads.

CIAO, TAO, and ZEN are open source [DOC] and have been used in many commercial distributed systems, ranging from avionics and vehtronics, factory automation and process control, telecommunication call processing, switching, network management, and medical engineering and imaging. Many of these systems need real-time support to meet their stringent computation time, execution period, and bandwidth/delay requirements. Due to its flexible, patterns-based design, however, CIAO, TAO, and ZEN are also well suited for distributed applications that require conventional 'best-effort' support. Using patterns that focus on both performance and configurability, including the pattern sequence outlined in this chapter, helped to create a product-line architecture for CIAO, TAO, and ZEN that meets all these requirements, while still being compact and comprehensible.

Further coverage on the patterns in TAO and ZEN appear in [SC99] [CSKO+02] and [KSS05].

7 Warehouse Topology

*Topology provides the synergetic means of ascertaining
the values of any system of experiences.
Topology is the science of fundamental pattern and
structural relationships of event constellations.*

Buckminster Fuller

The second chapter in our pattern story is about a specific domain object in the warehouse management process control system: the warehouse topology. We describe its internal design for the representation and access of physical warehouse storage, the extension and adaptation of this storage structure to warehouse-specific needs, and the integration of the warehouse topology design with the system's baseline architecture.

7.1   Warehouse Topology Baseline

Within a warehouse management process control system, the main responsibility of the warehouse topology DOMAIN OBJECT (208) is to provide a representation of the physical warehouse structures to other domain objects, mainly to the warehouse management and material flow control. The system's baseline architecture defines the fundamental structure for the warehouse topology domain object: its partitioning into an EXPLICIT INTERFACE (281) and an ENCAPSULATED IMPLEMENTATION (313), a HALF-OBJECT PLUS PROTOCOL (324) distribution architecture, and an ACTIVE OBJECT (365) concurrency model.

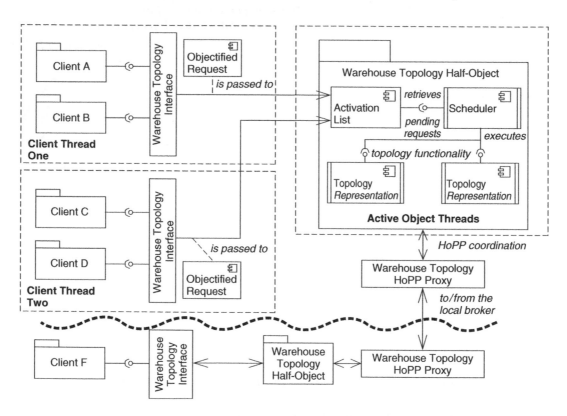

7.2 Representing Hierarchical Storage

When specifying the encapsulated implementation for the warehouse topology domain object, the first challenge that arises is to provide a model of physical storage hierarchies, transportation facilities, and the associations between the two that is suitable for representing any real-world warehouse structure. For example, warehouses can differ in size, organization of storage, and the types of storage that are available. Over time it can also happen that the structure of a warehouse is reorganized, for example because it is extended or modernized, or because new types of storage are installed that were not previously available. The corresponding software model of the warehouse structure must support such reorganizations without effects on any part that is not reorganized.

How can we represent arbitrary real-world storage structures within the warehouse topology DOMAIN OBJECT *(208) and support their flexible rearrangement and evolution?*

Capture the warehouse structures in a COMPOSITE *(319) arrangement to model their hierarchical organization transparently for clients using that structures.*

A Storage class defines the root of the representation and offers an EXPLICIT INTERFACE (281) that is shared by all elements of a concrete storage hierarchy, such as for storing and fetching items, checking the available storage capacity, and accessing information about the stored items. Two classes descend directly from `Storage`: `AggregateStorage` provide the data structures and methods common to all compound storage types, such as aisles, and `AtomicStorage` the data structures and methods common to all elementary storage types, such as bins. All concrete storage types are derived from these two classes: `Aisle`, `Side`, and `Rack`, for instance, represent aggregate storage, while `Bin`, `TransferBin`, `Door`, and `Dump` represent atomic storage.

Transportation facilities integrate seamlessly with this structure. From a general perspective, a transportation facility is just a special class of storage: you can store items on it, fetch items from it, check its available capacity, access information about the stored items, and so on. The only difference from 'real' storage is that transport facilities are mobile and proactive, as opposed to being immobile and reactive: a fork lift fetches and stores items, while a bin has items stored in it and fetched from it. There can also be aggregate transport facilities, such as trains with several carts.

A transportation facility can be associated with physical storage by a `transportationFacility` relationship between two `Storage` instances: if a specific transportation facility serves a specific (set of) physical storage, such as a stacker crane serving all bins and transfer bins in an aisle, this can be expressed by associating the corresponding stacker crane and aisle objects in the hierarchy.

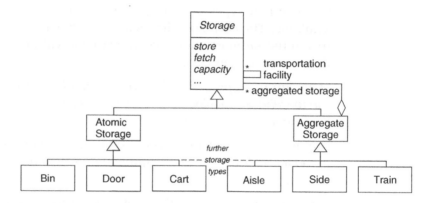

A COMPOSITE arrangement directly supports the creation of arbitrary storage hierarchies, such as the one illustrated in the following diagram, as well as their rearrangement:

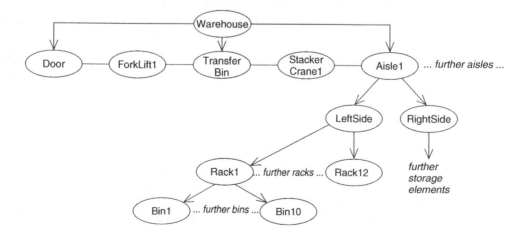

COMPOSITE also supports our extensibility and restructuring requirements: new storage and transportation facility types are realized by integrating corresponding new storage and transportation facility classes into the hierarchy. The modification or removal of existing storage and transformation facility classes does not affect other classes in this structure.

Last but not least, COMPOSITE arrangements map easily onto the HALF-OBJECT PLUS PROTOCOL (324) distribution strategy for realizing a federated warehouse topology domain object. The root composite elements of all half-objects are connected via an appropriate protocol. From a logical perspective, this allows clients of the warehouse topology to access the entire warehouse structure, regardless of how it is distributed across a network. Similarly, a concrete COMPOSITE hierarchy maps onto the ACTIVE OBJECT (365) concurrency model: different sub-trees are assigned to different active objects. For example, there could be an active object per warehouse site, per building, per aisle, or per side of an aisle, dependent on the corresponding parallelism in the real world.

Within an active object there is potential for further parallelism. For example, if an active object represents a warehouse site, it could contain a pool of threads in which each thread contains the COMPOSITE hierarchy of a different warehouse building at that site.

7.3 Navigating the Storage Hierarchy

One of the key operational requirements for the warehouse management process control system is performance. In the context of realizing the warehouse topology domain object, the essential measures to address performance are the HALF-OBJECT PLUS PROTOCOL (324) distribution strategy and the ACTIVE OBJECT (365) concurrency model. But performance also matters within the COMPOSITE (319) arrangement of the warehouse representation: the faster we can access specific storage elements in the hierarchy, the faster the corresponding requests can be served and processed, and the greater becomes the overall request throughput.

A Composite arrangement, however, most simply supports a strict top-down navigation: requests for access to a specific implementation of a storage element *always* enter the hierarchy at its top and 'fall down' a specific path until they arrive at their designated receivers. The deeper the hierarchy and the more legs in a path cross process or thread boundaries, the less feasible this strategy becomes. Specifically, it becomes problematic if a number of subsequent requests 'land' in the same area of the hierarchy, such as the same side or rack in an aisle, which is a common situation when processing large shipping or receiving orders for a specific item. In this case it would be better to navigate up the Composite hierarchy from the current storage element, which is typically a bin, to the next or second-next higher-level storage element, for example the aisle that contains the bin, and then down again to another lower-level storage element, such as another bin in the aisle. Compared to a strict top-down propagation of requests, this strategy would save a number of 'hops,' and in most cases there is also no need to cross thread or process boundaries.

How can we support bidirectional navigation through a Composite *storage hierarchy so that each storage element in this hierarchy can be reached from any other storage element most efficiently?*

Connect all storage elements in the hierarchy to their next higher-level storage element to form Chains of Responsibility *(440) from all leaves to the root. Navigate down the hierarchy via the* Composite *infrastructure and up via the* Chains of Responsibility.

Integrating Chain of Responsibility into our design for representing physical warehouse structures is straightforward: the class `Storage` is extended with a `parent` relationship to itself.

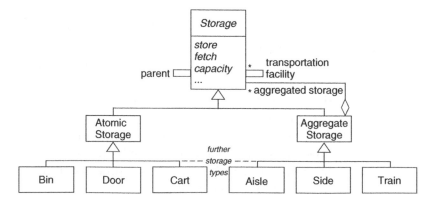

In a concrete warehouse configuration, storage elements in the hierarchy that represent 'real' storage are connected to their associated aggregate storage to support bidirectional navigation.

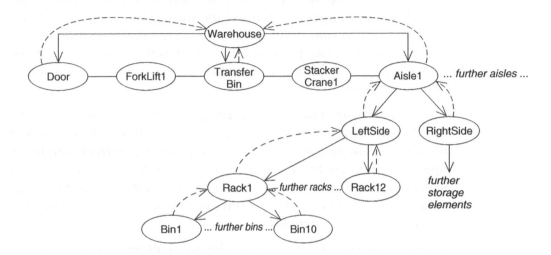

Bidirectional linkage of the storage elements in the COMPOSITE hierarchy ensures that each storage element can be reached by any other storage element with the minimal number of hops and thread boundary crossings.

7.4 Modeling Storage Properties

Each storage unit, transportation facility, and item in a warehouse is associated with specific properties. These properties are called storage organization criteria (SOC) and determine the type of items that can be stored in a particular storage unit, or which can be transported with a specific transportation facility. Examples for storage organization criteria are throughput class, hazard class, and temperature class. For each criteria there are specific, enumerable sets of allowed values, such as fast, medium, and slow runner for the throughput class. Domain functionality in a warehouse management process control system uses this information to determine the destination of an item that should be stored in the warehouse, the intermediate legs from the item's current location to its destination, and the transportation facilities to transport the item on each leg. For example, an item that is supposed to be stored for only a short time and fetched again quickly is a fast runner in terms of the throughput class, and should be stored only in storage intended for fast runners. Similarly, an item that has a certain hazard class value, such as flammable, should only be transported by transportation facilities suitable for transporting flammable items.

The storage organization criteria of a specific storage unit, transportation facility, and item change only rarely over time—if at all—such as when a warehouse gets modernized. During normal warehouse operation they are fixed and are not modifiable: once assigned to a specific storage unit, transportation facility, or item, a storage organization criterion can only be exchanged explicitly by corresponding administration functionality.

A problem arises, however, from the sheer mass of storage organization criteria that must be maintained in a concrete installation of the warehouse management process control system. Associating each storage unit, transportation facility, and item with its own, private collection of relevant storage organization criteria values could require an immense amount of memory: just consider a warehouse with over a million bins. In addition, much memory would be 'wasted' because many warehouse topology elements share the same storage organization criteria, but to ensure proper warehouse operation it is necessary that each of them actually *is* associated with a well-formed storage organization criteria collection.

How can we provide each storage, transportation facility, and item in a warehouse with a vector of relevant storage organization criteria, but avoid massive consumption of memory?

Realize the values of the storage organization criteria as IMMUTABLE VALUES *(555) that can be shared amongst multiple elements of a warehouse topology.*

Each storage, transportation facility, and item maintains a collection of immutable storage organization criteria that are assigned during the configuration of a concrete warehouse. This collection is maintained by the `Storage class` in our current design, the root of the COMPOSITE (319) hierarchy.

An IMMUTABLE VALUE (396) can be shared easily among different storage, transportation facilities, and items—even across multiple threads of control. In addition, immutable values cannot be modified by domain functionality in the warehouse management process control system, but must be exchanged explicitly by corresponding administration functionality via FACTORY METHODS (529).

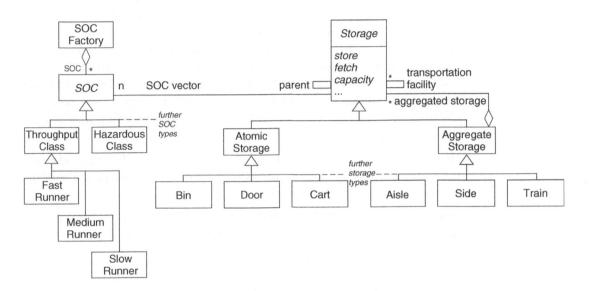

7.5 Varying Storage Behavior

The COMPOSITE (319) design for representing a concrete warehouse topology supports a common, explicit interface that can be realized differently for different types of storage and transportation facility. For example, storing an item in an aisle means selecting an appropriate side and rack in the aisle and then a specific bin in the selected rack, while storing an item in a bin means associating the item's identity with the bin.

However, the concrete behavior of a specific method in the common interface not only differs across different storage types: it can also vary among different instances of the same storage type. For example, in an almost empty aisle, items are stored in 'layers' from the bottom to the top across all racks, whereas in an aisle in which occupation exceeds a specific threshold, items can be stored in 'piles,' filling one rack after the other. The first storing strategy is less optimal in terms of throughput, because a transportation facility like a stacker crane must move longer distances to store and fetch a specific quantity of items, but it keeps the center of gravity towards the aisle's base and thus ensures the static stability of the racks. The second strategy stores items geographically densely, which ensures short moving distances when storing and fetching items, and thus a high throughput, but only works safely if piling up the racks does not endanger the stability of the aisle. Ideally the storage strategy of an aisle can change over time, dependent on its current state, so that at any time the most appropriate storage strategy is used.

How can we support multiple implementations for the methods of a class in the Composite *hierarchy as well as the runtime exchange of the 'active' method implementation?*

Provide Strategies *(455) for all methods that can vary, using polymorphism to configure and reconfigure storage elements in a* Composite *arrangement with appropriate method implementations.*

In terms of Strategy, the `Storage` class in our current design plays the role of the context. Methods whose behavior can differ across instances of a class in the Composite hierarchy are specified as an Explicit Interface (281) in the `StorageStrategy` class, for example `fetch` and `store`, and implemented in its subclasses, such as `StoreInLayers` and `StoreInPiles`. The class `Storage` is enriched with a method to configure a specific instance in a Composite arrangement with a concrete storage strategy.

Strategy supports the provision of instance-specific method implementations for the common Composite interface, as well as their runtime exchange. The latter is possible by both an explicit trigger through invoking the configuration method of the `Storage` class, or by some logic internal to the classes in the Composite hierarchy.

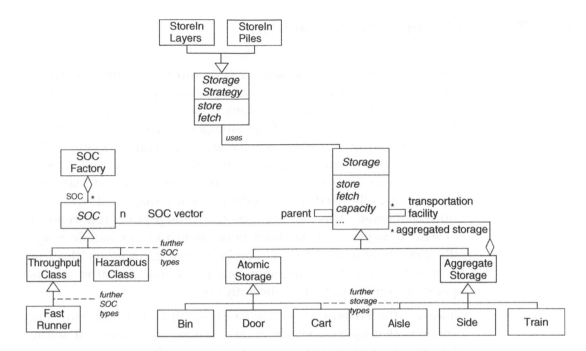

Template Method (453) is an alternative to Strategy that provides an equally feasible solution to support the variation of functional behavior in a class. Strategy resolves the problem via delegation, Template Method by inheritance. However, in accordance with the 'Scandinavian school of object-orientation,' the architecture directives for designing the warehouse management process control system favour delegation over inheritance in the case in which a relationship between classes is not purely structural. Strategy was therefore preferred over Template Method in the design of the warehouse topology domain object.

7.6   Realizing Global Functionality

Some warehouse topology management functions, such as gathering statistical information or reorganization, operate on the entire warehouse topology. These functions traverse all or a large number of storage elements and perform storage-specific actions on them. Reorganization of a warehouse, for example, can be compared to de-fragmenting a hard disk: over time many storing and fetching operations can 'fragment' the storage in a warehouse, so that racks are only sparsely filled and specific items are dispersed across the entire warehouse. This can decrease the throughput of a warehouse, because transportation facilities need more time to handle a specific quantity of items. Regular warehouse reorganizations 'clean-up' the warehouse by re-storing items such that subsequent warehouse operations can be executed efficiently again.

However, the current COMPOSITE-based (319) design supports only functions that operate locally on one or more (pre-selected) storage elements in a concrete warehouse topology, such as storing, fetching, and transporting an item. Functionality like reorganization that operates globally on many storage elements can hardly be modularized in this way: it must be split into different parts that are implemented across multiple classes. In consequence, such functions become hard to understand and maintain, because their logic and control flow is scattered across multiple elements of design and code. In addition, the coupling between the classes of the COMPOSITE hierarchy increases, because changes to the global functionality in one class may require subsequent changes in other classes. As this coupling is also implicit rather than explicit, it also violates fundamental design principles for well-structured software, and the design looks more decoupled than it actually is.

How can we support the realization of global topology management functionality in a strictly modular fashion but without violating the structural properties of the current COMPOSITE-based design?

Implement global topology management functionality as VISITORS (447) that traverse all storage elements of a concrete warehouse topology to perform (local) operations on selected storage elements.

The integration of visitors into our design is very similar to the integration of strategies for varying class-specific behavior. A `GlobalOp-eration` class declares the `visit` methods for each concrete storage class in the COMPOSITE design. It acts as an EXPLICIT INTERFACE (281) for all global warehouse topology management functions, which are realized by subclasses that implement the `visit` methods accordingly. The class `Storage` is extended with an `accept` method to accept a VISITOR, while the concrete storage classes in the COMPOSITE hierarchy implement this `accept` method by calling back the corresponding `visit` method on the visitor.

Using VISITOR to realize functions that operate on large portions of the warehouse topology helps to keep the design modularized and tangible: different concerns, such as storage-local and storage-global functions, are clearly separated from one another. For performance optimizations, visitors can run in their own thread of control, so that other operations can be executed while the visitors are active.

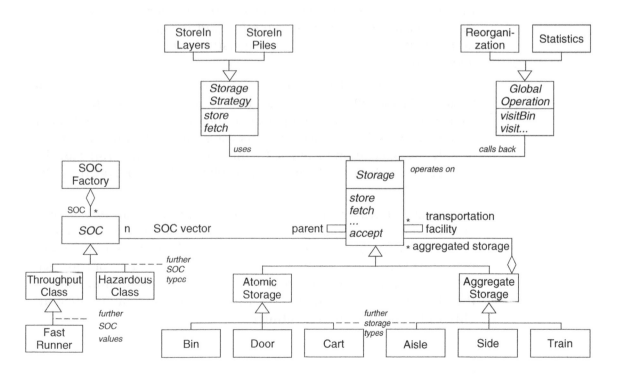

7.7   Traversing the Warehouse Topology

Many warehouse management operations, to execute properly, need to traverse the warehouse topology as a whole. For example, collecting statistical information requires visiting each storage unit in a warehouse, while storing or fetching an item requires selecting an appropriate specific storage.

However, integrating traversal functionality into the corresponding warehouse management operations would make them dependent on the concrete COMPOSITE (319) structure for representing the warehouse topology. Similarly, integrating the traversal functionality into the COMPOSITE hierarchy itself requires a complex infrastructure to support multiple simultaneous traversals.

How can we support sequential access to the storage elements of the warehouse topology without exposing its underlying structure?

Use ITERATORS *(298) to realize traversal strategies separately from both the warehouse topology representation and the operations that need access to it, and let concrete* ITERATOR *instances maintain the state of a specific traversal.*

An `Iterator` class defines an EXPLICIT INTERFACE (281), for example a COMBINED METHOD (296) called next, to access and traverse the storage elements of the warehouse topology. Concrete subclasses implement specific traversal strategies, such as traversing only atomic storage, or only transportation facilities. Clients can obtain an iterator for the storage hierarchy by calling a FACTORY METHOD (529) provided by the `Storage` class.

Factoring out traversal strategies into separate iterators not only keeps domain functionality and core data structures in our design free from 'utility aspects' such as accessing data in a specific manner. It also supports addition, removal, and modification of traversal strategies without affecting other classes in the design, and enables the (dynamic) configuration and reconfiguration of domain functionality with different traversal strategies.

The following diagram illustrates the use of ITERATOR in the design of the warehouse topology domain object.

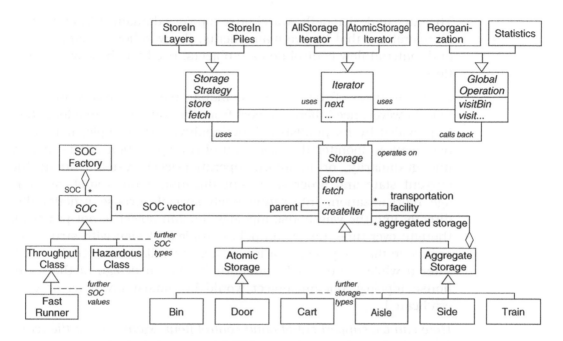

At first glance VISITOR (447) would seem to be an alternative to ITERATOR. Like an iterator, a visitor would allow us both to separate the warehouse topology representation from traversal functionality and to support multiple concurrent traversals. However, a visitor realizes its functionality using double-dispatch. This mechanism is appropriate in cases in which traversal is *paired* with (domain) functionality specific to the visited storage element, such as reorganization, but overly complex for realizing simple one-by-one access to elements of the warehouse topology.

7.8 Supporting Control Flow Extensions

The current design of the warehouse topology domain object supports all operations that its two main clients, the warehouse management and material flow control domain objects, need for their own execution.

Some instances of the warehouse management process control system, however, need more support from the warehouse topology than is provided by its published functionality. For example, it may be necessary to monitor the execution of transportation orders at very fine granularity, or to inform operation-level systems about the current state and progress of long-duration actions such as storage reorganization. Integrating such special-purpose functionality directly into the warehouse topology domain object is not practical, though: over time this would pollute its lean design with structures and code that only one or a few system installations actually need. After a while the original, thoughtfully chosen design of the warehouse topology domain object would be almost invisible, or even eradicated.

How can we support out-of-band control flow extensions for the warehouse topology Domain Object *(208) but avoid their direct integration into its core design?*

Realize out-of-band control flow extensions as pluggable Interceptors *(467) that are called when specific events internal to the warehouse topology* Domain Object *occur.*

An `Interceptor` class specifies an Explicit Interface (281) to which all interceptors must conform. Concrete interceptors implement this interface to perform a specific out-of-band functionality. For example, a `MonitoringInterceptor` could collect information about the current computational state of the warehouse topology domain object and provide it to a monitoring tool for further processing and display, while a `GatewayInterceptor` could report the progress of long-duration actions to the gateway for a system at the operation level, such as SAP. Concrete interceptors register with the `Storage` class as Observers (428) for events of interest, such as the start, end, and specific intermediate states of long-duration actions, so that specific storage classes in the COMPOSITE (319) hierarchy can call them back when these events occur. If necessary, information about the current computational state of the warehouse topology is passed along with the callback.

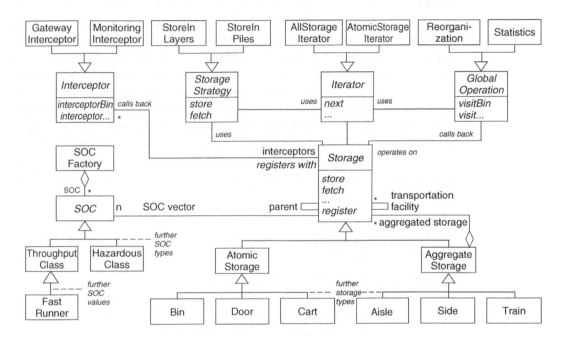

As a result of providing a framework for pluggable INTERCEPTORS, the core design of the warehouse topology domain object is opened to customer- and system-specific extensions to its existing functionality, while still remaining lean and stable, and therefore closed to uncontrolled changes.

Out-of-band control flow extensions can also be supported via a DECORATOR (449) design that wraps existing classes to provide additional functionality or behavior. However, decorators only allow new methods to be added to a class, or preprocessing and post-processing actions to existing methods, but not additional control flow within a given method. We therefore preferred interceptors over decorators in the design of the warehouse topology domain object.

7.9   Connecting to the Database

As outlined in Chapter 4, *Warehouse Management Process Control*, the topology of a warehouse is maintained persistently in a database. A DATABASE ACCESS LAYER (538) ensures that the architecture of the warehouse management process control system is independent of a concrete database interface and also of a specific database paradigm. However, performance and throughput requirements mean that it is not practical to manipulate the entire warehouse topology within the database: we also need an in-memory representation to be able to execute operations on the topology efficiently. On the other hand, keeping a *complete* model of the warehouse topology in memory is not practical: for larger warehouses, the amount of memory that is necessary to maintain the topology would exceed the available memory significantly, even if the topology is distributed across multiple hosts.

How can we ensure that whenever a specific storage element is accessed by an operation on the warehouse topology, the storage element is available in main memory?

Provide VIRTUAL PROXIES *(497) for all atomic storage in the warehouse topology. Whenever atomic storage is accessed via its* VIRTUAL PROXY, *its data is loaded from the database into main memory before the invoked operation is executed. Once a storage element is available in main memory, keep it there so that subsequent accesses can execute efficiently.*

Providing a PROXY-based solution for accessing atomic storage increases the structural complexity of the warehouse topology domain object, but the performance gained once storage data is loaded into main memory outweighs by far the penalties of this design. For performance optimizations, it is also possible to bypass the proxy once the data of the atomic storage is available in main memory. Providing virtual proxies for aggregate storage is technically possible, but because aggregate storage is accessed so frequently, it is more efficient to maintain its data constantly in memory rather than load it on demand. In addition, compared to the number of atomic storage elements, there are only very few aggregate storage elements in a concrete warehouse configuration, so that memory is not wasted.

Supporting virtual proxies for atomic storage is straightforward: a `StorageProxy` class derives from the `Storage` class and maintains a relationship to a specific `AtomicStorage`, for example via its primary key. When the proxy is accessed, it uses the primary key to load the storage's data and execute the operation invoked on it.

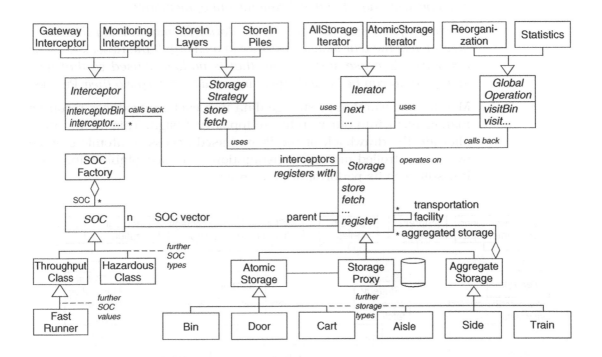

7.10 Maintaining In-Memory Storage Data

Although the introduction of proxies into the warehouse topology design supports performance and throughput goals, it also incurs a significant drawback. Storage data loaded into main memory via the proxies is not erased once the invoked operation terminates: instead it is kept in memory to support the efficient execution of subsequent operations. After a while all available memory could be in use, making it impossible to load further storage data from the database.

Modifying the behavior of the proxies so that they delete their associated data once an operation is executed is not an appropriate solution to this problem: we would face the same performance issues as we addressed with the original proxy realization!

How can we keep the original VIRTUAL PROXY *(497) design for representing atomic storage, but avoid running out of memory?*

Provide a fixed size RESOURCE CACHE *(505) for maintaining the representation of the warehouse structure in memory. If the* RESOURCE CACHE *becomes full, erase storage data that is no longer used so that new storage data can be loaded safely into main memory via their* PROXIES.

Maintaining warehouse storage data in a cache introduces resource management into our warehouse topology design. This allows us to alleviate the drawback of the PROXY-based access to atomic storage over uncontrolled memory consumption to an acceptable minimum, but still keep its performance advantages.

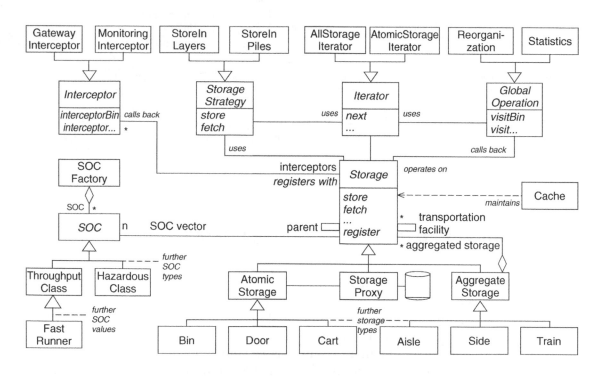

7.11   Configuring the Warehouse Topology

The design we created for the warehouse topology domain object offers a variety of configuration options: interceptors, visitors, strategies, and iterators support flexible adaptation to warehouse-specific behavior, while the COMPOSITE (319) hierarchy supports the integration of warehouse-specific storage structures.

However, configuring a specific instance of the warehouse topology domain object is non-trivial. Semantic dependencies can occur between configuration options—for example, specific visitors might require specific iterators to work correctly—and configuration options must often be installed in a defined order. A 'manual' and explicit configuration of each option via an appropriate interface is theoretically possible, but opens the door to subtle configuration errors that can remain unnoticed until the warehouse topology is misbehaving during system operation.

How can we configure the warehouse topology DOMAIN OBJECT *(208) both simply and correctly?*

Use a BUILDER *(527) internal to the warehouse topology* DOMAIN OBJECT *to check a specific set of configuration options for consistency, create each configuration option, and integrate all options at the right place and in the right order.*

The system's central COMPONENT CONFIGURATOR (490) infrastructure passes the set of storage classes, interceptors, visitors, strategies, and iterators that should be configured into the warehouse topology to its internal BUILDER arrangement via an appropriate configuration method in the explicit interface of the warehouse topology domain object. A ConfigurationDirector controls the configuration process: it checks the received configuration for consistency and, if it is valid, instructs a ConfigurationBuilder to install each element of the configuration in the correct order. The ConfigurationBuilder first creates the respective configuration element, then integrates it at the appropriate place in the warehouse topology structure. In terms of BUILDER, the concrete storage classes, interceptors, visitors, strategies, and iterators that are configured play the role of products.

The following diagram outlines a simplified example configuration for the warehouse topology domain object.

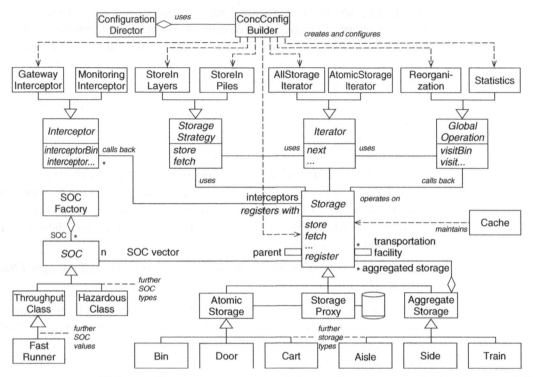

Using a BUILDER arrangement to configure concrete instances of the warehouse topology domain object supports simplicity, efficiency, and correctness. Simplicity is supported because neither clients of the warehouse topology nor its domain functionality are responsible for the correctness of the configuration. Instead, there is a separate dedicated entity: the builder. Efficiency is supported because the builder is internal to the warehouse topology domain object, so that the implementation of its configuration process can take advantage from having access to and knowledge of the warehouse topology's concrete design and implementation. Correctness is supported because the builder realizes an explicitly coded and tested configuration strategy that integrates the different configuration options in the right order and the right place.

7.12   Detailing the Explicit Interface

The baseline architecture of the warehouse management process control system specifies that each domain object must provide an explicit interface through which its functionality is remotely accessible.

However, domain objects like the warehouse topology offer a wide range of different functions to their clients, but different clients only use parts of this functionality. Providing a single explicit interface for the entire warehouse topology runs the risk of introducing undesirable implicit dependencies between domain objects of the system. For example, if a client domain object does not use all offered functions of the warehouse topology, but the signature of an unused function evolves, the client must be recompiled and relinked even though its usage of the warehouse topology is unchanged. Similarly, if the interface of the warehouse topology is extended with new functionality that is not used by the client, it must also be recompiled and relinked. Ideally, clients of the warehouse topology must only be changed if their usage of the warehouse topology changes, for example because they use new or additional functionality, or because they use existing functionality differently.

How can we ensure that changes to an EXPLICIT INTERFACE *(281)—be it the modification of the signature of an existing function or the provision of new functions—affect clients of the interface only if they are interested in such changes?*

Partition the EXPLICIT INTERFACE *into role-specific* EXTENSION INTERFACES *(284) with one or more extension interfaces per role. Never change a published extension interface: if a* DOMAIN OBJECT *(208) must provide additional roles, introduce corresponding new extension interfaces, and if an existing role evolves, offer an additional extension interface for the changed role, but still support the original extension interfaces.*

Within the EXTENSION INTERFACE arrangement for the warehouse topology, a RootInterface offers functionality to access any individual extension interface, as well as to navigate between all provided extension interfaces. Concrete and role-specific extension interfaces derive from this `RootInterface`, for example `Configuration`, `Routing`, and

Statistics interfaces. Clients can obtain an initial extension interface onto the warehouse topology via a TopologyInterfaceFactory. Once a client has access to a specific extension interface, it can use the interface's navigation functionality to access any other extension interface provided by the warehouse topology, provided that the client has appropriate access rights.

The diagram below sketches the EXTENSION INTERFACE design for the warehouse topology:

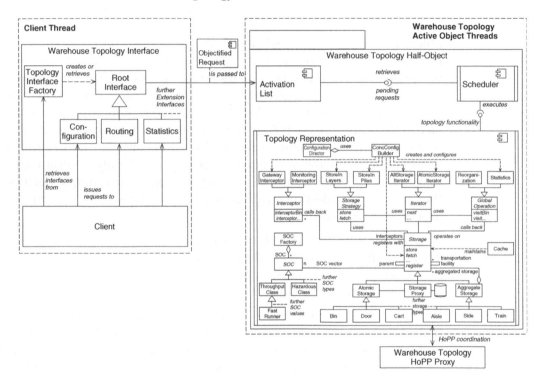

Providing role-specific extension interfaces for the warehouse topology contributes significantly to its openness to controlled evolution. The fundamental partitioning of this domain object into an explicit interface that is separated from its encapsulated implementation supports client stability if the implementation changes. Extension interfaces add to this and support client stability even in the case of specific changes and extensions to the warehouse topology's public contract. In particular, a client that uses a specific extension interface is unaffected by the addition of new extension interfaces to the warehouse topology or if other, unused extension interfaces change. The client is also unaffected if is not 'interested' in the evolution of an extension interface that it uses, because the old version is still supported. On the interface side, therefore, extension interfaces complete and complement the flexible design we created for the encapsulated implementation of the warehouse topology.

7.13 Warehouse Topology Summary

Taking a bird's-eye view of the pattern sequence we applied to design the warehouse topology DOMAIN OBJECT (208) reveals that even though this design is specific to the warehouse management domain, we received concrete guidance from our general pattern language for distributed computing to create this sequence.

Its first three patterns—COMPOSITE (319), CHAIN OF RESPONSIBILITY (440), and IMMUTABLE VALUE (396)—define the strategic core of the warehouse topology's ENCAPSULATED IMPLEMENTATION (313), the central structure that represents and hosts the spatial arrangement and functional behavior of physical storage and transportation facilities in a concrete warehouse.

Four patterns unfold this stable design center [Gam97] to support (tactical) behavioral variation. STRATEGY (455) enables the behavioral variation of a specific storage element or transportation facility. VISITOR (447) allows the expression of operations that act on multiple storage elements and transportation facilities. VISITOR also supports extension of the warehouse topology with functionality that was unanticipated during its original design and implementation. ITERATORS (298) supports strategies and visitors traversing the warehouse structure according to different traversal policies. Finally, INTERCEPTOR (444) supports controlled extension of the warehouse topology's core control flow to support customer-specific or system-specific out-of-band functionality.

The next two patterns address an important operational quality of the warehouse topology domain object: resource awareness. VIRTUAL PROXY (497) enables us to keep only the core structure of the warehouse topology in main memory, while the concrete data for specific storage or transportation facilities is maintained in the database and only loaded when operations need to access it. A RESOURCE CACHE (529) alleviates the main performance bottleneck of virtual proxies, that data loaded into main memory should not be stored and deleted from memory immediately after use, but kept in memory for a while for subsequent fast access. Such data should not however hog memory indefinitely.

A BUILDER (527) arrangement completes the design of the warehouse topology by offering a centralized mechanism for configuring a concrete instance of this DOMAIN OBJECT both correctly and in a controlled manner.

Finally, EXTENSION INTERFACE *(284)* partitions the EXPLICIT INTERFACE (281) of the warehouse topology into multiple, role-specific contracts, each of which can be accessed and evolved independently.

The table below summarizes the pattern sequence that helped in creating the warehouse topology domain object, as well as with the design challenges addressed by each pattern in the sequence.

Pattern	Challenges
COMPOSITE	Modeling the warehouse storage hierarchy
CHAIN OF RESPONSIBILITY	Navigating up a COMPOSITE structure
IMMUTABLE VALUE	Sharing state information
STRATEGY	Supporting storage-specific behavior
VISITOR	Providing warehouse-global functionality
ITERATOR	Traversing the warehouse structure
INTERCEPTOR	Providing control flow extensions
VIRTUAL PROXY	Accessing persistent data
RESOURCE CACHE	Maintaining in-memory data
BUILDER	Configuring the warehouse topology DOMAIN OBJECT
EXTENSION INTERFACE	Providing role-specific views of the warehouse topology functionality

It is important to note that although the design of the warehouse topology domain object appears to be 'reusable' for other systems that must maintain topological information, it is nevertheless a very specific design that is driven by very specific requirements. For example, if the entire warehouse topology could be maintained in a database both efficiently and without performance penalties, there would be no need for a dedicated warehouse topology domain object. A properly designed DATABASE ACCESS LAYER (538) for the persistence domain object, as outlined in Chapter 5, *Baseline Architecture*, would be sufficient to provide both the warehouse management and material flow control domain objects with appropriate topology information. Similarly, if the entire warehouse topology could be maintained completely in memory, there would be no need for virtual proxies and a cache. If there was only a fixed set of standard functionality to support, flexibility measures such as strategies, visitors, and interceptors could perhaps also not be necessary.

If requirements and constraints are related to those for our warehouse management process control system, the warehouse topology design can potentially serve as a role model for other topology management domain objects. But it is very important to check carefully if there are more, fewer, or different requirements to support that suggest other solutions. In fact several designs for topology management are possible, all of which are created by different pattern sequences whose selection is driven by different sets of requirements.

8 The Story Behind The Pattern Story

... and they all lived happily ever after ...

In this chapter we step back from the details of the warehouse management process control system to take a bird's-eye view of the pattern story that guided the creation of its architecture. We discuss how this story reinforces the properties of pattern languages, and how the pattern language for distributed computing from Part III of this book supported the selection of the specific pattern sequence that underlies the story.

Looking back at the pattern story about the architecture of the warehouse management process control system may give the impression that the selection and application of its constituent patterns was fairly obvious: perhaps just common sense, or even predetermined. The story has a natural, intuitive flow and we can easily follow its plot. It may therefore appear that creating this architecture was straightforward.

This impression, however, is simplistic and misleading, missing many of the subtleties that make the act of design anything but a handle-turning process, regardless of patterns. Analyzing the pattern sequence reveals that it was thoughtfully chosen rather than randomly picked. Most obviously, its individual patterns address the specific requirements of the warehouse management process control system—definitely a prerequisite for creating a well-defined software architecture. But just selecting the right patterns is by no means sufficient to achieve an effective and robust architecture. All patterns must also be applied in an appropriate order and integrated with one another so that they complement and reinforce rather than contradict one another. A set of individual patterns cannot give you such support, because each pattern focuses largely on resolving the specific problem that it addresses.

In a process of piecemeal growth, one pattern at a time, this pattern sequence created, unfolded, and gradually solidified the system's architecture until it was complete and consistent in all its different parts—not only from a functional perspective, but also from success-critical operational and developmental aspects such as throughout, scalability, flexibility, and portability.

At the baseline architectural level, and also for the fundamental structures of the communication middleware and warehouse topology, all patterns in the sequence address system-wide and strategic issues to define the architecture's backbone. Local and tactical issues, such as variations in algorithms and control flow, were addressed later in the sequence, after the respective stable, strategic design centers were created. The patterns in the sequence were applied one at a time, and each pattern was first integrated into the existing design before it was implemented in detail. In other words, each pattern in the sequence transformed an existing design into a new design that strengthened and extended the original design's properties.

All patterns were also tightly integrated with one another based on their roles, so that they could effectively balance the forces of their respective problems and mutually support and reinforce their individual properties. For example, many components in our CCM-based ORB participate in several pattern implementations. As we showed in Chapter 6, *Communication Middleware*, the `Acceptor` components introduced by ACCEPTOR-CONNECTOR (265) are event handlers from the perspective of REACTOR (259). In addition, they are context components from the perspective of STRATEGY (455), because Acceptors can implement different concurrency strategies for the service handlers on whose behalf they listen for new connection requests. Equally, the `Storage` class of the warehouse topology design presented in Chapter 7, *Warehouse Topology*, implements the roles of nine patterns: COMPOSITE (319), CHAIN OF RESPONSIBILITY (440), IMMUTABLE VALUE (396), PROXY (290), ITERATOR (298), STRATEGY (455), VISITOR (447), INTERCEPTOR (444), and RESOURCE CACHE (505). This merging of responsibilities results in high pattern density, which helps ensure powerful but compact and comprehensible designs.

Other patterns, such as LAYERS (185), COMPONENT CONFIGURATOR (490), and STRATEGY (455), were also used to guide the design of different portions of the warehouse management process control system. LAYERS, for example, was used to separate different levels of application functionality from one another in the system's baseline architecture, as well as different levels of granularity associated with communication in the design of our CCM-based ORB. We used COMPONENT CONFIGURATOR to orchestrate configuration and deployment of functionality, both at the baseline level of the system as well as inside the communication middleware. STRATEGY was applied throughout the system to support the variation of algorithmic behavior and internal middleware mechanisms for different scenarios and for many layers in the warehouse management process control system.

The ability of patterns to apply at multiple levels of abstraction and granularity in a large-scale software architecture provides a powerful tool that helps to ensure the conceptual integrity of complex systems. In particular, common and related problems are resolved similarly using the same patterns across the entire system. Consequently, it is no surprise that the pattern sequence we applied created not only a well-balanced, sustainable software architecture for our warehouse management process control system, but one that was also easy to understand and use.

In addition, the pattern sequence we selected allowed us to create a multi-layered product-line architecture for the warehouse system—a software architecture that is suitable for supporting multiple system variants and versions. On the domain side, for example, we can support variants with different functionality sets: some system configurations include the full set of warehouse management and material flow control functionality, others only the material flow control functionality, and still others the material control flow functionality and selected warehouse management functionality. Similarly, on the infrastructure side, our communication middleware can be strategized and (re)configured to satisfy a myriad of different application requirements and operational environments.

Such flexibility can only be supported because the pattern sequence that helped to generate the software architecture for the warehouse management process control system follows the principles of loose coupling. Other domain-specific variation points include warehouse types, warehouse sizes, and warehouse operation modes. On the technical side, the architecture, and particularly the design of its communication middleware, supports integration with different operating systems and network protocols, and configuration with different communication and quality of service strategies. The design and implementation of the communication middleware is also independent of the warehouse management process control domain, thus forming a reusable asset by itself that can be used as the basis of architectures and implementations for distributed systems in many other domains.

We can therefore conclude that key quality aspects of the warehouse management process control system architecture have come from a successful and sound pattern sequence. This pattern sequence was well suited to the problem and the creation of a system in a systematic manner. Yet it is just one possible sequence of many through our pattern language for distributed computing, and also just one of many for the design of warehouse management process control systems. We can see that for a pattern language capable of addressing a specific domain more broadly, many, many such sequences must be supported. In other words, the quality of a pattern language is characterized by the quality of its possible sequences. Only then can a pattern language inform us of the important challenges in developing software for a specific domain, and tell us in what order these challenges should be addressed, what design alternatives exist for addressing specific challenges, and when to use specific alternatives to resolve a challenge.

As a result of integrating coherent and complementary sets of quality pattern sequences, pattern languages become important tools for designing, implementing, customizing, and applying reusable product-line architectures, platform architectures, and frameworks. Pattern stories, in turn, help developers understand the design and implementation of existing software systems, so that they can use these systems effectively in their own projects, such as applying off-the-shelf communication middleware, or to maintain and evolve software towards new requirements, such as our warehouse management process control system.

III The Language

"I wish life was not so short," he thought,
"Languages take such a time,
and so do all the things one wants to know about."

J.R.R. Tolkien, The Lost Road

In the third part of the book we present one possible pattern language for distributed computing. We distilled it from our own experiences in realizing distributed systems, as well as from the distribution patterns that skillful software architects, designers, and developers contributed to the software community. The language has been used to develop many real-world distributed object computing middleware and distributed applications. You can use it with your colleagues and project team-mates to guide the design of new distributed systems, and also to improve and refactor existing ones.

Over the past fifteen years we have participated in the development of many industrial networked, concurrent, and distributed systems, ranging from industrial process automation systems, medical imaging, and large-scale telecommunication systems, to high-performance communication middleware. The pattern language for distributed computing that we present in this part of the book distils this experience in a tangible, ready-to-use form. You can use it to build new distributed systems, to evolve, re-engineer, or refactor existing systems, or simply to understand the architectures of distributed software systems or middleware that you are using in your work.

Our pattern language for distributed computing includes 114 patterns, which are grouped into thirteen problem areas. A problem area addresses a specific technical topic related to building distributed systems, and comprises all those patterns in our language that address the challenges associated with that technical topic. The main intent of the problem areas is to make the language and its patterns more tangible and comprehensible: patterns that address related problems are presented and discussed within a common and clearly scoped context. The problem areas are presented in their approximate order of relevance and application when building distributed systems.

Each problem area and its constituent patterns forms a separate chapter in this part of the book:

- Chapter 9, *From Mud To Structure*, includes the ten root patterns of our pattern language for distributed computing. They help transform the 'mud' of requirements and constraints we usually start with into a coarse-grained software structure with clearly separated, tangible parts that make up the system being developed.

- Chapter 10, *Distribution Infrastructure*, describes twelve patterns pertaining to *middleware*, distribution infrastructure software that helps to simplify distributed computing applications.

- Chapter 11, *Event Demultiplexing and Dispatching*, comprises four patterns that provide efficient and flexible infrastructures for demultiplexing, dispatching, and responding to events received from the network.

- Chapter 12, *Interface Partitioning*, offers eleven patterns that help in the design and specification of meaningful component interfaces that are easy to use for common component usage scenarios, but also allow for special-purpose and out-of-band scenarios.

- Chapter 13, *Component Partitioning*, includes six patterns for partitioning components. The focus of the patterns is on supporting visible component quality properties such as performance, scalability, and flexibility.

- Chapter 14, *Application Control*, addresses eight patterns that help in transforming user input for an application into concrete service requests to its functionality, executing those requests, and transforming any results back into an output meaningful for users—which can be a challenging task.

- Chapter 15, *Concurrency*, comprises four patterns for concurrency that help servers and server-side software to handle requests from multiple clients simultaneously.

- Chapter 16, *Synchronization*, describes nine patterns that help with synchronizing the access to shared components, objects, and resources, either by outlining efficient synchronization strategies, or by minimizing the need for synchronization.

- Chapter 17, *Object Interaction*, comprises eight patterns that support efficient collaboration and data exchange between interacting components and objects of an application.

- Chapter 18, *Adaptation and Extension.* describes thirteen patterns that help in preparing components and objects in long-lived systems, in particular distributed systems, for their own configuration, adaptation, and evolution.

- Chapter 19, *Modal Behavior*, offers three patterns for structuring components and objects that are inherently state-driven.

- Chapter 20, *Resource Management.* includes twenty-one patterns that help with explicit management of components and resources in a distributed system.

- Chapter 21, *Database Access*, 'closes' our pattern language by presenting five patterns for mapping an object-oriented application design to a relational database schema efficiently, *and* without introducing tight dependencies between the two worlds.

The main intent of our pattern language for distributed computing is to serve as an overview about, introduction to, guide through, and communication vehicle for the best practices and state-of-the-art in major areas of the construction of distributed software systems. It is not a tutorial for distributed computing in general, however, but has a clear focus on the *design* of distributed software systems. We therefore assume readers have some familiarity with core distributed computing concepts and mechanisms, as described in the body of the relevant literature [TaSte02] [Bir05].

9 From Mud To Structure

Kasbah Ait Benhaddou, Atlas Mountains, UNESCO world cultural heritage
© Lutz Buschmann

This chapter presents the root and entry point to our pattern language for distributed computing. Its featured patterns help to transform the mud of requirements and constraints we usually start with into a coarse-grained software structure with clearly separated, tangible parts that make up the system being developed, and address several key concerns of sustainable software architectures: operational aspects such as performance and availability, as well as developmental qualities like extensibility and maintainability.

Large distributed systems tend to be complex. In the beginning, all we have is a set of requirements and constraints that must be transformed into a working software system. A naive approach to development is likely to result in a 'big ball of mud' [FoYo99], a software clump whose design and code is so messy that it is hard to see any coherent architecture in it. Such software is hard to understand, maintain, and evolve, and over time it also tends to suffer from poor stability, performance, scalability, and other essential operational architecture qualities [Bus03].

One of the keys to successful software development is *structure*. We need structure that can be understood by developers, structure that is resilient to the forces to which the system and its development are subjected, structure that favors the development process surrounding and creating it, structure that respects the business and individuals who will make it and shape it. In short, structure that provides a habitable environment for developers and other stakeholders of a software system. Without vision and a guiding hand, however, the structure of a software system is likely to be complicated rather than just complex, leading not only to the loss of the big picture, but the small picture as well—the code can become mired in accidental detail and assumptions.

In undertaking such software development, therefore, a coarse-grained conception of the system is needed that—with the help of abstraction and separation—omits unnecessary details and organizes the system's key concepts at a broader level.

First and foremost, a software architecture must be a meaningful expression of the system's application domain. Specifically, the functionality and features provided by the system must support a concrete business, otherwise it has no practical value for its users. If the system's software architecture does not scope and portray the application domain appropriately, however, it will be hard, if not impossible, to provide user-level services and features that correctly address the functional requirements of the system.

A further concern when modeling the functional architecture of a system is *variability*. Variations can arise in regard to different feature sets, alternatives in business processes, choices for concrete business algorithms, and options for the system's appearance to the user. Without a clear knowledge of what can vary in an application domain, and also of what variations must be supported, it is hard to provide the right level and degree of flexibility in a software system or product.

The root pattern of our pattern language addresses the challenge of creating a model of the application domain that both reflects the functional responsibilities of a software system and can serve as a solid basis for the further elaboration of its technical architecture.

> The DOMAIN MODEL pattern (182) [Fow03a] defines a precise model for the structure and workflow of an application domain— including their variations. Model elements are abstractions meaningful in the application domain; their roles and interactions reflect domain workflow and map to system requirements.

The following diagram illustrates how DOMAIN MODEL connects to the body of our pattern language for distributed computing and orchestrates the patterns that help with its refinement.

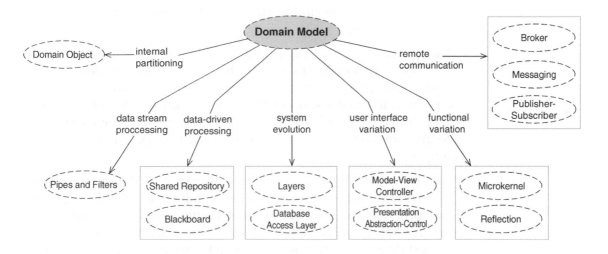

DOMAIN OBJECT is also described in the collection of *Patterns Of Enterprise Application Architecture* [Fow03a], but its focus there is solely on technical aspects of the realization of a domain model, and it does not address the explicit modeling of the domain.

Dividing the core structure of a distributed software system purely along lines visible in the application domain, however, will not always help to define a feasible baseline architecture. On one hand, a software system needs to include many components and exhibit many properties that are unrelated to its domain. For example, quality-of-service requirements, such as performance and predictable resource utilization, are cross-cutting issues and therefore cannot be addressed through component decomposition alone. Similarly, the need for responsive user interaction can conflict with the latency and partial-failure modes associated with networks. On other hand, we as developers want more than a system that simply meets the visible user requirements. User's indifference to developmental qualities such as portability, maintainability, comprehensibility, extensibility, testability, and so on should not be shared by developers.

Finding a suitable application partitioning depends on framing answers to several key questions and challenges:

- *How does the application interact with its environment?* Some systems interact with different types of human user, others with other systems as peers, and yet others are embedded within even more complex systems. Inevitably, there are also systems that have all of these interactions.

- *How is application processing organized?* Some applications receive requests from clients to which they react and respond. Other applications process streams of data. Some applications perform self-contained tasks without receiving stimuli from their environment. Indeed, for some applications, it may not even be possible to identify any concrete workflow and explicit cooperation among its components.

- *What variations must the application support?* Flexibility is a major concern in software development, especially when developing software products, or software product families, that are intended to serve a whole range of different customer needs. Some systems must support different feature sets, such as for small, medium, and large enterprises, to address different markets and customer groups. Other systems must support variations in business processes, so that each customer can model the workflow of its specific business appropriately. Yet other systems must support variations in algorithmic behavior and visual appearance to be attractive to a broad range of customers.

- *What is the life expectancy of the application?* Some systems are short-lived and thrown away when they are no longer used, such as an online trading program designed to exploit a transient market trend. Other systems will be in operation for thirty years or more and must respond to changing requirements, environments, and configurations, such as Telecommunication Management Network (TMN) system.

Our pattern language for distributed computing, therefore, includes nine strategic patterns that help in the transformation of a DOMAIN MODEL into a technical software architecture that can serve as the basis for further development. Each pattern provides its own answers to the questions raised above:

The LAYERS pattern (185) [POSA1] helps to structure applications that can be decomposed into groups of subtasks in which each group of subtasks is at a particular level of abstraction, granularity, hardware-distance, or other partitioning criteria.

The MODEL-VIEW-CONTROLLER pattern (MVC) (188) [POSA1] [Fow03a] divides an interactive application into three parts. The model contains the core functionality and data. Views display information to the user. Controllers handle user input. Views and controllers together comprise the user interface. A change-propagation mechanism ensures consistency between the user interface and the model.

The PRESENTATION-ABSTRACTION-CONTROL pattern (PAC) (191) [POSA1] defines a structure for interactive software systems in the form of a hierarchy of cooperating agents. Each agent is responsible for a specific aspect of the application's functionality and consists of three components: presentation, abstraction, and control. This subdivision separates the human-computer interaction aspects of an agent from its functional core and its communication with other agents.

The MICROKERNEL pattern (194) [POSA1] applies to software systems that must adapt to changing system requirements. It separates a minimal functional core from extended functionality and customer-specific parts. The microkernel also serves as a socket for plugging in these extensions and coordinating their collaboration.

The REFLECTION pattern (197) [POSA1] provides a mechanism for changing the structure and behavior of software systems dynamically. It supports the modification of fundamental aspects, such as type structures and function call mechanisms. In this pattern an application is split into two parts. A base level includes the core application logic. Its runtime behavior is observed by a meta level that maintains information about selected system properties to make the software self-aware. Changes to information kept in the meta level thus affect subsequent base-level behavior.

The PPIPES AND FILTERS pattern (200) [POSA1] [HoWo03] provides a structure for systems that process data streams. Each processing step is encapsulated in a filter component. Pipes are used to pass data between adjacent filters.

The SHARED REPOSITORY pattern (202) [HoWo03] helps to structure applications whose functionality and collaboration is purely data-driven. A shared repository maintains the common data on which the application's components operate, the components themselves access and modify the data in the shared repository, and the state of that data in the shared repository instigates the control flow of specific components.

The BLACKBOARD pattern (205) [POSA1] is useful for problems for which no deterministic solution strategies are known. In Blackboard several specialized subsystems assemble their knowledge to build a possibly partial or approximate solution.

The DOMAIN OBJECT (208) pattern encapsulates a self-contained, coherent functional or infrastructural responsibility into a well-defined entity that offers its functionality via one or more explicit interfaces while hiding its inner structure and implementation.

The nine patterns above address a whole range of different concerns in refining DOMAIN MODEL towards a sustainable software baseline architecture.

LAYERS defines a general approach for partitioning the responsibilities of an application according to a (sub) system-wide property, such that each group of functionalities can be developed and evolved independently. The specific partitioning criteria can be defined along one or more dimensions, such as abstraction, granularity, hardware distance, and rate of change. LAYERS is probably the most fundamental pattern for separating different, and grouping related, concerns in a software architecture.

LAYERS integrates with our pattern language for distributed computing as follows.

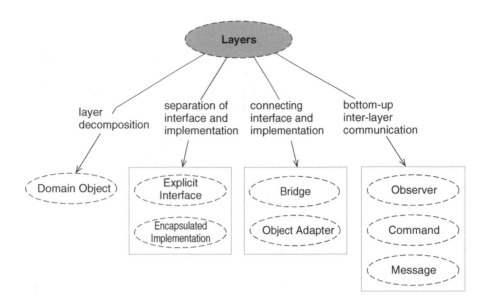

The next two patterns, MODEL-VIEW-CONTROLLER and PRESENTATION-ABSTRACTION-CONTROL, address the problem of support for variability in user interfaces. Though both patterns are related in several ways, they are not necessarily alternatives. In a nutshell, MODEL-VIEW-CONTROLLER supports variability within one specific user interface, while PRESENTATION-ABSTRACTION-CONTROL supports the use of multiple, distinct user interfaces and their independent variation. As most software systems need only one user interface paradigm, MODEL-VIEW-CONTROLLER should always be your first choice.

PRESENTATION-ABSTRACTION-CONTROL, in contrast, is (only) useful if a software system is partitioned into multiple, largely independent but sometimes cooperating subsystems, each of which suggests its own user interface paradigm. Examples for such systems include software that is used off-shore by users both on board a ship and underwater, robot control systems, or applications that are partly operated via virtual reality devices. Only few types of system fall into this category, thus the applicability of PRESENTATION-ABSTRACTION-CONTROL is significantly narrower than that of MODEL-VIEW-VIEW-CONTROLLER.

The following diagram illustrates how these two patterns integrate with our pattern language for distributed computing.

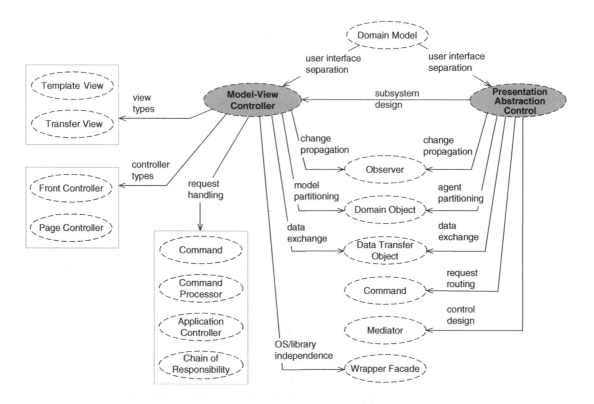

The MODEL-VIEW-CONTROLLER pattern is also described in *Patterns of Enterprise Application Architecture* [Fow03a], where it has the same intent, structure, and behavior as the POSA version. The MODEL-VIEW-PRESENTER pattern [Fow06] is also related to MODEL-VIEW-CONTROLLER, but works better for rich client development than MVC because it does not delegate all view behavior to the model. An intermediate presenter component receives all user actions, such as when clicking a checkbox, or if the involvement of the model is necessary, such as when clicking an 'Apply' button, and decides whether it can handle them without consulting the model. This improves composability of complex views and the testability of the different roles.

The next two patterns, MICROKERNEL and REFLECTION, both foster the construction of flexible software systems. Both patterns address different aspects of flexibility, however. MICROKERNEL, in general, provides a plug-in architecture that supports flexibility in terms of *what* functionality a system provides to its users. MICROKERNEL has thus evolved as a popular architecture for operating systems, middleware, and product-line architectures.

REFLECTION, in contrast, defines an architecture that objectifies specific aspects of a system's structure and behavior, which supports flexibility in terms of *how* its functionality executes and/or can be used by its clients. It is thus often used in the context of application and service integration scenarios, in which client applications must be able to use or control the functionality of other applications without having an explicit, built-in knowledge of their interfaces and internal behavior.

The following diagrams outline how MICROKERNEL and REFLECTION connect to the patterns of our language.

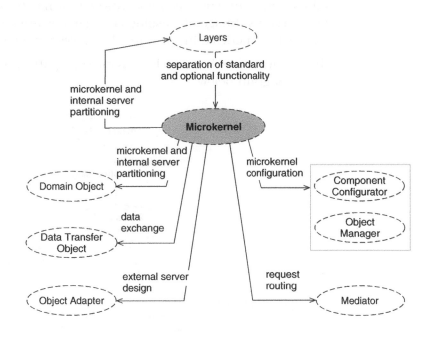

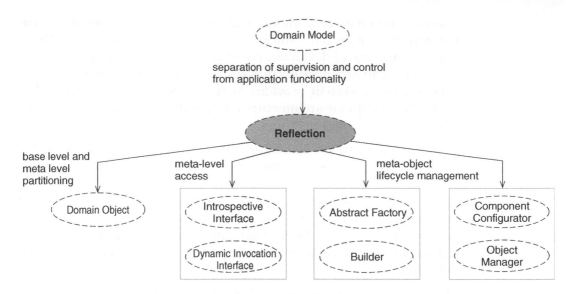

The PIPES AND FILTERS pattern is suited for applications that process data streams, or whose components communicate via the exchange of data streams. Image processing is a prime example of a domain that can best be modeled in software via a PIPES AND FILTERS architecture.

The integration of PIPES AND FILTERS into our pattern language is shown in the diagram below.

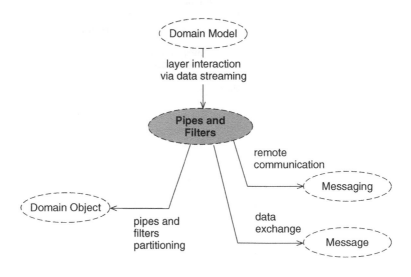

Some sources also see PIPES AND FILTERS as a fundamental style for interprocess communication [HoWo03] [VKZ04], but in the context of our pattern language for distributed computing we consider it more as an approach for *orchestrating the collaboration* of an application's services, rather than a style they can use to *exchange information*. In a PIPES AND FILTERS arrangement the latter is done with help of messaging, which, as we outline in Chapter 10, *Distribution Infrastructure*, we consider of equal importance to remote method invocation and publish/subscribe as one of three communication styles.

Another version of PIPES AND FILTERS is published in *Enterprise Integration Patterns* [HoWo03], where it is used to enable stepwise transformation of message formats and content in message-oriented middleware. The scope of PIPES AND FILTERS in POSA is broader, because there the pattern is used to structure entire data stream processing *applications*. The use of PIPES AND FILTERS in this pattern language follows the POSA scope.

The SHARED REPOSITORY and BLACKBOARD patterns help in designing applications whose components work largely on a common set of (structured) data. By separating the data from the functionality of a system, data exchange between components of the application is simplified, and coordination of the components via Change of Value (CoV) notifications in that data becomes possible.

Their integration with our pattern language for distributed computing is as follows:

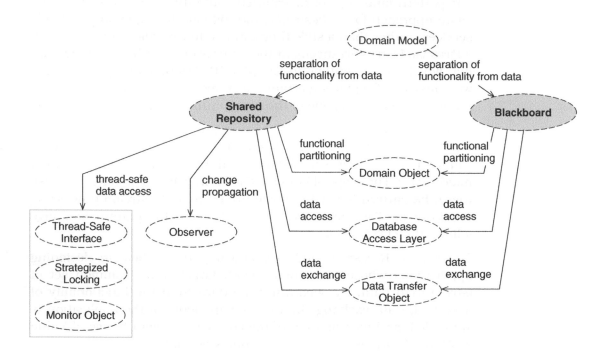

The difference between the two patterns is in their computational approach. In a SHARED REPOSITORY architecture, application components realize a deterministic control flow and cooperate in an explicitly coded or configured manner. It is thus a suitable approach for applications in the network management and control system domains, which typically operate on a large amount of data from field devices, such as Telecommunication Management Network (TMN) systems or industrial process control systems.

A BLACKBOARD architecture, in contrast, implements a computational model based on heuristics, which is able to produce useful results even when no deterministic algorithms are known or feasible in an application domain, or if input data is fuzzy, inaccurate, or otherwise questionable in its quality. For example, BLACKBOARD is a fairly popular architectural approach for bio-information systems, which typically operate on large bases of fuzzy, incomplete, or partly erroneous data. It was also popular in speech recognition applications until appropriate deterministic solutions were discovered.

From a general perspective, BLACKBOARD is a specialized variant of SHARED REPOSITORY, but one that addresses a different set of forces whose resolution requires a different computational approach. Although the applicability of BLACKBOARD is definitely narrower than that of SHARED REPOSITORY, these differences justify its description as a pattern in its own right.

The SHARED REPOSITORY pattern is also described in *Enterprise Integration Patterns* [HoWo03], under the name SHARED DATABASE. Its focus there is on (enterprise) application integration—in contrast to coordinating the control flow of a data-driven applications, which is the scope of the pattern in the context of our pattern language. As with PIPES AND FILTERS, some sources also see SHARED REPOSITORY as a fundamental style for interprocess communication [Fow03a] [HoWo03] [VKZ04]. We do not share this perspective in the context of our pattern language for distributed computing. and consider the pattern as an approach to partitioning the functionality of an application.

The final pattern we present in this chapter, DOMAIN OBJECT, supports the encapsulation of self-contained responsibilities in an application within a defined software realization. Such encapsulation allows us to address the specific functional, operational, and developmental requirements of this responsibility explicitly, directly, and independently of other DOMAIN OBJECT realizations.

The next diagram illustrates the integration of DOMAIN OBJECT into our pattern language for distributed computing.

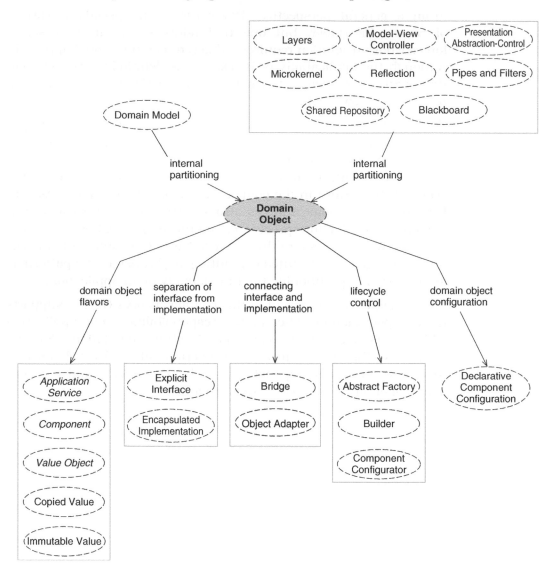

Some of the patterns referenced are not described in this book, but are nevertheless included in our pattern language because they represent different DOMAIN OBJECT flavors. APPLICATION SERVICE is the key pattern in *Core J2EE Patterns* for partitioning the business logic of an enterprise application [ACM01], and Component is one of the two root patterns of *Server Component Patterns* [VSW02]. The two patterns, therefore, connect our pattern language to all patterns in *Server Component Patterns* and *Core J2EE Patterns* of which they are composed. A Value Object, finally, is a small object whose identity is based on its state rather than its type [PPR] [Fow03a]

Most real-world software systems cannot be formed reasonably from a single pattern from the above application partitioning patterns. Different patterns offer different architectural properties, and a system may find that it must grow from multiple strategic patterns to meet its system requirements. For example, you may have to build a system that has two distinct and sometimes conflicting design goals, such as adaptability of its user interface *and* portability to multiple platforms. For such systems you must combine several patterns to form an appropriate structure. When scaling to a distributed environment, these application infrastructure patterns must also be integrated with suitable distribution patterns.

However, the selection of an application partitioning pattern, or a combination of several, is just one step of many when designing a software system. A selection of partitioning patterns is not yet a complete software architecture in the sense of being whole and addressing all the significant decisions that characterize the design. Instead it remains a structural framework for a software system that must be further specified and refined. This process includes the task of expressing the application's concrete functionality within the framework, detailing its components and relationships. We support this with the patterns presented in the subsequent chapters of our pattern language.

Domain Model **

When starting to build a (distributed) application ...

... we need an initial structure for the software being developed.

Requirements and constraints inform the functionality, quality of service, and deployment aspects of a software system, but do not themselves suggest a concrete structure to guide development. Without precise and reasoned insight into a system's scope and application domain, however, its realization is likely to be a 'big ball of mud' that is hard to understand and convey to customers, and a poor architectural basis on which to build.

A list of requirements shows the problem domain of an application, but not its solution domain. Yet requirements in a working system must be addressed by concrete software entities. If these entities and their interactions are unrelated to the application's core business, however, it will be hard to understand and communicate what the system actually does. Similarly, it will be hard to meet system quality of service requirements, since they cannot be mapped clearly to the software elements where they are relevant. Without a clear vision of a system's application domain, therefore, software architects cannot determine if their designs are correct, complete, coherent, and sufficiently bounded to serve as the basis for development.

Therefore:

Create a model that defines and scopes a system's business responsibilities and their variations: model elements are abstractions meaningful in the application domain, while their roles and interactions reflect the domain workflow.

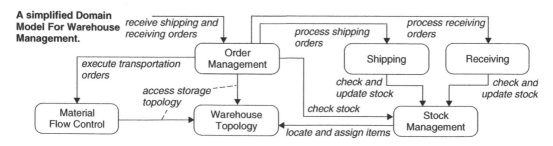

A simplified Domain Model For Warehouse Management.

The domain model serves as the foundation for a system's software architecture, which becomes an expression of the model as it evolves.

A DOMAIN MODEL provides the initial step in transforming requirements into a sustainable software architecture and implementation. Defining a precise model for the structure and workflow of an application domain, including their variations, helps to map requirements to concrete software entities and check whether requirements are complete and self-consistent. Missing requirements can be identified, fuzzy requirements clarified, and unnecessary requirements removed. As a result, the responsibilities and boundaries of a system's architecture are scoped properly. A well-formed domain model also makes it easier meet a system's quality of service requirements, because they can be assigned to the specific elements and workflows to which they apply in the model. A domain model also fosters communication between software professionals, domain experts, and customers, because its elements are based on the terminology used in the application domain.

In general, a domain model is created using an appropriate method, such as *Domain-Driven Design* [Evans03] or *Domain Analysis* [CLF93]. Several specialized methods support the expression of variabilities in a domain, such as *Commonality/Variability Analysis* [Cope98] and *Feature Modeling* [CzEi02]. Domain-specific patterns can further support the creation of a domain model: they offer representations for recurring arrangements of common abstractions and workflows within a domain, including their potential variations. Domain-specific patterns are documented in a variety of domains, such as telecommunication, health care, and corporate finance [Fow97] [Ris01] [PLoPD1] [PLoPD2] [PLoPD3] [PLoPD4] [PLoPD5].

Once the domain model has matured to the point where it adequately portrays the functional responsibilities of an application, as well as their variations, the next step is to transform the model into a concrete architecture that expresses and supports this functionality, and which addresses a range of quality of service requirements such as performance, scalability, availability, adaptability, and extensibility.

Several patterns help to arrange and connect the elements of a domain model to support specific styles of computation. For example,

PIPES AND FILTERS (200) is suitable for applications that process data streams, SHARED REPOSITORY (202) helps to organize data-driven applications, and BLACKBOARD (205) is appropriate for applications that operate on incomplete or fuzzy data, or for which no deterministic solution algorithm is known or feasible.

Other patterns help group and separate elements of a domain model to support specific aspects of system adaptation, extension, and evolution. For example, LAYERS (185) groups elements of the domain model that share similar responsibilities, properties, or granularity into separate layers, so that each layer can evolve independently. MODEL-VIEW-CONTROLLER (188) and PRESENTATION-ABSTRACTION-CONTROL (191) separate user interfaces from domain functionality, to support customer-specific interface adaptations without the need to change or modify the realization of business logic. MICROKERNEL (194) partitions applications into core functionality, version-specific functionality, and version-specific APIs, to support different product variants. REFLECTION (197) objectifies specific aspects of a system's structure and behavior to supports runtime flexibility in terms of how its functionality executes and/or can be used by its clients. Finally, DATABASE ACCESS LAYER (538) decouples application functionality from a relational database, to make it easy to replace the database.

In production systems, several of the patterns outlined above can be applied in combination to form a structural baseline architecture for an application. For example, a MODEL-VIEW-CONTROLLER arrangement may be combined with REFLECTION and a SHARED REPOSITORY-based computational model.

Typically, each self-contained and coherent entity or responsibility within the application's baseline is represented as a separate DOMAIN OBJECT, to provide a defined software realization that addresses its specific functional, operational, and developmental requirements.

In a distributed system, the domain objects in an application's baseline can communicate via middleware. For example, BROKER (237) supports applications whose components communicate via remote method invocation, MESSAGING (221) supports systems in which components exchange asynchronous messages, and PUBLISHER-SUBSCRIBER (234) mediates communication between components that coordinate their processing via notifications of changes to their state.

Layers **

When transforming a DOMAIN MODEL (182) into a technical software architecture, or when realizing BROKER (237), DATABASE ACCESS LAYER (438), MICROKERNEL (194), or HALF-SYNC/HALF-ASYNC (359) ...

... we must support the independent development and evolution of different system parts.

Regardless of the interactions and coupling between different parts of a software system, there is a need to develop and evolve them independently, for example due to system size and time-to-market requirements. However, without a clear and reasoned separation of concerns in the system's software architecture, the interactions between the parts cannot be supported appropriately, nor can their independent development.

The challenge is to find a balance between a design that partitions the application into meaningful, tangible parts that can be developed and deployed independently, but does not lose itself in a myriad of detail so that the architecture vision is lost and operational issues such as performance and scalability are not addressed appropriately. An ad hoc, monolithic design is not a feasible way to resolve the challenge. Although it allows quality of service aspects to be addressed more directly, it is likely to result in a spaghetti structure that degrades developmental qualities such as comprehensibility and maintainability.

Therefore:

Define one or more layers for the software under development, with each layer having a distinct and specific responsibility.

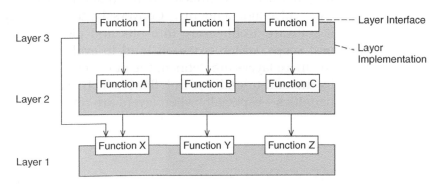

Assign the functionality of the system to the respective layers, and let the functionality of a particular layer only build on the functionality offered by the same or lower layers. Provide all layers with an interface that is separate from their implementation, and within each layer program using these interfaces only when accessing other layers.

A LAYERS architecture defines a horizontal partitioning of a software's functionality according to a (sub)system-wide property, such that each group of functionalities is clearly encapsulated and can evolve independently. The specific partitioning criteria can be defined along various dimensions, such as abstraction, granularity, hardware distance, and rate of change. For example, a layering that partitions an architecture into presentation, application logic, and persistent data follows the abstraction dimension. A layering that introduces a business object layer whose entities are used by a business process layer follows the granularity dimension, while one that suggests an operating system abstraction layer, a communication protocol layer, and a layer with application functionality follows the hardware distance dimension. Using rate of change as a layering criteria separates functionalities that evolve independently of one another.

In most applications we find multiple dimensions combined. For example, decomposing an application into presentation, application logic, and persistent data layers is a layering according to both levels of abstraction and rate of change. User interfaces tend to change at a higher rate than application logic, which evolves faster than data schemes such as tables in a relational database. Regardless of which layering dimensions an application follows, each layer uses the functionality offered by lower layers to realize its own functionality.

A key challenge is to find the 'right' number of layers. Too few layers may not separate sufficiently the different issues in the system that can evolve independently. Conversely, too many layers can fragment a software architecture into bits and pieces without a clear vision and scope, which makes it hard to evolve them at all. In addition, the more layers are defined, the more levels of indirection must cross in an end-to-end control flow, which can introduce performance penalties—especially when layers are remote.

Typically, each self-contained and coherent responsibility within a layer is realized as a separate DOMAIN OBJECT, to further partition the layer into tangible parts that can be developed and evolved independently.

Split each layer into an EXPLICIT INTERFACE (281) that publishes the interfaces of those domain objects whose functionality should be accessible by other layers, and connect it with an ENCAPSULATED IMPLEMENTATION (313) that realizes this functionality. This separation of concerns minimizes inter-layer coupling: each layer only depends on layer interfaces, which makes it possible to evolve a layer implementation with minimal impact on other layers, and also to provide remote access to a layer. A BRIDGE (436) or an OBJECT ADAPTER (438) supports the separation of the explicit interface of a layer from its encapsulated implementation.

Control and data can flow in both directions in layered systems. For example, data is exchanged between adjacent layers in layered protocol stacks such as TCP/IP or UDP/IP. However, LAYERS defines an acyclic downward dependency: lower layers must not depend on functions provided by higher layers. Such a design avoids accidental structural complexity, and supports the use of lower layers in other applications independently of the higher layers. Therefore, control flow that originates from the 'bottom' of the stack is often instigated via an OBSERVER-based (399) callback infrastructure. Lower layers can pass data and service requests to higher layers via notifications realized as COMMANDS (412) or MESSAGES (420), without becoming dependent on specific functions in their interfaces.

Model-View-Controller **

When transforming a DOMAIN MODEL (182) into a technical software architecture, or specifying an agent in a PRESENTATION-ABSTRACTION-CONTROL (191) configuration ...

... we must consider that the user interface of an application changes more frequently than its domain functionality.

♦♦♦

User interfaces are prone to change requests: some must support multiple look-and-feel skins, others must address specific customer preferences. However, changes to a user interface must not affect an application's core functionality, which is generally independent of its presentation, and also changes less frequently.

Changes to a user interface should be both easy and local to the modified interface part. A changeable user interface must however not degrade the application's quality of service: at any time it must display the current state of computation, and respond to state changes immediately. To further complicate matters, in a system that supports multiple look-and-feel skins, each skin can change at a different rate, which requires additional decoupling of different user interface parts.

Therefore:

Divide the interactive application into three decoupled parts: processing, input, and output. Ensure the consistency of the three parts with the help of a change propagation mechanism.

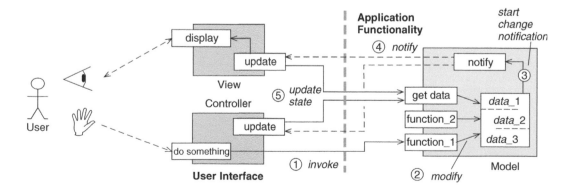

Encapsulate the application's functional core inside a model whose implementation is independent of specific user interface look-and-feel and mechanics. For each aspect of the model to be presented in the application's user interface, introduce one or more self-contained views. Associate each view with a set of separate controllers that receive user input and translate this input into requests for either the model or the associated view. Let users interact with the application solely through the controllers.

Connect the model, view, and controller components via a change propagation mechanism: when the model changes its state, notify all views and controllers about this change so that they can update their state accordingly and immediately via the model's APIs.

A MODEL-VIEW-CONTROLLER arrangement separates responsibilities of an application that tend to change at a different rate, to support their independent evolution.

The model defines the functional heart of the interactive application, thus its internal structure depends strongly on the application's specific domain responsibilities. Often the model is partitioned into one or more application DOMAIN OBJECTS (208), one for each self-contained responsibility. The implementation of the model should not rely on specific I/O data formats or view and controller APIs, to avoid having to change the model when the user interface changes.

Each coherent piece of information that is presented in the application's user interface is encapsulated within a self-contained view, together with functionality to retrieve the respective data from the model, transform this data into its output format, and display the output in the user interface. This self-containment allows views to evolve without affecting one another or the model. Two typical types of view are TEMPLATE VIEW (345) and TRANSFORM VIEW (347). A TEMPLATE VIEW renders model information into a predefined output format. A TRANSFORM VIEW creates its output by rendering each data element individually that it retrieves from the model.

Each view of the system is associated with one more controllers to manipulate the model's state. A controller receives input through an associated input device such as a keyboard or a mouse, and translates it into requests to its associated view or the model. There are three common types of controller: a controller associated with a specific function in the application's user interface, a PAGE CONTROLLER (337) that handles all requests issued by a specific form or page in the user interface, and a FRONT CONTROLLER (339) that handles all requests on the model. A controller per function is most suitable if the model supports a wide range of functions. A PAGE CONTROLLER is appropriate for form-based or page-based user interfaces in which each form or page offers a set of related functions. A FRONT CONTROLLER is most usable if the application publishes functions to the user interface whose execution can differ for each specific request, such as the HTTP protocol of a Web application.

The requests issued by controllers may be encapsulated into COMMAND (412) objects that are passed to a dedicated COMMAND PROCESSOR (343) for execution. Such a design allows controllers to change transparently to both the views and the model. In addition, it supports the treatment of requests as first class objects, which in turn enables an application to offer 'house-keeping' services like undo/redo and request scheduling.

If a controller is in doubt over which concrete command to create, for example in a workflow-driven application, an APPLICATION CONTROLLER (341) helps to avoid dependencies on the model's internal state. In most applications, multiple controllers are active at the same time, but each user input can only be processed by one particular controller. A CHAIN OF RESPONSIBILITY (440) that connects all controllers simplifies the dispatching of the 'right' controller in response to a specific input.

Using WRAPPER FACADES (459) for accessing low-level device driver APIs and graphical libraries enables the views and controllers to be kept independent of the system's platform, as well as of its input and output devices. DATA TRANSFER OBJECTS (418) help to encapsulate the data that views and controllers retrieve from the model.

To support efficient collaboration between model, views, and controllers without breaking the model's independence of user interface aspects, connect them via an OBSERVER (405) arrangement. The model is a subject, while the views and controllers are its observers. When the model changes its state, it notifies all registered views and controllers, which in turn update their own state by retrieving the corresponding data from the model.

Presentation-Abstraction-Control

When transforming a DOMAIN MODEL (182) into a technical software architecture ...

... we must at times consider that different functional responsibilities of an application can require different user interface paradigms.

A human-computer interface allows users to interact with an application via a specific 'paradigm,' such as forms or menus and dialogs. However, some applications are best operated via a distinct interface paradigm for each functionality type on offer.

For example, in a robot control system, the functionality for defining a mission requires a different user interface than the functionality for controlling a mobile robot during a mission. Yet we must ensure that all functions and their user interfaces form a coherent system. In addition, changes to any user interface should neither affect the implementation of its corresponding functionality, nor that of other functions and their associated user interfaces. Similarly, changes to the implementations of a distinct function should not affect user interfaces and implementations of other functions.

Therefore:

Structure the interactive application as a hierarchy of decoupled agents: one top-level agent, several intermediate-level agents, and many bottom-level agents. Each agent is responsible for a specific functionality of the application and provides a specialized user interface for it.

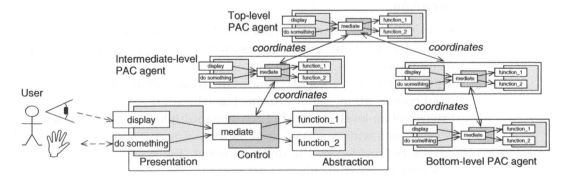

Bottom-level agents implement self-contained functionality with which users can interact, for example administration, error handling, and data manipulation. Mid-level agents coordinate multiple related bottom-level agents, for example all views that visualize a particular type of data. The top-level agent provides core functionality that is shared by all agents, such as access to a data base.

Split each agent into three parts. A presentation part defines the agent's user interface. An abstraction part provides agent-specific domain functionality. A control part connects the presentation with the abstraction and allows the agent to communicate with other agents. Connect the agents in the hierarchy via their controls.

Users interact with an agent via its presentation. All user requests to the respective functionality in its abstraction are mediated by the agent's control. If a user action requires accessing or coordinating other agents, mediate this request to the controls of these agents, either up or down the hierarchy, and from there to their abstractions.

A PRESENTATION-ABSTRACTION-CONTROL architecture helps to connect multiple self-contained subsystems, or even whole applications, with specialized human-computer interaction models to a coherent (distributed) system. The downside of such an arrangement is its complexity: multiple user interfaces must be provided, and actions instigated by a specific user interface must be coordinated carefully and explicitly if control flow spans multiple subsystems and causes reactions or view changes in their associated user interfaces. Consequently, a PRESENTATION-ABSTRACTION-CONTROL architecture only pays off if a software system cannot be implemented by a single user interface paradigm.

To specify a PRESENTATION-ABSTRACTION-CONTROL (PAC) architecture, identify all the self-contained responsibilities the application should offer to its users. Each responsibility is then encapsulated within a separate bottom-level agent. If several agents share functionality or need coordination, factor out this (coordination) functionality into an intermediate-level agent. There can be multiple levels of intermediate-level agents within a PAC architecture. Functionality shared by all agents is provided by the top-level agent. Such decoupling supports independent modification of agents without affecting other agents, and allows each agent to provide its own user interface. Provide all agents with a MODEL-VIEW-CONTROLLER (188) architecture: the abstraction corresponds with the model and its partitioning into DOMAIN OBJECTS (208), and the presentation to the views and controllers. Changes to an agent's interface will therefore affect its realization.

Decouple an agent's abstraction from its presentation via a control component that is a MEDIATOR (410) with a twofold responsibility. First, it must route all user requests from the agent's presentation to the appropriate functionality in its abstraction. It must also route all change propagation notifications from the abstraction to the views in the presentation. Second, the control must coordinate the cooperation between agents. If a user request received by a particular agent cannot be handled by the agent alone, the control routes the request to the controls of appropriate higher- or lower-level agents, together with its associated input data. Results are returned in the same way, but in reverse. Similarly, the control of an agent can receive requests and data from the controls of other agents. The requests to be routed can be encapsulated inside COMMAND (412) objects, and the data inside DATA TRANSFER OBJECTS (418). Controls are the key to a loose coupling between agents: if an agent's abstraction changes, effects on other agents are limited to their controls.

To keep agents consistent with one another, connect them via an OBSERVER (405) arrangement. An agent that is dependent on the state of its associated higher- or lower-level agents registers its control as a subscriber of the other agents' controls, which play the role of subjects. Whenever one of these 'subject' agents changes its state, its control notifies the control of the 'observing' agents, which can then react appropriately to update their own state.

Microkernel **

When transforming a DOMAIN MODEL (182) into a technical software architecture ...

... we must design support for functional scalability and adaptability in different deployment scenarios.

◆◆◆

Some applications exist in multiple versions. Each version offers a different set of functionality to its users, or differs from other versions in specific aspects, such as its user interface. Despite their differences, however, all versions of the application should be based on a common architecture and functional core.

The goal is to avoid architectural drift between the versions of the application and to minimize development and maintenance effort for shared functionality. In addition, upgrading one version of the application to another by adding and removing features, or by changing their implementation, should require no or only minimal modifications to the system. Similarly, it should be easy to provide a particular application version with different user interfaces, and also to run the version on different platforms, allowing clients to use it most appropriately within their specific environments.

Therefore:

Compose different versions of the application by extending a common but minimal core via a 'plug-and-play' infrastructure.

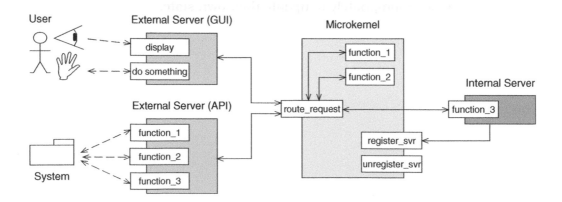

A microkernel implements the functionality shared by all application versions and provides the infrastructure for integrating version-specific functionality. Internal servers implement self-contained version-specific functionality, and external servers version-specific user interfaces or APIs. Configure a specific application version by connecting the corresponding internal servers with the microkernel, and providing appropriate external servers to access its functionality. Consequently, all versions of the application share a common functional and infrastructural core, but provide a tailored function set and look-and-feel.

Clients, whether human or other software systems, access the microkernel's functionality solely via the interfaces or APIs provided by the external servers, which forward all requests they receive to the microkernel. If the microkernel implements the requested function itself, it executes the function, otherwise it routes the request to the corresponding internal server. Results are returned accordingly so that the external servers can display or deliver them to the client.

A MICROKERNEL architecture ensures that every application version can be tailored exactly for its purpose. Users or client systems only get the functionality and look-and-feel that they require, but do not have to incur the cost of anything they do not need. In general, evolving a particular version towards new or different functions and aspects 'only' requires reconfiguring it with appropriate internal and external servers: the microkernel itself is unaffected by such upgrades. Existing internal and external servers and other application versions are similarly unaffected. In addition, a MICROKERNEL architecture minimizes development and maintenance efforts for all members of the application family: each service, user interface, or API is implemented only once.

The internal structure of the microkernel is typically based on LAYERS (185). The bottommost layer abstracts from the underlying system platform, thereby supporting the portability of all higher levels. The second layer implements infrastructure functionality, such as resource management, on which the microkernel depends. The layer above hosts the domain functionality that is shared by all application versions. The topmost layer includes the mechanisms for configuring internal servers with the microkernel, as well as for routing requests from external servers to their intended recipient.

Each specific and self-contained function and responsibility within the microkernel can be realized as a DOMAIN OBJECT (208), which supports its independent implementation and evolution. The routing functionality of the microkernel is often implemented as a MEDIATOR (410) that receives requests through a uniform interface and dispatches these requests onto corresponding domain functions in the microkernel or the internal servers. To minimize resource consumption, particularly memory, the routing layer can use a COMPONENT CONFIGURATOR (490) or an OBJECT MANAGER (492) to load internal servers on demand, unload them after use, and control their lifecycle. This design also supports the upgrade of a particular application version with new, different, or modified functionality dynamically at runtime.

Internal servers follow a similar LAYERS design as the microkernel, but do not usually provide a routing layer. In addition, if the functionality of an internal server builds on system services and platform abstractions that are offered by the layers in the microkernel, they can avoid implementing these services and abstractions themselves, and instead call back the corresponding layers in the microkernel. This keeps the server's footprint small, but at the expense of additional runtime overhead to perform the callbacks. To minimize network traffic in a distributed system, and to increase the performance of internal servers, therefore, it may be beneficial to provide them with all the system services and platform abstractions that they need.

The design of an external server strongly depends on its complexity and purpose. It can range from a simple OBJECT ADAPTER (438) that maps the application's published APIs onto its internal APIs, to a complex user interface.

The application-specific data exchanged between external servers, the microkernel, and its configured internal servers can be encapsulated inside DATA TRANSFER OBJECTS (418).

Reflection *

When transforming a DOMAIN MODEL (182) into a technical software architecture ...

... we must sometimes provide a design that is prepared for evolution and integration of unanticipated changes.

Support for variation is the key to sustainable architectures for long-lived applications: over time they must respond to evolving and changing technologies, requirements, and platforms. However, it is hard to forecast what can vary in an application and when it must respond to a specific variation request.

To complicate matters, the need for variation can occur at any time, specifically while the application is in productive use. Variations can also be of any scale, ranging from local adjustments of an algorithm to fundamental modifications of distribution infrastructure. Yet, while the variation of the application should be possible at appropriate times, the complexity associated with particular variations should be hidden from maintainers, and there should be a uniform mechanism for supporting different types of variation.

Therefore:

Objectify information about properties and variant aspects of the application's structure, behavior, and state into a set of metaobjects. Separate the metaobjects from the core application logic via a two-layer architecture: a meta level contains the metaobjects, a base level the application logic.

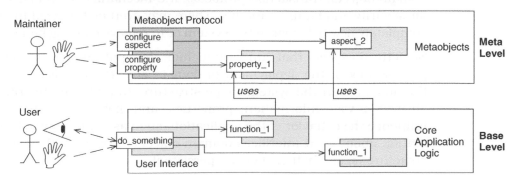

Provide the meta level with a metaobject protocol, which is a specialized interface that administrators, maintainers, or even other systems can use to *dynamically* configure and modify all metaobjects under the supervising control of the application. Connect the base level with the meta level such that base-level objects first consult an appropriate metaobject before they execute behavior or access state that potentially can vary.

REFLECTION supports a high degree of runtime flexibility in a software architecture. Almost any information about a software system can be made accessible; and any aspect that can change can be made (ex)changeable. Some programming languages, therefore, support specific flavors of REFLECTION directly, such as `Java` with the `java.lang.reflect` package and C# with the `System.Reflection` namespace. Note, however, that the heavyweight measures of a REFLECTION architecture only pay off if there are similarly heavyweight flexibility requirements that justify these measures.

To realize a REFLECTION architecture, first specify a stable design for the application that does not consider flexibility at all: stability is the key to flexibility [Bus03]. Typically, each self-contained responsibility of the application is encapsulated within a DOMAIN OBJECT (208), which together form the base level of the REFLECTION architecture.

Using a suitable method, such as *Open Implementation Analysis and Design* [KLLM95], *Commonality/Variability Analysis* [Cope98], or *Feature Modeling* [CzEi02], identify all the structural and behavioral aspects of the application that can vary. Variant behavior often includes algorithms for application functionality, lifecycle control of domain objects, transaction protocols, IPC mechanisms, and policies for security and failure handling. There may even be the need to add completely new behavior to the system or to remove existing behavior.

Structural aspects that can vary include the application's thread or process model, the deployment of domain objects to processes and threads, or even the system's type structure. In addition, determine all system-wide information, properties, and global state that can influence the behavior of the application, such as runtime type information about what interfaces domain objects offer, what their inner structure is, or whether they are persistent.

Realize each variant behavioral and structural aspect, system property, and state identified in the analysis as a separate metaobject, and assign all metaobjects to the meta level of the REFLECTION architecture. Such a strict encapsulation makes the aspects explicitly accessible, and thus (ex)changeable at any time. Changes to metaobjects also cannot ripple through to the implementation of the application's base level.

Open the implementation of each DOMAIN OBJECT at the base level such that it consults an appropriate metaobject for each aspect encapsulated in the meta level. Changes to the metaobjects thus immediately impact the base level's subsequent behavior.

To support the creation, configuration, exchange, and disposal of metaobjects at runtime, introduce a metaobject protocol that serves as the sole interface to manage the meta level. The metaobject lifecycle infrastructure that is necessary for these activities can be realized with help of ABSTRACT FACTORIES (525) and BUILDERS (527) to create and dispose of metaobjects, and a COMPONENT CONFIGURATOR (490) or an OBJECT MANAGER (492) to control the execution of specific metaobject lifecycle steps. Such a design also enables the integration of metaobjects that were developed after the reflective application went live with the meta level. An INTROSPECTIVE INTERFACE (286) and a DYNAMIC INVOCATION INTERFACE (288) support application-external clients such as test frameworks or object browsers, to obtain information about base-level domain objects without becoming dependent on their internal structure, as well as invoking methods on them without the need to use their functional interfaces.

The metaobject protocol in conjunction with the two-layer structure of a REFLECTION architecture is a prime example of how the open/close principle [Mey97] can be realized. The metaobject protocol hides the complexity of software evolution behind a 'simpler' interface, making it easy, uniform, and dynamic, but allows the reflective application to supervise its own evolution so that uncontrolled changes are minimized. The separation of a REFLECTION architecture into a base level and a meta level strictly separates variant from invariant aspects in an application: metaobjects can be managed without implications for the internal design and implementation of the domain objects at the base level.

Pipes and Filters **

When transforming a DOMAIN MODEL (182) into a technical software architecture . . .

. . . we must sometimes provide a design that is suitable for processing data streams.

Some applications process streams of data: input data streams are transformed stepwise into output data streams. However, using common and familiar request/response semantics for structuring such types of application is typically impractical. Instead we must specify an appropriate data flow model for them.

Modeling a data-flow-driven application raises some non-trivial developmental and operational challenges. First, the parts of the application should correspond to discrete and distinguishable actions on the data flow. Second, some usage scenarios require explicit access to intermediate yet meaningful results. Third, the chosen data flow model should allow applications to read, process, and write data streams incrementally rather than wholesale and sequentially so that throughput is maximized. Last but not least, long-duration processing activities must not become a performance bottleneck.

Therefore:

Divide the application's task into several self-contained data processing steps and connect these steps to a data processing pipeline via intermediate data buffers.

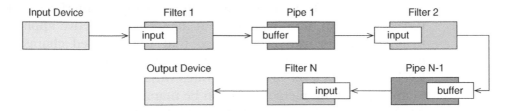

Implement each processing step as a separate filter component that consumes and delivers data incrementally, and chain the filters such that they model the application's main data flow. In the data processing pipeline, data that is produced by one filter is consumed by its subsequent filters. Adjacent filters are decoupled using pipes that buffer data exchanged between the filters.

A PIPES AND FILTERS architecture decouples different data processing steps so that they can evolve independently of one another and support an incremental data processing approach.

Within a PIPES AND FILTERS architecture, filters are the units of domain-specific computation. Each filter can be implemented as a DOMAIN OBJECT (208) that represents a specific, self-contained data processing step. Filters with a concurrent DOMAIN OBJECT implementation enable incremental and concurrent data processing, which increases the performance and throughput of a PIPES AND FILTERS arrangement. If a filter performs a long-duration activity, consider integrating multiple parallel instances of the filter into the processing chain. Such a configuration can further increase system performance and throughput, as some filter instances can start processing new data streams while others are processing previous data streams.

Pipes are the medium of data exchange and coordination within a PIPES AND FILTERS architecture. Each pipe is a DOMAIN OBJECT that implements a policy for buffering and passing data along the filter chain: data producing filters write data into a pipe, while data consuming filters receive their input from a pipe. The integration of pipes decouples adjacent filters so that the filters can operate independently of one another, which maximizes their individual operational performance.

In a single-process PIPES AND FILTERS arrangement, pipes are typically implemented as queues. Pipes with a concurrent DOMAIN OBJECT implementation enable incremental and concurrent data processing, as do concurrent filters. In a distributed arrangement, pipes are realized as some form of MESSAGING (221) infrastructure that passes data streams between remote filters. Pipes that are implemented as a DOMAIN OBJECT shield filters from a knowledge of their specific implementation, which also allows transparent swapping of implementation forms. Such a design supports a flexible (re-)deployment of filters in a distributed PIPES AND FILTERS arrangement. MESSAGES (420) help to encapsulate the data streams that are passed along the pipes.

Shared Repository **

When transforming a DOMAIN MODEL (182) into a technical software architecture ...

... we must sometimes provide a design for applications whose parts operate on, and coordinate their cooperation via, a set of shared data.

Some applications are inherently data-driven: interactions between components do not follow a specific business process, but depend on the data on which they operate. However, despite the lack of a functional means to connect the components of such applications, they must still interact in a controlled manner.

One example of a data-driven system is a network management and control application, such as a Telecommunication Management Network (TMN) system. Such systems operate on massive amounts of data provided by field devices. Core responsibilities like monitoring and control, alarming, and reporting are largely independent of one another, and it is the state of the data that determines the control flow and collaboration of these tasks. Connecting the tasks directly would hard-code a specific business process into the application, which may be inappropriate if specific data is unavailable, not of the required quality, or in a specific state. However, we need a coherent computational state across the entire application.

Therefore:

Maintain all data in a central repository shared by all functional components of the data-driven application and let the availability, quality, and state of that data trigger and coordinate the control flow of the application logic.

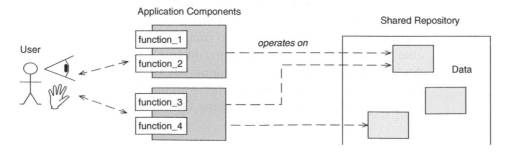

Components work directly on the data maintained by the shared repository, so that other components can react if this data changes. If a component creates new data, or if the application receives new data from its environment, is also stored in the shared repository, to make it accessible to other components.

A SHARED REPOSITORY architecture allows integration of application functionality with a data-driven control flow to form coherent software systems. It also supports coherent integration of applications that operate on the same data, but neither share nor participate in common business processes. Coordinating components via the state of shared data can introduce performance and scalability bottlenecks, however, if many concurrent components need access to the same data exclusively and are thus serialized.

The shared repository is the central control coordination entity and data access point of a data-driven application. It can be as simple as an in-memory data collection, or as complex as an external data repository that is accessed via a DATABASE ACCESS LAYER (438). If the shared repository is implemented as a DOMAIN OBJECT (208), its concrete implementation is hidden from the application's components and can be swapped or modified transparently. DATA TRANSFER OBJECTS (418) help to encapsulate the data passed between the shared repository and the components of the application.

The data maintained by the shared repository is often encapsulated inside managed objects: DOMAIN OBJECTS that hide the details of concrete data structures and offer meaningful operations for their access and modification. Managed objects allow the application's components to use specific data without becoming dependent on its concrete representation, and support the modification of data representations without effects on the components that use the data. Managed objects can also indicate the quality of the represented data via a corresponding quality attribute, for example that the data is up-to-date, out-of-date, uncertain, or corrupted. Components can use this information to control the specific treatment of that data.

In general, access to the shared repository and its managed objects must be synchronized, because multiple components of the application can access it concurrently. In most configurations, this synchronization happens at the level of managed objects, which maximizes the potential concurrency within the data-driven application. Providing a managed object with a THREAD-SAFE INTERFACE (406) enforces synchronization at the interface of the managed object. If only small portions of its methods are critical sections, synchronization via STRATEGIZED LOCKING (388) is a possible alternative. Realizing a managed object as a MONITOR OBJECT (390) supports cooperative concurrency control of multiple components that access the managed object simultaneously.

Many shared repositories offer a mechanism for notifying application components about data changes within the repository. For example, new data may have been inserted, existing data modified, or data may have been dropped. Components can therefore react immediately to changes to the data in the repository. In most cases, the change notification mechanism is realized by an OBSERVER (405) arrangement: the shared repository is the subject, the application's components are its observers. Similarly, managed objects can also offer an OBSERVER-based change propagation mechanism, which allows them to notify components about specific value changes.

Which of the two options best suits a data-driven application depends on its concrete responsibilities. The trade-off to consider is simplicity versus granularity: change notification at the level of the shared repository is simple to implement, but could cause overhead due to notification of components that are not interested in the changes reported. Vice versa, a mechanism implemented at the level of managed objects avoids unnecessary notifications and data transfer, but is of higher complexity. The more components of an application that operate on the entire data maintained by the shared repository, the more feasible a notification mechanism at the repository level becomes, while the more selectively components access managed objects, the more notification at the level of managed objects is the best fit.

The data-driven service components of the application are typically implemented as DOMAIN OBJECTS that realize a specific responsibility by accessing and manipulating data in the shared repository. Cooperation between the components happens purely at the data level, by notifying other components when a specific managed object changes its state, or when data is inserted into, or deleted from, the shared repository.

Blackboard

When transforming a DOMAIN MODEL (182) into a technical software architecture ...

... we must sometimes provide a design suitable for applications that resolve tasks for which no deterministic solution strategy is known.

◆◆◆

For some tasks no deterministic solution algorithms are known, only approximate or uncertain knowledge is accessible. However, despite this lack of proper algorithmic support, trial-and-error techniques can be sufficiently successful and it is necessary to develop productive applications for these types of task.

Examples of such systems include speech recognition, submarine detection based on sonar signals, and the inference of protein molecule structures from X-ray data. Such tasks must resolve several hard challenges: input data is often fuzzy or inaccurate, the path towards a solution must be explored, every processing step can generate alternative results, and often no optimal solution is known. Nevertheless, it is important to compute valuable solutions in a reasonable amount of time.

Therefore:

Use heuristic computation to resolve the task via multiple smaller components with deterministic solution algorithms that gradually improve an intermediate solution hypothesis.

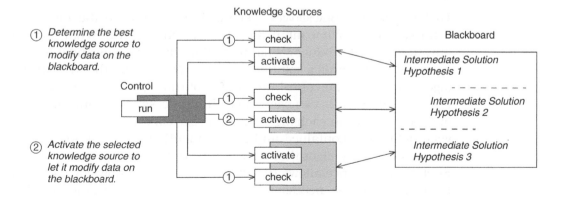

Divide the overall task of the system into a set of smaller, self-contained subtasks for which deterministic solution algorithms are known, and assign the responsibility for each subtask to an independent knowledge source. To allow the knowledge sources to execute independently of one another and in arbitrary order, let them cooperate via a non-deterministic data-driven approach. Using a shared data repository, the blackboard, knowledge sources can evaluate whether input data is available for them, process this input, and deliver their results, which may then form the input for any other knowledge source in the system.

Coordinate the computation with a control component that uses an opportunistic heuristic to select and activate adequate knowledge sources if the data on the blackboard does not yet represent a useful final result, and finishes the computation if it does. Such a strategy works towards a solution via incremental improvement of partial results and evaluation of alternative hypothesis, instead of using a deterministic algorithm.

A BLACKBOARD architecture helps in the construction of software systems that must resolve tasks on the basis of uncertain, hypothetical, or incomplete knowledge and data. It also helps to discover and optimize strongly deterministic solutions for tasks that lack such solutions. On the other hand, there is no guarantee that a BLACKBOARD-based system actually produces a useful result. In addition, a computational approach based on heuristics is often not feasible for systems that demand a predictability in terms of result quality and the time in which a result is produced.

To implement a BLACKBOARD system, first decompose the task that it must resolve. What input does the system receive? What form of output should it produce? What potential solution paths and intermediate results towards a solution are known? What are the well-known algorithms that can contribute to the solution (path)? What input or intermediate results can each algorithm process? What intermediate or final results can each algorithm deliver? On the basis of this analysis, define self-contained and independently executable knowledge sources for every algorithm that is involved in the tasks's solution. Such independence allows the execution order of knowledge sources to be *arbitrary*—a necessary precondition for a heuristic solution strategy. To allow a heuristic to determine a *particular* execution order, split each knowledge source into two separate parts. A condition part examines whether the knowledge source can make a contribution to the computation's progress by inspecting the data written on the blackboard. An action part implements the knowledge source's functionality: it reads one or more inputs from the blackboard, processes it, and writes one or more outputs back to the blackboard. Alternatively, the action part could erase data from the blackboard because it identifies the data as not contributing to the overall task's solution. Typically, a knowledge source is implemented as a DOMAIN OBJECT (208), which supports its independent evolution and optimization when more knowledge about the application's overall task becomes available.

The blackboard is a data repository that maintains all partial and final results that the knowledge sources produce. It can be designed as an in-memory data collection, or as an external data repository that is accessed via a DATABASE ACCESS LAYER (538). If the blackboard is implemented as a DOMAIN OBJECT, its concrete implementation is hidden from the knowledge sources and can be swapped or modified transparently. DATA TRANSFER OBJECTS (418) help to encapsulate the data passed between the blackboard and the knowledge sources.

A control component realizes the heuristic solution strategy of a BLACKBOARD system. First it reads the system's input and stores it on the blackboard, then it enters a loop that executes three steps. The initial step calls the condition parts of all knowledge sources to determine whether they *can contribute* in the current state of computation. The second step uses a heuristic that analyzes the results returned by the condition parts to determine the particular knowledge source that can *best contribute* to the progress of the computation. The final step invokes the action part of the selected knowledge source, which then modifies the blackboard's content. Once this knowledge source finishes its execution, the loop starts over again.

The loop ends if the blackboard contains a valid final result, or if none of the knowledge sources can improve the quality of any intermediate solution hypothesis on the blackboard. Implementing the control component as a DOMAIN OBJECT allows the chosen heuristics to be modified and evolved transparently for the knowledge sources and the blackboard of a concrete BLACKBOARD arrangement.

Domain Object **

When realizing a DOMAIN MODEL (182), or its technical architecture in terms of LAYERS (185), MODEL-VIEW-CONTROLLER (188), PRESENTATION-ABSTRACTION-CONTROL (191), MICROKERNEL (194), REFLECTION (197), PIPES AND FILTERS (200), SHARED REPOSITORY (202), or BLACKBOARD (205) …

… a key concern of all design work is to decouple self-contained and coherent application responsibilities from one another.

◆◆◆

The parts that make up a software system often expose manifold collaboration and containment relationships to one another. However, implementing such interrelated functionality without care can result in a design with a high structural complexity.

Separation of concerns is a key property of well-designed software. The more decoupled are the different parts of a software system, the better they can be developed and evolved independently. The fewer relationships the parts have to one another, the smaller the structural complexity of the software architecture. The looser the parts are coupled, the better they can be deployed in a computer network or composed into larger applications. In other words, a proper partitioning of a software system avoids architectural fragmentation, and developers can better maintain, evolve and reason about it. Yet despite the need for clear separation of concerns, the implementation of and collaboration between different parts in a software system must be effective and efficient for key operational qualities, such as performance, error handling, and security.

Therefore:

Encapsulate each distinct functionality of an application in a self-contained building-block—a domain object.

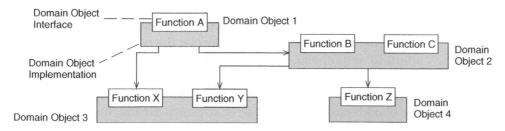

Provide all domain objects with an interface that is separate from their implementation, and within each domain object program only using these interfaces when accessing other domain objects.

DOMAIN OBJECT separates different *functional* responsibilities within an application such that each functionality is well encapsulated and can evolve independently. The specific partitioning of an application's responsibilities into domain objects is based on one or more granularity criteria. An APPLICATION SERVICE [ACM01] is a domain object that encapsulates a self-contained and complete business feature or infrastructure aspect of an application, such as a banking, flight booking, or logging service [Kaye03]. A COMPONENT [VSW02] is a domain object that either encapsulates a functional building block such as an income tax calculation or a currency conversion, or a domain entity such as a bank account or a user. A VALUE OBJECT [PPR] [Fow03a], a COPIED VALUE (394), and an IMMUTABLE VALUE (396) are small domain objects whose identity is based on their state rather than their type, such as a date, a currency exchange rate, or an amount of money. A domain object can also aggregate other domain objects of the same or smaller granularity. For example, services are often created from components that use value objects.

Split each domain object into an EXPLICIT INTERFACE (281) that exports its functionality and an ENCAPSULATED IMPLEMENTATION (313) that realizes the functionality. This separation of interface and implementation minimizes inter-domain-object coupling: each domain object only depends on domain object interfaces, but not on domain object implementations. It is thus possible to realize and evolve a domain object implementation with minimal effect on other domain objects. The explicit interface of a domain object defines a contract for key operational properties, such as error behavior and security aspects, on which other domain objects can rely.

There are several options for connecting the explicit interface of a domain object with its encapsulated implementation. For example, Java and C# support the concept of explicit interface in the core language, and classes (encapsulated implementations) can implement them directly. In other statically typed languages such as C++, an explicit interface can be expressed as an abstract base class from which the explicit implementation derives.

A BRIDGE (436) or an OBJECT ADAPTER (438) explicitly decouples the explicit interface of a domain object from its encapsulated implementation so that the two can vary independently. The degree of decoupling between the explicit interface of a domain object and its encapsulated implementation depends on its granularity and likelihood of change. The smaller the domain objects, for example when realizing a VALUE OBJECT or an IMMUTABLE VALUE, the less beneficial strict decoupling becomes. Similarly, the more often an encapsulated implementation evolves, the more strongly the explicit interface should be decoupled.

Explicit interfaces also enable remote access to domain objects. Note, however, that remoting is generally feasible only for 'larger' domain objects such as services and coarse-grained components, but not for 'small' domain objects like a value object. The smaller are the domain objects, the more adverse is the ratio of networking overhead versus computation time inside the domain object, with corresponding penalties on operational quality factors such as performance, availability, and scalability.

Domain objects are often associated with an ABSTRACT FACTORY (525) or BUILDER (527) that allows clients to obtain access to their explicit interface and to manage their lifetime transparently. On platforms like CCM [OMG02], EJB [MaHa99], and. NET [Ram02], domain objects are controlled by a DECLARATIVE COMPONENT CONFIGURATION (461) that specifies how their lifecycle, resource management, and other technical concerns like transactions and logging should be handled by their hosting environment. A COMPONENT CONFIGURATOR (490) helps with loading, replacing, (re)configuring, and unloading domain objects at runtime.

10 Distribution Infrastructure

Zhaoqing power converter station for high-voltage direct-current transmission line, Guangdong province, China Siemens press picture, © Siemens AG

It is hard to meet complex distributed system requirements such as scalability and dependability if only the application, host operating system, and network perspectives are considered. The application should focus on 'business logic' rather than 'plumbing,' and the operating system and network should focus on endsystem resource management and communication protocol processing respectively. To address other key perspectives, this chapter describes twelve patterns pertaining to *middleware*, which is distribution infrastructure software that shields applications from many inherent and accidental complexities of operating systems and networks.

Several trends influence the way we conceive and construct distributed systems [ScSc01]:

- Information technology is becoming commoditized: hardware and software are generally getting more powerful, cheaper, and better at a relatively predictable rate. The commoditization of hardware, such as CPUs and storage devices, and networking elements such as IP routers and WiFi devices, has been underway for decades. More recently, software is being commoditized due to the maturation of object-oriented languages such as Java, C#, and C++, and commercial-of-the-shelf operating environments, such as Linux, Windows, and Java virtual machines.

- There is a growing acceptance of the service-oriented software paradigm, in which distributed systems with a range of requirements are constructed by integrating separate services that are connected by various forms of network protocols. The nature of these interconnections can range from very small and tightly coupled applications, such as anti-lock braking systems, to very large and loosely coupled systems, such as the Internet and World Wide Web.

The interplay of these two trends has yielded new architectural concepts and services embodying layers of *middleware*, such as MQ Series, CORBA, Enterprise Java Beans, DDS, and Web Services. Middleware is distribution infrastructure software that resides between the applications and the underlying operating systems, network protocol stacks, and hardware. Its primary role is to bridge the gap between application programs and the lower-level hardware and software infrastructure, to coordinate how parts of applications are connected and how they inter-operate. Middleware also enables and simplifies the integration of components developed by different technology suppliers.

When implemented and applied properly, middleware addresses many of the challenges described in Chapter 2. For example, it shields developers from many low-level platform details, such as socket-level network programming, thereby enabling them to focus on their application's business logic requirements. Middleware can also amortize software lifecycle costs by leveraging previous development expertise via reusable frameworks and services that are needed to operate effectively in a networked environment, rather than handcrafting them for each use.

Developing communication middleware that masters the challenges outlined above and in Chapter 2 is complex and time-consuming. Fortunately, there is rarely a need to design and implement your own approaches. A wide range of communication middleware standards and commercial off-the-shelf platforms are now available, such as CORBA [OMG04a], .NET Remoting [Ram02], the Microsoft Communication Framework [Pal05], and JMS [HBS+02], which are used successfully in many distributed systems.

The drawback of having so many different standards and products, of course, is that you now have to consider more options for your projects and systems. Selecting the 'best' communication paradigm, middleware standard, and product depends on many factors, including price, support, quality, and the requirements of the systems being developed. Rarely does one middleware solution work optimally for all applications in a distributed system.

To enhance productivity in a given distributed application, the selected middleware must also be used correctly. Several projects have failed [Bus03] due to insufficient understanding of the communication paradigm and a lack of knowledge about the key structure and behavior of chosen middleware. Selecting and using specific communication middleware therefore requires thoughtful consideration and explicit decisions.

The main intent for including this chapter in our pattern language for distributed computing is to help you understand different communication middleware approaches and their internal designs. Armed with a knowledge of the fundamental properties of each approach and their benefits and liabilities, you can choose the right communication paradigm and middleware for applications in your distributed system.

Despite their detailed differences, middleware technologies typically follow one or more of three different communication styles: *messaging*, *publish/subscribe*, and *remote method invocation*, which are reflected by the following three entry-point patterns in this chapter:

> The MESSAGING pattern (221) [HoWo03] structures distributed software systems whose services interact by exchanging messages. A set of interconnected message channels and message routers manages the exchange of messages between services across the network, including passing request and reply messages that contain information, metadata, and error information.

> The PUBLISHER-SUBSCRIBER pattern (234) structures distributed software systems whose services or components interact by exchanging events asynchronously in a one-to-many configuration. Publishers and subscribers of events are generally unaware of one another. Subscribers are interested in consuming events, not in knowing their publishers. Similarly, publishers just supply events, and are not interested in who subscribes to them.

> The BROKER pattern (237) [POSA1] [VKZ04] structures distributed software systems whose components interact by remote method invocations. A federation of brokers manages key aspects of interprocess communication between components, ranging from forwarding requests to transmitting results and exceptions.

Several criteria distinguish these patterns from one another, including their communication models—such as many-to-one versus one-to-many—and the degree of coupling between an application's components. In particular:

- In BROKER, many clients can make remote method invocations on specific remote component objects hosted by a server. Clients thus communicate with the server objects in a many-to-one fashion, and their functional interfaces are often statically typed. The remote method invocation style of communication provided by BROKER is best suited for systems that try to hide the presence of the network.

- MESSAGING relaxes this coupling and typing: clients send dynamically typed messages to specific remote services that reside at communication endpoints, not (necessarily) to specific methods. MESSAGING thus enables many-to-one communication without statically predefining the interface dependencies of clients to services.

- PUBLISHER-SUBSCRIBER decouples an application's components even more: they can exchange events in a one-to-many manner without knowing one another's identity explicitly, and without having to make a request each time new events are available. PUBLISHER-SUBSCRIBER middleware is therefore responsible for tracking which subscribers receive specific events sent asynchronously by publishers. Subscribers react when receiving an event by performing some action, but publishers do not directly initiate the execution of a specific method on the subscribers.

The following table summarizes these differences:

Pattern	Communication Style	Communication Relationships	Component Dependencies
Broker	Remote Method Invocation	One-to-one	Component interfaces
Messaging	Message	Many-to-one	Communication endpoints Message formats
Publisher-Subscriber	Events	One-to-many	Event formats

Though achieving completely location-transparent communication in a distributed system is infeasible [WWWK96], BROKER makes invocations on remote component objects look and act as much as possible like invocations on component objects in the same address space as their clients. MESSAGING and PUBLISHER-SUBSCRIBER are most appropriate for integration scenarios in which multiple, independently developed and self-contained services or applications must collaborate and form a coherent software system. MESSAGING still allows services to exchange requests and responses, whereas the entire collaboration between components in PUBLISHER-SUBSCRIBER is coordinated by notifying subscribers about state changes and other events of interest.

In practice, middleware platforms and products often implement one or more of these patterns. For example, Web Services implements PUBLISHER-SUBSCRIBER via WS-NOTIFICATION and MESSAGING via SOAP, whereas CORBA implements PUBLISHER-SUBSCRIBER via the

Notification Service and Broker via the ORB itself. Some CORBA Broker implementations, such as BEA's Web Logic Enterprise, are even implemented on top of the Tuxedo Messaging middleware. In general, the CORBA ORB Core can be viewed as the Messaging layer of the CORBA Broker architecture.

Other distributed computing literature lists additional communication styles, such as shared databases, data streaming, file transfer, and peer-to-peer [Fow03a] [HoWo03] [VKZ04]. We consider these more as approaches for *orchestrating the collaboration* of an application's services, however, rather than a style they use to *exchange information*. This distinction explains why we present patterns like Pipes and Filters (200) and Shared Repository (202) in Chapter 9 rather than in this chapter. The data streaming style, for example, can be realized via a Pipes and Filters design with the pipes being middleware based on Messaging or Broker. Similarly, the shared repository style can be realized with a Shared Repository design using middleware based on Broker or Publisher-Subscriber.

Messaging, Broker, and Publisher-Subscriber are just the entry points into the patterns in this chapter. To be usable for a distributed application, each type of middleware must address many different issues, each representing its own problems and offering a coherent solution space. It is therefore natural to document these problems and their solutions as separate patterns—in fact, the architecture of many middleware platforms today are guided and documented by many such patterns [SC99] [ACM01] [VSW02] [VKZ04] [MS03].

Middleware based on Messaging can be refined by the following four distribution infrastructure patterns:

> The Message Channel pattern (224) [HoWo03] connects application services that interact by exchanging messages. One service writes information to the channel and the other reads that information from the channel.

> The Message Router pattern (231) [HoWo03] allows a client to send messages to other services of an application depending on a set of conditions.

The MESSAGE TRANSLATOR pattern (229) [HoWo03] supports the translation of a message into another form if the sender of a message and its reader expect different message formats.

The MESSAGE ENDPOINT pattern (227) [HoWo03] helps application services connect with the messaging infrastructure by encapsulating and implementing the necessary adaptation code.

MESSAGING middleware is defined by other distribution infrastructure patterns beyond MESSAGE, MESSAGE CHANNEL, MESSAGE ROUTER, MESSAGE TRANSLATOR, and MESSAGE ENDPOINT. Each of these four patterns references other finer-grained patterns that assist their further decomposition and implementation. We do not cover these patterns in detail, but instead refer to their original source, *Enterprise Integration Patterns* [HoWo03]. Nonetheless, all these patterns form an integral part of our pattern language for distributed computing.

The following diagram outlines how the MESSAGING and PUBLISHER-SUBSCRIBER patterns integrate with our pattern language.

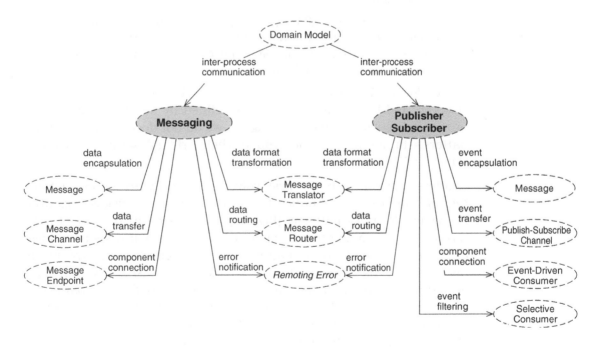

The responsibilities of BROKER middleware can be decomposed into the following five distribution infrastructure patterns, which are described in the order they are applied from client to server:

The CLIENT PROXY pattern (240) [VKZ04] offers clients a local interface as a remote component with which they interact. Clients can access the remote component in a location-independent manner, as if it were collocated with the client.

The REQUESTOR pattern (242) [VKZ04] encapsulates the details of client-side remote communication, such as marshaling and sending a request across the network, and allows clients to access remote components in a location-independent manner.

The CLIENT REQUEST HANDLER pattern (246) [VKZ04] encapsulates the details of client-side interprocess communication behind a uniform interface.

The SERVER REQUEST HANDLER pattern (249) [VKZ04] encapsulates the details of server-side interprocess communication behind a uniform interface.

The INVOKER pattern (244) [VKZ04] shields a server component application from dealing with networking issues, such as receiving, demarshaling, and dispatching requests, when a request arrives from a remote client.

CLIENT PROXY, REQUESTOR, CLIENT REQUEST HANDLER, SERVER REQUEST HANDLER, and INVOKER are themselves refined by several other distribution infrastructure patterns. Again, we do not describe these other patterns in detail, but refer you to their original source, *Remoting Patterns* [VKZ04].

Readers familiar with the first volume of the POSA series, *A System of Patterns*, might notice that the CLIENT-DISPATCHER-SERVER and FORWARDER-RECEIVER patterns [POSA1] are missing in the list of patterns above. We omit these two patterns because their responsibilities are better covered by other patterns in our language. Our experience also revealed that these patterns were too broad in scope, which suggested refactoring them into multiple smaller, more focused patterns. The responsibilities of CLIENT-DISPATCHER-SERVER are thus addressed by a BROKER configuration that uses a LOOKUP (495) service, and a CLIENT REQUEST HANDLER (246) and SERVER REQUEST HANDLER (249) association forms a FORWARDER-RECEIVER arrangement.

The diagram below illustrates how the BROKER pattern connects with other patterns in our pattern language for distributed computing

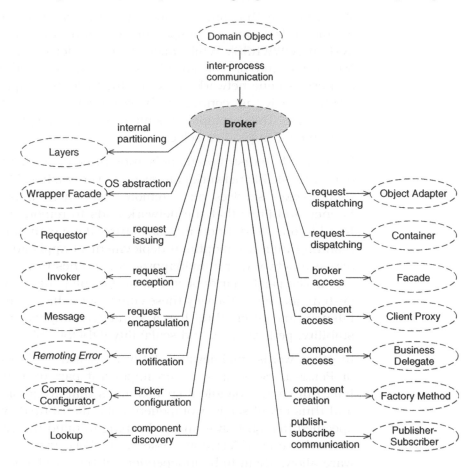

The diagram above and the earlier one on page 217 show the relationship of PUBLISHER-SUBSCRIBER with MESSAGING and BROKER. PUBLISHER-SUBSCRIBER can be viewed as a specialized form of these two patterns, since its anonymous and asynchronous group communication model can be implemented using either MESSAGING or BROKER. We present it as a separate pattern in our pattern language because it addresses a different set of forces than MESSAGING or BROKER. These forces result in more loosely coupled—and often more scalable—communication between distributed application components. Describing PUBLISHER-SUBSCRIBER as a separate pattern enables us to discuss these forces and consequences more prominently and explicitly than if it were presented as a special case of other patterns.

We recognize that our distribution infrastructure patterns do not enable fully location-transparent communication in a distributed system [WWWK96]. While middleware platforms based on BROKER, MESSAGING, and/or PUBLISHER-SUBSCRIBER can off-load many tedious and error-prone network programming tasks from applications, they are ultimately just connectors between components of a distributed application. These components must therefore be prepared to handle certain challenges themselves.

For example, a distributed application must be resilient against cases of non-maskable network failures or server crashes. Likewise, a client that invokes services on a remote component must consider the latency and jitter that the network adds to remote communication. In addition, distribution infrastructure alone cannot solve problems resulting from a suboptimal deployment of application components across a network, or from inappropriate orchestration of their cooperation. The particular deployment of the components of a distributed system, as well as the way these components handle network failure, latency, and jitter, thus has a significant impact on this system's stability, performance, and scalability [DBOSG05].

In other words, middleware platforms based on MESSAGING, BROKER, or PUBLISHER-SUBSCRIBER are an important part of a distributed system, but cannot handle responsibilities that are application-specific and thus out of scope. Components of a distributed system must be specified thoughtfully—always keeping in mind the properties of the network—even if MESSAGING, BROKER, or PUBLISHER-SUBSCRIBER middleware allows them to be independent of the specific location of other components.

Messaging **

When deploying a DOMAIN MODEL (182), or a PIPES AND FILTERS (200) arrangement, to multiple processors or network nodes ...

... we often need a communication infrastructure that integrates independently developed services into a coherent system.

Some distributed systems are composed of services that were developed independently. To form a coherent system, however, these services must interact reliably, but without incurring overly tight dependencies on one another.

Application integration is a key technique for composing solutions—often at the enterprise level—from existing, self-contained, special-purpose services. Each service provides its own business logic and value, but together they can provide the business processes and value chain of an entire enterprise. Integrating independent services into a coherent application naturally requires reliable collaboration with one another. Since services are developed independently, however, they are generally unaware of each other's specific functional interfaces. Each service may also participate in multiple integration contexts, so using it in a specific context should not preclude its use in other contexts.

Therefore:

Connect the services via a message bus that allows them to transfer data messages asynchronously. Encode the messages so that senders and receivers can communicate reliably without having to know all the data type information statically.

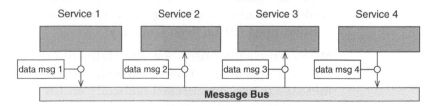

The services that form the distributed system connect with the message bus to exchange data messages with other services. Clients can initiate collaborations with remote services by sending them data messages asynchronously. The remote services process the received messages and return their responses—if there are any—asynchronously to the clients via messages containing the processing results. The messages are often *self-describing*: they contain both metadata that describes the message schema, and the values corresponding to the schema.

Middleware based on MESSAGING enables services in a distributed application to interact without having to deal with remoting concerns by themselves, and without depending on statically defined service interfaces and data structures. In addition, the asynchronous nature of MESSAGING communication allows distributed application services to handle multiple requests simultaneously without blocking, as well as participate in multiple application integration and usage contexts. MESSAGING thus enables loose coupling, which is a key to *Enterprise Application Integration* (EAI) [Lin03] and *Service-Oriented Architectures* (SOA) [Kaye03]. The primary drawbacks of MESSAGING are its lack of statically typed interfaces, which makes it hard to validate system behavior prior to runtime, and the potential for high time and space overhead necessary to process self-describing messages [Bell06].

Data exchanged between application services are often encapsulated inside MESSAGES (420). A message hides the concrete data format of its contents from both the sender and the receiver, as well as from the MESSAGING middleware itself, which enables the transparent modification of its format. XML is a popular format for representing both the metadata and data values of self-describing messages. It enables clients to generate and send messages whose form and content need not be fixed statically.

MESSAGING clients only know the endpoints of the services they use, not their specific interfaces. Consequently the form and content of a message cannot be checked statically on the client before sending it to a specific service. Instead, the service that *receives* a message is responsible for understanding the message's form and content. This process typically involves parsing the message dynamically to validate and extract its contents. If the service does not understand some of the message fields, it can simply ignore them, thereby simplifying the integration of services whose message formats were not originally designed to work together.

A concrete MESSAGING arrangement typically consists of several specialized parts. MESSAGE CHANNELS (224) support point-to-point communication between interacting remote services and enable reliable message exchange. MESSAGE ENDPOINTS (227) connect application services with the MESSAGING middleware: these can send and receive messages without depending on concrete messaging APIs, which enables the transparent exchange and evolution of the underlying MESSAGING infrastructure.

If the sender and the receiver of a message do not share a common message format, a MESSAGE TRANSLATOR (229) can convert messages issued by the sender into a format understood by the receiver. If the sender does not know where to address a message, a MESSAGE ROUTER (231) can help to direct it to its intended receiver. A communication failure that cannot be handled internally by the MESSAGING middleware can be returned as a REMOTING ERROR [VKZ04] to the client that sent the message.

Message Channel **

When developing a MESSAGING (221) infrastructure or a CLIENT REQUEST HANDLER (246) and SERVER REQUEST HANDLER (249) in a BROKER (237) arrangement ...

... we must provide a means to connect a set of clients and services that communicate by sending and receiving messages.

Message-based communication supports loose coupling between services in a distributed system. Messages only contain the data to be exchanged between a set of clients and services, however, so they do not know who is interested in them.

Loose coupling makes it easier to integrate diverse information systems, but somehow the loose ends must tie back together. It is not sufficient for a client to send messages randomly while other services randomly receive whatever messages they come across. A client that sends out messages knows what sort of information these messages contain and often also knows who it wants to receive the messages. Similarly, services that receive messages look for particular messages they can process, and often for messages from specific senders. In other words, clients and services need to exchange messages in predictable and reliable ways.

Therefore:

Connect the collaborating clients and services using a message channel that allows them to exchange messages.

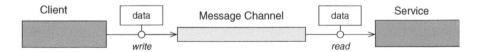

When a client has a message to communicate, it writes that message to the message channel. Services interested in the message can pick it up from there and process it.

A message channel connects a set of interacting clients and services, thereby allowing them to exchange messages in a well-defined and reliable manner. Clients that write messages to the channel can be sure that the services reading the messages from the channel are interested in the information they contain, while services that read messages are sure they have received information that they can use and process.

A message channel is thus a logical address to which clients and services can write messages and/or from which they can receive messages. Several types of message channels are common. A POINT-TO-POINT CHANNEL [HoWo03] connects exactly one client and one service and ensures that only they can read the messages written to it. In contrast, a PUBLISH-SUBSCRIBE CHANNEL [HoWo03] enables publishers to broadcast messages to multiple subscribers using the PUBLISHER-SUBSCRIBER pattern (234).

An INVALID MESSAGE CHANNEL [HoWo03] decouples the handling of erroneous messages separately from the rest of the application logic, whereas a DEAD LETTER CHANNEL [HoWo03] handles messages that were sent successfully but which could not be delivered. Finally, a DATATYPE CHANNEL [HoWo03], ensures that all messages on a channel are of the same type, which helps to reduce message validation overhead in the intended receiver.

A message channel is shared by at least two concurrent entitles: a client that sends messages to the channel, and a service that obtains messages from the channel. Depending on a channel's implementation and use, therefore, it may require synchronization. A THREAD-SAFE INTERFACE (384) enforces synchronization at the channel's interface, and a realization as a MONITOR OBJECT (368) supports cooperative concurrency control for simultaneous access to the channel.

In general, the operational requirements of a distributed application determine which specific message channel configuration is most appropriate. For example, information assurance requirements may dictate separate SECURE CHANNELS [SFHBS06] for selected security-sensitive collaborations. Performance and scalability requirements may equally dictate separate message channels for each type of message, or even for each use case.

A message channel does not come without cost, however, since it needs memory, networking resources, and persistent storage to support GUARANTEED DELIVERY [HoWo03]. Developers must therefore plan and configure the number and types of message channels explicitly and thoughtfully to ensure the desired quality of service in a given system deployment. A well-designed set of message channels forms a MESSAGE BUS [HoWo03] that acts like a messaging API for the clients and services in the distributed system.

Clients and services that are not designed to use a message channel or message bus can connect to it via a CHANNEL ADAPTER [HoWo03]. A MESSAGING BRIDGE [HoWo03] helps to connect clients and services that are designed to use different channel or bus implementations.

Message Endpoint **

When developing a MESSAGING (221) infrastructure ...

... we must enable clients and services in an application to send and receive messages.

Clients and services in a stand-alone application usually collaborate by passing data to one another. When clients and services are connected by a messaging infrastructure, however, such direct collaboration is impossible: data must be transformed into messages and vice versa.

Performing the data-to-message transformation directly within the applications would tightly couple them with the specific message format required by the messaging middleware. It would therefore be hard to use the services in other applications, and the mix of domain-specific code with infrastructure code would complicate their evolution and maintenance. Even if messaging is incorporated as a fundamental part of the application, replacing the underlying messaging infrastructure is time-consuming, tedious, and error-prone.

Therefore:

Connect the clients and services of an application to the messaging infrastructure using specialized message endpoints that allow clients and services to exchange messages.

When a client has data to communicate, it passes this data to its associated message endpoint, which first converts the data into a message understood by the messaging middleware, then sends that message to an endpoint representing the message's receiver. This endpoint converts the message into data that is understood by the receiver service and passes the data to that service in an appropriate format.

MESSAGE ENDPOINTS encapsulate the messaging middleware from the application clients and services and customize the middleware's general messaging API for them. Modifications to the messaging API, and even an exchange of the entire messaging infrastructure, can therefore be transparent to applications. In addition, all necessary changes are localized within the endpoints.

In general, a messaging endpoint should be designed as a MESSAGING GATEWAY [HoWo03], to encapsulate the messaging-specific code and expose a domain-specific interface to the service it represents. Internally, the endpoint can deploy a MESSAGING MAPPER [HoWo03] to transfer data between the service and the messages. To provide asynchronous access to a synchronous method, a message endpoint can be structured as a SERVICE ACTIVATOR [HoWo03]. A TRANSACTIONAL CLIENT [HoWo03] allows a message endpoint to control transactions explicitly in the messaging middleware.

Message endpoints can select among several different approaches for receiving messages. A POLLING CONSUMER [HoWo03] provides a *proactive* message reception strategy that reads messages only when the represented service is ready to consume them. In contrast, an EVENT-DRIVEN CONSUMER [HoWo03] supports a *reactive* message reception strategy that processes a message immediately upon arrival. If a service implements stateless functionality, the message endpoint can be a COMPETING CONSUMER [HoWo03], to allow multiple service instances to process messages concurrently. A MESSAGE DISPATCHER [HoWo03] helps to dispatch incoming messages to the 'right' recipient if several services share the same message endpoint.

Designing a message endpoint as a SELECTIVE CONSUMER [HoWo03] enables the filtering of incoming messages: a service only processes messages that comply to the filter's criteria. A message endpoint can also be a DURABLE SUBSCRIBER [HoWo03], so that messages received while the represented service is unavailable are not lost. Finally, an endpoint realized as an IDEMPOTENT RECEIVER [HoWo03] can handle messages that were accidentally received multiple times.

The type and functionality of the represented service generally dictates which of the message reception strategies outlined above are most appropriate for a specific endpoint. The development of the message endpoint can be customized for 'its' service.

Message Translator **

When developing a MESSAGING (221) infrastructure . . .

. . . we often must transform messages from the format delivered by the client to the format understood by the service that receives them.

Messages enable a loosely coupled style of communication between an application's clients and services. As a consequence of this decoupling, however, the client that sends a message cannot assume that the services that receive it understand the same message format.

In complex integration scenarios in which existing and independently developed components are composed into new applications, it is likely that many services will require a specific message format. Resolving such a 'Tower of Babel' confusion of 'languages' inside the services would introduce explicit and mutual dependencies between them, which contradicts the idea of loose coupling and degrades the benefits of message-based communication. Unifying the message formats across all services is often infeasible, however, because it can degrade their usability in other applications and integration scenarios.

Therefore:

Introduce message translators between clients and services of an application that convert messages from one format into another.

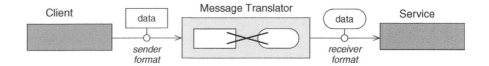

A message translator provides a bidirectional translation of message formats. In a specific collaboration, clients can send messages in any format they use. The message translator ensures that services get these messages in the formats they understand.

A Message Translator maintains the loosely coupled style of communication introduced by Messaging even if the clients and services of an application do not share a common message format. In addition, all message transformation code is localized within a dedicated entity. This design supports evolution that is independent of, and transparent to, the clients and services that exchange messages via the translator.

In many integration scenarios, message exchange can be supported by placing specific requirements on the format and contents of a message header. An Envelope Wrapper [HoWo03] helps encapsulate the message payload so that it complies with the format required by the messaging infrastructure. When the message arrives at its destination the payload can be unwrapped. A Content Enricher [HoWo03] is needed if the target service requires data fields in a message that the originating client cannot supply: it has the ability to locate or compute the missing information from the available data. The opposite action—removing unneeded data from a message—is supported by a Content Filter [HoWo03]. A Claim Check [HoWo03] is similar to a Content Filter, but stores the removed data for later retrieval. A Normalizer [HoWo03] helps convert multiple different message format into one common format, and a Canonical Data Format [HoWo03] that is independent of any specific service can be used inside the messaging middleware to minimize the message transformations within an application.

Message Router **

When developing a MESSAGING (221) infrastructure ...

... we must select a route to propagate messages through a system from their source to their destination.

Messages exchanged between collaborating clients and services must be routed through the messaging infrastructure. None of these entities, however, should have knowledge about the routing path to choose.

Making application clients and services responsible for determining the paths that messages should take through the system is not an effective solution to the routing problem, nor should they have to redirect messages they receive that were not intended for them. Such designs would tightly couple application code with infrastructure code, with clients and services depending on the internal structure and configuration of the messaging infrastructure, thereby causing maintenance problems when changes occurred. Similarly, making messages responsible for their own routing introduces the same problems for the data exchanged between collaborating components.

Therefore:

Provide message routers that consume messages from one message channel and reinsert them into different message channels, depending on a set of conditions.

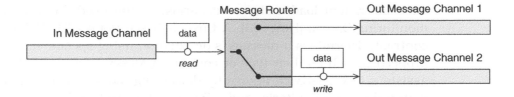

A message router connects a set of message channels to a message channel network. Messages it reads from one channel are routed to a different channel that directs them to their intended receiver.

The key benefit of a MESSAGE ROUTER is that it maintains the decision criteria for the destination of messages in a designated location, separate from application clients, services, and the data they exchange. If new message types are defined, the routing criteria within the message router can be modified easily and locally. If necessary, new message routers can be inserted into the messaging middleware. A message router thus increases the options developers have to send messages between application clients and services, as well as to change routing strategies independently of, and transparently to, applications.

The downside of MESSAGE ROUTER is that it adds extra processing steps to an application, which may degrade its performance. A message router also must know all the message channels it connects, which may become a maintenance problem if configurations change frequently. Moreover, the more message routers a system contains, the harder it is to analyze and understand the overall flow of messages through the system without additional tools.

Developers must therefore plan and configure the number and types of message routers carefully to meet quality of service requirements in a given system deployment. The more message routers a system configuration contains, the more flexibly messages can be routed between the components of the application, but the less efficient the message exchange becomes. In general, therefore, select the minimal set of message routers that meet application requirements to balance the needs for simplicity, flexibility, and quality of service.

There are many types of message routers. A CONTEXT-BASED ROUTER [HoWo03] bases its routing decisions on environmental conditions, such as system load, failover scenarios, or the need for a system monitoring DETOUR [HoWo03]. A CONTENT-BASED ROUTER [HoWo03], in contrast, determines a message's destination using specific message properties such as their type or content. A MESSAGE FILTER [HoWo03] assists a CONTENT-BASED ROUTER by discarding messages that do not match the routing criteria, and a RECIPIENT LIST [HoWo03] determines a list of recipients from the messages it receives. A PROCESS MANAGER [HoWo03] routes messages based on intermediate results it receives in response to previously routed messages. A MESSAGE BROKER [HoWo03] provides a central hub-and-spoke architecture for routing messages throughout an application.

Additional message routers help in managing messages exchanged between components. A SPLITTER [HoWo03] converts a single large message into several smaller messages that can be routed individually. An AGGREGATOR [HoWo03] provides the opposite functionality, by integrating multiple messages into a single message. A RESEQUENCER [HoWo03] helps to collect and reorder out-of-sequence messages so that they can be republished in the correct order. A ROUTING SLIP [HoWo03] adds explicit routing information to a message before it is sent to its receiver. A COMPOSED MESSAGE PROCESSOR [HoWo03] splits a message into multiple parts using SPLITTER, performs some processing on each message part, and reassembles the parts into a single message via AGGREGATOR before directing it to an output channel. Finally, a SCATTER-GATHER [HoWo03] broadcasts a message to multiple recipients and creates a single aggregated response message from the individual responses of each recipient.

There are two general options for implementing the control logic of a message router: it may be either statically or dynamically configurable. Statically configured message routers have less run-time overhead but are less flexible; dynamically configured message routers have the inverse properties. Dynamic configuration can be realized with help of a central CONTROL BUS [HoWo03], or by implementing the router as a DYNAMIC ROUTER [HoWo03] that configures itself based on control messages from potential message recipients.

A message router that receives messages from multiple input channels must be synchronized. A THREAD-SAFE INTERFACE (384) enforces synchronization at the router's interface, while realization as a MONITOR OBJECT (368) supports cooperative concurrency control of all message channels, enabling the router to receive messages simultaneously.

Publisher-Subscriber **

When deploying a DOMAIN MODEL (182) to multiple processors or network nodes ...

... we often need an infrastructure that allows application components to notify each other about events of interest.

Components in some distributed applications are loosely coupled and operate largely independently. If such applications need to propagate information to some or all of their components, however, a notification mechanism is needed to inform the components about state changes or other interesting events that affect or coordinate their own computation.

Nevertheless, this notification mechanism should not couple application components too tightly, or they will lose their independence. Such application components only want to know that another component in the system is in a specific state, not which specific component is involved. Similarly, components that disseminate events often do not care which other components want to receive the information. In addition, components should not depend on how other components can be reached, or on their specific location in the system.

Therefore:

Define a change propagation infrastructure that allows publishers in a distributed application to disseminate events that convey information that may be of interest to others. Notify subscribers interested in those events whenever such information is published.

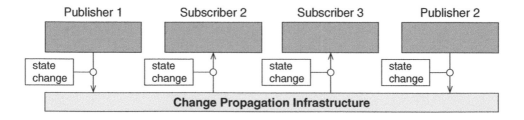

Publishers register with the change propagation infrastructure to inform it about what types of events they can publish. Similarly, subscribers register with the infrastructure to inform it about what types of events they want to receive. The infrastructure uses this registration information to route events from their publishers through the network to interested subscribers. Subscribers receiving events from the infrastructure can use information in the events to guide or coordinate their own computation.

Like MESSAGING, PUBLISHER-SUBSCRIBER supports *asynchronous communication*, in which publishers transmit events to subscribers without blocking to wait for a response. Asynchrony decouples publishers and subscribers so that they can be active and available at different points in time, and also leverages the parallelism inherent in a distributed system. In addition, PUBLISHER-SUBSCRIBER allows components in an application to coordinate their computation *anonymously* without introducing explicit dependencies to one another: they are unaware and independent of each other's location and identity, since they only send and receive events about changes of their state and/or the changed state itself.

Only the infrastructure has the knowledge of how the components connect, where they are located, and how events is routed through the system. PUBLISHER-SUBSCRIBER also supports *group communication*, in which publishers of events need not inform each subscriber explicitly, and the infrastructure forwards the events to all interested subscribers.

A drawback of anonymous communication is that it can cause unnecessary overhead if subscribers are interested in a specific type of event, and will only react if the event's content meets specific criteria. One way to address this problem is by filtering based on the type or content of events. Filtering can incur other costs, however. For example, filtering inside PUBLISHER-SUBSCRIBER middleware decreases its throughput, filtering within the subscribers can result in unnecessary notifications, and filtering inside publishers can break the anonymous communication model.

The information exchanged between the components connected by PUBLISHER-SUBSCRIBER middleware is encapsulated inside events, which are realized as MESSAGES (420). An event hides its concrete message format from both the publisher and subscriber(s), as well as from the PUBLISHER-SUBSCRIBER middleware itself, which enables transparent modification of the message's format.

PUBLISHER-SUBSCRIBER middleware can be implemented in various ways. One approach involves the reuse of MESSAGING and BROKER middleware. For example, PUBLISHER-SUBSCRIBER middleware has been implemented on top of MESSAGING and BROKER middleware, as is the case with many WS-NOTIFICATION [OASIS06c] [OASIS06c] and CORBA Notification Service [OMG04c] products, respectively. Another approach is to implement PUBLISHER-SUBSCRIBER using fundamental concurrency and network programming patterns [POSA2], as is the case with many DDS [OMG05b] products. In general, the former approach simplifies the efforts of the middleware developers, whereas the latter approach yields better performance.

To support anonymous and asynchronous group communication, a set of PUBLISH-SUBSCRIBE CHANNELS [HoWo03] or Event Channels [HV99] can broadcast or multicast event messages from publishers to subscribers. Components can inform a specific channel about which events they publish and which events they would like to receive. EVENT-DRIVEN CONSUMERS [HoWo03] support the transparent adaptation of a consumer to a specific notification publish/subscribe APIs. Such a design enables transparent exchange and evolution of the underlying PUBLISHER-SUBSCRIBER infrastructure. Designing subscribers as SELECTIVE CONSUMERS [HoWo03] enables the filtering of incoming event messages: a subscriber only processes events whose content complies with the filter's criteria.

If the publisher and subscriber of an event do not share a common message format, a MESSAGE TRANSLATOR (229) can convert events issued by a publisher into the format understood by its subscribers. MESSAGE ROUTERS (231) help maintain information about how to route events through the middleware to their registered subscribers. A communication failure that cannot be handled internally by the PUBLISHER-SUBSCRIBER middleware can be returned as a REMOTING ERROR [VKZ04] to the publisher that sent the event.

Broker **

When deploying a DOMAIN MODEL (182) to multiple processors or network nodes …

… we often need a communication infrastructure that shields applications from the complexities of component location and IPC.

Distributed systems face many challenges that do not arise in single-process systems. Application code, however, should not need to address these challenges directly. Moreover, applications should be simplified by using a modular programming model that shields them from the details of networking and location.

Sending requests to services in distributed systems is hard. One source of complexity arises when porting services written in different languages onto different operating system platforms. If services are tightly coupled to a particular context, it is time-consuming and costly to port them to another distribution environment or reuse them in other distributed applications. Another source of complexity arises from the effort required to determine where and how to deploy service implementations in a distributed system. Ideally, services should interact by calling methods on one another in a common, location-independent manner, regardless of whether the services are local or remote.

Therefore:

Use a federation of brokers to separate and encapsulate the details of the communication infrastructure in a distributed system from its application functionality. Define a component-based programming model so that clients can invoke methods on remote services as if they were local.

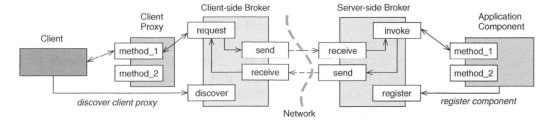

At least one broker instance is defined per participating network node. Component interfaces and locations are registered with their local broker to gain visibility within the distributed system. To invoke functionality on a component, clients ask their local broker for a proxy, which acts as the remote component's surrogate. A client calls a method on the proxy to initiate a request to a component. The proxy collaborates with the client and server-side brokers to deliver the request to the component and receive any results.

A BROKER enables components of a distributed application to interact without handling remoting concerns by themselves. It can also optimize communication mechanisms, such as using remote method invocation versus collocated method calls, depending on the location of client and server components. For example, if the client and component are in the same address space, the broker can optimize the communication path to alleviate unnecessary overhead.

Most BROKER realizations are based on a LAYERS (185) architecture to manage complexity, such as CORBA [OMG04a] and Microsoft's .NET Remoting [Ram02]. These layers are further decomposed into 'special-purpose' components for specific networking and communication tasks. We illustrate this partitioning using the CORBA layering [SC99]—other layering schemes and middleware may involve different assignments [VKZ04].

An OS adaptation layer shields a broker from its underlying execution platform. In languages that use virtual machines, such as Java, this layer *is* the virtual machine. In other languages, such as C++, it usually contains a set of WRAPPER FACADES (459) that provide a uniform interface to specific OS APIs.

An ORB core layer forms the heart of a BROKER arrangement. In general it is a *messaging infrastructure* consisting of two components. A REQUESTOR (242) forwards request MESSAGES (420) from a client to the local broker of the invoked remote component, while an INVOKER (244) encapsulates the functionality for receiving request messages sent by a client-side broker and dispatching these requests to the addressed remote components. If a communication failure cannot be resolved internally by a BROKER infrastructure, a REMOTING ERROR [VKZ04] is signaled to the client that issued the failed request. A

Component Configurator (490) can configure Requestor and Invoker implementations with specific communication strategies and protocols. This supports the transparent exchange and evolution of functionality within a Broker, as well as a protocol-level integration of heterogeneous or legacy components into a distributed system.

Additional Lookup (495) functionality allows components to register their interfaces and location with a Broker infrastructure. Clients can similarly use Lookup to find these components and the access to them. Using Lookup, clients need not know the concrete location of components, but can connect to them at runtime. Lookup also enables a flexible deployment of components, which supports both an optimal utilization of network resources and different application deployment scenarios. To complement remote procedure call invocation, a Broker may interact with an *event channel* to support event-based notifications, which is in essence a Publisher-Subscriber (234) service.

An ORB adapter typically provides a Container (488) that manages the technical environment of remote components. It interacts with a set of skeletons, which are Object Adapters (438) that map between the generic messaging infrastructure of the broker and the specific interfaces of remote components. A Facade (294) presents a simple interface that components can use to access their local broker.

A Client Proxy (240) represents a component in the client's address space. The proxy offers an identical interface that maps specific method invocations on the component onto the broker's message-oriented communication functionality. Proxies allow clients to access remote component functionality as if they were collocated, and can be used to implement collocation optimizations transparently [ScVi99].

Client proxies increase location-independent communication in a distributed system, but do not achieve full transparency. Before clients can use a client proxy they must obtain it from their local broker, for example via a Lookup. This activity is not necessary for local components unless they use a Factory Method (529) to access the components they use. In addition, client proxies may be unable to handle all Remoting Errors transparently to their clients. A Business Delegate (292) can encapsulate such 'infrastructural concerns,' and thus help to provide more complete location-independent communication among the components of a distributed system.

Client Proxy **

When constructing a client-side BROKER (237) infrastructure, realizing PROXY-based (290) interfaces for distributed components, or implementing a BUSINESS DELEGATE (292) for a remote component ...

... we must provide an abstraction that allows clients to access remote components using remote method invocation.

◆◆◆

Accessing the services of a remote component requires the client side to use a specific data format and networking protocol. Hard-coding the format and protocol directly into the client application, however, makes it dependent on the remoteness of its collaboration partner, because invocations on remote components will differ from invocations on local components.

Ideally, access to a component should be location-independent. There should be no functional difference between a method invocation on a local component and a method invocation on a remote component.

Therefore:

Provide a client proxy in the client's address space that is a surrogate for the remote component. The proxy provides the same interface as the remote component, and maps client invocations to the specific message format and protocol used to send these invocations across the network.

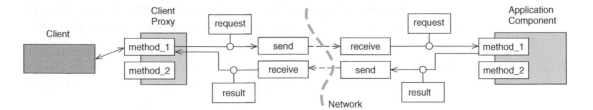

Ensure client applications issue requests to the remote component only via its client proxy. The proxy then transforms the concrete method invocation and its parameters into the data format understood by the network, and uses an IPC mechanism to send the data to the remote component. The client proxy also transforms results returned from the component represented by the proxy back into the format understood by its clients.

Client proxies support a remote method invocation style of IPC. As a result there is no API difference between a call to a local or a remote component, which enhances location-independent communication within a distributed application. In addition, a client proxy can shield its clients from changes in the represented component's 'real' interfaces, which avoids rippling effects in the case of component evolution. If the proxy interface is designed in a network-unaware style, however, it may incur excessive overhead. For example, it could offer many fine-grained methods, such as accessors for each visible attribute of the represented component. Accessing all attributes would require a client to invoke many proxy calls, each of which incurs network overhead.

In addition, client proxies can only support, but not fully achieve, location-independent communication. Before clients can use a client proxy they must obtain it from their local broker—thus clients are aware of the potential remoteness of the represented component. Moreover, a client proxy may not be able to handle all errors returned by the network transparently for its clients.

A client proxy can use a RESOURCE CACHE (505) to maintain immutable data and state of the represented remote component, once this data and state is first accessed and transferred. Caching avoids unnecessary performance penalties and network traffic for subsequent accesses to the data and state. If the immutable state and data is encapsulated within IMMUTABLE VALUES (396), the client proxy can pass it directly to clients. A client proxy can also use AUTHORIZATION (351) to enforce access rights to the remote component on the client side, which helps minimize unnecessary performance penalties and network traffic if access is denied.

Designing the client proxy as a REMOTE FACADE [Fow03a] helps to address performance problems by coalescing related fine-grained methods into a single coarser-grained method, such as a method that returns all visible attributes of the represented component in response to a single call.

Requestor **

When constructing a client-side Broker (237) infrastructure ...

... we must provide a means for sending method invocations over the network to remote components.

The client-side invocation of a method on a remote component involves many administrative and infrastructure tasks. Implementing these tasks repeatedly within each client is tedious, error-prone, and pollutes application code with infrastructure code that may be non-portable.

Invoking a method on a remote component requires the client side to marshal invocation information, manage network connections, transmit the invocation over the network, and handle invocation results and errors. These activities are unnecessary for local method invocations. If client applications handle these issues directly, they can become dependent on specific networking protocols and IPC mechanisms, thereby decreasing their portability and reusability in other deployment scenarios and applications. Moreover, client developers would be distracted from their primary tasks: implementing application functionality correctly and efficiently.

Therefore:

Create a requestor that encapsulates the creation, handling, and sending of request messages to remote components.

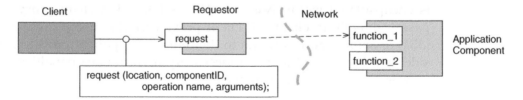

Clients that want to access a remote component supply the requestor with information about the component's location, a reference to the component, the operation to be invoked, and its arguments. The requestor uses the information to construct a corresponding request message and send it over the network to the remote component.

A requestor shields application logic in a distributed system from the details of client-side networking and IPC activities and tasks.

A requestor can delegate some of its sub-activities to other components. A MARSHALER [VKZ04] serializes concrete service requests into request MESSAGES (420) and de-serializes corresponding result messages into concrete responses. A CLIENT REQUEST HANDLER (246) manages connections and encapsulates specific IPC mechanisms, thereby simplifying sending request messages across a network and receiving result messages.

Some applications require additional requestor activities, such as adding a security token, which an INTERCEPTOR (467) can encapsulate via a uniform interface. In general, a MARSHALER, CLIENT REQUEST HANDLER, and INTERCEPTOR manipulate client-side request processing aspects without affecting the requestor's core algorithm for creating, handling, and sending requests. An ABSOLUTE OBJECT REFERENCE [VKZ04] can encapsulate information about the location and identity of the remote component that is the target of the request. Similarly, a REMOTING ERROR [VKZ04] is returned to the client when a failure cannot be handled transparently by the requestor.

In general there are three deployment options for a requestor [SMFG00]. The simplest option is to deploy one requestor for all client threads or processes on a node. The more clients access the requestor, however, the more it becomes a throughput and scalability bottleneck. To alleviate this drawback, there could be a separate requestor per client, or several clients could share a requestor. A requestor that is shared by multiple concurrent clients must be synchronized. Providing the requestor with a THREAD-SAFE INTERFACE (384) is a simple, coarse-grained synchronization option, because it enforces synchronization at the interface of the requestor, even if only small portions of its methods are critical sections. In this case, synchronization via STRATEGIZED LOCKING (388) is an alternative. Realizing a requestor as a MONITOR OBJECT (368) supports cooperative concurrency control of multiple clients that access the requestor simultaneously. If there are multiple requestors per client application, they must synchronize their internal use of shared resources, such as connections or cached request objects.

Invoker **

When constructing a server-side BROKER (237) infrastructure ...

... we must provide a means for receiving method invocations from the network and dispatching them to remote components.

◆◆◆

The server side must perform many administrative and infrastructure tasks to transform data received from clients into an invocation on a specific method of a remote component. Implementing these tasks repeatedly within each component implementation is tedious, error-prone, and pollutes application code with infrastructure code that is often non-portable.

Invoking a specific method of a component implementation in response to a client request requires a server to manage network connections, receive data on the connections, demarshal that data to receive the associated invocation information, identify the intended component implementation, invoke the appropriate method on that component, and return its results or errors. If remote components handled these concerns directly, they would be tightly coupled to specific networking protocols and IPC mechanisms, thereby decreasing their portability and reusability in other deployment scenarios and applications. Moreover, server developers would be distracted from their primary tasks: implementing application functionality correctly and efficiently.

Therefore:

Create an invoker that encapsulates the reception and dispatch of request messages from remote clients in a specific method of a component implementation.

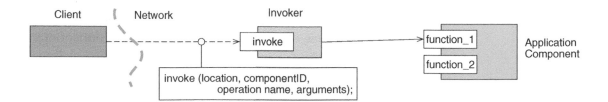

An invoker listens to network connections for request messages to arrive from remote clients, receives the request messages when they arrive, demarshals the received information to determine which method and parameters to invoke on which component implementation, and dispatches that method on the identified component.

An invoker shields the application logic of a distributed system from the details of server-side networking and IPC tasks and activities.

An invoker can delegate several sub-activities of its responsibility to other components. A MARSHALER [VKZ04] can de-serialize request MESSAGES (420) into a concrete service and serialize corresponding services results into result messages. A SERVER REQUEST HANDLER (249) manages connections and encapsulates a specific IPC mechanism, thereby simplifying the process of receiving requests and sending results across a network.

Some applications also require additional invocation activities, such as interpreting an embedded security token, which an INTERCEPTOR (444) can encapsulate via a uniform interface. In general, a MARSHALER, SERVER REQUEST HANDLER, and INTERCEPTOR manipulate server-side request processing aspects without affecting the invoker's core algorithm for the reception and dispatch of client requests on component implementations.

An ABSOLUTE OBJECT REFERENCE [VKZ04] encapsulates the identity of a specific component implementation. A REMOTING ERROR [VKZ04] is returned to the client that issued a request if failures occur that cannot be handled by the invoker. The invoker can also delegate its invocation to a LOCATION FORWARDER [VKZ04] if it cannot find the component implementation, for example if the component was redeployed, or is temporarily unavailable due to high machine load.

An invoker has several deployment options, the simplest of which is to deploy one invoker for all components implementations in a server application. The more components are accessed via one invoker, however, the more it becomes a throughput and scalability bottleneck. To alleviate this drawback, several remote components could share an invoker, or each component could have its own invoker.

Client Request Handler **

When developing a REQUESTOR (242) . . .

. . . we must send requests to, and receive replies from, the network.

Sending client requests to and receiving replies from the network involves various low-level IPC tasks, such as connection management, time-out handling, and error detection. Writing and performing these tasks separately for each client uses networking and endsystem resources ineffectively.

The more clients access the network, and the more requests and replies must be handled simultaneously, the more efficiently network resources must be managed to achieve appropriate quality of service in a distributed application. Network connections and bandwidth, for example, are limited resources and must be shared and used judiciously by all clients to ensure acceptable latency and jitter. In addition, writing error detection and time-out handling tasks separately for each client duplicates code and pollutes the application with non-portable networking code.

Therefore:

Provide a specialized client request handler that encapsulates and performs all IPC tasks on behalf of client components that send requests to and receive replies from the network.

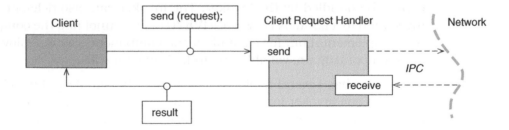

The functional responsibilities of a client request handler include connection establishment, request sending and result dispatching, and time-out and error handling, which it performs with help of specific IPC mechanisms. In addition, the client request handler is responsible for efficient management and utilization of networking and computing resources, such as network connections, memory, and threads.

The centralized execution and management of all client-side networking activities within a CLIENT REQUEST HANDLER can improve distributed application quality of service, such as latency, throughput, scalability, and resource utilization. The encapsulation of specific IPC mechanisms makes communication transparent for clients that issue requests to remote components.

To establish concrete connections to remote components, the client request handler implements the connector role of ACCEPTOR-CONNECTOR (265), which supports the evolution of network connection establishment strategies independently of other client request handler responsibilities. If the client request handler is shared by multiple concurrent clients, the connector must be synchronized. Providing the connector with a THREAD-SAFE INTERFACE (384) is a simple but coarse-grained synchronization option, because it enforces synchronization at the interface of the connector, even if only small portions of its methods are critical sections. In this case, consider using STRATEGIZED LOCKING (388) to parameterize the synchronization mechanisms. Realizing a connector as a MONITOR OBJECT (368) supports cooperative concurrency control when multiple clients access the connector simultaneously.

A connection created by a connector can be encapsulated within a connection handler that plays the service handler role in ACCEPTOR-CONNECTOR. This design treats a connection as a first-class entity, which supports efficient maintenance of connection-specific state, as well as the handling of REMOTING ERRORS [VKZ04] that occur on the connection. Scalability is also supported, since each connection handler can run in its own thread, thereby processing requests from and replies to multiple clients simultaneously.

A connection handler can implement a synchronous or asynchronous communication strategy. Synchronous communication can simplify the client programming model, but reduces performance and throughput, whereas asynchronous communication has the inverse properties. Four patterns—FIRE AND FORGET, SYNC WITH SERVER, POLL OBJECT, and RESULT CALLBACK [VKZ04]—help realize an asynchronous communication model. These four patterns provide different strategies for addressing the following three aspects: whether or not a result is sent to the client, whether or not the client receives an acknowledgement, and, if a result is sent to the client, whether it is the client's responsibility to obtain the result or whether it is informed using a callback.

If a client expects a result or an acknowledgement, a connection handler can use time-outs to detect potential failures of asynchronous communication. Depending on whether a connection handler processes data serially or is interrupt-driven, it can register with a REACTOR (259) or PROACTOR (262), respectively, which will notify it when a specific result arrives.

The specific IPC mechanism used by the connector and the connection handlers of a client request handler can be encapsulated by a PROTOCOL PLUG-IN [VKZ04] or a set of WRAPPER FACADES (459). Both patterns hide IPC mechanism details behind uniform, platform-independent interfaces. A PROTOCOL PLUG-IN allows runtime (re)configuration of IPC mechanisms, but incurs some runtime overhead. WRAPPER FACADE, in contrast, avoids runtime overhead, but only supports compile-time configuration. The requests are encapsulated within MESSAGES (420) and sent over the network via a MESSAGE CHANNEL (224). If security is required, the IPC mechanism should use a SECURE CHANNEL [SFHBS06] to transmit requests.

An OBJECT MANAGER (492) can enhance client request handler performance via caching. For example, if a specific connection is no longer needed, it need not be destroyed, but can instead be kept 'alive' for a predetermined time and reused for another collaboration between the client and server it connects.

Results of specific invocations, as well as any REMOTING ERRORS [VKZ04] that cannot be resolved by the client request handler, are returned to the client that issued the corresponding request.

Server Request Handler **

When developing an INVOKER (244) . . .

. . . we must receive requests send replies across the network.

Receiving client requests from and sending replies to the network involves several low-level IPC tasks, including connection management, time-out handling, and error detection. Writing and performing these tasks separately for each client uses networking and endsystem resources ineffectively.

The more remote requests and replies must be handled simultaneously by a server part of a distributed application, the more efficiently network resources must be managed and utilized to achieve an appropriate quality of service. Network connections and bandwidth, for example, are limited resources, and must be shared and used effectively by all remote components to provide an appropriate performance, throughput, and scalability on the server-side of a distributed system. In addition, writing error detection and time-out handling tasks separately for each component duplicates code and pollutes the application with non-portable networking code.

Therefore:

Provide a specialized server request handler that encapsulates and performs all IPC tasks on behalf of remote components that receive requests from and send replies to the network.

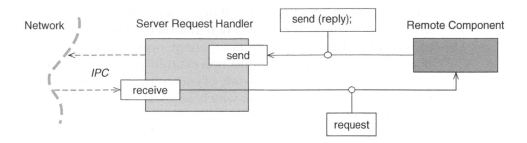

The functional responsibilities of a server request handler include connection establishment, request reception and dispatching, result sending, and error handling, which it performs with the help of specific IPC mechanisms. In addition, the server request handler is responsible for efficient management and utilization of networking and computing resources such as network connections, memory, and threads.

The centralized execution and management of all server-side networking activities within a SERVER REQUEST HANDLER can improve the distributed application's quality of service, in particular, latency, throughput, scalability, and resource utilization. The encapsulation of specific IPC mechanisms makes communication transparent for application components that receive requests from and send responses back to remote clients.

The client request handler needs an event-handling infrastructure that listens on the network for connection requests to arrive, establishes the requested connections, and dispatches service requests to methods on the appropriate application components. This infrastructure must allow multiple connection and service requests to be received and processed simultaneously to achieve appropriate latency, throughput, and scalability. Its core can be realized by a REACTOR (259) or PROACTOR (262), depending on whether the processing of received events is handled serially, or driven by interrupts, respectively.

The event handlers of a REACTOR or PROACTOR can be realized as an ACCEPTOR-CONNECTOR (265) to separate connection establishment from request and reply handling. A dedicated acceptor listens on the network for connection requests to occur, accepts these requests, and creates a connection handler that encapsulates the newly established connection. The connection handler then performs the IPC on behalf of the application component accessed via that connection. This design enables connection establishment and data transfer strategies to evolve independently of each other. Connections are also treated as first class entities, which supports efficient maintenance of connection-specific state and handling of any REMOTING ERRORS [VKZ04] that occur on the connection. In addition, scalability is supported: each connection handler can run in its own thread, which allows a server request handler to handle requests from, and replies for, multiple clients concurrently.

A connection handler can implement a synchronous or asynchronous communication strategy. Synchronous communication can simplify the client programming model but reduces performance, whereas asynchronous communication has the inverse properties. The SYNC WITH SERVER pattern [VKZ04] can help to return acknowledgements for an asynchronous communication model.

The specific IPC mechanism used by the acceptor and the connection handlers of a server request handler can be encapsulated by a PROTOCOL PLUG-IN [VKZ04] or a set of WRAPPER FACADES (459). Both patterns hide IPC mechanism details behind uniform and platform-independent interfaces. A PROTOCOL PLUG-IN allows runtime (re)configuration of IPC mechanisms, but incurs some runtime overhead. WRAPPER FACADE, in contrast, enhances performance, but only supports compile-time configuration. The requests are encapsulated within MESSAGES (420) and sent over the network via a MESSAGE CHANNEL (224). If security is required, the IPC mechanism should use a SECURE CHANNEL [SFHBS06] to transmit requests.

An OBJECT MANAGER (492) can enhance client request handler performance via caching. For example, if a specific connection is no longer needed, it need not be destroyed, but can instead be kept 'alive' for a predetermined time and reused for another collaboration between the client and server it connects.

11 Event Demultiplexing and Dispatching

Taxi stand in Munich
© Frank Buschmann

At its heart distributed computing is all about handling of, and responding to, events received from the network. This chapter, therefore, presents four patterns that describe different approaches for initiating, receiving, demultiplexing, dispatching, and processing events in distributed and networked systems.

Distributed computing is ultimately event-driven, even when middleware platforms offer applications with a more sophisticated communication model, such as request/response operations or asynchronous messaging. There are a number of challenges that differentiate event-driven software from software with a 'self-directed' flow of control [PLoPD1]:

- *Asynchronous arrival of events.* Behavior in event-driven software is triggered largely by external or internal events that can arrive asynchronously. Most events must be handled promptly, even if the application is under heavy workload, or while it is executing long-duration services. If not, response time will suffer, and hardware devices with real-time constraints will fail or corrupt data.

- *Simultaneous arrival of multiple events.* Event-driven software typically receives events from multiple independent event sources, such as I/O ports, sensors, keyboards or mice, signals, timers, or asynchronous software components. Consequently, multiple events can arrive at the application simultaneously. To react promptly to any event from any event source, event-driven software must therefore be able to listen for events on all its event sources.

- *Non-deterministic arrival of events.* Although event-driven software generally has little control over the order in which events arrive, it must handle events properly regardless of their order of arrival. Software that processes events in a specific order must be able to detect illegal event sequences in order to prevent improper state transitions. These requirements motivate flexible and effective event demultiplexing and dispatching infrastructure within event-driven software.

- *Multiple event types.* Most event-driven software handles multiple types of events, where each type requires a particular behavior. For example, a *Connect* event indicates a request to establish a connection between two peers, whereas a *Data* event indicates an operation request and its parameters. Dispatching the correct handler in response to events is the responsibility of the event-handling infrastructure, which requires an efficient mechanism to demultiplex events onto their intended handler, and to dispatch the correct service or operation to process the event.

- *Hiding the complexity of event demultiplexing and dispatching.* Low-level operating system mechanisms for detecting, receiving, and demultiplexing events are often tedious and error-prone to program [SH03]. To simplify the development of event-driven software, higher-level abstractions are needed that hide the complexity of demultiplexing and dispatching events to application services.

To master the challenges described above both elegantly and efficiently, event-driven software is often structured as a LAYERS architecture (185) with an inverted flow of control [John97]. Each layer in this architecture is responsible for handling a particular aspect of event-driven computation, and hides the complexity that is associated with this aspect from higher layers. Event-driven software typically exhibits three layers:

- *Event sources* such as sockets [Ste98] occur at the lowest level, which detect and retrieve events from various hardware devices or low-level services that reside within an operating system.

- In the next layer up is an *event demultiplexer, which uses functions* such as `WaitForMultipleObjects`, `GetQueuedCompletionStatus` [Sol98], select [Ste98], or poll [Rago93] to wait for events to arrive on the various event sources, and then dispatch events to their corresponding *event handler* callbacks.

- The *event handlers*, together with the application code, form a further layer, which performs application-specific processing in response to callbacks.

Though a LAYERS approach decouples different concerns in event-driven software in a way that handles each concern separately, it does not explain how to resolve a particular concern optimally under a given set of forces. For example, an event-demultiplexing layer alone does not ensure efficient yet simple demultiplexing and dispatching of events to event handlers.

The four event-handling patterns in our pattern language for distributed computing help to fill this gap. They provide efficient, extensible, and reusable solutions to key event demultiplexing and dispatching problems in event-driven software:

> The REACTOR pattern (259) [POSA2] allows event-driven software to demultiplex and dispatch service requests that are delivered to an application from one or more clients.

> The PROACTOR pattern (262) [POSA2] allows event-driven software to demultiplex and dispatch service requests triggered by the completion of asynchronous operations efficiently, thereby achieving the performance benefits of concurrency without incurring some of its liabilities.

> The ACCEPTOR-CONNECTOR pattern (265) [POSA2] decouples the connection and initialization of cooperating peer services in a networked system from the processing performed by the peer services after they are connected and initialized.

> The ASYNCHRONOUS COMPLETION TOKEN pattern (268) [POSA2] allows event-driven software to demultiplex and process the responses of asynchronous operations it invokes on services efficiently.

This chapter focuses solely on patterns for event demultiplexing and dispatching that are relevant to distributed computing. Patterns related to other areas of event-driven software, such as handling user interface events, are not included.

The REACTOR and PROACTOR patterns define event demultiplexing and dispatching infrastructures that can be used by event-driven applications to detect, demultiplex, dispatch, and process events they receive from the network. Although both patterns resolve essentially the same problem in a similar context, and also use similar patterns to implement their solutions, the concrete event-handling infrastructures they suggest are distinct, due to the orthogonal forces to which each pattern is exposed.

REACTOR focuses on simplifying the programming of event-driven software. It implements a *passive* event demultiplexing and dispatching model in which services wait until request events arrive and then react by processing the events synchronously without interruption. While this model scales well for services in which the duration of the response to a request is short, it can introduce performance penalties for long-duration services, since executing these services synchronously can unduly delay the servicing of other requests. PROACTOR, in contrast, is designed to maximize event-driven software performance. It implements a more *active* event demultiplexing and dispatching model in which services divide their processing into multiple self-contained parts and proactively initiate asynchronous execution of these parts. This design allows multiple services to execute concurrently, which can increase quality of service and throughput.

Consequently, REACTOR and PROACTOR are not really equally weighted alternatives, but rather are complementary patterns that trade-off programming simplicity and performance. Relatively simple event-driven software can benefit from a REACTOR-based design, whereas PROACTOR offers a more efficient and scalable event demultiplexing and dispatching model.

The following diagram illustrates how REACTOR and PROACTOR integrate into our pattern language.

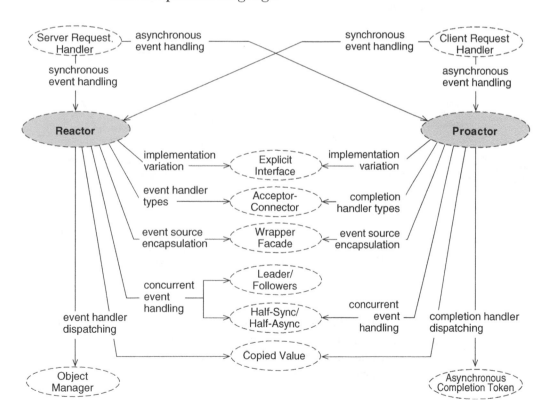

ACCEPTOR-CONNECTOR and ASYNCHRONOUS COMPLETION TOKEN help in refining the event-handling infrastructures introduced by REACTOR and PROACTOR. In its essence, ACCEPTOR-CONNECTOR partitions event handlers according to specialized responsibilities: initiating a connection to a remote peer handler, accepting a connection request from a remote peer, and event processing. This separation supports the variation of connection establishment and initialization behavior independently of service handler functionality. In addition, it shields application developers from dealing with low-level issues of connection management. ASYNCHRONOUS COMPLETION TOKEN supports the correlation of responses to asynchronous service invocations with the corresponding requests so that the sender of the request can determine the actions to perform on the response in constant time.

The second diagram illustrates how ACCEPTOR-CONNECTOR and ASYNCHRONOUS COMPLETION TOKEN connect with other patterns in our language.

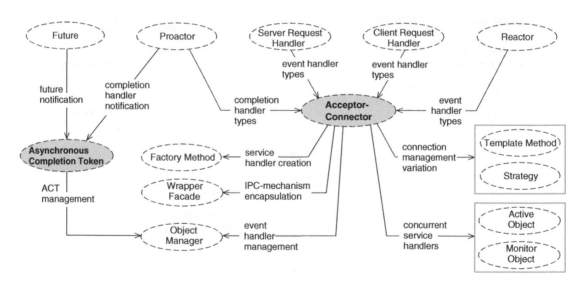

All four patterns, however, have broader applicability than merely handling network events. For example, REACTOR and PROACTOR can also be applied in demultiplexing and dispatching user input events to user interface elements.

Reactor **

When developing event-driven software, or designing a CLIENT REQUEST HANDLER (246) or a SERVER REQUEST HANDLER (249) ...

... we must decouple infrastructure behavior associated with detecting, demultiplexing, and dispatching events from short-duration components that service the events.

◆◆◆

Event-driven software often receives service request events from multiple event sources, which it demultiplexes and dispatches to event handlers that perform further service processing. Events can also arrive simultaneously at the event-driven application. However, to simplify software development, events should be processed sequentially and synchronously.

Efficiently and flexibly processing events that arrive concurrently from multiple sources is hard. For example, using multi-threading to wait for events to occur in a set of event sources can introduce overheads due to synchronization, context switching, and data movement. In contrast, blocking indefinitely on a single event source can prevent the servicing of other event sources, degrading the quality of service to clients. In addition, it should be easy to integrate new or improved event handlers into the event-handling infrastructure.

Therefore:

Provide an event handling infrastructure that waits on multiple event sources simultaneously for service request events to occur, but only demultiplexes and dispatches one event at a time to a corresponding event handler that performs the service.

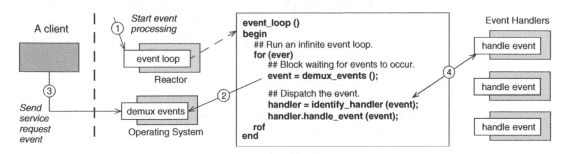

A reactor component coordinates the processing of events within the event-driven application. It defines an event loop that uses an operating system event demultiplexer to wait synchronously for service request events to occur on a set of event sources. By delegating the demultiplexing of events to the operating system, the reactor can wait for multiple event sources simultaneously without a need to multi-thread the application code. When events arrive, the event loop dispatches them one at a time to event handlers that implement the requested application functionality. Each event handler then reacts and services 'its' event synchronously.

◆◆◆

There are several benefits to a REACTOR design. First, operating system event demultiplexing mechanisms can wait on a set of event sources while avoiding the performance overhead and programming complexity associated with multi-threading. Second, encapsulating the software event loop within the reactor shields service event handlers from complexities in the synchronous event demultiplexing and dispatching infrastructure. Third, event serialization becomes transparent for an application's components, which can execute sequentially and synchronously without the need for explicit locking.

A reactor component forms the heart of event-driven software: it encapsulates a reusable event demultiplexing and dispatching infrastructure. In particular, the reactor defines an event loop that uses an event demultiplexer provided by the underlying operating system, such as select or `WaitForMultipleObjects`, to wait for service request events to occur on a set of event sources that are identified by handles. Calling the event demultiplexer blocks the reactor until one or more events arrive on the event sources and it is possible to process these events without blocking. The event demultiplexer returns the handles of all event sources on which service request events occurred to the reactor, which then dispatches these events, one at a time, as COPIED VALUES (394) to the handlers that react and process the events synchronously.

Different reactor implementations are often required when platforms offer different event demultiplexers. In such a situation, an EXPLICIT INTERFACE (281) may be needed to separate the reactor interface from its implementations. Event handlers are often arranged in an ACCEPTOR-CONNECTOR (265) configuration, in which service handlers provide domain-specific functionality and acceptors and connectors establish connections on behalf of service event handlers. An extensible event handling infrastructure can be supported by defining a common EXPLICIT INTERFACE for all event handlers that specifies the set of operations available for processing service request events. This design minimizes the coupling between the reactor and the signatures and logic of specific services, which all use a generic event handler interface.

Processing a service request event often requires an event handler to perform additional I/O on the event source on which the event arrived, for example to read parameter values associated with a client request, or to return results to the client that issued the event. WRAPPER FACADES (459) can be used to simplify communication between event handlers and event sources and to remove dependencies on platform-specific I/O functions. The I/O handles and event handlers within a reactor are typically stored and retrieved using an OBJECT MANAGER (492).

An event handler does not return control to the reactor until it is done processing a service request event. If an event handler blocks for an extended period, therefore, no other event handlers can be dispatched to service events. As a result, a single-threaded REACTOR configuration is best suited for event handlers that perform short-duration services that do not block on I/O handles or locks, but is infeasible for event handlers that perform long-duration actions.

To alleviate this drawback, event-driven software can implement concurrent event handlers, which allow the event-driven application to process multiple events simultaneously. The HALF-SYNC/HALF-ASYNC (359) pattern can work in conjunction with REACTOR to process long-duration client requests and replies concurrently in separate threads of control. Similarly, the LEADER/FOLLOWERS (362) pattern is suitable for event-driven software that uses a thread pool to process a high volume of short-duration, repetitive, and atomic actions.

Proactor *

When developing event-driven software, or designing a CLIENT REQUEST HANDLER (246) or a SERVER REQUEST HANDLER (249) . . .

. . . we must decouple infrastructure behavior associated with the detection, demultiplexing, and dispatch of events from long-duration components that service the events.

♦♦♦

To achieve the required performance and throughput, event-driven applications must often be able to process multiple events simultaneously. Resolving this problem via multi-threading, however, may be undesirable, due to the overhead of synchronization, context switching, and data movement.

Nevertheless, service processing should not be delayed unduly by long-duration activities on event sources, such as awaiting service request events from remote clients or performing I/O with clients or other components such as a database. Performance and throughput should also be maximized. In addition, it should be easy to integrate new or improved components into the existing event-handling infrastructure.

Therefore:

Split an application's functionality into asynchronous operations that perform activities on event sources and completion handlers that use the results of asynchronous operations to implement application service logic. Let the operating system execute the asynchronous operations, but execute the completion handlers in the application's thread of control.

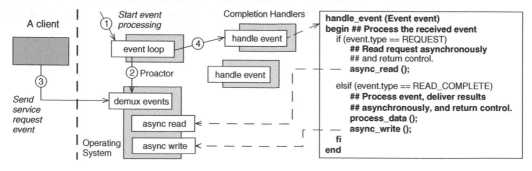

A proactor component coordinates the collaboration between completion handlers and the operating system. It defines an event loop that uses an operating system event demultiplexer to wait synchronously for events that indicate the completion of asynchronous operations to occur. Initially all completion handlers 'proactively' call an asynchronous operation to wait for service request events to arrive, and then run the event loop on the proactor. When such an event arrives, the proactor dispatches the result of the completed asynchronous operation to the corresponding completion handler. This handler then continues its execution, which may invoke another asynchronous operation.

A PROACTOR event-handling infrastructure allows multiple long-duration services to be executed simultaneously within a single application thread, which enhances the performance and throughput of event-driven software by avoiding multi-threading overhead, such as synchronization, context switching, and data movement—as long as completion handlers do not operate on the same resources at the same time. Encapsulating the software event loop within the proactor also shields completion handlers from complexities in the asynchronous event demultiplexing and dispatching infrastructure.

To implement a PROACTOR arrangement, most modern operating systems offer asynchronous operations, such as the `aio_*` API in Real-time POSIX [POSIX95], and Overlapped I/O in Windows [Sol98]. Without blocking their callers, the operating system executes these asynchronous operations on event sources identified via handles. Completion handlers can use the operations to delegate the execution of long-duration I/O activities to the operating system, which enables the handlers to process other requests until the operations complete. A downside of the Proactor is its reliance on operating system support for asynchronous I/O to run efficiently.

For efficiency reasons, the collaboration between completion handlers and asynchronous operations is often based on ASYNCHRONOUS COMPLETION TOKENS (ACTs) (268). When a completion handler invokes an asynchronous operation, it also passes an ACT that contains unambiguous identification of the calling handler, as well as the handle of the event source on which the operation should execute. When the asynchronous operation completes, it fills the ACT with its results, and the operating system generates a completion event on the respective event source to indicate that the operation has finished. This completion event also contains the corresponding ACT.

Completion events are returned to completion handlers via the proactor, whose event loop uses an event demultiplexer provided by the operating system, such as `GetQueuedCompletionStatus` in the Windows API [Sol98]. This event demultiplexer waits for completion events to occur on event sources that can be identified via handles. When such events occur, the event demultiplexer returns them to the proactor, which uses their ACTs to dispatch each event to the associated completion handler as a COPIED VALUE (394), to process the results of the asynchronous operation. Once a completion handler calls another asynchronous operation, control returns to the proactor, so that it can wait for and dispatch the next completion event.

Different platforms often require different proactor implementations, so the proactor interface should be separated from its realization via an EXPLICIT INTERFACE (281). Completion handlers are often designed as an ACCEPTOR-CONNECTOR (265) configuration, in which service handlers provide domain-specific functionality and acceptors and connectors establish connections asynchronously on behalf of service handlers. To support an extensible event-handling infrastructure, define a common EXPLICIT INTERFACE for all completion handlers that specifies the set of operations available for processing service request events. This design minimizes the coupling between the proactor and the signatures and logic of specific services, which all use a generic completion handler interface.

Processing a service request event often requires a completion handler to perform additional I/O on the event source on which the event arrived, for example to read parameter values asynchronously that are associated with a client request, or to return results to the client that issued the event. WRAPPER FACADES (459) can be used to simplify the communication between completion handlers and event sources and to remove dependencies on platform-specific I/O functions.

The HALF-SYNC/HALF-ASYNC (359) pattern can work in conjunction with PROACTOR to process long-duration clients requests and replies synchronously and sequentially, which simplifies application programming without degrading the performance of the PROACTOR event-handling infrastructure.

Acceptor-Connector **

When implementing event handlers in a connection-oriented networked system, such as event handlers in a REACTOR (259) architecture or completion handlers in a PROACTOR (262) architecture, or when designing a CLIENT REQUEST HANDLER (246) or a SERVER REQUEST HANDLER (249) . . .

. . . we want to decouple infrastructure behavior associated with establishing connections and initializing event handlers from the application-specific processing within these handlers.

◆◆◆

Before peer event handlers in a networked system can execute their functionality with other peer event handlers they must first be connected and initialized. The connection establishment and initialization code of a peer event handler, however, is largely independent of the functionality that it performs.

To complicate matters, the application functionality of an event handler usually changes more frequently than its connection and initialization strategies. In addition, an event handler may change its connection role dynamically: in one scenario it initiates a connection to a remote peer actively, while in another scenario it accepts a connection request passively from a remote peer.

Therefore:

Decouple the connection and initialization of peer event handlers in a networked system from the processing that these peers subsequently perform.

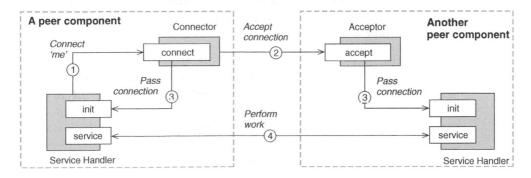

A client service handler can initiate a connection to a remote service handler by calling its local connector, a factory that actively initiates new connections to remote peers. The connector sends the request to a corresponding acceptor, a factory on the server side that accepts connection requests passively from remote peers. After the factories establish a connection between two peers, they initialize the associated service handlers and pass the connection to the handlers. The service handlers then use the connection to execute their application functionality cooperatively.

An ACCEPTOR-CONNECTOR arrangement encapsulates connection establishment within separate acceptor and connector components, which shields service handlers from complexities in the underlying network programming infrastructure. In addition, connection establishment and initialization behavior can vary independently of service handler functionality. Note, however, that an ACCEPTOR-CONNECTOR arrangement may add unnecessary complexity for simple client applications that connect with only one server and perform one service using a single network programming interface.

Design acceptors to use an event demultiplexer to listen for the arrival of connection requests passively. If an ACCEPTOR-CONNECTOR arrangement is built on top of a REACTOR or PROACTOR, the acceptors can use the event demultiplexer that is provided by these event-handling infrastructures. When a connection request arrives, the event demultiplexer dispatches the request to the acceptor, which performs three steps to establish a connection with the remote peer that issued the request. First, a FACTORY METHOD (529) creates the service handler instance that should be connected to the remote peer. Second, the acceptor establishes the connection with the remote peer, and third, it passes the connection to the associated service handler and finishes initializing it.

In general, a connector factory can support a synchronous or an asynchronous connection establishment strategy to service handlers. Synchronous connection establishment is most useful if the connection establishment latency is low, if service handlers must be initialized in a fixed order, and if service handlers can deploy a thread-per-connection model to connect to remote peers. Otherwise, an asynchronous connection establishment strategy is more beneficial.

Both synchronous *and* asynchronous connection establishment can be supported transparently to service handlers by dividing connectors into a `connect` method that is called by a service handler to establish a new connection actively, and a `complete` method that passes this connection to the service handler that requested it after the connection is established [POSA2].

Each activity in the connector and acceptor factories can be realized with help of TEMPLATE METHODS (453) or STRATEGIES (455). Such a design supports flexible evolution and exchange of connection establishment and initialization policies transparently to service handlers. TEMPLATE METHODS are most appropriate if the flexibility is needed at compile time, whereas typical STRATEGIES support a runtime configuration and reconfiguration of acceptors and connectors. In C++, a STRATEGY can also be expressed as a compile-time policy, in which case the choice is simply between using an inheritance-versus a delegation-based approach—binding time need not be a consideration.

The I/O handles and event handlers used by a connector component to support asynchronous connection establishment are typically stored and retrieved using an OBJECT MANAGER (492).

The acceptor and connector factories perform their connection establishment functionality, and the service handlers their application functionality, by exchanging messages with their peers via an IPC mechanism. Encapsulating the IPC mechanism inside a set of WRAPPER FACADES (459) ensures its correct and portable use within the acceptor and connector factories and service handlers.

Concurrent service handlers can improve the throughput of an event-driven application because multiple events can be processed simultaneously. A concurrent service handler can be implemented as an ACTIVE OBJECT (365) if it represents a coarse-grained component or service, or as a MONITOR OBJECT (368) if it is a fine-grained (distributed) object.

Asynchronous Completion Token **

When developing a PROACTOR (262) infrastructure, a FUTURE (404) arrangement, or in general using asynchronous communication within an application ...

... we must demultiplex and process the responses of asynchronous operations invoked on services efficiently.

♦♦♦

A two-way operation that a client invokes asynchronously returns its response via a completion event. This response can then be processed within the client. The client does not block, however, after calling the operation. The state of the client when the completion event arrives can therefore differ from the state it had when the operation was invoked.

To behave correctly, however, the client must process the result of the operation in its appropriate context. To enhance performance, the client should also spend as little time as possible in identifying how responses of asynchronous operations must be processed. In addition, if the client calls multiple asynchronous operations, the order in which responses arrive may not be identical to the order in which the operations were called.

Therefore:

Along with each call that a client issues on an asynchronous operation, transmit an asynchronous completion token (ACT) that contains the minimum amount of information needed to identify how the client should process the operation's response.

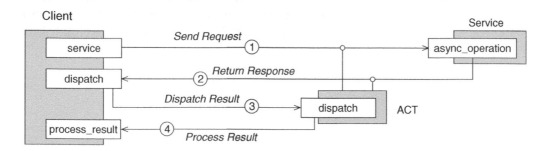

An ACT associates an individual invocation of an asynchronous operation with the specific behavior that should be executed in the client when the operation completes. When a client invokes an operation on a service asynchronously, it also passes an ACT to that service. The service holds the ACT within the operation while it executes, but does not modify it. When the operation finishes, the ACT is returned to the client along with any results. The client uses the ACT to indicate efficiently and unambiguously which behavior to execute in response to the completed operation. In particular, the client uses the ACT to demultiplex and dispatch control flow to a method or handler that is responsible for processing the operation's result.

Using ASYNCHRONOUS COMPLETION TOKENS to dispatch and process the results of asynchronous operations allows clients to demultiplex and dispatch the methods or handlers that process the results in constant time. In addition, ACTs use the minimum amount of space needed to match responses with the corresponding requests. On the other hand, using ACTs can make an application more vulnerable to accidental mistakes or malicious attacks, because it is assumed that asynchronous operations treat them opaquely and do not modify their data structures.

There are several ways to implement an ASYNCHRONOUS COMPLETION TOKEN. One option, which is specific to system-level languages like C++, is to encode the memory address of the method or handler that is responsible for processing the result of the associated asynchronous operation as the value of the ACT. When the ACT is returned, the pointer is downcast and the appropriate method or handler invoked. However, if the method handler was re-mapped in virtual memory—a situation that can occur for objects allocated from a memory-mapped address space—using a memory address as an ACT can lead to subtle failures. If passing the memory address as an ACT is risky, use a proxy identifier, such as an object reference or an index into a table. Keep the 'real' ACT within the client, for example within an OBJECT MANAGER (492). When the ACT's proxy identifier is returned, use it to retrieve the 'real' ACT and process it.

To reclaim ACTs robustly, even when asynchronous operations fail, let the OBJECT MANAGER control the lifetime of all ACTs within the client, for example by disposing of them if errors are returned on an invocation, or if a given time-out expires.

12 Interface Partitioning

Maskebærere (Mask Bearers) by Hilde Mæhlum, on display at Bærum Verk near Oslo
© Kevlin Henney

Specifying component interfaces is a significant activity in a software project. Interfaces should reflect component responsibilities and usage protocols clearly, provide meaningful services for clients, and hide clients from the cost of change and evolution of component implementations. Otherwise, components become hard to use and their collaborations tend to be complex. This chapter presents eleven patterns for specifying well-defined component interfaces that expose the qualities listed above.

Interfaces are the 'business card' of a component. They should inform clients about the component's responsibilities, offered services, and usage protocols, and should make it easy for clients to collaborate with the component effectively and correctly. Consequently, designing and specifying usable and meaningful component interfaces is a key to successful software development. In addition, the productive use of software development and deployment approaches such as *Component-Based Development* [Szy02] and *Service-Oriented Architectures* (SOA) [Kaye03] depends strongly on the quality of the available service and component interfaces. Ultimately, inappropriately specified interfaces decrease the usability of a component, while increasing the structural complexity of applications using it, which makes the component hard and costly to understand, maintain, and evolve [Bus03].

Designing quality interfaces for components in an application requires that developers address the following challenging—and sometimes conflicting—aspects:

* *Component responsibilities and contract specification.* Developers of components—particularly multi-use components—often have no control over which applications will use their components. They also often have limited control over how their components will be used by such applications. This lack of control requires component developers to specify the concrete responsibilities, functionality, and usage protocols of components with care. Different component responsibilities must be clearly separated from one another to avoid confusion about the component's purpose and usage. A component should be easily (re)usable in all situations where it applies, while also preventing undesirable usage.

* *Quality attributes.* A component that behaves correctly for its intended uses and also fails robustly when errors occur is easier to use and reuse than components that do not possess these quality attributes. Other quality attributes must also be considered in concurrent and distributed application deployments, including the performance of remote invocations, the synchronization of shared, concurrent components, a component's proper creation and disposal, and the secure access to component functionality. These concerns are not limited to implementation details: they must often be reflected in the design and specification of component interfaces.

Ideally, an interface defines a contract that specifies the qualities that are relevant to the effective and correct use of the component.

- *Expressiveness and simplicity.* The more expressive and simpler is a component's interface, the easier the component is to use. Concrete methods should therefore reflect the intended usage scenarios of clients, without breaking the component's encapsulation. Ideally, simple and common functionality should be easy to use, yet complex usage scenarios should also be possible, albeit with additional effort.

- *Loose coupling and stability.* Clients are often uninterested in the internal design and implementation of the components they use. Nor should they depend on component interfaces and usage protocols they do not use. In addition, interface versioning and stability is a key issue for successful component use: clients should not be affected if signatures evolve in methods they do not use, or if the component is extended with new functionality and roles they do not care about. In general, the published interfaces of a component should remain stable, protecting clients from changes within the component implementation as much as possible.

  This property is particularly important for components in distributed systems, and even more so for components in systems designed using a Service-Oriented Architecture. In such systems it is hard to determine a component's clients in advance, and client implementations cannot always be changed whenever component interfaces change. Moreover, many clients may access a component at runtime, which complicates online upgrades. A loose coupling between components, in conjunction with interface stability, is therefore a key factor for building software systems that are both sustainable and open to controlled evolution.

Resolving these challenges is hard and requires deep domain knowledge, design expertise, and implementation skills.

Scaling up components to distributed systems makes interface design even more challenging, due to the following problems:

- *Component distribution.* Component implementations may not share the same address space as their clients. This distribution requires powerful mechanisms for locating components within a distributed system and accessing their services. However, the distribution of components should be transparent to clients.

- *Heterogeneity of components and their clients.*   Components in a distributed system can be implemented using different programming paradigms and languages, which may differ from those used by their clients. Despite this heterogeneousness, however, clients and components within a distributed system should be configurable seamlessly with one another, without exposing (mutual) hard-coded dependencies to the implementation details of their respective partners.

Many patterns support the resolution of the above challenges. Some of these patterns are domain-specific, for example, patterns that help to define a component's concrete responsibilities and contracts. Describing these patterns would go beyond the scope of our distributed computing pattern language, which would explode if we were to cover all 'patternized' application domains. We instead refer to the appropriate body of literature [Fow97] [PLoPD1] [PLoPD2] [PLoPD3] [PLoPD4] [PLoPD5] [Ris01]. This chapter focuses solely on patterns that help to partition component interfaces and resolve key challenges related to component distribution. There are eleven such patterns in our pattern language:

The EXPLICIT INTERFACE pattern (281) separates component usage from realization details. Clients only depend on the contract that a component interface defines, but not on the component's internal design, implementation specifics, location, synchronization mechanisms, and other realization details.

The EXTENSION INTERFACE pattern (284) [POSA2] allows multiple interfaces to be exported by a component, to prevent bloating of interfaces and breaking of client code when developers extend or modify the functionality of the component.

The INTROSPECTIVE INTERFACE (286) pattern offers a supplementary interface that supports clients in accessing information about a component's type, functionality, public interface, internal structure, behavior, and computational state. Clients or application-external tools can use this information to monitor a component or control their use of the component.

The DYNAMIC INVOCATION INTERFACE (288) pattern offers a supplementary interface that allows clients to invoke methods on components dynamically, composing the calls at runtime rather than selecting them from declarations.

The BUSINESS DELEGATE (292) [ACM01] pattern encapsulates infrastructure concerns associated with access to a remote component, such as lookup, load balancing, and network error handling, from clients that use the component. A business delegate enables location transparency when invoking components in a distributed application.

The PROXY pattern (290) [POSA1] [GoF95] enables clients of a component to communicate transparently via a surrogate rather than with the component itself. This surrogate can serve many purposes, including simplified client programming, enhanced efficiency, and protection from unauthorized access.

The FACADE pattern (294) [GoF95] provides a unified, higher-level interface to a set of interfaces in a subsystem that makes the subsystem easier to use.

The COMBINED METHOD pattern (296) [Hen00c] arranges methods that are commonly used together into a single method to ensure correctness and improve efficiency in multi-threaded and distributed environments.

The ITERATOR pattern (298) [GoF95] provides a way to access the elements of an aggregate component sequentially without exposing its underlying representation.

The ENUMERATION METHOD pattern (300) [Beck97] [Hen01c] encapsulates iteration over an aggregate component to execute an action on each element of the component into a method on the aggregate. The goal is to reduce the costs of multiple individual accesses to the elements that result from external iteration over the aggregate.

The BATCH METHOD pattern (302) [Hen01c] folds together repeated accesses to the elements of an aggregate object to reduce the costs of multiple individual accesses.

The EXPLICIT INTERFACE pattern describes the basic idea of all interface design strategies: when defining an expressive and intuitive interface to a component, separate the interface from the implementation strictly and explicitly. EXPLICIT INTERFACE addresses the most fundamental of interface partitioning challenges outlined above: contract specification, simplicity, expressiveness, quality, loose coupling and component distribution. Hence, it is used by many other patterns in our pattern language for distributed computing, as shown in the following diagram.

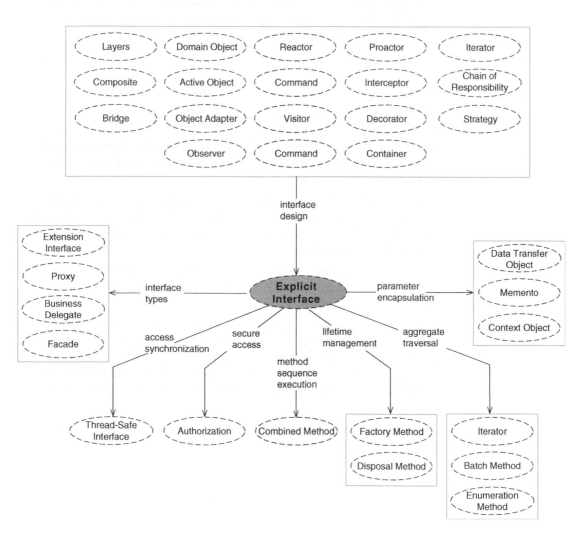

EXPLICIT INTERFACE is refined by the EXTENSION INTERFACE pattern, which introduces role specific interfaces—and thus role-specific client perspectives—to a component.

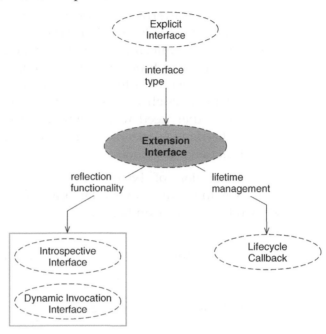

The notion of role-specific interfaces helps to address a variety of different challenges and issues in interface design:

- *Stability.* Clients do not break if a role-specific interface that they do not use changes.

- *Versioning.* If a particular role-specific interface evolves, for example by modifying, adding, or removing method signatures, it can be realized as a separate role-specific interface, and its old version can still be supported.

- *Extensibility.* If a component is extended with a new role, it can be offered to clients via a separate interface, thus clients not interested in the new role do not break.

- *Special purpose usage.* Advanced component usage scenarios often require reflection capabilities, which are not necessarily part of a component's core contract. Specialized reflection interfaces help to separate the 'standard' use of a component from its 'special-purpose' use, so that 'standard' clients can use it in an explicit and type-safe manner. Similarly, a separate lifecycle management interface allows component middleware such as containers to manage the lifecycle of a component transparently to its clients.

The next two patterns, INTROSPECTIVE INTERFACE and DYNAMIC INVOCATION INTERFACE, define 'advanced' interfaces for components that allow clients to obtain information about component-internal details and to invoke component functionality by composing requests to it dynamically. These reflective interfaces are particularly useful for application-external tools, such as testing frameworks, system monitors, and debuggers, that need to monitor, control, and access components without becoming dependent on specific component details, including their functional interfaces.

The integration of INTROSPECTIVE INTERFACE and DYNAMIC INVOCATION INTERFACE into our pattern language for distributed computing is shown by the diagram below:

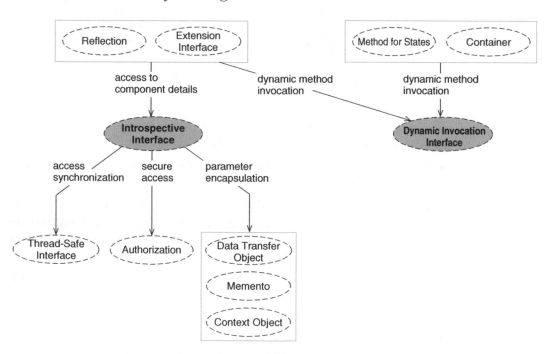

Three patterns, BUSINESS DELEGATE, PROXY, and FACADE, then capture different but related design flavors for component interfaces:

- BUSINESS DELEGATE helps to hide infrastructure aspects from those related to distribution, such as load balancing and replication.

- PROXY provides a surrogate for a component that cannot be accessed directly, for example because it is remote, stored in a database, or requires secure access.

- FACADE provides a defined access point to a group of components that together provide a broad service to their clients.

The following diagram outlines the integration of BUSINESS DELEGATE, PROXY, and FACADE into our pattern language:

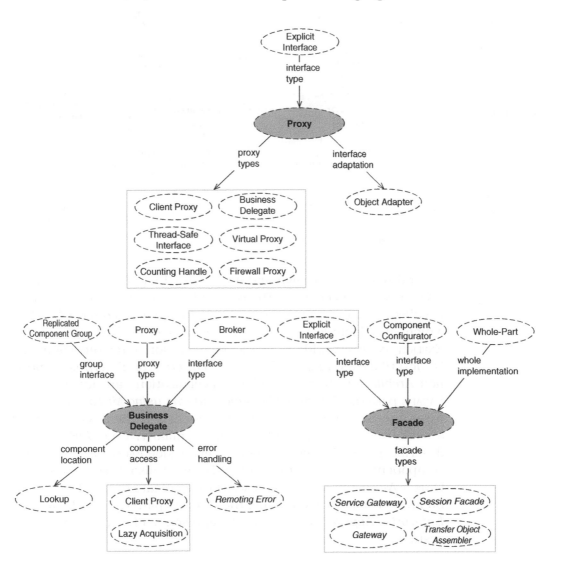

The four remaining patterns, COMBINED METHOD, ITERATOR, BATCH METHOD, and ENUMERATION METHOD, deal with designing specific methods within a component interface, specifically in the context of building concurrent and/or distributed systems. Their integration into our pattern language for distributed computing is as follows:

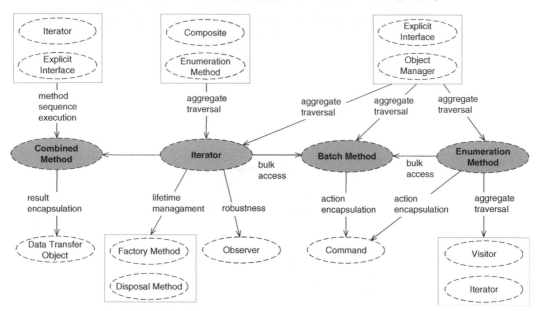

Several flavors are known and documented for some of the patterns presented in this chapter. The EXPLICIT INTERFACE pattern, for example, is called COMPONENT INTERFACE in *Server Component Patterns* [VSW02], which also include COMPONENT PROXY, a special form of PROXY. An EXPLICIT INTERFACE with COMBINED METHODS for a remote component is described as REMOTE FACADE in *Patterns of Enterprise Application Architecture* [Fow03a]. Many specializations are known for the FACADE pattern. *Enterprise Solution Patterns using Microsoft. NET* features the SERVICE GATEWAY pattern, which is a client-side FACADE to a set of remote components [MS03]. Similarly, *Core J2EE Patterns* describe SESSION FACADE, which is a server-side FACADE to a set of EJB components [ACM01]. *Core J2EE Patterns* also describes TRANSFER OBJECT ASSEMBLER, which is a FACADE to aggregate results from several business components. Finally, the GATEWAY pattern from *Patterns for Enterprise Application Architecture* represents a FACADE to an external system.

Explicit Interface **

When designing a Layers (185), Domain Object (208), Reactor (259), Proactor (262), Iterator (298), Composite (319), Active Object (365), Command (412), Interceptor (444), Chain of Responsibility (440), Bridge (436), Object Adapter (438), Visitor (447), Decorator (453), Strategy (455), Wrapper Facade (459), Observer (405), or Container (488) arrangement ...

... a major concern of all software architecture work is the effective and appropriate expression of component interfaces.

A component represents a self-contained unit of functionality and deployment with a published usage protocol. Clients can use it as a building block in providing their own functionality. Direct access to the full component implementation, however, would make clients dependent on component internals, which ultimately increases application internal software coupling.

Ideally a client should only depend on a component's published interface. If this interface remains stable, modifications to the component's implementation should not affect its clients. Encapsulating components within ordinary concrete classes is impractical: these class interfaces are always bound to their implementations. Even with abstract classes, the typical inclusion of a partial implementation is more binding than is appropriate for loose coupling and stability. Location independence is a further concern: clients of a component may reside in remote address spaces, and a component's location may change at runtime, so client dependencies on a component's location should therefore be avoided. Finally, the methods offered by a component should be meaningful for clients and support its effective and correct usage, especially in distributed or concurrent deployments.

Therefore:

Separate the declared interface of a component from its implementation. Export the interface to the clients of the component, but keep its implementation private and location-transparent to the client.

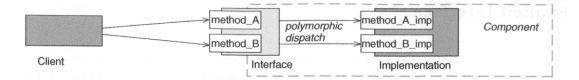

A call from the client through this explicit interface will be forwarded to the component, but the client code will depend only on the interface and not on the implementation. An EXPLICIT INTERFACE is associated with a contract [Mey97] that clients *must* follow to use such a component correctly. This contract includes operations offered by the component, the protocol for calling the operations, and any other constraints and information that clients must know to use the component correctly and effectively.

♦♦♦

An EXPLICIT INTERFACE enforces a strict separation of the component's interface from its concrete implementation, which separates component usage issues from concrete realization and location details. This separation also enables the transparent modification of component implementations independently of the clients using it, as long as the contract defined by the interfaces remains stable.

Several patterns help in structuring a component's explicit interface. An EXTENSION INTERFACE (284) supports the partitioning of an explicit interface into multiple smaller interfaces, one for each role of the component. EXTENSION INTERFACE also enables the extension of the component with new role-specific interfaces. In general, an EXTENSION INTERFACE supports interface evolution while minimizing the effect of this evolution on the component's clients.

A PROXY (290) helps to encapsulate specific house-keeping tasks associated with invoking a component. For example, it can transform a method call into a message that can be sent across the network to the component implementation, load it from the database on the first access, or cache immutable state for efficient client access. A BUSINESS DELEGATE (292), in contrast, is most useful in dynamic distributed environments, which typically require a range of infrastructure tasks to be performed when accessing the component. For example, before a component can be invoked, its implementation must first be located and a connection to its implementation must be established. A

BUSINESS DELEGATE can execute these tasks transparently for clients when they invoke a method on the component. A FACADE (294) shields clients from the internal structure of the component, which can consist of even smaller parts. It provides a single, defined entry point into the component, which allows the component's structure to be varied without effects onto its clients.

A key issue when specifying an explicit interface is operational quality: clients must be able to use the component effectively and correctly. Designing an explicit interface as a THREAD-SAFE INTERFACE (384) serializes the access to a component in concurrent usage scenarios, keeping locking overhead to a minimum and, in the case of non-recursive locks, avoiding self-deadlock should a component invoke methods on itself. AUTHORIZATION (351) ensures secure access to the component's functionality. A COMBINED METHOD (296) represents a series of method invocations on the component that are always called together and in a specific order, which makes an explicit interface more expressive, because it reflects common component usage. FACTORY METHODS (529) and DISPOSAL METHODS (531) allow clients to create and dispose of a component without being dependent on either its internal structure or the processes for constructing and destroying it.

If an interface represents an aggregate structure such as a collection, clients may need access to the elements or want to execute actions on them. An ITERATOR (298) allows clients to traverse these elements one at a time without breaking the component's encapsulation. A BATCH METHOD (302) is similar in intent to an ITERATOR, but sends or returns multiple elements on each invocation, which is beneficial for distributed and concurrent systems, because networking and synchronization overhead is minimized. An ENUMERATION METHOD (300) helps to execute a specific action on each element without requiring the caller to manage the traversal explicitly, which minimizes synchronization overhead in concurrent usage scenarios.

The parameters and results of an invocation on an explicit interface can be encapsulated into DATA TRANSFER OBJECTS (418), which avoids clients or the component having to depend on concrete data representations. If clients need access to the component's internal state, it can be returned as a MEMENTO (414) to maintain encapsulation. If the component needs client-specific information to execute its services, it can be passed as a CONTEXT OBJECT (416) to the component.

Extension Interface **

When specifying an EXPLICIT INTERFACE (281) ...

... we may want to ensure client stability and type-safety in the face of interface evolution.

Clients can use a component effectively only if it provides a stable and coherent interface. The interface of a component is often affected, however, when its functionality is modified or extended, which can break the client code—in some cases even if the new functionality is not used.

Ideally, clients of a component should not break when parts of the component's interface that they do not use change, or if they are not interested in new services added to the component. Even when interface parts that they actually do use change, clients should not break if they do not use the changes. Similarly, the existing interface of a component should remain stable when its implementation is extended with new services, or when existing service signatures are updated.

Therefore:

Let clients access a component only via specialized extension interfaces, and introduce one such interface for each role that the component provides. Introduce new extension interfaces whenever the component evolves to include new functionality or updated signatures within existing extension interfaces.

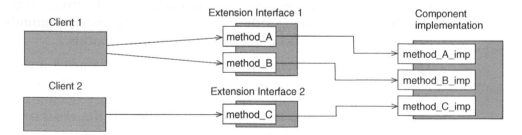

Clients interested in a specific role of the component issue requests through the corresponding extension interface, which forwards the request to the associated component implementation. When implementing a component's extension interfaces, first identify the different roles that it can play within its envisioned usage scenarios. Encapsulate each role into a separate extension interface and allow clients to access only those extension interfaces that they actually need to do their job. Avoid modifying existing extension interfaces, and instead create new extension interfaces when extending the component with new functionality or when updating existing service signatures.

An EXTENSION INTERFACE design offers several benefits. First, it minimizes client coupling to the component: clients only depend on the interfaces of those roles they actually use, which ensures that they do not break when signatures change or new services are added to the component. Second, clients can still access component functionality via concise and strongly typed interfaces, without resorting to accessing bloated 'one-size-fits-all' interfaces or inefficient dynamically typed message-oriented interfaces. In particular, each role-specific extension interface of an EXTENSION INTERFACE arrangement can be an EXPLICIT INTERFACE that specifies the methods—and only those methods—necessary to fulfill its respective role.

To manage a component's extension interfaces, introduce a special root interface that offers functionality to retrieve and access each extension interface of the component. Optionally, the root interface can offer an INTROSPECTIVE INTERFACE (286) that allows clients to obtain information about the component, and a DYNAMIC INVOCATION INTERFACE (288) through which client can issue requests to the component without the need to use one of its role-specific extension interface. Both types of interface are especially useful if the component is monitored or accessed by external tools, such as testing tools or system monitors, or if it must be integrated dynamically into applications that originally were not designed to use the component.

LIFECYCLE CALLBACKS (499) and configuration functionality are optional functionality for the root interface, which an application can use to initialize the component and control its lifecycle actively. Make sure that the root interface functionality is accessible through all extension interfaces of the component, for example by deriving all extension interfaces from the root interface, or by implementing its functionary within all extension interfaces.

Introspective Interface **

When specifying a REFLECTION (197) architecture or the root functionality of an EXTENSION INTERFACE (284) ...

... we must sometimes allow clients to access information, also known as *metadata*, about the components they are using.

◆◆◆

Using a component correctly may require clients to access information about it, such as its type, identity, supported interfaces, or current state. However, allowing clients to access such mechanistic details directly could break component encapsulation and reduce dependency stability.

In addition, clients would become dependent on the component's structure, which increases an application's complexity and complicates its maintenance and evolution. Subsequent changes to the component's implementation and interface could potentially ripple through to all its clients. Avoiding such ripple effects is particularly important for application-external tools such as debuggers and system monitors, which are unaware of the specific properties of the components they control, but need to access their mechanisms without introducing dependencies on their implementation details. A component should therefore be a self-contained, well-encapsulated, building block—regardless of how clients want or need to use it.

Therefore:

Introduce a special introspective interface for the component that allows clients to access information about its mechanisms and structure. Keep the introspective interface separate from the component's 'operational' interfaces.

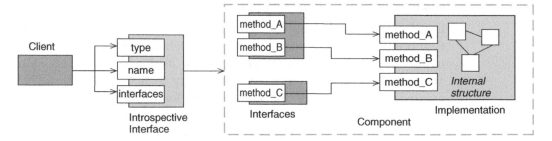

By calling the introspective interface, clients can access information that helps them to control how they use the component and/or monitor and reason about it. General metadata provided by an introspective interface could include the component's type, name, location, version, interfaces, configuration and deployment parameters, as well as its dependencies to other components. An introspective interface could also provide metadata useful for managing the component, such as the number of clients, load, and resource usage. An introspective interface supports the calling a component through a DYNAMIC INVOCATION INTERFACE.

An INTROSPECTIVE INTERFACE provides controlled access to a component's details without breaking its encapsulation. In addition, it separates component usage from the process of obtaining information about it, which makes it ideal for tools to obtain information without becoming dependent on their specific interfaces, internal design, and implementation details. However, most component usage scenarios actually do not need introspective access to component metadata, so providing an INTROSPECTIVE INTERFACE should be considered an option, not a mandatory requirement, for a component.

Some languages offer standard introspective interfaces for obtaining metadata about objects and classes, such as the `java.lang.reflect` package in Java and the `System.Reflection` namespace in C#. Other languages, such as C and C++, require framework support for introspective interface, as is the case in CORBA and COM. AUTHORIZATION (351) ensures secure access to the component's details: in general, not every client is allowed to obtain this information.

The parameters and results of an invocation on an introspective interface can be encapsulated into DATA TRANSFER OBJECTS (418), which avoids dependencies of clients or the component on concrete input/output data representations. If clients need to access the component's internal state, it can be returned as a MEMENTO (414) to maintain component encapsulation. Similarly, if client-specific information is needed to obtain the 'right' information, for example if it maintains sessions with its clients, this information can be passed to the component as a CONTEXT OBJECT (416).

Dynamic Invocation Interface *

When specifying a REFLECTION (197) architecture, the root functionality of an EXTENSION INTERFACE (284), a METHODS FOR STATES (469) arrangement, or a CONTAINER (488) ...

... we may need to allow access to the functionality of a component without knowing or using any of its statically typed interfaces.

A component may need to support calls of its methods outside the declared and enumerated protocol of an explicit interface. Such openness is needed when clients have to invoke additional capabilities on the component that cannot necessarily be known by the component's client in advance.

A component may be loaded dynamically into a framework environment, such as a user-interface component in a client, a business-logic component on a server, or a set of test cases in an automated testing tool. The loaded component can support a variety of methods suitable for its task, but not specifically relevant to its calling framework—except that the framework must be aware of the methods and be able to forward events or translate calls to them.

In principle, the features exported by the component may be unbounded, such as the many possible names of test cases a component may offer. Alternatively, features may form a coherent model, but not one for which a generic framework would be specialized. For example, user-interface controls can choose to support only a handful of the events and properties picked up by a GUI framework. An EXPLICIT INTERFACE (281) can capture the specific detail of what is offered, but not necessarily in a way that such dynamic clients can use. An INTROSPECTIVE INTERFACE supports querying of methods, but not necessarily in a way that allows calling by dynamic clients.

Therefore:

Introduce an invocation interface for the component that allows clients to compose calls on the component dynamically. Methods are identified at runtime by strings, and arguments are passed

as generally typed collections. Keep the dynamic invocation interface separate from the component's 'operational' interfaces.

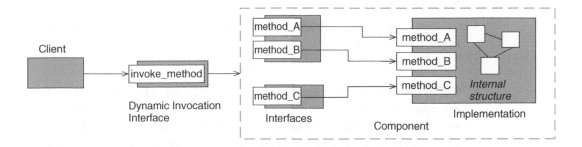

Calls on the component through a dynamic invocation interface are dispatched to specific methods on the component's declared interface.

◆◆◆

A DYNAMIC INVOCATION INTERFACE opens up the options available to a client when calling a component. Interface usage based on a dynamic protocol, rather than on static explicit interfaces, is open and non-intrusive, which enhances client application flexibility.

In addition to such benefits, however, with any form of late binding there is also the liability of late error detection for incorrect implementation or incorrect use of a protocol. It is important to establish a protocol for naming or annotating methods that components can follow, but this still offers no guarantee of correctness. It is possible for some checking tools to detect incorrect usage of dynamic interface invocation, but the options are more constrained than for statically checked invocations. Similarly, automated refactoring through dynamic invocations does not have the same guarantee of correctness as automated refactoring through statically checked interfaces.

The evolvability and flexibility of a dynamic invocation interface may also be associated with a performance overhead. Heavy use of reflection-based inspection and invocation in languages with statically checked type systems contrasts with the cheap execution of methods through declared interfaces. This overhead is less problematic in interpreted languages such as Smalltalk, Ruby, and Python, whose type systems and normal execution model are already based on a dynamic model.

Proxy **

When specifying an EXPLICIT INTERFACE (281) ...

... we often want to avoid accessing services of a component implementation directly.

Software systems consist of cooperating components: client components access and use the services provided by other components. It is often impractical, or even impossible, to access the services of a component directly, for example because we must first check the access rights of its clients, or because its implementation resides on a remote server.

Including 'housekeeping' functionality such as authorization *within* a component is undesirable, for two reasons. First, we might not need such functionality for every use of the component. Second, it mixes multiple orthogonal concerns within a single implementation, thereby making it hard to modify each concern separately and independently. A component's functionality should always be independent of any housekeeping activities. For similar reasons it is undesirable for component clients to perform this housekeeping functionality, since it would couple them tightly with the component's implementation. For example, if clients are to access a remote component directly, they become dependent on the component's location, as well as on the networking protocols that are used to access its functionality, which should be transparent to a component's clients.

Therefore:

Encapsulate all component housekeeping functionality within a separate surrogate of the component—the proxy—and let clients communicate only through the proxy rather than with the component itself.

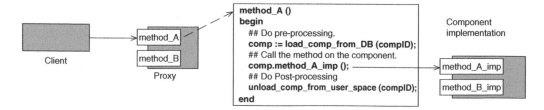

Design the proxy so it offers the same public interface as the component. When a client calls a method on the proxy, first perform all housekeeping preprocessing that must be done before forwarding the client's request to the 'real' component, then let the proxy call the corresponding method on the component. When control flow returns, first perform all necessary housekeeping postprocessing before returning any results of the method to the client.

A PROXY frees both the client and the component from implementing component-specific housekeeping functionality. It is also transparent to clients whether they are connected with the component or its proxy, because both publish an identical interface. The primary liabilities of a proxy are the hidden costs it can introduce for clients, although for many uses these costs are negligible compared to the execution time of the component's services.

There are many types of proxy [POSA1]. A CLIENT PROXY (240) shields the clients of a remote component from network addresses and IPC protocols to enable location independence within a distributed system: clients can use the client proxy as if it were a local component. A BUSINESS DELEGATE (292) goes one step further: it shields clients from all IPC, as well as locating remote components, load balancing when multiple component instances are available in a distributed application, and handling of specific networking errors. A THREAD-SAFE INTERFACE (384) is a proxy that serializes access to concurrent components transparently for both the client and the components. A COUNTING HANDLE (522) is normally expressed as a proxy that helps to access the functionality of shared heap objects whose lifetime must be managed explicitly by an application, to avoid memory leaks when the object is no longer used. A VIRTUAL PROXY (497) loads or creates an expensive component on demand and may delete it from memory after use. Finally, a FIREWALL PROXY (349) protects a software system from specific types of external attack.

If it is impossible or impractical to provide the proxy with an interface identical to that of the represented component, implement an OBJECT ADAPTER (438) that maps between the two interfaces.

Business Delegate **

When specifying a BROKER-based (237) distribution infrastructure, an EXPLICIT INTERFACE (281) or PROXY (290), or a REPLICATED COMPONENT GROUP (326) ...

... we must often consider that a component is, or can be, accessed from another address space.

Due to performance and reliability properties of networks, accessing remote components differs significantly from accessing local components. Ideally, however, clients should not need to care whether the components they use are collocated or remote.

An invocation across a network involves specific infrastructure tasks, such as retrieving the location of the remote component, error handling, and load balancing. Many of these tasks are unnecessary for collocated components. If clients depended on specific locations of components, or even on their remoteness, they would have to perform these tasks themselves, which would mix networking code with domain-specific code and increase application complexity. Moreover, clients would need to be modified if the location of components they used changed, for example due to fault recovery or load balancing. Consequently, client code should be as independent of the location and plumbing support of invoked components as possible.

Therefore:

Introduce a business delegate for each remote component that can be created, used, and disposed of like a collocated component, and whose interface is identical to that of the component it represents. Let the business delegate perform all networking tasks transparently for clients using the component.

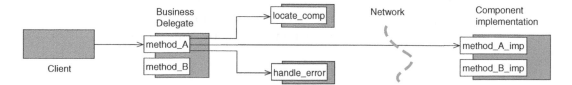

On creation or access by a client, the business delegate locates the remote component it represents. Subsequent method calls on the business delegate are forwarded to the remote component using that location information. In addition, the business delegate handles errors that can occur when communicating with the remote component. If multiple instances of the component are deployed, the business delegate can also perform load balancing before issuing a request to a specific component instance. A business delegate is also an ideal access point for system management functionality, to monitor and control all client-side communication and interaction with the remote component.

A BUSINESS DELEGATES supports location-independent component invocation in a distributed system: networking tasks and issues are hidden from the delegate's clients. In addition, each business delegate follows the same lifetime and usage protocol as components collocated with its clients: it can be created and disposed of via constructors and destructors or garbage collection, and it can be called via 'ordinary' method invocation. The primary liability of a business delegate is the hidden cost it can introduce for clients, though for most usage scenarios this cost is negligible compared to the execution time of the business delegate's primary responsibilities.

Typically, a business delegate uses a LOOKUP (495) service to retrieve the location of one or more instances of the remote component it represents. The access to a specific remote component instance is often encapsulated inside a CLIENT PROXY (240), which shields the business delegate from the details of the networking protocol used to access the instance. LAZY ACQUISITION (507) helps to defer connection to the represented component to the time when it is first accessed by a client calling the business delegate.

If calling the remote component returns a REMOTING ERROR [VKZ04], the business delegate can take appropriate action to resolve the error before it signals a failure to clients. For example, if the connection to the component breaks, the business delegate can try to re-establish the connection and try to issue the call again. Similarly, if a specific component instance is overloaded, the business delegate can try calling a more lightly loaded instance of the same component.

Facade **

When developing a Broker (237), an Explicit Interface (281), a Whole-Part (317) structure, or a Component Configurator (490) . . .

. . . we must sometimes access a group of components that together provide a broad service to their clients.

Complex services are often provided by a group of components, each of which can offer its own self-contained services to clients. If clients that want to invoke a complex service must maintain explicit relationships to each component in the group, however, they become dependent on the group's internal structure.

If this structure changes, all clients are affected. In addition, the more such dependencies exist, the greater the physical and logical complexity of the software system [Lak95]. Ideally, clients should have a single entry point to a group of related components that simplifies the invocation and execution of common tasks from the client's perspective. On the other hand, there could be clients that use only one specific component in the group. Forcing these clients to invoke methods on that component through a separate component entry point would introduce an unnecessary level of indirection, with corresponding performance penalties. In addition, there could be clients that want to execute specific, more sophisticated tasks on the component group, which require the means to integrate and invoke its components differently than in the common usage scenarios.

Therefore:

Specify a single point of access for the component group—the facade—that mediates client requests to the appropriate components in the group for common usage scenarios, but can be bypassed for specific, more sophisticated scenarios.

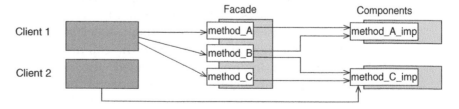

In addition to routing requests, the facade performs all necessary adaptation between the signatures of its published services and the interfaces of the 'protected' components. A facade can also aggregate features of different components to new, 'higher-level' services. Nevertheless, clients are not forced to call the components through the facade: direct access to each specific component is still possible.

Clients that call the component group through its FACADE are independent of the group's internal structure and relationships, so they are not affected when this structure changes. In addition, clients that want to access a specific component in the group can bypass the facade to call that part directly, which avoids performance penalties for such clients.

In a remote application setting, a facade can be deployed as a SERVICE GATEWAY [MS03] to the address spaces of its clients, or as a SESSION FACADE [ACM01] to the (server-side) address space of its component group. A SERVICE GATEWAY supports throughput and scalability. All overhead of deciding which component of the group to invoke, as well as all adaptation of requests on the facade to the interfaces of the corresponding components, is located on the client side. The downside of a SERVICE GATEWAY is that each component in the group is accessed remotely, which can increase the networking overhead, as well as the structural complexity of a distributed application.

A SESSION FACADE avoids these penalties: remote clients can access the component group only via its facade. The more frequently clients access the component, however, and the more routing and adaptation overhead is necessary to mediate requests appropriately to the corresponding components in the group, the more a SESSION FACADE can become a performance and scalability bottleneck.

A GATEWAY [Fow03a] is another form of FACADE, which represents an access point to an external system used by an application. The application thus becomes independent of the specific interfaces of the external system and also of its internal structure. A TRANSFER OBJECT ASSEMBLER [ACM01] is a FACADE that combines results received from several components into an aggregated result that can be returned wholesale to the clients of the components.

Combined Method **

When specifying an EXPLICIT INTERFACE (281) or an ITERATOR (298) ...

... we often need to invoke multiple methods on a component together and in the same order.

Clients often must invoke multiple methods on a component in the same order to perform a specific task. From a client's perspective, however, it is tedious and error-prone to call the method sequence explicitly each time it wants to execute the task on the component.

Repeating the same method call sequence across an entire application makes it harder to develop, understand, and maintain. It is easy to call the methods in the wrong order, forget to call a specific method, or pass incorrect parameters to them. Changes to the calling order, or changes to the signatures of the called methods, affects all the code executing the method sequence.

Additional problems arise in distributed and concurrent systems in which each remote call incurs networking overhead, and a sequence of calls on a mutable component may not have the desired outcome if the component is shared across threads, even if each individual method is safe against race conditions. Moreover, if any of the methods in the sequence fails, it is the responsibility of the calling client to handle this failure and to undo or roll-back the changes on the component caused by method calls prior to the one that failed.

Therefore:

Combine methods that must be, or commonly are, executed together on a component into a single method.

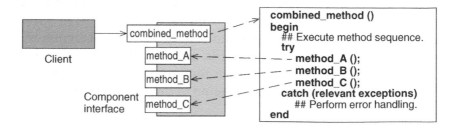

Clients that want to execute the method sequence issue a request to the combined method, which then executes that sequence on behalf of the clients. In addition, the implementation of the combined method handles all necessary distribution, concurrency, and failure management aspects associated with invoking the method sequence.

Using a COMBINED METHOD makes the interface of a component or an object more expressive and cohesive, because it reflects common use. Similarly, the robustness of the application improves, because there is only one place, rather than many, where the method sequence is programmed and failures are handled. Consequently, from a client's perspective, the component or object becomes easier to use.

Distribution overhead also occurs only once for calls to a combined method, as it replaces many remote calls by a single one. Similarly, concurrency hazards that can result from non-determinism are eliminated, because the entire calling sequence is synchronized, rather than each individual method call. Finally, failure handling and recovery strategies are encapsulated within the combined method, leading to a more transaction-like style of method design: either the entire sequence is executed successfully, with corresponding effects on the component or object, or, if any method in the sequence fails, it appears to clients as if the entire sequence was not executed at all, leaving the component or object unchanged.

A combined method that is based on querying or setting a group of values at once can be expressed with a DATA TRANSFER OBJECT (418). If the access is to traverse all the elements of an aggregate, such as a collection, a BATCH METHOD (302) can be seen as a generalization of COMBINED METHOD, in which, instead of combining calls to different methods on an object, it is the whole loop and access of successive elements of the target object that is folded into a single call.

Iterator **

When specifying EXPLICIT INTERFACE (281), ENUMERATION METHOD (300), COMPOSITE (319), or OBJECT MANAGER (492) ...

... we often need to access elements of an aggregate object sequentially without exposing its underlying structure.

♦♦♦

Clients often want to traverse elements that are encapsulated within an aggregate, such as the elements maintained by a collection. Clients may not wish, however, to depend on the aggregate's internal structure to access components of interest, nor do aggregates want to expose their internal structure to clients.

To complicate matters, clients often need to traverse the components in a specific order that best fits their needs. Multiple clients may also want to access the aggregate simultaneously, and it is even possible that a single (multi-threaded) client needs to run multiple simultaneous traversals. Supporting multiple traversal strategies as well as simultaneous traversal directly within the aggregate, however, would complicate its internal structure. For example, the aggregate must maintain the concrete state of each active traversal within a separate session. Developers would also be distracted from realizing the aggregate's domain responsibility.

Therefore:

Objectify the strategy to access and traverse the components maintained by the aggregate into a separate iterator component. Let this iterator be the only means for clients to access the component, and allow the iterator access to the representation of the aggregate necessary for it to carry out the traversal.

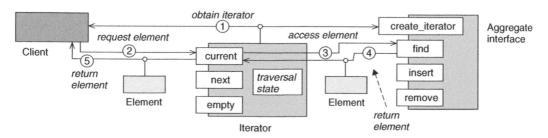

Clients that want to traverse the aggregate's contained elements must first obtain an iterator from the aggregate. Clients can then use this iterator to access the elements in sequence.

An ITERATOR preserves the encapsulation of the aggregate and keeps clients independent of its internal structure. In addition, the reification of access and traversal strategies allows multiple clients to maintain their own traversal over the aggregate's content, and single clients to run several independent traversals simultaneously. An ITERATOR arrangement is however most suitable in single-process, single-threaded component deployments.

A common ITERATOR arrangement is based on an abstract iterator that is declared as an EXPLICIT INTERFACE (281) for accessing and traversing components maintained by the aggregate. Concrete iterators derive from or implement this interface to realize particular access and traversal strategies, such as breadth-first or depth-first for tree-like hierarchies. Such a design helps to encapsulate different traversal strategies behind a uniform interface, as well as integrating new or evolving existing iterator types without modification to the existing iterator management infrastructure within the aggregate.

A COMBINED METHOD (296) on the iterator's interface avoids subtle race conditions when accessing the aggregate via iterators running in separate threads. Similarly, a BATCH METHOD (302) on the iterator's interface that supports 'chunky' access to the aggregate's elements avoids performance penalties and unnecessary network load when the iterator is remote to the aggregate.

Provide the aggregate's interface with a FACTORY METHOD (529) and a DISPOSAL METHOD (531) to create and dispose of concrete iterators on client request. Both methods separate and encapsulate the lifetime control of iterators behind a common interface, and separate it from the aggregate's domain logic. If the aggregate's internal structure can be modified during a traversal, there may be a need for robust iterators. Robustness can be achieved with an OBSERVER (405) arrangement: the aggregate plays the role of a subject that notifies all active iterators whenever its internal structure changes, such as on the deletion of an aggregated component [Kof04].

Enumeration Method **

Within an EXPLICIT INTERFACE (281), BATCH METHOD (302), or OBJECT MANAGER (492) . . .

. . . we may want to iterate over the elements of an aggregate component, invoking an action on each element.

Some types of aggregate components, such as graphs or trees, have representations that do not conveniently support ITERATOR-based traversal. Similarly, using an ITERATOR approach to access the elements of an aggregate that is shared between threads can incur unnecessary overhead from repeated locking. Remote aggregate access incurs an even greater overhead. It must be possible, however, to access the elements of the aggregate efficiently to execute actions on them.

To further complicate matters, there are times when an aggregate requires pre- and post-iteration code to be executed before and after the traversal. The most obvious and common case is synchronization against threaded interruption. Expecting the clients of the aggregate to write this code themselves is tedious and error-prone. In the specific case of Java thread synchronization in distributed systems, an external synchronized block is problematic, because it can give you the illusion of safety without any of the actual safety [Hen01c].

Therefore:

Bring the iteration inside the aggregate and encapsulate it in a single enumeration method that is responsible for complete traversal. Pass the task of the loop—the action to be executed on each element of the aggregate—as an argument to the enumeration method, and apply it to each element in turn.

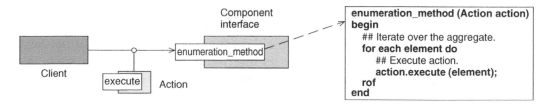

In contrast to an Iterator approach, Enumeration Method performs a complete traversal, including the invocation of an action on each element of the traversed aggregate, wholesale, rather than in many separate bits and pieces.

In distributed and networked environment, reducing many remote calls to a single Enumeration Method improves performance, incurs less network errors, and saves precious bandwidth. The key to these benefits is that an Enumeration Method realizes the principle of inversion of control—it is not the client that controls the iteration, but the aggregate itself. In addition, an Enumeration Method applies any of the relevant pre- and post-iteration activities on the aggregate itself, such as synchronization, performing the loop in between. This approach allows the aggregate to keep control of how it behaves: its design becomes more complete, explicit, encapsulated, and self-contained.

The action passed to an enumeration method is a Command object (358), or some kind of method reference such as a function pointer in C++ or a delegate in C#. Such a design allows the provision of a 'generic' enumeration method for the aggregate, to which clients can pass arbitrary actions. However, one liability can work against it for remote access. For the inversion of control to be efficient, calls to the Command must be local rather than remote. This means that the Command object must be copied from the client to the server, and should not be accessed indirectly as a remote object. This constraint also has implications for the Command's code, which must also be local at the point of call, either already present or transferred on the first call. Such code transfer implies that this pattern does not apply in heterogeneous systems. Enumeration methods are, however, particularly effective in multi-threaded situations. A Batch Method may be more suitable in remote cases.

A Visitor (447) can help an enumeration method to simplify the traversal of non-linear aggregate structures such as graphs without becoming dependent on the structure. Alternatively, if the aggregate's structure is linear, such as in a double-linked list, an Iterator (298) can help to achieve this independence.

Batch Method **

Within an EXPLICIT INTERFACE (281), ITERATOR (298), or OBJECT MANAGER (492) . . .

. . . we may need to perform bulk accesses on an aggregate component.

Clients sometimes perform bulk accesses on an aggregate component, for example to retrieve all elements in a collection that meet certain properties. If access to the aggregate is expensive, for example because it is remote or concurrent, accessing it separately for each element can incur significant performance penalties and concurrency overhead.

If the aggregate is remote, each access incurs latency and jitter, decreases the available network bandwidth, and introduces additional points of failure. If the aggregate is a concurrent component, synchronization and thread management overhead must be added to the cost of each access. Similarly, any other per-call housekeeping code, such as for authorization, further decreases performance. Nevertheless, it must be possible to perform bulk accesses to an aggregate efficiently and without interruption.

Therefore:

Define a single batch method that performs the action on the aggregate repeatedly. The method is declared to take all the arguments for each execution of the action, for example via an array or a collection, and to return results by similar means.

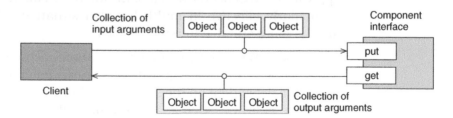

A batch method folds repetition into a data structure, rather than a loop within the client, so that looping is performed before or after the method call, in preparation or follow-up respectively.

A BATCH METHOD reduces the cost of accessing the aggregate to a single access or a few 'chunked' accesses. In distributed systems this can significantly improve performance, incur less network errors, and save precious bandwidth. Although by using a BATCH METHOD each access to the aggregate becomes more expensive, the overall cost for bulk accesses has been reduced. Bulk accesses can also be synchronized as appropriate within the method call.

The trade-off in complexity is that a batch method performs significantly more housekeeping to set up and work with the results of the call, and requires more intermediate data structures to pass arguments and receive results. The higher are the costs for networking, concurrency, and other per-call housekeeping, however, the more affordable this overhead becomes. BATCH METHOD can be seen as a generalization of COMBINED METHOD, in which a whole loop traversal is folded into the target, not simply a short sequence of different methods.

Simplistically, the parameters of a batch method are either *in* or *out*, and these may be expressed as simple collections, such as arrays of values or name–value pairs, or even variable argument lists, assuming appropriate type-safe language support exists. *In* parameters list elements that are to be sent from the caller to the aggregate, such as elements to add or keys to query. *Out* parameters, possibly expressed as return values, list results returned from the aggregate, such as found values.

Typically, batch methods are specific rather than general. That is, they are named after a particular action and their arguments reflect the inputs and results directly. For example, finding values that match keys can be expressed as a single method. However, if more generalization is required, further parameters that control the encapsulated loop are needed. Examples finding all entries that are older than a particular date, or greater than a particular value. The most generalization that is possible is to pass in a predicate or some control code in the form of a COMMAND object (412), which makes a BATCH METHOD more like an ENUMERATION METHOD (300), and with similar liabilities in a distributed environment.

13 Component Partitioning

Anna Buschmann, partitioning a Lego building
© Frank Buschmann

Components are the implementation building blocks that provide
well-defined services to their clients. How these services are realized
is generally of no interest to the clients. While this black-box view is
beneficial for component users, component developers cannot ignore
the need for a internal component design. This chapter, therefore,
presents six patterns that help to structure the implementation of
a component. The focus of these patterns is on general component
decomposition and the support for various component deployment
scenarios in a distributed system.

Component-based software development is a key technology in modern software construction. The core idea is that software can be composed of well-defined modular building blocks, each providing a specific, coherent, and self-contained service through an interface. A defining characteristic of components and their composability is that they are based on a strong form of encapsulation and a range of choices concerning application binding time and location. This strong encapsulation of implementation details yields the two primary benefits of component-based software development:

- *Productivity.* If the components that are used in the development of an application already exist or can be purchased as third party products, this can markedly improve the productivity of software development.

- *Quality.* (Re-)using existing components with a well-established pedigree can improve software quality. Such components are tested, debugged, and tuned, and developers know and can rely on their properties.

Providing an appropriate component realization, one that keeps its implementation details well-encapsulated, can however be hard in practice, due to the following challenges:

- *Component partitioning.* From an outside view, a component is a monolithic building block that provides well-defined services to its clients. Such a view is impractical, however, from a component-internal and development perspective. Large components in particular would be hard to understand, evolve, and maintain, and their implementation would be likely to involve a big chunk of 'spaghetti' code. To support the internal qualities of a component, such as understandability and maintainability, it is thus necessary to partition it into more fine-grained structures. Achieving the right partitioning can however be a challenge: the component's constituent parts, and their relationships and interactions, should portray the component's main responsibility well, but each specific part by itself should also be semantically meaningful to, and maintainable, by the programmer.

- *Component quality.* Although clients are largely uninterested in the specific implementation of the components they use, they care about the functional behavior and operational quality of the services they invoke on these components—basic functionality, performance, scalability, throughput, and so on. Achieving the required quality of service is not just a matter of sophisticated algorithms and optimized code, it is also strongly influenced by the internal component design.

- *Component flexibility.* To serve a wide range of applications, a component must model its respective application domain properly. Its internal structure must also support specific tactical design aspects, such as adaptability to selected customer-specific requirements, extensibility with new features, and portability to new platforms. These requirements necessitate a thoughtful analysis of component responsibilities, such as what remains invariant in its supported usage scenarios, and what can vary.

- *Distribution of component functionality.* By definition, a component forms a particular logical or functional unit or self-contained entity [Szy02]. Extending this definition to distributed systems, each component also needs a defined home: it resides at one particular network node. Such a monolithic view, however, is not always feasible, and particularly not if (remote) clients expect a high quality of service from the components they use, for example in performance, availability, or scalability.

In such situations it is often beneficial to partition a component into a group of smaller, more specialized components, and let these smaller components reside at different network nodes. Alternatively, we could deploy multiple instances of the component within the system. To their clients, however, such distributed component groups should still appear to be cohesive units, offering a single entry point and a set of meaningful services. Preserving this view requires the cooperation within distributed component groups to be conducted explicitly via appropriate mechanisms and protocols.

- *Concurrency and parallelism within a component implementation.* Distributed systems and multi-core processors offer the possibility of executing independent parts of a component's implementation in parallel, which yields better performance of a single invocation and supports the component's general scalability and through-put. Taking advantage of the available parallelism in a network or on a computer, however, requires an appropriate partitioning of the component's implementation into smaller parts that are coordinated appropriately to allow its functions to execute in parallel, or such that the execution of long-duration functions can be parallelized.

Many patterns support the resolution of the challenges described above. Some of these patterns are domain-specific, in particular patterns that help to define a component's concrete responsibilities. Describing *all* these patterns explicitly would exceed the scope of our pattern language for distributed computing, so instead we refer to the appropriate body of literature, such as [Fow97] [PLoPD1] [PLoPD2] [PLoPD3] [PLoPD4] [PLoPD5] [Ris01]. Patterns that support the construction of adaptable and extensible components are presented separately in Chapter 18, *Adaptation and Extension*: the topic of adaptation and extension is relevant for many parts of a distributed system, not only component implementations. Similarly, patterns that support concurrent execution are described in Chapter 15, *Concurrency*.

This chapter focuses solely on patterns that help to partition components and help to resolve the challenges related to component distribution. There are six such patterns in our pattern language:

> The ENCAPSULATED IMPLEMENTATION pattern (313) addresses the fundamental and typical design of a component so that it can fulfill its interface's contractual obligations without leaking its implementation assumptions through its interface, and by minimizing the assumptions that are exposed as configuration and creation options.

The WHOLE-PART pattern (317) [POSA1] helps in composing component objects from multiple distinct and self-contained internal objects. An aggregate encapsulates the component object's constituent parts, organizes their collaboration, and provides a common interface to its functionality. Clients cannot directly access the parts: they only see the functionality offered by the aggregate.

The COMPOSITE pattern (319) [GoF95] defines a partitioning for component objects representing whole-part hierarchies composed of similar types of object. Clients can treat individual objects and compositions of objects uniformly.

The MASTER-SLAVE pattern (321) [POSA1] supports fault tolerance, parallel computation, and computational accuracy. A master component distributes work to a group of slave components and computes a final result from the results returned by the slaves.

The HALF-OBJECT PLUS PROTOCOL pattern (324) [Mes95] structures logical objects that are used in multiple address spaces into two or more cooperating 'half-objects.' Each half-object implements a specific part of the component's functionality. Half-objects coordinate their execution via synchronization protocols.

The REPLICATED COMPONENT GROUP pattern (326) [Maf96] provides fault-tolerance through client-transparent component replication. Replicated component implementations reside at different network nodes and together form a component group. Clients interact with the component group via a single point of access as if it were one logical component

The ENCAPSULATED IMPLEMENTATION pattern serves as the general integration point for all component partitioning patterns in our language, be they described in this chapter, in other chapters, or in other sources. In particular, ENCAPSULATED IMPLEMENTATION addresses the problem of how to realize the concrete responsibilities of a component appropriately, but without compromising operational qualities such as performance, scalability, availability, and extensibility. It is thus the key pattern to start with when specifying a concrete component realization.

The diagram below outlines how Encapsulated Implementation is connected with our pattern language for distributed computing and how it integrates the many patterns that support high-quality component partitioning and realization.

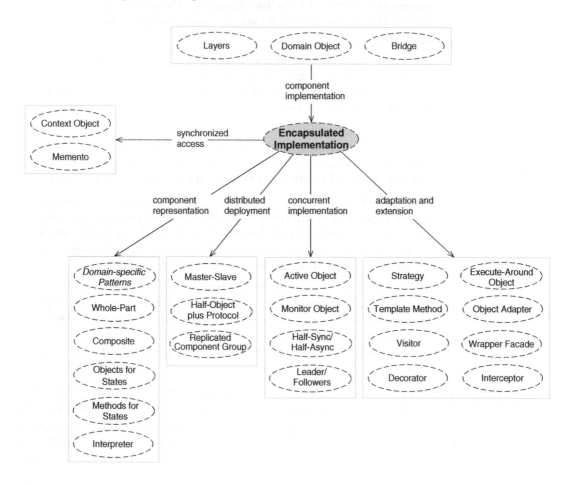

The next two patterns in this chapter, WHOLE-PART and COMPOSITE, define ways of organizing whole-part hierarchies of objects within a component. Their integration into our pattern language for distributed computing is shown in the following diagram.

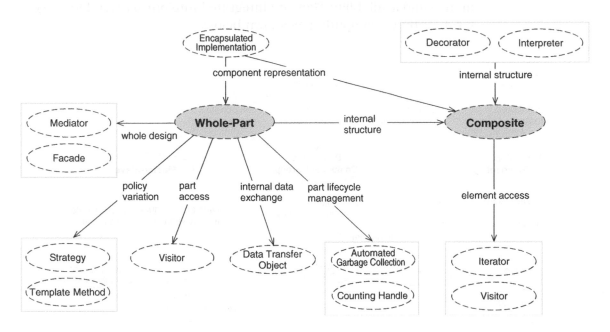

In general, COMPOSITE is a specific, yet common and widely-used, form of WHOLE-PART. The key difference between the two patterns is that WHOLE-PART organizes hierarchies of completely distinct objects, whereas COMPOSITE constitutes hierarchies of objects with similar or even identical responsibilities, interfaces, and properties.

The three remaining patterns, MASTER-SLAVE, HALF-OBJECT PLUS PROTOCOL, and REPLICATED COMPONENT GROUP, describe component partitionings that are suitable for distributed deployment so that a component can maximize its operational qualities, such as performance and availability They are integrated into our pattern language for distributed computing as shown below.

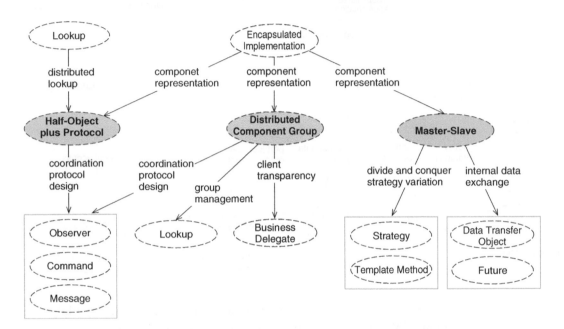

Encapsulated Implementation **

When developing a Layers (185) architecture, an application's Domain Objects (208), a Bridge (436) arrangement, or generally when designing components for a component-based system . . .

. . . a significant decision involves the realization of component implementations against component interfaces.

A component offers its services through interfaces that define its usage protocols, published functionality, and quality of service properties. However, an interface is only a promise: a component must provide fulfillment. Thus a component implementation is often subjected to assumptions, considerations, and constraints that cannot be exposed through its interface.

Regardless of the contract defined by a component's interface, its realization is exposed to constraints and requirements that are of little interest for component users, but are crucial in fulfilling the contract. For example, the component may need to be prepared for distributed deployment without decreasing its performance and throughput properties. Or, depending on its concrete usage and deployment scenarios, different algorithms, additional functionality, or additional quality properties may be required, such as different tax calculation algorithms, a user-specific business activity, or stronger security measures. Finally, almost all components are subject to evolution; their implementation can change over time. Nevertheless, clients should be shielded from all these aspects—they are only interested in the contract, not in how it is fulfilled.

Therefore:

Ensure that all component implementation details remain hidden behind its interfaces to shield clients from representation choices that may change during the lifetime of an application, or are dependent on the component's specific deployment.

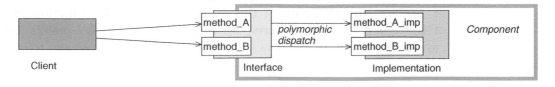

A component's client cannot programmatically assume more than is exposed through its official interface, which supports the component implementor's ability to change the implementation without breaking clients.

A component implementation that respects the boundary defined by its interfaces ensures that the dependency of its clients is on its interface, its whole interface, and nothing but its interface. The ENCAPSULATED IMPLEMENTATION is free to evolve, while preserving the stability of its clients. Developers of client code are still presented with a simple and stable interface to use.

The interface boundary seals the component implementation from its environment, and vice versa, but it is possible that the component has a dependency on some features of its calling environment. To avoid introducing a reverse dependency, pass CONTEXT OBJECTS (416) from the caller to the component when such information or behavior is needed. A component may also need to pass out implementation-dependent state to the client for later use with respect to the component, for example a position in a traversal or a callback handler for a registered event of interest. In this case, preserve the component's encapsulation by returning a MEMENTO (414).

In general, an ENCAPSULATED IMPLEMENTATION should provide a well-encapsulated software representation of the component's specific functional responsibilities. Domain-specific patterns can support the creation of this representation, such as those for health care, corporate finance, telecommunication, and public transportation applications [Fow97] [Ris01] [PLoPD1] [PLoPD2] [PLoPD3] [PLoPD4] [PLoPD5].

Sometimes the representation of the component's functionality can also be defined on the basis of more general patterns that are not bound to a specific (application) domain. For example, components that represent a hierarchy of elements can be realized using a WHOLE-PART (317) or COMPOSITE (319) design, dependent on how distinct or uniform the elements of the hierarchy are. If the functionality of the component is centered on a state machine, its realization can be based on an OBJECTS FOR STATES (467) or METHODS FOR STATES

(469) design, dependent on the size of the state machine and the amount of data and context information shared between states. If the component's responsibility is to interpret structured files or sentences of a given language, such as in a parser, an INTERPRETER (442) design could be considered as its fundamental structure.

A key concern of all ENCAPSULATED IMPLEMENTATIONS is fulfilling the operational qualities specified in the component's contract: performance, scalability, and so forth. Providing the 'right' structure and behavior is simply not enough to ensure a component's usability and acceptance. Two techniques that help in achieving key operational qualities are distribution and concurrency.

Deploying an ENCAPSULATED IMPLEMENTATION to multiple hosts in a distributed system allows a component to take advantage of the resources available in the entire network, rather than only of those available on a single network node. The more resources are available, the better the component's operational quality. Which particular qualities can be supported by distributed deployment depends on the chosen component partitioning. MASTER-SLAVE (321), HALF-OBJECT PLUS PROTOCOL (324), and REPLICATED COMPONENT GROUP (326) offer different trade-offs for the support of performance, availability, scalability, fault tolerance, and computational accuracy.

A concurrent ENCAPSULATED IMPLEMENTATION impacts the operational qualities of a component—specifically its performance and throughput—because multiple client requests can be handled and processed simultaneously. An ACTIVE OBJECT (365) arrangement supports the implementation of components in their own set of threads, whereas a MONITOR OBJECT (368) helps in realizing components that are collocated within their client threads. HALF-SYNC/HALF-ASYNC (359) and LEADER/FOLLOWERS (362) configurations are most suitable for components that process network I/O.

However, all the above deployment and concurrency models come with certain costs, which are mainly due to duplicated functionality, increased resource usage, more intricate implementation, and the coordination between the concurrent parts of the ENCAPSULATED IMPLEMENTATION or other distributed components. Before introducing any of these models, it is important to assess whether their costs outweigh their benefits.

Another key concern for almost all ENCAPSULATED IMPLEMENTATIONS is support for evolution, extension, and adaptation. These developmental qualities enable the effective use of components within different application deployments and variants, and also their reuse within completely different applications.

STRATEGIES (455) and TEMPLATE METHODS (453), for example, support the separation of variant from invariant behavior, STRATEGY by using delegation, and TEMPLATE METHOD by inheritance. In contrast, a VISITOR (447) allows functionality to be added to an ENCAPSULATED IMPLEMENTATION that was not envisioned during its original development. The control flow inside a component can be extended by INTERCEPTORS (444), DECORATORS (472) and, if C++ is used to realize the ENCAPSULATED IMPLEMENTATION, EXECUTE-AROUND OBJECTS (451). INTERCEPTORS can inject out-of-band behavior into a function's control flow, whereas DECORATORS help in wrapping a function with specialized behavior that is to be executed before or after a function. An EXECUTE-AROUND OBJECT is similar in this respect to a DECORATOR: it allows additional functionality to be executed before or after a sequence of statements in an exception-safe manner, which makes it a preferred C++ idiom for resource acquisition and release. Finally, OBJECT ADAPTERS (438) and WRAPPER FACADES (459) support the integration of an ENCAPSULATED IMPLEMENTATION with its environment by adapting the *provided* interfaces of components, libraries, and operating systems to those *expected* or *required* by the ENCAPSULATED IMPLEMENTATION. The difference between the two design options is that OBJECT ADAPTER does not hide the adapted interfaces, which are still accessible by the ENCAPSULATED IMPLEMENTATION, whereas in a WRAPPER FACADE arrangement these interfaces are fully sealed.

While a certain degree of flexibility is necessary to use an ENCAPSULATED IMPLEMENTATION effectively in concrete applications, too much flexibility could result in exactly the opposite: a component that is so flexible that it is of no use at all [Bus03]. It is thus important that only mandatory variability is supported by an ENCAPSULATED IMPLEMENTATION, not all 'nice-to-have' variability. The mandatory variability for a component can be identified with the help of appropriate methods, such as *Open Implementation Analysis and Design* [KLLM95], *Commonality/Variability Analysis* [Cope98], or *Feature Modeling* [CzEi02].

Whole-Part **

When partitioning an ENCAPSULATED IMPLEMENTATION (313) ...

... at times we need to, or are able to, decompose complex component objects into several smaller parts.

Some component objects aggregate so much functionality that it is impractical to realize them as monolithic units. Instead, they should be partitioned into smaller parts with defined responsibilities. However, despite the need for partitioning, clients typically do not want to deal with such a community of smaller parts.

In particular, the component should not allow direct access to its constituent parts, because in general they do not provide services that are meaningful for its clients. In addition, clients should not be affected if the partitioning of these parts is changed. On the other hand, it is often necessary to design the parts so that they are also usable elsewhere, which requires avoiding tight dependencies of the parts on specific components, because each component will probably combine the parts differently, or with other parts.

Therefore:

Partition the component object into a whole that encapsulates and orchestrates multiple independent parts, and define an interface for the whole that is the only means to access the component's functionality.

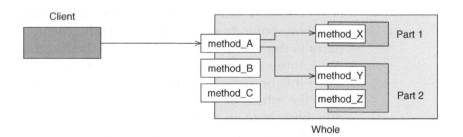

The parts implement self-contained *entities* or *mechanisms* from which higher-level functionality can be composed. The whole, in contrast, represents an aggregate that implements a *policy* that uses the functionality offered by the parts to provide the required component behavior. When a client calls a method on the whole, the method executes its policy, using one or more parts encapsulated by the whole to realize its behavior.

A WHOLE-PART design prevents clients from accessing any of the aggregate's constituent parts directly, thus allowing it to appear as a self-contained semantic unit. The strict separation of policies from mechanisms within a WHOLE-PART arrangement enables the aggregate to combine and use its constituent parts transparently for both its clients and parts, as well as to reuse the parts within other aggregate components.

There are many ways to implement a particular WHOLE-PART structure. The whole is often a MEDIATOR (410) or a FACADE (294), and the parts are independent components by themselves. Functionality that traverses multiple parts in a specific order can be implemented as a VISITOR (447), which avoids this functionality being scattered across the parts. Finally, a part can also be a WHOLE-PART arrangement by itself, which leads to recursive WHOLE-PART structures. The data exchanged between the whole and its parts is often encapsulated within DATA TRANSFER OBJECTS (418), which avoids dependencies of the whole on specific data representations, and increases the reusability of parts in other WHOLE-PART arrangements.

Two important issues to consider when realizing a WHOLE-PART structure are the sharing and lifecycle management of parts. In many arrangements, such as a representation of a drive in a factory process control system, parts are neither shared with other wholes, nor are they visible from outside the arrangement. The lifecycle of the parts is thus bound to the lifecycle of their aggregating whole—they come into existence when the whole is created, and cease to exist when it is destroyed. In other arrangements, parts can also live outside the whole or can be shared among several wholes, such as attachments to an e-mail. Such parts must be able to manage their lifecycle themselves, including all constraints that apply when being bound to a whole or set of wholes. In environments that do not support AUTOMATED GARBAGE COLLECTION (517), COUNTING HANDLES (522) can help in managing the lifetime of independent and shared parts.

Composite **

When implementing an ENCAPSULATED IMPLEMENTATION (313), or when realizing an INTERPRETER (442) configuration ...

... we sometimes need to treat atomic elements and aggregate elements of a whole-part hierarchy uniformly.

Sometimes whole-part hierarchies are recursively composed of objects that all support the same interface. However, clients are often uninterested in either the concrete arrangement or the recursive nature of the structure—instead they want to use, and act on, the whole-part hierarchy as if it were a single entity.

Nevertheless, within the whole-part arrangement the hierarchical structure must often be preserved. For example, it may represent a corresponding hierarchy in an application domain, such as a network or warehouse topology, or a hierarchical file system. To complicate matters, the transparency of the hierarchy to clients should not break if its constituent objects are rearranged, for example when moving a directory or file in a file system structure to another directory or volume. In addition, an extension of the hierarchy with new object types that implement the common interface should have minimal effect on other types in the hierarchy. For example, the hierarchy should remain stable when extending a file system structure with a recycle bin or a new file type.

Therefore:

Declare a component interface that specifies the functionality common to all objects in the whole-part hierarchy, and subclass from this interface to realize the hierarchy's specific objects and their recursive composition.

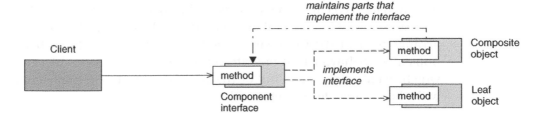

There are two types of object in a Composite hierarchy: leaves and composites. *Leaf* objects realize behavior for atomic entities that cannot be decomposed, such as concrete file types. *Composite* objects define behavior for aggregates in the hierarchy and the functionality to maintain multiple objects that support the shared interface, such as volumes and directories in a file system.

Clients refer to and manipulate the aggregate through the component interface. If the interface represents a leaf, the request is executed by the leaf's implementation. In contrast, if the interface represents a composite, the request is forwarded to one or more of its children, which execute the request if they are leaves, or forward the request recursively to their own children if they are composites. In addition, the composite can perform its own activities before and after forwarding the request to any aggregated component. Results of an invocation on the component interface are returned back along the recursive call chain of composites and leafs.

A Composite design supports the representation of arbitrary whole-part hierarchies of objects that implement the component interface. This hierarchy is transparent to clients: they only see objects that support a uniform contract. In addition, the hierarchy is easy to evolve: an extension or rearrangement of an existing Composite configuration does not require modification of existing leaves and composites. On the other hand, a Composite design is only useful if all objects in the whole-part hierarchy implement the same functionality. To hide the hierarchical nature of the Composite arrangement from clients, its component interface must accumulate all methods offered by its leaf and composite objects. The more diverse these functions are, the more the component interface becomes bloated with functions implemented only by few leaf and composite objects, making the interface useless for clients.

A composite typically accesses its children via an Iterator (298) or an Enumeration Method, which avoids dependencies on their concrete arrangement in the Composite structure. A Visitor (447) can help to implement behavior that operates on the entire Composite hierarchy, which avoids tight coupling of the functionality to be implemented with the strategy for traversing the object hierarchy.

Master-Slave *

When implementing an ENCAPSULATED IMPLEMENTATION (313) . . .

. . . we must sometimes provide increased performance, fault-tolerance, or result accuracy for a component implementation.

♦♦♦

Some components must meet high performance, fault-tolerance, or accuracy requirements, in particular if they are responsible for critical or complex activities, such as a monitoring service in a nuclear power plant control system, or a service for DNA analysis in a medical system. Addressing these requirements using more powerful computing resources can help, but such solutions may be too expensive, or simply insufficient.

For example, performance can be improved by optimized algorithms and faster hardware, but do not really help for NP-hard or NP-complete problems that operate on large amount of data, such as DNA analysis. Accuracy can be improved by algorithm and code verifications, but in the case of complex algorithms, such verifications are often barely possible, or offer the possibility of errors. Fault-tolerance can be improved by increasing the stability and robustness of code, but does not help in the case of failures in the component's hosting environment. Yet components are only useful if they meet their requirements and resolve these with reasonable cost.

Therefore:

Meet the performance, fault-tolerance, or accuracy requirements of the component via a 'divide and conquer' strategy. Split its services into independent subtasks that can be executed in parallel, and combine the partial results returned by these subtasks to provide the service's final result.

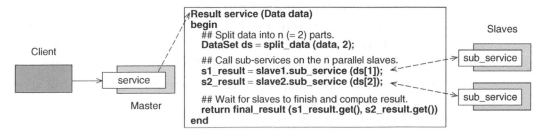

The component is partitioned into a master that implements a specific 'divide and conquer' strategy and serves as its access point for clients, and at least two slaves that realize the subtasks to be executed in parallel. When the master receives a client request, it splits the work to be done into as many parts as slaves are available, delegates the processing of each part to a separate slave, waits until all slaves finish their execution, and computes a final result from the partial results that the slaves return.

A MASTER-SLAVE design can significantly improve the performance of long-duration services due to the parallel execution of independent subtasks. For this reason, MASTER-SLAVE arrangements are specifically popular and beneficial for components deployed on multi-core processors [IBM06]. Other operational qualities supported by a MASTER-SLAVE configuration are fault tolerance, availability, and computational accuracy. Fault tolerance and availability is supported by enabling slaves to run as replicas, so that if one slave fails, others can continue to process requests and return results. Computational accuracy is supported by voting on the results of multiple slaves that all realize the same service, often using different algorithms.

As its downside, a MASTER-SLAVE configuration is only feasible for services that can be processed using a 'divide and conquer' strategy with parallel execution of subtasks. For example, if there is a high degree of independence between the data to be processed, it can be partitioned into multiple chunks of equal volume, and a set of slaves replicating the service's functionality then process these chunks. Operations on large or clustered databases fall into this category [DeGe04]. If the data cannot be divided, it may be possible to partition the service itself into multiple independent steps that can be executed in parallel by a set of slaves. Many algorithms on graphs belong to this category, in particular those for routing or collecting status information. If any form of meaningful service partitioning requires coordination and synchronization activities between the subtasks, a MASTER-SLAVE arrangement is probably inappropriate for addressing the component's performance, fault-tolerance, or accuracy requirements.

In a MASTER-SLAVE arrangement, the master acts as the central access point for clients and encapsulates the component's specific 'divide and conquer' strategy. This strategy is primarily determined by the intent of the MASTER-SLAVE arrangement. If, for example, the intent is performance, the master partitions the workload or data to process it into as many parts of identical volume as slaves are available, executes all slaves in parallel, and assembles the final result from the partial results that the slaves return. If the component's intent is to provide computational accuracy or fault tolerance, all slaves process the entire data. A voting strategy like '*n of m slaves must return the same result*' helps the master to determine the final result. A TEMPLATE METHOD (453) or STRATEGY (455) provide design support for configuring and varying the 'divide and conquer' strategy without affecting component clients, slaves, and the master's invariant core algorithm for slave coordination.

In most MASTER-SLAVE arrangements there is only one master. However, such a design introduces a single point of failure, which cannot always be tolerated. An alternative implementation is, therefore, to merge the roles of master and slave into a single object and to define a particular MASTER-SLAVE arrangement by specifying which role a particular instance in this arrangement embodies. Using a suitable mechanism such as heartbeats, the master regularly notifies all slaves that it is alive. If this notification is not received by a slave, it assumes that the master failed, claims the master role, and notifies the remaining slaves about this take-over. In cooperation with the underlying communication infrastructure, subsequent client requests are then redirected to the new master. Alternatively, a watchdog can relaunch the master in the case of failure.

The number of slaves in a MASTER-SLAVE configuration is largely dependent on the amount of available computing resources such as memory, threads, and CPUs. The more CPUs are available, the greater the potential parallelism, and the more slaves can be assigned to a MASTER-SLAVE arrangement.

The data exchanged between master and slaves is often encapsulated within DATA TRANSFER OBJECTS (418) to avoid dependencies to specific data representations. Access to slave results can be coordinated conveniently via FUTURES (382). When a slave is invoked, it returns a future that represents the result the slave will compute. When the slave finishes execution, it fills the future with the corresponding data. If the master accesses a future before the corresponding slave has filled it, it will block until the slave's result is available.

Half-Object plus Protocol **

When realizing an ENCAPSULATED IMPLEMENTATION (313) or a LOOKUP (495) service . . .

. . . at times we need to ensure reduced response time when accessing a single object from multiple address spaces.

♦♦♦

Distributed systems often use designs in which clients access objects of components that reside in other address spaces. However, due to the latency and jitter incurred when exchanging requests and responses across the network, this design can be impractical when requirements demand rapid response.

Resolving the problem via replication is not always feasible. For example, a component may need access to information from multiple address spaces to carry out its behavior. Obtaining this information from each replicated component would result in significant network load and traffic, which can decrease or even eliminate the performance advantages of the component's replication. The same effect occurs for replicated components that represent a single stateful entity within the distributed system. If the state of any of the replicas is modified, the state of the other replicas must be updated accordingly across the network.

Therefore:

Divide the objects into multiple 'half objects,' one for each address space in which they is used. Each half object implements the functionality and data required by the clients that reside in 'its' address space. A protocol between the half objects helps to coordinate their activities and keep their state consistent.

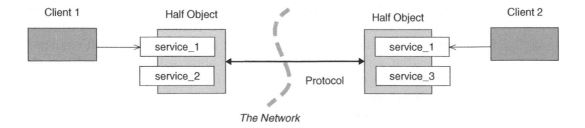

When a client invokes a service on the component that does not involve information maintained in other address spaces, the corresponding half object executes this service locally in the client's address space without involving the network at all. Otherwise the client-local half object obtains the necessary information from the other address spaces of the system via the protocol that connects the distributed half objects.

A HALF-OBJECT PLUS PROTOCOL arrangement optimizes performance by minimizing the use of the network, but at the expense of duplicating functionality and perhaps data. All the services of the logical object that can be executed locally within the address spaces of its clients are executed locally by the corresponding half object. Only if multiple address spaces need to be involved in a service execution is the protocol that connects the half objects necessary to coordinate the distributed computation. In general, the more functionality that can be executed locally in the address space of clients, and the less data need to be exchanged between the half objects to keep them consistent, the better the performance of an HALF-OBJECT PLUS PROTOCOL arrangement. The greater the need for distributed computation, and the more data that needs to be exchanged via the protocol, the less beneficial a HALF-OBJECT PLUS PROTOCOL design becomes. As a general rule of thumb, duplication of internal state should be reduced to minimize the need for data exchange and synchronization via the protocol.

A side-benefit of a HALF-OBJECT PLUS PROTOCOL design is scalability. A new half object is added to the arrangement with every new client address space, which avoids the use of computing resources in other address spaces.

The concrete design of the protocol between the half objects depends on what particular coordination they need. Simple data exchange protocols can be based on an OBSERVER (405) design to avoid unnecessary updates and coordination activities. Actions that the half objects in the arrangement can invoke on one another can be encapsulated into COMMANDS (412) or MESSAGES (420), to keep the protocol independent of a specific action set.

Replicated Component Group *

When realizing an ENCAPSULATED IMPLEMENTATION (313) ...

... we must sometimes support fault tolerance and high availability for component implementations.

Some components in a system must meet high availability and fault tolerance requirements, in particular if they execute or coordinate central activities, such as a directory service in a telecommunication system. Brute force solutions to this problem, however, such as complete hot or cold stand-by system replication, are often too expensive for many applications due to their high total cost of ownership.

In most systems only a few components are exposed to extreme availability and fault tolerance requirements, which hardly justifies expensive hardware-based system-level solutions. Providing high availability and fault tolerance within a low cost environment, however, is a challenge. Commodity hardware and standard networks are sources of failure—and thus unavailability—in themselves, which components with high availability and fault-tolerance requirements must take into account explicitly: network connections and inter-process communication can fail, hosts can be down. Figuratively speaking, the components must be strong in a weak environment.

Therefore:

Provide a group of component implementations instead of a single implementation, and replicate these implementations across different network nodes. Forward client requests on the component interface to all implementation instances, and wait until one of the instances returns a result.

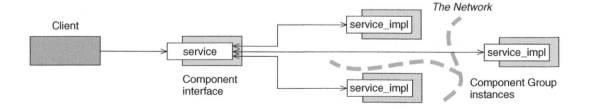

The first result returned by any of the component instances in the group is returned to the client.

The key benefit of a REPLICATED COMPONENT GROUP is that it enhances the fault-tolerance of a component: as long as at least one of the component instances within the group is accessible, client requests can be serviced. A REPLICATED COMPONENT GROUP also supports availability, because if a component instance in the group cannot execute a request immediately due to high workload, other, less overloaded object implementations can service the request instead.

One downside of a REPLICATED COMPONENT GROUP configuration is that it requires all component instances to maintain consistent state, which can lead to 'chatty' communication, resulting in heavy network traffic. The more state there is to maintain, and the higher its rate of change, the more networking overhead is necessary to keep the group state consistent. In addition, a request to a REPLICATED COMPONENT GROUP is executed by all its constituent component implementations, which can consume a significant amount of computing resources. As a result a REPLICATED COMPONENT GROUP design should only be considered for components that play a central role in a distributed system and whose availability and fault tolerance is crucial for the system's operability.

A BUSINESS DELEGATE (292) that serves as the component's interface helps to keep a concrete REPLICATED COMPONENT GROUP transparent to its clients. Additional LOOKUP (495) functionality allows component implementations to join and leave the group dynamically, which enables runtime redeployment of group members without compromising the component's availability.

The protocol for keeping the state of instances in the group consistent is often based on an OBSERVER (405) design, which avoids unnecessary updates and coordination activities. Requests that the arrangement should execute can be encapsulated into COMMANDS (412) or MESSAGES (420), to keep the communication within the group independent of a specific request set.

14 Application Control

Remote-controlled fast car
© Kevlin Henney

Separating the user interface from an application's core functionality enables its deployment across a network. This decoupling also allows independent modification of, and access to, the user interface and the application's core functionality. But how do you separate these two concerns effectively in practice? The eight patterns in this chapter address this topic, covering the areas of transforming user input into concrete service requests, converting the results of invocations into user output, and ensuring secure access to an application's functionality.

It is hard to transform user input into service requests to application functionality, execute these requests, and convert any results back into meaningful output for presentation to users. These aspects of application control are even harder if the application's user interface is separated from its functionality. This separation of concerns is often done to support decoupled evolution of user interface or application functionality, simplify changes in underlying software or hardware technologies, and enable distributed deployment on heterogeneous platforms.

The specific issues to consider when separating an application's user interface from its other functionality include:

- *Data structure decoupling.* Separating user interface and application functionality implies that data structures used by application components should be independent of control and presentation-specific concerns. For example, a mouse-click on a user interface element must be transformed into a service request to one or more of the application's components. Similarly, data returned in response to a user request must be converted into a specific output format that can be rendered on a designated output device. Without this decoupling, it is hard to change the look-and-feel of a user interface without modifying the implementation of the underlying application functionality.

- *Location decoupling.* The simplest GUI frameworks assume that the user interface, application logic, and data are collocated on the same machine and accessed by a single user. This assumption is rarely valid in distributed applications, particularly multi-tier systems, in which user interfaces may execute remotely, application logic and state is often shared by many users, and data is physically located in different hosts than the application logic and user interface.

- *Workflow decoupling.* Many applications are workflow-driven, leading their users through a specific sequence of forms, or showing specific forms only under certain conditions. Implementing this workflow logic directly in either the user interface or the application logic can tightly couple these two issues. This coupling makes it hard to change the workflow without changing user interface elements, or to change user interface elements without affecting core application functionality.

- *Technology decoupling.* User interfaces are built using specific user-interface technologies, which can change independently of the desired look-and-feel of the user interface itself. If user-interface technologies are expected to change during an application's lifetime, its architecture should separate technology-independent aspects of the user interfaces from technology-specific aspects.

- *Explicit coordination and control of requests.* The handling and execution of requests to an application or component often involves coordination and housekeeping tasks. For example, there may be a need to schedule the execution sequence of invocations received from multiple clients, a requirement to support logging and undo/redo functionality, or a policy-based approach for handling failures. The specific policies and configurations for these activities should depend on the needs of specific application *instances*, rather than being inherent properties of the application's user interface and core functionality. The independence of the user interface and the invocation of components should therefore be preserved.

- *Security.* Although securely accessing application services is increasingly important for user acceptance, networked applications—particularly those accessible via the Internet—are vulnerable to cyber attacks. For example, malicious users may try to access and execute functionality for which they are not authorized. Other users who are authorized to access specific applications, or parts of application functionality, may intentionally or unwittingly embed attacks in their service requests. Since user interfaces typically run on the client side of an application, usually on user-owned or administered machines that are vulnerable to exploitation, the trust boundary for most networked applications occurs between their user interface and their core (domain) functionality.

The issues described above must be addressed appropriately and consistently. If they are handled poorly, changes in an application's user interface can ripple through to the implementation of its functionality, and vice versa. Moreover, these issues are often dependent on each another, so choosing a solution that addresses one may constrain the solutions for others.

Eight patterns in our pattern language, drawn largely from *Patterns of Enterprise Application Architecture* [Fow03a], address the issues described above, providing common approaches to handle the implied or explicit introduction of control entailed by these various separations:

> The PAGE CONTROLLER pattern (337) [Fow03a] introduces a defined entry point—the page controller—for each form in a form-based user interface, to consolidate the handling and execution of service requests issued through each form.

> The FRONT CONTROLLER pattern (339) [Fow03a] establishes a single entry point into an application—the front controller—that consolidates the handling and execution of service requests issued through its user interface.

> The APPLICATION CONTROLLER pattern (341) [Fow03a] separates user interface navigation from controlling and orchestrating an application's workflow. An application controller receives service requests from the application's user interface, decides which service to invoke on its functionality, depending on the current state of its workflow, and determines which view to present at the user interface in response to the executed service.

> The COMMAND PROCESSOR pattern (343) [POSA1] separates the request for a service from its execution. A command processor component manages requests as separate objects, schedules their execution, and provides additional services such as logging and storing request objects for later undo/redo.

> The TEMPLATE VIEW pattern (345) [Fow03a] introduces a template view component for each view that renders application data or other information into a predefined view format using a specific user interface technology.

> The TRANSFORM VIEW pattern (347) [Fow03a] introduces a dedicated transform view component that converts data received

from the application in response to specific user requests into concrete views onto the data.

The Firewall Proxy pattern (349) [SFHBS06] helps protect an application from external attacks by introducing a proxy that inspects the payload of service requests to identify and remove suspicious content.

The Authorization pattern (351) [SFHBS06] evaluates client access rights to ensure only authorized clients that comply with designated access rules can access specific application functionality.

These patterns help to realize the goal of separating the user interface from core functionality presented earlier by the application partitioning patterns, in particular Model-View-Controller (188) and Presentation-Abstraction-Control (191). As described below, the patterns outlined above are not fully independent of one another, but can be paired to complement one another, with each pair addressing different aspects and forces of a common problem.

Page Controller and Front Controller aim to minimize the number of controllers accessing the functionality of an application. The two patterns differ primarily in their scope. A Page Controller is appropriate for form- or page-based user interfaces that have a simple control flow to access application's functionality, such as those in static HTML pages. Instead of having a separate controller for each action that can be invoked via a specific form or page, a dedicated Page Controller handles these actions consistently and uniformly. A Front Controller, in contrast, is most effective if service requests issued by a user interface must be transformed into invocations on an application's functional interfaces before they can execute. An example of this approach is requests issued to a Web server via the HTTP protocol.

The following diagram shows how PAGE CONTROLLER and FRONT CONTROLLER are connected with other patterns in our pattern language for distributed computing.

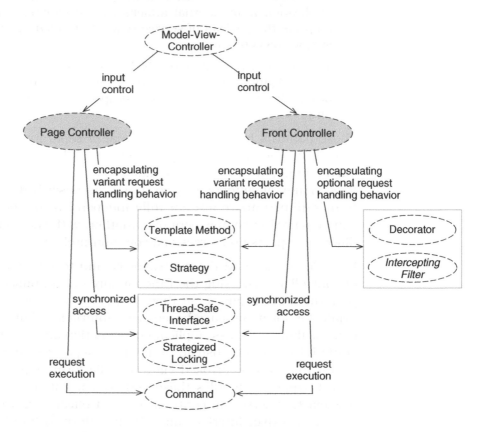

APPLICATION CONTROLLER and COMMAND PROCESSOR help orchestrate access to application functionality. APPLICATION CONTROLLER addresses workflow-based systems whose current computational state determines which function to execute in response to a particular service request. COMMAND PROCESSOR, in turn, supports scheduling of the execution order of requests issued by multiple clients according to a specific scheduling criteria such as priorities and deadlines. The goal of COMMAND PROCESSOR is to enforce specific quality of service aspects or maximize application throughput.

The following diagram shows the integration of APPLICATION CONTROLLER and FRONT CONTROLLER into our pattern language for distributed computing:

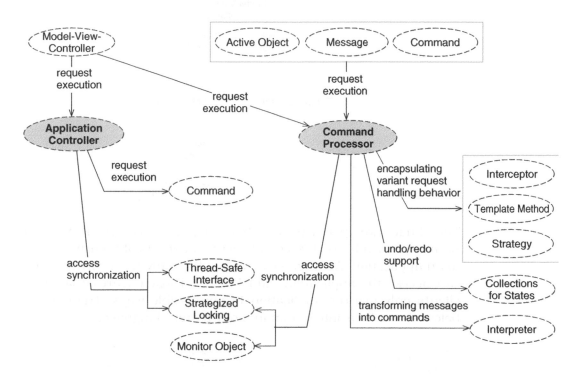

TEMPLATE VIEW and TRANSFORM VIEW both help to transform application data into a specific view onto the application. These patterns differ largely in their perspective. TEMPLATE VIEW takes a user-interface-centric perspective: it is the concrete user-interface technology, such as JSP or ASP.NET, that determines how to obtain data from the application. TRANSFORM VIEW, in contrast, takes an application-centric-perspective: data is retrieved from the application and then transformed into a specific view using a particular user-interface technology.

The following diagram shows how TEMPLATE VIEW and TRANSFORM VIEW are embedded in our pattern language for distributed computing:

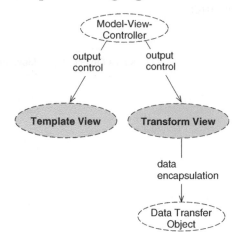

The final two patterns in this chapter, FIREWALL PROXY and AUTHORIZATION, address two complementary aspects of securing access to an application. AUTHORIZATION ensures that only trustworthy clients can access the application, and FIREWALL PROXY ensures that these clients only use the application in permissible ways. The diagram below shows their integration into our pattern language:

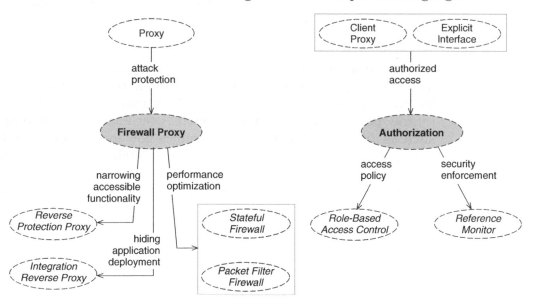

Page Controller **

When developing a MODEL-VIEW-CONTROLLER (188) architecture where the view is remote from the model . . .

. . . we may need a mechanism to consolidate the handling and execution of service requests issued by a specific form in a form-based user interface.

♦♦♦

Some applications offer form-based user interfaces, with each form invoking a coherent, interrelated set of application functions. Encapsulating the handling of each type of client request in a separate controller, however, could complicate controller implementations and duplicate functionality that is common to handling the requests issued from a specific form.

For example, in Web applications with static HTML pages, some pages handle the input and processing of specific data records by taking the input, loading data from the database if the record already exists, and checking the integrity of the record's data before processing it in the application. Similarly, results of data processing may be displayed to users. There could also be common constraints on the execution of specific functions, such as security, logging, and other housekeeping functionality. A strict encapsulation of each type of function offered by a page into a separate controller, however, would ignore their interdependencies and common execution constraints, yielding complicated and redundant code that is hard to maintain and evolve.

Therefore:

For each form offered by an application's user interface, introduce a page controller to control the execution of all requests issued from that form.

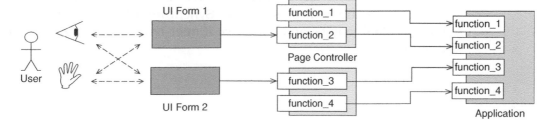

All client requests from a specific form are channelled through their associated page controller. The page controller transforms each request into a more specific request on the application's components, for example by extracting information from the client request parameters. The page controller also performs any housekeeping functionality associated with requests issued from the form. In addition, if the form includes a small and form-local workflow, the page controller can maintain the necessary session state information.

A PAGE CONTROLLER centralizes access to an application's domain services from a specific user interface form, which avoids duplication of functionality associated with handling an individual client request issued through that form. As a result, common request-handling code becomes easier to maintain and evolve. In addition, the request handling of different forms is separated, which supports form-based request handling strategies and rearranging the forms within another user-level workflow.

Request handling functionality that follows a common core algorithm with variant policies can be realized with TEMPLATE METHOD (453) or STRATEGY (455). The functionality performed by a page controller results in a service request on the application's components. These requests are often realized as COMMANDS (412) that support the managed execution of the requests on the application logic, as well as other features such as scheduling, logging, and undo/redo.

There are two general deployment options for a page controller: per-client and per-application. Per-client deployment is more scalable, but requires additional resources on the client side. Per-application deployment, in contrast, helps to minimize client footprint. A page controller shared by multiple clients must usually be synchronized. Providing it with a THREAD-SAFE INTERFACE (384) is a simple yet coarse-grained synchronization option, because it enforces synchronization at the page controller's interface, even if only small portions of its methods are critical sections. Synchronization via STRATEGIZED LOCKING (388) may be an alternative if finer levels of serialization are required.

Front Controller **

When developing a MODEL-VIEW-CONTROLLER (188) architecture where the view is remote from the model . . .

. . . we often need a mechanism to consolidate the handling and execution of service requests issued to an application.

When handling a request, networked applications often perform similar actions, including pre- and post-processing actions such as authorization and logging, and context-specific behavior such as providing particular views for specific users. Implementing this transformation functionality within each controller of an application, however, can duplicate code and thus complicate maintenance and evolution.

As the number of controllers grow, it also becomes hard to identify all the sites where code is duplicated. As a result, the complexity of modifying each duplicate code fragment correctly opens a floodgate to incorrect and inconsistent application behavior. In addition, the memory footprint of the application, especially its controllers, can increase significantly as the transformation from general to specific requests becomes more complicated. This problem becomes even worse if common infrastructure functionality such as authorization and logging must be performed with each request.

Therefore:

Introduce a front controller that publishes the application's functionality and transforms client service requests into specific requests that can be invoked on the application's components.

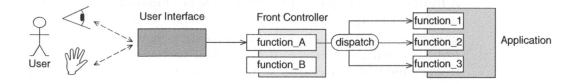

All client requests are channelled through the front controller. This controller transforms each request into a more specific request to the application's components, for example by extracting information from the client request parameters.

A FRONT CONTROLLER centralizes access to an application's domain services, which avoids duplicated implementations of functionality associated with handling individual client requests. As a result, not only does the common request handling code become easier to maintain and evolve, but the application memory footprint is also minimized. In addition, a FRONT CONTROLLER can provide common housekeeping functionality, such as authorization and logging. One downside of a FRONT CONTROLLER is that its centralized design can create a performance and scalability bottleneck if many clients requests arrive simultaneously. Similarly, it can be a single point of failure in an application.

Common request transformation and housekeeping functionality can be implemented via TEMPLATE METHOD (453) or STRATEGY (455). Alternatively, if a specific housekeeping or transformation feature is completely optional, it can be added to the core request transformation functionality via a DECORATOR (449), also known as INTERCEPTING FILTER [ACM01]. The transformation performed by a front controller results in a concrete service request to the application's components. These requests are often encapsulated in COMMAND (412) objects that support the managed execution of the requests on the application logic, as well as other features such as scheduling, logging, and undo/redo.

There are two general deployment options for a front controller: per-client and per-application. Per-client deployment alleviates the performance, scalability, and failure penalties of a front controller, but requires additional client resources, such as memory and CPU time. Per-application deployment, in contrast, helps minimize the footprint of clients, but at the expense of the drawbacks outlined above.

A front controller shared by multiple clients must often be synchronized. Providing it with a THREAD-SAFE INTERFACE (384) is a coarse-grained synchronization option that enforces synchronization at the front controller's interface. If only small portions of the front controller's methods are critical sections, synchronization via STRATEGIZED LOCKING (388) provides a finer level of serialization. The COMMAND (412) objects, however, are created per request and are not shared, so they need not offer thread-safe interfaces.

Application Controller **

When developing a MODEL-VIEW-CONTROLLER (188) architecture where the view is remote from the model ...

... we must often provide an access point for handling user interface navigation and the workflow of an application.

◆◆◆

Some applications lead their users through a series of screens or forms following a specific workflow, or present specific screens or forms only under certain conditions. Placing such logic in the application's controllers, however, mixes user-interface code with application-specific workflow logic.

Moreover, different controllers could instigate the same workflow, which would lead to duplicated logic that is hard to maintain and evolve. Another approach is to implement the logic of the screen or form to display next in response to a specific action directly within the application logic. This approach is not practical, however, since application components, which are generally independent of presentation aspects, would become dependent on the partitioning and screen ordering of a specific user interface.

Therefore:

Encapsulate the application's workflow within a separate application controller. User-interface controllers use the application controller to determine the appropriate actions to invoke on application logic, as well as the correct view to display after the action has been executed.

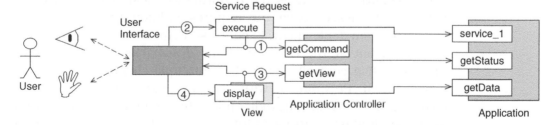

The application controller acts as a central access point for user-interface elements, unifying access to the functionality of an application with its workflow. When invoked by an user-interface controller, the application controller identifies the correct function to execute on the application. The function selected depends both on the input received from the controller and on the application controller's current workflow state. Similarly, after the invoked function has been executed, the workflow transitions into a new state, which allows the application controller to determine the specific view to display in the user interface in response to the executed function.

An APPLICATION CONTROLLER helps to encapsulate parts of an application where user-interface aspects and domain-logic aspects are interwoven. As a result, the core domain logic of the application remains independent of any user-interface considerations, such as its structure, and user-interface controllers and views are independent of the workflow and state of the application logic. If the application's workflow or the user-interface structure changes, the corresponding modifications to the application's code are limited largely to the application controller. In a distributed application, the liabilities of an APPLICATION CONTROLLER design include potential performance and scalability bottlenecks, due to its central role within an application. It can also be a single point of failure.

An application controller typically transforms requests received from a user-interface controller into a concrete COMMAND (412) object. COMMAND supports the managed execution of the requests to the application logic, as well as other features, such as scheduling, logging, and undo/redo.

There are two deployment options for an application controller. Per-client deployment reduces the performance, scalability, and failure penalties discussed above, but requires additional client resources. Per-application deployment, in contrast, helps minimize the footprint of clients, but at the expense of the drawbacks described above. An application controller shared by multiple clients must often be synchronized. Providing it with a THREAD-SAFE INTERFACE (384) is a coarse-grained synchronization option that enforces synchronization at the application controller's interface. If only small portions of its methods are critical sections, synchronization via STRATEGIZED LOCKING (388) provides a finer level of serialization.

Command Processor **

When developing a MODEL-VIEW-CONTROLLER (188) architecture or an ACTIVE OBJECT (365), or when encapsulating service requests for an application into COMMANDS (412) or MESSAGES (420) ...

... we need a mechanism for executing service requests.

If an application can receive requests from multiple clients, they may need to manage the execution of these requests, for example to handle request scheduling, logging, and undo/redo. An individual client, however, generally has no knowledge about when and under what conditions its requests execute.

Allowing a client to obtain this information from an application would increase its logical and physical complexity [Lak95], with corresponding degradation in modularity, extensibility, and understandability. A client should therefore be able to issue requests without needing to know the conditions under which the requests execute. To complicate matters, many distributed applications must also support additional housekeeping and system management functionality, such as logging, authorization, and multiple undo/redo. Neither application clients nor application components should be responsible for these tasks. Making the clients responsible would increase their coupling to the component and reduce client cohesion., while making the components responsible would clutter their intent with additional complexity, thereby complicating future development.

Therefore:

Introduce a command processor to execute requests to the application. The command processor acts on behalf of the clients and within the constraints of the application.

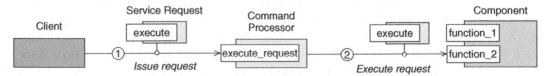

The command processor is the only means for clients to issue requests to the application. In addition, the command processor can access information about the computational state of its components, so it can schedule the execution sequence of pending service requests in terms of specific criteria such as priorities and throughput. The command processor can also offer useful housekeeping and system management functionality, such as history-based functionality and persistence.

Since a COMMAND PROCESSOR manages the functionality of a component, the component's clients and the component itself are freed from organizing the execution of concrete service requests. As a result the degree of coupling between the two parties is minimized.

Removing the responsibility of invoking services on the component from its clients implies that the clients cannot call the component's functionality directly. Instead, they send 'objectified' requests, such as COMMANDS (412) or MESSAGES (420), to the command processor, which then executes the requests on the component. This request reification is the key to handling requests explicitly and centrally within the command processor.

Internally, the command processor can manage the requests it receives via multiple COLLECTIONS FOR STATES (471). For example, a do collection can hold all requests that have yet to execute, as well as all requests that have been undone and can now be redone. An undo collection can maintain all requests that have been executed on the component that can be rolled back. If the command processor receives requests as COMMAND objects, it can simply invoke these objects to execute the encapsulated requests on the component. If requests are received as MESSAGES, an INTERPRETER (442) can help to transform their content into COMMANDS.

Scheduling and other housekeeping functionality, such as logging and authorization, can be realized and configured via TEMPLATE METHOD (453), STRATEGY (455), or INTERCEPTOR (442). These patterns allow the configuration of a command processor with different request execution policies, considering different trade-off options in terms of binding time and looseness of coupling. If the command processor is shared by multiple clients it should be implemented using MONITOR OBJECT (368). STRATEGIZED LOCKING (388) offers another dimension of configuration for synchronization.

Template View **

When specifying a MODEL-VIEW-CONTROLLER (188) architecture . . .

. . . we often need to render application data or other information into a predefined view format.

Many views onto an application present dynamic content, such as the results of database queries, so their appearance can change with each display and update. Providing separate view implementations for each possible appearance of the view, however, inflates the number of views and duplicates code.

Ideally a view whose content can vary should be designed and implemented similarly to static views—that is, views whose content, structure, and appearance is fixed and therefore simple to develop. Variations in a view's appearance, however, suggest multiple implementations. In contrast, the potential variations are not arbitrary, so there should be a way to handle such bounded variation within a single implementation.

Therefore:

Introduce a template view that predefines the view's structure and which contains placeholders for dynamic application data.

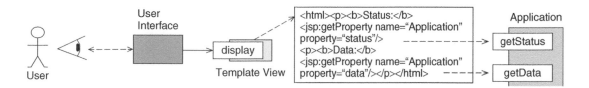

When the view is invoked to display or update itself, the placeholders for application data are filled in, for example as a result of some computation or of database queries. The view is displayed to the user after the application data to display has been determined.

A TEMPLATE VIEW simplifies the development of views that follow a common structure and format but whose content is dynamic. A single class encapsulates the structure of the view, the code to access and compute the content, and the code to display that content at the appropriate places in the view.

Popular forms of TEMPLATE VIEW are server pages, such as ASP.NET, JSP, and PHP-based page generation. These technologies actually go further than a pure TEMPLATE VIEW, because they allow embedding of arbitrary active content, i.e. programming logic. Using that capability carelessly, however, can yield template views that contain excessive application logic, which contradicts the goal of having views that only display information. This problem can be resolved by inserting a *helper* class between the view and the application's components that contains the necessary programming logic [Fow03a]. The same problem can occur if the template view contains conditional display and iterations. Although such constructs cannot always be avoided, their use should be minimized, and if possible factored out to the helper class associated with the view [Fow03a].

Transform View **

When specifying a MODEL-VIEW-CONTROLLER (188) architecture ...

... we often need to transform the data received from the application in response to user requests into specific views onto the data.

♦♦♦

Many views onto an application present content collected from different and often complex data structure returned by application services. The data structures, however, generally contain no knowledge about what specific data fields should be presented and how that data should be formatted.

Implementing the inspection of the data and its transformation into a specific output format within the views themselves is a clumsy solution to the problem, because it mixes application logic with user-interface code. The clear separation of application logic and user interface would be blurred. In addition, the larger and more complex the data inspection and transformation code, the less suitable the views become for low-footprint thin clients, which is often a requirement for Web applications.

Therefore:

Introduce a transform view that walks the structure of the data received from the application, recognizes the data to display, and transforms it into a specific output format.

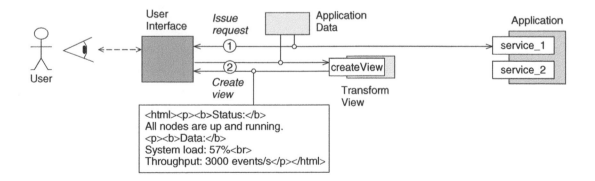

A transform view is an adapter that converts a specific type of input into a specific type of output. A controller can pass the data it receives in response to a service request for the application to the transform view and receive the concrete view to display as a result.

A TRANSFORM VIEW helps to simplify the development of views that must be assembled from complex data sets. Application logic for data inspection is clearly separated from specific user-interface technologies and view-specific data-rendering code, which also allows these two aspects to vary independently. A TRANSFORM VIEW is also a good candidate for being a pluggable component, thereby affording a high degree of flexibility in application configuration.

The application data converted by a TRANSFORM VIEW is typically encapsulated inside DATA TRANSFER OBJECTS (418) to keep the transform view independent of concrete data structures. To simplify the programming of a specific transformation, the data transfer objects could serialize their content into a standard representation, such as XML. This design also supports the use of popular data transformation technologies such as XSLT.

The downside, however, is that transformation logic is code in its own right, and metacode at that, and does not necessarily have the tool support of more direct approaches such as TEMPLATE VIEW. It can therefore be more general than is strictly necessary, and the subtlety of testing or debugging a transformation may dissuade some developers from using it.

Firewall Proxy **

When designing the PROXY-based (290) interfaces of an application that is accessible via the Internet or other public networks ...

... we must protect components from external attacks.

An application that is accessible via a public network such as the Internet has little reliable knowledge about who is using it, since virtually anybody can invoke its functionality. There is a need, however, to protect the application from potential cyber attacks embedded in service requests from clients.

Protecting publicly accessible applications against cyber attacks is hard. On one hand such applications should be available for public access, so we cannot require that all users be known by the application before they can access it. At least some services—a home page, a registration page, or basic query functionality—should be available without already being a registered user. On the other hand, if application services are publicly accessible, cyber attacks can be embedded within the payload of service requests. Depending on the security policies for the application, potential cyber attacks should be identified and access to the application denied.

Therefore:

Introduce a firewall proxy for the publicly accessible functionality of the application. This proxy enforces security policies on each client request to protect the components that implement this functionality from cyber attacks.

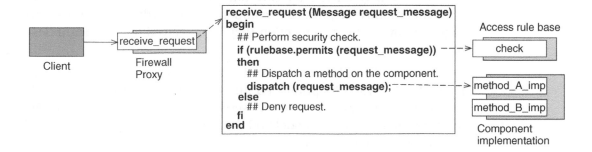

An external client can access application functionality only via the firewall proxy. When a client issues a request to that proxy, the proxy checks the request against applicable access rules, for example by inspecting the payload of the request message. If the request is accepted, the firewall proxy forwards the request to the protected component, otherwise it denies access to the client's request.

A Firewall Proxy supports the detailed filtering of service requests for components on a packet and payload level, which helps to identify cyber attacks at a higher level than that of networking protocols. In addition, security checks are separated from the components, which allows clients internal to the application or behind the firewall to access components directly, without incurring the performance overhead of security checks.

The security policy applied by a firewall proxy is often captured in a rule base that is separate from the proxy itself. This design supports variation in security policies without modifying the proxy implementation. As with any security mechanism based on denial of service for access identified as malicious, however, there is the risk of misidentification. The perceived effectiveness of a firewall proxy thus depends heavily on the quality of the rule base.

Implementing the firewall proxy as a Packet Filter Firewall [SFHBS06] supports request forwarding from trusted clients directly to the components, without inspecting request payloads. An implementation as a Stateful Firewall [SFHBS06] avoids payload inspections for requests received from already established and checked connections. Both designs can improve external client quality of service. Configuring the firewall proxy as a Reverse Protection Proxy [SFHBS06] adds another security barrier for external clients that limits the accessible functionality of protected components regardless of who sends requests, over which connection they are received, or the cleanliness of a request payload.

Finally, the firewall proxy can also act as an Integration Reverse Proxy [SFHBS06] if its published functionality is realized by multiple components deployed to multiple servers. This design helps hide the application deployment model and the network topology from external clients and potential attackers.

Authorization **

When realizing a CLIENT PROXY (240) or an EXPLICIT INTERFACE (281) ...

... we must ensure that only specific clients can access the functionality of a subsystem.

A subsystem must provide well-defined and meaningful functionality to its clients, otherwise it is of little value to them. Clients can invoke this functionality by sending service requests. Not all clients that potentially can send requests to the subsystem, however, may be entitled to invoke its functionality.

Subsystems that maintain sensitive information, such as medical or financial data, must be protected from unauthorized access. Not all users of an application or internal clients of a subsystem should be allowed to access or manipulate this information, otherwise the confidentiality, integrity, or availability of the data could be endangered. The same situation holds for components that offer 'manipulation' functionality, such as administration and configuration tasks. Hardcoding information about the 'trusted' clients directly within the components is a clumsy and high-maintenance solution, however, because significant effort and cost would be required to redeploy the components in multiple applications with different clients, change the set of authorized clients, or evolve the authorization rights of clients.

Therefore:

Assign access rights to each client that can send service requests to the security-sensitive subsystem and check these rights before executing any requests on the subsystem.

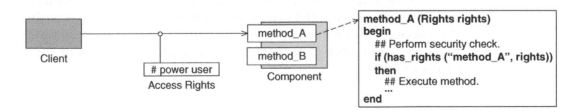

Access rights specify the operations or categories of operations clients are allowed to invoke on the subsystem. If a client issues a service request to the subsystem, its access rights are checked. If they have sufficient rights, the requested service is executed, otherwise their access to the subsystem is denied.

The key benefit of AUTHORIZATION is that subsystems can only be accessed by authorized clients, which is important for security-sensitive applications. A secondary benefit is that specific access rights, as well the policies for checking them, can evolve transparently for both clients and components of an application.

A common form of implementation for an AUTHORIZATION infrastructure is ROLE-BASED ACCESS CONTROL [SFHBS06]. Instead of assigning individual access rights to each client, there is a defined set of user roles in an application, such as administrator, power user, user, and guest, with specific access rights associated with each role. Users and client components must be assigned to, or act under the perspective of, one or more roles. Depending on the access rights of these roles they can—or cannot—access the application's components and their functionality. ROLE-BASED ACCESS CONTROL simplifies the realization and evolution of an AUTHORIZATION infrastructure by limiting the number of specified access rights specified to a small set of roles. In addition, a ROLE-BASED ACCESS CONTROL design can enforce structures and policies of the organization that owns or hosts the application.

A REFERENCE MONITOR [SFHBS06] complements an AUTHORIZATION structure with a defined access right decision and enforcement point. All client requests are intercepted by a central reference monitor to check their access rights for compliance with the application's authorization rules. This design strictly enforces an application's security policies by checking all client service requests. A reference monitor avoids code duplication and simplifies maintenance by centralizing the checking of access rights for each component that requires authorized access. Multiple reference monitor instances can be deployed in a system to minimize performance or scalability bottlenecks or single points of failure.

15 Concurrency

Autobahn A3, exit Duisburg-Wedau at night
Siemens press picture, © Siemens AG

The choice of concurrency architecture has a significant impact on the design and performance of multi-threaded software in general, and distributed software in particular. No single concurrency architecture is suitable for all workload conditions and platforms, however. The four concurrency patterns in this chapter therefore address a variety of concurrency problems, ranging from combining asynchronous with synchronous concurrent processing to synchronizing access to shared components, while maximizing performance and throughput.

Software for distributed systems can often benefit from concurrency, in particular servers and server-side software that handles requests from multiple clients simultaneously. In addition, an increasing number of multi-core CPUs and multi-CPU computers are designed to run multiple threads of control in parallel to compensate for the stall in Moore's Law [Sut05a]. Developers of software for distributed systems therefore need to become proficient with process and thread management mechanisms.

A process is a collection of resources, such as virtual memory, I/O handles, and threads of control, that provide the context for executing program instructions. Each process serves as a *unit of protection and resource allocation* within a hardware-protected address space [StRa05]. In contrast, a *thread* is a single sequence of instruction steps executed in the context of a process [Lew95]. In addition to an instruction pointer, a thread consists of resources, such as a runtime stack of function activation records, a set of registers, and thread-specific data. Each thread serves as a *unit of execution* that runs inside a process and shares its address space with other threads.

Distributed system software uses multiple processes and threads for a number of purposes, including:

- *Improving performance transparently* by using the concurrent processing capabilities of today's hardware and software platforms.

- *Improving performance explicitly* by allowing programmers to overlap computation and communication in their service processing.

- *Shortening perceived response time* for interactive software such as graphical user interfaces by associating separate threads with different service processing tasks, so that users are able to perform useful work while some tasks are blocked.

- *Simplifying application design* by allowing multiple service processing tasks to run independently using synchronous programming abstractions, such as two-way method invocations and operations that block on I/O and locks.

It is remarkably hard to develop efficient, predictable, scalable, and robust concurrent software, however [Lea99]. Effective concurrent programming requires much more than just starting individual components, objects, or services in their own threads of control and letting these threads run at their own discretion. This is due to the following challenges:

- *Software diversity.* There is no 'one-size-fits-all' concurrency model, since different types of distributed system software exhibit different structural and behavioral characteristics. For example, some software uses a mixture of asynchronous and synchronous service processing, other software is event-driven, and still other software must handle service requests at different priorities. Each type of software may therefore require a particular concurrency model so that it can provide the required quality of service to users and the appropriate programmer model to developers.

- *Multi-threading costs.* Designers of concurrent software must account for the fact that multi-threading incurs costs such as context switching, synchronization, and data movement between CPU caches. Naive uses of threading mechanisms can therefore result in overhead that reduces or even outweighs the benefits of concurrency. It is therefore essential to design concurrent software that minimizes the costs of using multiple threads.

- *Portability.* Additional accidental complexity in concurrent programming arises from limitations with existing development methods, tools, and operating system platforms. For example, the heterogeneity of today's hardware and software platforms complicates the development of concurrent software and tools that run on multiple operating systems.

Effectively resolving these challenges and complexities requires developers to know and apply the appropriate concurrency patterns. These patterns must be understood and applied consciously and thoughtfully throughout the design of the software's baseline architecture, subsystems, and components.

Our distributed computing pattern language, therefore, includes four patterns that offer proven solutions to various concurrency architecture and design problems:

> The HALF-SYNC/HALF-ASYNC pattern (359) [POSA2] decouples asynchronous and synchronous service processing in concurrent systems, to simplify programming without unduly reducing performance. The pattern introduces two intercommunicating

layers, one for asynchronous and one for synchronous service processing.

The LEADER/FOLLOWERS pattern (362) [POSA2] provides an efficient concurrency model in which multiple threads take turns sharing a set of event sources in order to detect, demultiplex, dispatch, and process service requests that occur on the event sources.

The ACTIVE OBJECT pattern (365) [POSA2] decouples service requests from service execution to enhance concurrency and simplify synchronized access to objects that reside in their own threads of control.

The MONITOR OBJECT pattern (368) [POSA2] synchronizes concurrent method execution to ensure that only one method at a time runs within an object. It also allows an object's methods to schedule their execution sequences cooperatively.

This chapter restricts its coverage to patterns for developing concurrent communication middleware and application components for distributed systems. Our intention is not to cover every aspect of concurrency. In particular, we focus on patterns that define how to *structure* and *partition* concurrent software into multiple cooperating threads, or how to *organize* the access to components that are shared by multiple threads. We deliberately do not aim to present a general guide to the many documented concurrency models available in both theory and practice.

Patterns that deal with thread synchronization techniques are not included in this chapter, but instead are covered in Chapter 16, *Synchronization*. Although THREAD-SPECIFIC STORAGE (392) was originally classified as a concurrency pattern [POSA2], our experience using THREAD-SPECIFIC STORAGE over the years has revealed that it is less about concurrency and more about avoiding locking overhead, so we have assigned it to the *Synchronization* chapter.

MONITOR OBJECT is another pattern that could arguably be classified either as a concurrency or a synchronization pattern. We placed it in this chapter, since its primary purpose is to enable concurrency in object-oriented programs: its use of synchronization mechanisms, such as mutexes and condition variables, can be considered subordinate to this role. It is also worth noting that MONITOR OBJECT acts as a complement to ACTIVE OBJECT.

The patterns presented in this chapter fall into to two groups: *concurrency infrastructures* and *access synchronization.*

HALF-SYNC/HALF-ASYNC and LEADER/FOLLOWERS define higher-level concurrency architectures. HALF-SYNC/HALF-ASYNC decouples asynchronous and synchronous processing in concurrent systems, to simplify application programming without unduly reducing performance at the operating system and network level. Due to the simplicity of its programming model, HALF-SYNC/HALF-ASYNC is used in many concurrent applications, ranging across operating systems, middleware, and industrial process control and telecommunication applications [POSA2]. LEADER/FOLLOWERS provides a concurrency model for event-driven systems. It is especially suitable for systems that process a high volume of events within short-duration, atomic, and repetitive actions, such as receiving and dispatching network events or storing high-volume data records in a database.

The following diagram illustrates how the HALF-SYNC/HALF-ASYNC and LEADER/FOLLOWERS patterns integrate with our pattern language for distributed computing.

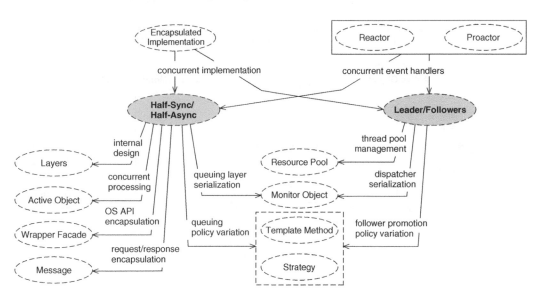

ACTIVE OBJECT and MONITOR OBJECT help to synchronize and schedule methods invoked concurrently on objects and components. The main difference is that an ACTIVE OBJECT executes its methods in a different thread than its clients, whereas a MONITOR OBJECT executes its methods by borrowing the thread of its clients. As a result an ACTIVE OBJECT can perform more sophisticated—albeit expensive—scheduling to determine the order in which its methods execute. Consequently ACTIVE OBJECT is mainly used to support concurrency in large components and subsystems, while MONITOR OBJECT in mainly used to realize (small) concurrent objects.

The diagram below illustrates the integration of ACTIVE OBJECT and MONITOR OBJECT into our pattern language for distributed computing.

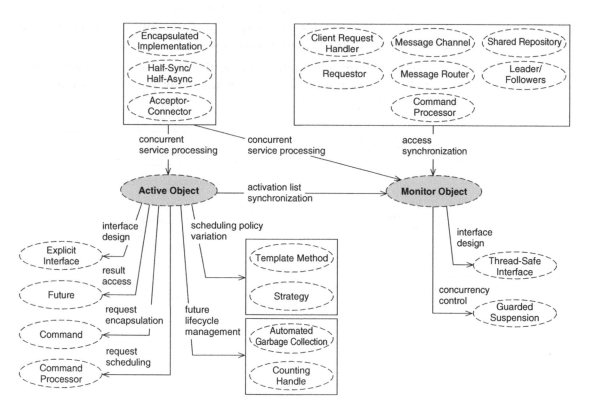

Half-Sync/Half-Async **

When developing concurrent software, specifically a concurrent ENCAPSULATED IMPLEMENTATION (313) or a network server that employs a REACTOR (259) or PROACTOR (262) event handling infrastructure ...

... we need to make performance efficient and scalable while ensuring that any use of concurrency simplifies programming.

Concurrent software often performs both asynchronous and synchronous service processing. Asynchrony is used to process low-level system services efficiently, synchrony to simplify application service processing. To benefit from both programming models, however, it is essential to coordinate asynchronous and synchronous service processing efficiently.

Asynchronous and synchronous service processing is usually interrelated. For example, the I/O layer of Web servers often uses asynchronous read operations to obtain HTTP GET requests [HPS97]. Conversely, the processing of the GET requests at the CGI layer often runs synchronously in separate threads of control. The asynchronous arrival of requests at the I/O layer must therefore be integrated with synchronous processing of the requests at the CGI layer. From a different point of view, similar observations can be made about AJAX—the use of asynchronous JavaScript and XML to increase the perceived responsiveness of Web clients [Gar05]. In general, asynchronous and synchronous services should cooperate effectively and be encapsulated against either other's deficiencies.

Therefore:

Decompose the services of concurrent software into two separated layers—synchronous and asynchronous—and add a queueing layer to mediate communication between them.

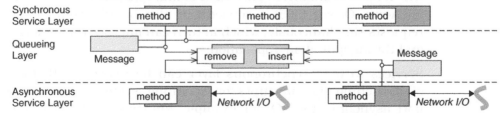

Process higher-level services, such as domain functionality, database queries, or file transfers, *synchronously* in separate threads or processes. Conversely, process lower-level system services, such as short-lived protocol handlers driven by interrupts from network hardware, *asynchronously*. If services in the synchronous layer must communicate with services in the asynchronous layer, have them exchange messages via a queueing layer.

A HALF-SYNC/HALF-ASYNC design enforces a strict separation of concerns between the three layers, which makes concurrent software easier to understand, debug, and evolve. In addition, asynchronous and synchronous services do not suffer from each other's liabilities: asynchronous service performance does not degrade due to blocking synchronous services, and the simplicity of programming synchronous services is unaffected by asynchronous complexities such as explicit state management. Finally, using a queueing layer avoids hard-coded dependencies between the asynchronous and synchronous service layers, as well as making it easy to reprioritize the order in which messages are processed. The strict decoupling of the asynchronous layer from the synchronous layer, however, requires that data exchanged between the two layers must be either communicated as COPIED VALUES, which can introduce performance penalties and resource management overhead the more data there is to pass, or represented as IMMUTABLE VALUES, which are lighter in weight but perhaps more intricate to construct.

In general, a HALF-SYNC/HALF-ASYNC arrangement employs LAYERS (185) to keep its three distinct execution and communication models independent and encapsulated.

Services in the synchronous layer, such as database queries, file transfers, or domain functionality, generally run in their own threads, which allows concurrent execution of multiple services. If realized as an ACTIVE OBJECT (365) a service can also handle multiple service requests simultaneously, which in turn can improve the performance and throughput of an application.

Services in the asynchronous layer can be realized with the help of asynchronous interrupts or operating system APIs that support asynchronous I/O, for example Windows overlapped I/O and

I/O completion ports [Sol98], or the POSIX aio_* family of asynchronous I/O system calls [POSIX95]. WRAPPER FACADES (459) help to encapsulate platform-specific asynchronous I/O functions behind a uniform interface, which simplifies their correct use and the portability of the asynchronous layer to another operating system. Alternatively, if a HALF-SYNC/HALF-ASYNC arrangement is designed in conjunction with a PROACTOR or REACTOR event-handling infrastructure, this event-handling infrastructure *is* the asynchronous layer. Although a REACTOR is not truly asynchronous, it shares key properties with asynchrony if its services implement short-duration operations that do not block for long periods of time.

The queueing layer often consists of a message queue shared by all services in the synchronous and asynchronous layers. Sophisticated queueing layers can provide multiple message queues, for example one message queue for every message priority or communication endpoint. Message queues can be implemented as MONITOR OBJECTS (368) to serialize access to the message queues transparently for asynchronous and synchronous services. TEMPLATE METHODS (453) and STRATEGIES (455) support the setting of various aspects of the message queues, for example configuring their behavior for ordering, serialization, notification, and flow control. STRATEGIES are the more flexible option, offering loose coupling and runtime configuration and re-configuration of the message queues. TEMPLATE METHODS can be appropriate if only compile-time flexibility is needed. The information routed by the queueing layer is encapsulated within MESSAGES (420).

Leader/Followers **

When developing concurrent software, specifically a concurrent
ENCAPSULATED IMPLEMENTATION (313) or a network server that employs
a REACTOR (259) event-handling infrastructure . . .

. . . we must often react on and process multiple events from multiple
event sources both concurrently and efficiently.

**Most event-driven software uses multi-threading to process mul-
tiple events concurrently. It is surprisingly hard, however, to
allocate work to threads in an efficient, predictable, and simple
manner.**

In event-driven software, particularly server software, it is often necessary to define efficient demultiplexing associations between threads
and event sources. It is also necessary to prevent race conditions if
multiple threads demultiplex events on a shared set of event sources.
For example, a Web server may use multiple threads to service multiple GET requests scalably on multiple I/O handles. Some methods
of associating threads and event sources are inefficient because they
incur high levels of overhead. For example, creating a thread for each
request, or dedicating a separate thread for each event source, can
be inefficient due to scalability limitations of operating systems and
hardware. What is needed is an architecture for concurrent reactive
software that is both easy to use and efficient.

Therefore:

**Use a pre-allocated pool of threads to coordinate the detection,
demultiplexing, dispatching, and processing of events. In this
pool only one thread at a time—the *leader*—may wait for an
event on a set of shared event sources. When an event arrives,
the leader promotes another thread in the pool to become the
new leader and then processes the event concurrently.**

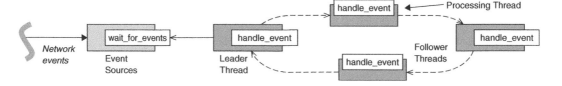

While the *leader* is listening on the event sources for an event to occur, other threads—the *followers*—can queue up and sleep until they are promoted to be the leader. When the current leader thread detects an event from the event sources it does two things. It first promotes a follower thread to become the new leader, then it morphs itself into a *processor* thread that demultiplexes and dispatches the event to a designated event handler that runs in the same thread that received the event. Multiple processing threads can handle events concurrently while the current leader thread waits for new events to occur on the shared event sources. After handling its event, a processing thread reverts to the follower role and sleeps until it becomes the leader again.

By pre-allocating a pool of threads, a LEADER/FOLLOWERS design avoids the overhead of dynamic thread creation and deletion. Having threads in the pool self-organize and not exchange data between themselves also minimizes the overhead of context switching, synchronization, data movement, and dynamic memory management. Moreover, letting the leader thread perform the promotion of the next follower prevents performance bottlenecks arising from having a centralized manager make the promotion decisions.

The price to pay for such performance optimizations is limited applicability. A LEADER/FOLLOWERS configuration only pays off for short-duration, atomic, repetitive, and event-based actions, such as receiving and dispatching network events or storing high-volume data records in a database. The more services the event handlers offer, the larger they are in size, while the longer they need to execute a request, the more resources a thread in the pool occupies and the more threads are needed in the pool. Correspondingly fewer resources are available for other functionality in the application, which can have a negative impact on the application's overall performance, throughput, scalability, and availability.

In most LEADER/FOLLOWERS designs the shared event sources are encapsulated within a dispatcher component. If a LEADER/FOLLOWERS arrangement is designed in conjunction with a REACTOR event-handling infrastructure, its reactor component *is* the dispatcher. Encapsulating the event sources separates the event demultiplexing and dispatching mechanism from the event handlers. Providing the dispatcher with methods for deactivating and reactivating a specific event source avoids race conditions if a new leader thread is selected simultaneously with completion of processing of the most recent event.

Specify the threads as a RESOURCE POOL (503), and use a MONITOR OBJECT (368) to maintain the dispatcher and synchronize access to the shared event sources. This design enhances performance by using a self-organizing concurrency model that avoids the overhead of a separate queueing layer between event sources and event handlers.

Inside the thread pool the monitor object offer two methods to its threads. A join method allows newly initialized threads to join the pool. The joining thread first waits to become the new leader by suspending its own execution on the thread pool's monitor condition. After it becomes the leader, it accesses the shared event sources to wait for and process an incoming event. A `promote_new_leader` method allows the current leader thread to promote a new leader by notifying a sleeping follower via the thread pool's monitor condition. The notified follower resumes execution of the thread pool's join method and accesses the shared event sources to wait for the next event to occur.

Multiple promotion protocols, such as last-in/first-out, first-in/first-out, and highest priority, can be supported via TEMPLATE METHODS (453) and STRATEGIES (455).

Active Object **

When developing an ENCAPSULATED IMPLEMENTATION (313), the synchronous service layer in a HALF-SYNC/HALF-ASYNC (359) architecture, or service handlers in an ACCEPTOR-CONNECTOR (265) configuration ...

... we must often ensure that the operations of components can run concurrently within their own threads of control.

Concurrency can improve software quality of service, for example by allowing components to process multiple client requests simultaneously without blocking. Developers, however, must decide how to express the units of concurrency in their software and how to interact with them as they run.

In particular, clients should be able to issue requests on components without blocking until the requests execute. It should also be possible to schedule the execution of client requests according to specific criteria, such as request priorities or deadlines. To keep service requests independent, they should be serialized and scheduled transparently to the component and its clients, thereby enabling the reuse of software implementations that require different synchronization strategies.

Therefore:

Define the units of concurrency to be service requests on components, and run service requests on a component in a different thread from the requesting client thread. Enable the client and component to interact asynchronously to produce and consume service results.

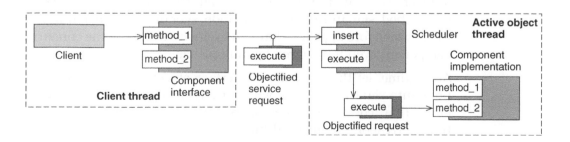

Clients can initiate a service request on the component by calling a method on its interface, which is exposed to the clients' thread(s). Design the component's interface without subjecting it to synchronization constraints and return control immediately to clients after they issue their requests. In addition, objectify the requests, pass them to the component implementation running in one or more separate threads, and let the implementation schedule the execution of the requests independently of the point in time at which they were initiated. Provide a way for the component to return results to the client when the service is complete.

An ACTIVE OBJECT design enhances concurrency in an application by allowing clients threads and the execution of service requests to run simultaneously: clients are not blocked while their service requests are executed. In addition, synchronization complexity is reduced by using a scheduler that evaluates synchronization constraints to serialize access to the component's implementation. The separation of request scheduling from the actual component implementation also supports the reuse of the component in scenarios that do not require synchronization, as well as enhancing legacy components that are not designed for concurrent access to be adapted for use in a concurrent application. Finally, the order of service request execution can differ from service request invocation, which can better account for priorities, deadlines, and other synchronization constraints—but at the cost of complicated debugging. An ACTIVE OBJECT arrangement also introduces a heavyweight request handling and execution infrastructure, which can cause performance penalties for components that only implement short-duration methods.

Use an EXPLICIT INTERFACE (281) to expose the component's interface to client threads. This design allows clients to access the component is if it were collocated in their own thread. Design the interface so that its method signatures do not include synchronization parameters. Clients therefore appear to have an exclusive access to the concurrent component even if it shared by multiple client threads.

At runtime, let the component interface objectify all method invocations into service requests, which are typically realized as COMMANDS (435) that convey the necessary synchronization constraints of their corresponding method invocations. This request objectification decouples service requests from service execution in time and space, so that each client can invoke services on the component without blocking itself or other clients. Store the created service requests into a shared activation list that maintains all pending service requests on the concurrent component. Implementing the activation list as a Monitor Object (368) helps to ensure thread-safe concurrent access.

One or more threads host the component's implementation. Within each thread, a servant implements the component's functionality. A scheduler dequeues pending service request objects from the shared activation list and executes them on the servants. Such a design allows service requests and executions to run concurrently, that is, service requests are invoked in client threads, while service executions run in different threads. In addition, the scheduler separates component functionality from scheduling and synchronization mechanisms, which supports independent realization and evolution of both concerns.

Design the scheduler as a Command Processor (343) that implements the component's event loop. This monitors the activation list to identify service requests that become executable, removes these requests from the activation list, and executes them on their servant. Template Methods (453) and Strategies (455) can support multiple scheduling policies within the scheduler. Template Methods are most appropriate if the configuration of the scheduler is possible at compile time. Strategies, in contrast, support runtime configuration and reconfiguration of scheduling policies.

Clients can obtain the result of a service request on the concurrent component via a Future (382). The interface of the concurrent component returns the future to the client after the service's invocation, while the associated service request fills the future after the servant has finished with the service's execution. If the client accesses the future before it contains the service's result, the client can block or poll until the result is available. When futures are no longer needed they can be reclaimed safely via Automated Garbage Collection (517) if this strategy is supported by the programming language, or via a Counting Handle (522) if the reclaim must be coded manually.

Monitor Object **

When developing a SHARED REPOSITORY (202) architecture, a REQUESTOR (242), CLIENT REQUEST HANDLER (246), MESSAGE CHANNEL (224), MESSAGE ROUTER (231) distribution infrastructure, ENCAPSULATED IMPLEMENTATION (313), ACCEPTOR-CONNECTOR (265) arrangement, HALF-SYNC/HALF-ASYNC (359), LEADER/FOLLOWERS (362), or ACTIVE OBJECT (368) concurrency model ...

... we must consider that objects can be shared between threads.

◆◆◆

Concurrent software often contains objects whose methods are invoked by multiple client threads. To protect the internal state of shared objects, it is necessary to synchronize and schedule client access to them. To simplify programming, however, clients should not need to distinguish programmatically between accessing shared and non-shared components.

Instead, each object accessed by multiple client threads should ensure that its methods are serialized transparently without requiring explicit client intervention. To ensure the quality of service of its clients, a shared object should also relinquish its thread of control voluntarily if any of its methods must block during execution, leaving the component in a stable state so that other client threads can access it safely.

Therefore:

Execute a shared object in each of its client threads, and let it self-coordinate a serialized, yet interleaved, execution sequence. Access the shared object only through synchronized methods that allow execution of only one method at a time.

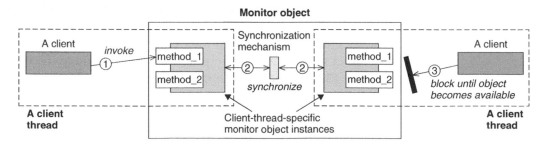

Monitor object

Each monitor object contains a monitor lock that it uses to serialize access to the object's state. Within a synchronized method, first acquire the monitor lock to ensure no other synchronized methods can execute. Once the lock is held, evaluate whether the shared object's current state allows the synchronized method to run. If it does, execute it, otherwise suspend the execution of the synchronized method on a condition. If called, a monitor condition should suspend the thread of its caller until it is notified to wake it. When suspending a thread, the monitor condition should also release the monitor lock, and when resuming this thread, re-acquire the monitor lock.

Suspending a synchronized method allows other client threads to access the shared object via its synchronized methods. Any synchronized method that executes, completing execution, may affect the validity of monitor conditions, in which case it should notify the corresponding monitor condition so that suspended method invocations can resume execution. Before terminating a synchronized method, release the monitor lock so that other synchronized methods called by other threads can execute.

Designing a shared object type as a MONITOR OBJECT simplifies concurrency control by sharing the object among cooperating threads and combining state synchronization with method invocation. A MONITOR OBJECT also helps in implementing a cooperative method execution sequence that ensures the availability of the shared object to its clients, and maximizes its availability within the constraints of serialization, to ensure that state changes are complete and free of race conditions. A liability of this pattern, however, is that it couples domain functionality tightly with synchronization aspects. It can be hard to compose or nest monitor objects without risking deadlock, for example, if one monitor object makes callbacks into objects that in turn use other monitor objects.

A monitor object can use a THREAD-SAFE INTERFACE (384) to decouple synchronization from its functionality. Such a design also allows both concerns to vary independently. GUARDED SUSPENSION (380) can be used to coordinate threads running in the object. The execution of methods is scheduled via monitor conditions and monitor locks that determine the circumstances under which they should suspend or resume their execution and that of collaborating components.

16 Synchronization

Kevlin and Frank at JAOO 2006, synchronizing their watches
© Mai Skou Nielsen

Concurrency mechanisms for dividing up and executing tasks across different threads present only one part of the concurrency story. Where objects are shared between threads, there is the question of thread-safe use of their methods. This chapter presents nine patterns that address synchronization or reduction of state change to minimize the need for synchronization.

In Chapter 15, *Concurrency* we discussed how the structure, efficiency, and responsiveness of software for distributed systems can benefit from concurrency. We also showed that well-structured, efficient, and responsive concurrent software is surprisingly hard to design: 'Multithreading is one thing after, before, or simultaneously with another' [MeAl04a]. To address these challenges, we therefore included patterns for effective concurrent design in our language. But not only is *designing* concurrent systems challenging, *programming* them is too—when present, concurrency is a concern that runs through all levels and across all aspects of an architecture.

One reason why concurrent programming is harder than sequential programming is the need to synchronize access to shared resources. Threads that run concurrently may share access to the same objects. Without appropriate safeguards, therefore, methods that change the internal state of a shared object have the potential to corrupt this state when called from different threads. To avoid this problem, code that should not run concurrently on the same object state can be synchronized within a *critical section*. A critical section is a sequence of instructions that obeys the following invariant: while one thread or process is executing in the critical section, no other thread or process can execute in the same critical section [Tan95].[6]

A common way to safeguard a critical section in object-oriented programs is to associate some type of lock object with a class or component. For example, a mutual exclusion object (mutex) is a type of lock that must be acquired and released serially within the same thread, embracing the critical section, so that if multiple threads attempt to acquire the mutex simultaneously, only one thread will succeed. The others must wait until the mutex is released, after which the waiting threads can compete for the lock again [Tan92]. Other types of locks, such as file locks, semaphores, and reader–writer locks, use a similar acquire–release protocol [McK96].

Although the use of locks with threads appears to be straightforward at a *conceptual* level, programming locks in *practice* are not always so

---

6 Note that this formal definition of *critical section* should not be confused with the Microsoft Windows synchronization primitive `CRITICAL_SECTION`. The former defines a region of code that must satisfy an invariant, while the latter is an API mechanism that can be used to satisfy such an invariant. A `CRITICAL_SECTION` is a lightweight, in-process mutual exclusion type.

[Lee06]. For example, if a lock is held longer than actually needed, it can degrade the availability of a shared component unduly by making the lock scope—the statements between the acquisition of the lock and its release—larger than the critical section, the statements that must be guarded from concurrent access. Similarly, acquiring and releasing locks at too fine a level of granularity can degrade the performance of a component: the acquisition and release of locks does not come free.

As an example, consider how a lock scope can easily be made broader than necessary in Java. In Java a lock scope is an explicit concept, introduced using `synchronized` to mark a whole method or block of code. Syntactically, it is more convenient to mark a whole method as `synchronized`, which also has the benefit of being more visible because the act of mutual exclusion is captured in the method's signature. However, it is common for the statements that form a critical section to be preceded and followed by statements that are concerned with operations on local variables or arguments, rather than the modification of private object state, and which therefore do not need locking. Where locking is necessary, it must be used to ensure program correctness: where locking is unnecessary, it should be avoided to help program performance. In our example, the method scope is larger than the critical section, so only the critical section should be surrounded by a `synchronized` block, not the whole method.

Using locks in an *ad hoc* manner also runs the risk of introducing *deadlock*, a deadly embrace in which two concurrent tasks wait on each other for completion. Consider two threads and two shared resources: thread 1 acquires a lock on shared resource 1, and thread 2 acquires a lock on shared resource 2. To progress, however, thread 1 then needs to lock and use shared resource 2 and thread 2 needs to lock and use shared resource 1. Thus there is no progress, and the deadlock results in the two threads hanging indefinitely. Design strategies and algorithms that ensure that locks are always acquired and released in the same order address many of these issues, but ultimately the surest course is to reduce the need for synchronous actions and locking, and to encapsulate locking behavior where possible [CMH83].

Programming with locking primitives requires some knowledge of their basic constraints and limitations to avoid both pessimization and deadlock. The simplest kind of lock is a semaphore, an exclusive lock that can be locked and unlocked from any thread. A more disciplined construct is a mutex, which must be unlocked in the same thread in which it was locked. In either case, it is easy to introduce a defect by forgetting to match the lock with a corresponding unlock. Sometimes this is obvious: the unlock is actually absent from the source code. But sometimes it can be more subtle: the unlock is present, but it is bypassed when an exception is thrown from within the critical region. Such subtle problem cases emphasize the need to wrap the use of such primitives, either within library code or through language mechanisms.

To add to the subtlety, mutexes come in two basic flavors: recursive and non-recursive. A recursive mutex allows re-entrant locking, in which a thread that has already locked a mutex can lock it again and progress. Non-recursive mutexes, in contrast, cannot: a second lock in the same thread results in self-deadlock. Non-recursive mutexes can be potentially much faster to lock and unlock than recursive mutexes, but the risk of self-deadlock means that care must be taken when an object calls any methods on itself, either directly or via a callback, because double-locking will cause the thread to hang. Recursive mutexes were designed explicitly for such scenarios, simplifying the composability of components by ensuring that something as simple and common as a callback does not lead to deadlock.

Another common synchronization mechanism is a condition variable, which collaborating threads can use to suspend themselves temporarily until condition expressions involving data shared between the threads attain desired states. A condition variable is always used in conjunction with a mutex, which the thread must acquire before evaluating the condition expression. If the condition expression is false, the thread atomically suspends itself on the condition variable and releases the mutex, so that other threads can change the shared data. When a cooperating thread changes the data, it can notify the condition variable, which atomically resumes a thread that had previously suspended on the condition variable and acquires its mutex again.

Our interest in synchronization is often focused on lock-based programming, and in particular how to use locks effectively, rather than merely adequately. Correctness, safety, and efficiency drive our vocabulary of techniques. Locks are not, however, the only path to thread-safe code. Designing software to reduce the opportunities for state change reduces the need to perform synchronization. Threads that work on disjoint data need not synchronize changes. Threads that work on shared, immutable data similarly need not synchronize changes, because there are none. Threads that work on data that can be updated atomically are able to share state changes. This last approach motivates lock-free programming, which is underpinned by guaranteeing that certain primitive operations, such as integer increment or compare-and-swap (CAS), are atomic and non-locking on a given platform. Lock-free programming, however, is a subtle and complex topic—'lock-based programming is hard for experts to get right, and lock-free programming is hard for geniuses to get right' [Sut05b]—and does not form a key theme in the patterns we present.

Nine patterns in our pattern language for distributed computing help to ensure that the interactions between threads and state are free of race conditions and deadlocks, but are still as efficient as possible:

The GUARDED SUSPENSION pattern (380) [Lea99] coordinates transparent client access to shared objects whose methods can only execute when certain conditions hold.

The FUTURE pattern (382) [Lea99] provides a 'virtual' data object that blocks clients automatically when they try to invoke its fields before its concurrent computation is complete.

The THREAD-SAFE INTERFACE pattern (384) [POSA2] minimizes locking overhead and ensures that intra-component method calls do not incur self-deadlock by trying to reacquire a non-recursive lock that is held by the component already.

The DOUBLE-CHECKED LOCKING pattern (386) [POSA2] reduces contention and synchronization overhead whenever a critical section of code must be executed the first time the section is encountered, but not subsequently, and yet still remain thread-safe.

The STRATEGIZED LOCKING pattern (388) [POSA2] parameterizes a component to enable user selection of the most appropriate synchronization mechanism to serialize the component's critical sections.

The SCOPED LOCKING pattern (390) [POSA2] ensures that a lock is acquired when control enters a scope and is released automatically when control leaves the scope, regardless of the return path from the scope.

The THREAD-SPECIFIC STORAGE pattern (392) [POSA2] allows multiple threads to use one 'logically global' access point to retrieve an object that is local to a thread, without incurring locking overhead on each object access.

The COPIED VALUE pattern (394) [Hen00b] ensures that value objects are passed by copy between threads. Value objects are therefore not shared between threads, so there are no opportunities for data races and no need for synchronization.

The IMMUTABLE VALUE pattern (396) [Hen00b] sets the internal state of value objects at construction and disallows subsequent changes of their state. Immutable values can be shared in a concurrent program without synchronization.

The first two patterns in this list, GUARDED SUSPENSION and FUTURE, help coordination of threads that try to execute methods or access data, but cannot succeed because certain conditions are not met or data they need is not yet available. GUARDED SUSPENSION orchestrates the effective use of one or more condition variables to implement cooperative concurrency control, while FUTURE suspends threads that try to access data that is yet to be computed until the data is available.

The next diagram illustrates how GUARDED SUSPENSION and FUTURE integrate with our pattern language for distributed computing.

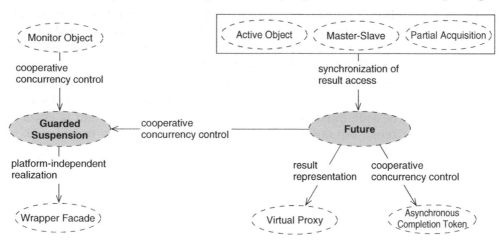

The next three patterns we present in this chapter, THREAD-SAFE INTERFACE, STRATEGIZED LOCKING, and SCOPED LOCKING, address concrete serialization techniques. THREAD-SAFE INTERFACE realizes a 'coarse-grained' locking policy: it serializes directly at the interface of a component, regardless of how much of the entire processing time of the invoked methods is spent in critical regions. The more time is spent in 'uncritical regions' of code, the less applicable THREAD-SAFE INTERFACE becomes, because it can block threads unnecessarily. In such a situation, STRATEGIZED LOCKING and SCOPED LOCKING are a better choice, because they serialize directly at the scope of the critical region. The two patterns are also complementary: STRATEGIZED LOCKING defines pluggable lock types, which can be configured according to an application's needs, such as semaphores, (recursive) mutexes, and reader/writers locks. SCOPED LOCKING helps in automating lock acquisition and—even more importantly—lock release, which is especially beneficial if a critical region is left unexpectedly, for example due to an exception.

The next diagram illustrates how the three patterns are connected with other patterns of our pattern language.

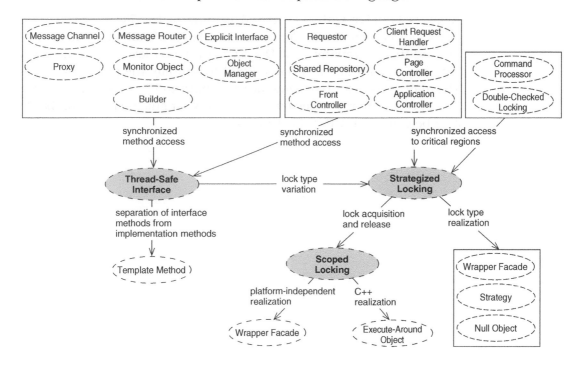

In contrast to its original classification as a concurrency pattern [POSA2], we assign the THREAD-SPECIFIC STORAGE pattern to the synchronization patterns in our language. The reason for this re-classification is that THREAD-SPECIFIC STORAGE, like DOUBLE-CHECKED LOCKING, is less about concurrency and more about avoiding locking overhead. THREAD-SPECIFIC STORAGE avoids locking overhead if thread-local variables are accessed via a global variable or access point, such as Unix `errno`. In contrast, DOUBLE-CHECKED LOCKING avoids this overhead if a critical region is guarded by a conditional expression whose evaluation depends on state that is modified within the critical section, such as the initialization of SINGLETONS [GoF95].

Similarly, COPIED VALUE and IMMUTABLE VALUE eliminate locking overhead by avoiding the need for locking altogether. In the case of COPIED VALUE, communicating a value by replicating an object rather than sharing it ensures that threads see disjoint objects that need no synchronization. Alternatively, once an object has been constructed, it may offer no methods that would cause internal state change. This restriction makes IMMUTABLE VALUES intrinsically thread-safe and ideal for exchanging data between threads.

Readers familiar with the second volume of the POSA series, *Patterns for Concurrent and Networked Objects* [POSA2], might also have noticed that we renamed the DOUBLE-CHECKED LOCKING OPTIMIZATION pattern as DOUBLE-CHECKED LOCKING (386) to simplify the pattern's name. The main reason for removing the word 'optimization,' however, is that if we keep it, many other patterns in our language should probably also be extended with this attribute.

The final diagram in this chapter illustrates how DOUBLE-CHECKED LOCKING, THREAD-SPECIFIC STORAGE, IMMUTABLE VALUE, and COPIED VALUE are integrated into our pattern language.

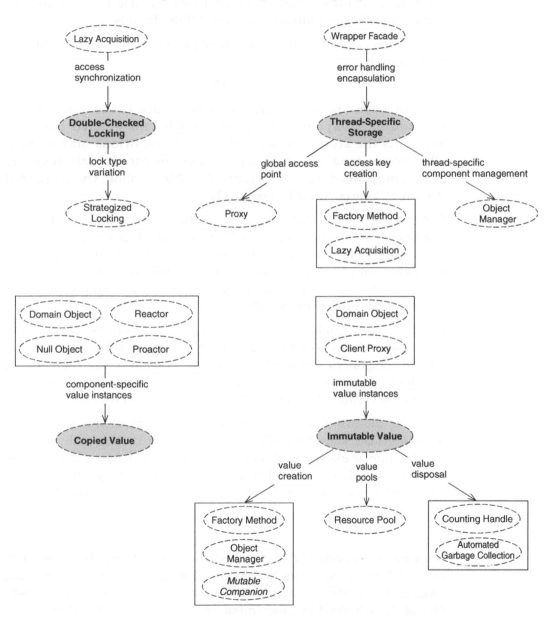

Guarded Suspension **

When implementing a MONITOR OBJECT (368), a FUTURE (382), or another component that is shared between multiple threads ...

... we must schedule the execution sequence of two or more threads cooperatively.

In concurrent programs we can often only execute a method invoked on component if specific conditions—called guards—apply. As the state of a method's guard conditions may eventually become true as a result of another concurrent action on the same component, it is not always feasible to abort the method if it cannot be executed immediately.

For example, we can remove a message from a synchronized message queue only when the queue is not empty, which is the guard condition. If another client thread inserts a message into the queue, it is not longer empty. A previously invoked removal method that could not execute because its guard condition is 'queue empty' can now proceed and finish successfully.

Blocking indefinitely is not really an option, because it prevents other client threads from performing potentially useful work on the shared component. Unconditional blocking can also create a potential deadlock situation by locking out *all* client threads, including ones that could change the state of the guard condition to true.

Aborting the attempt to access the critical section has the benefit of failing fast, signaling failure to the calling thread with a status result value or exception. It is intrusive for code in the client thread, however, which must implement some kind of retry strategy that will clutter the client code with mechanistic detail that is better encapsulated elsewhere.

Therefore:

Instead of aborting the method, suspend its client thread so that other client threads can access the shared component safely and change the state of the method's guard condition. If this state changes, resume the suspended thread so that the thread can try to continue the execution of the interrupted method.

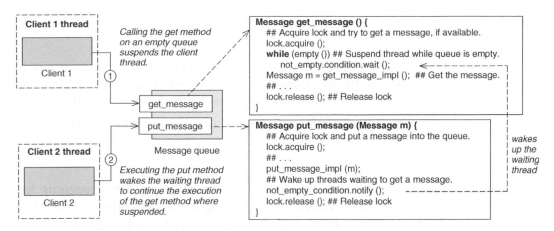

Guarded suspension allows a shared component to control and schedule the execution sequence of its client threads transparently to these threads.

◆◆◆

The key benefit of a GUARDED SUSPENSION design is that it is non-intrusive for the client. The called method encapsulates the policy and mechanism for access, leaving the calling code free of clutter and potentially duplicated mechanisms. An unexceptional and common situation is no longer flagged as a failure. The blocking behavior is such that the shared component continues to be available. If the suspension is at OS level, there is also no CPU wastage. As a result, GUARDED SUSPENSION minimizes concurrency overhead in the client threads and increases the shared component's availability.

Guarded suspension implementation primitives are offered in many OS APIs, but should be used via a WRAPPER FACADE (459) rather than directly. There are multiple ways to realize a guarded suspension [Lea99]: waits and notifications via condition variables and associated mutexes, busy-waits via spin-loops, and suspending and resuming client threads directly.

Although non-intrusive and non-failing blocking can simplify client code, a client may want the choice between blocking or doing something else, particularly if the suspension is long. This can be resolved by also providing non-blocking and time-out variants of the method. For example, a queue could provide a blocking get method and a non-blocking `try_get` method.

Future **

When implementing a MASTER-SLAVE (321) arrangement, an ACTIVE OBJECT (365), PARTIAL ACQUISITION (511), or software in which client and server run concurrently and communicate via method calls ...

... at times we must access data that is computed concurrently with the control flow of a client.

Services that are invoked concurrently on a component may need to return a result to the calling client. However, if the client does not block after calling the service, continuing instead with its own computation, the service's result may not be available when the client needs to use it.

A common use of concurrency is to optimize performance by over-lapping computation and communication. This optimization can be simple for one-way calls that return no results: invocation can be as simple as 'fire and forget.' A client, however, may want to invoke one or more two-way methods on one or more servers without having to wait synchronously for the server response(s). A call–return procedural model is simple to use but cannot, in this case, be used to return a result. Nevertheless, when the client needs a result to continue its processing, there must be a straightforward way to obtain it.

Therefore:

Immediately return a 'virtual' data object—called a future—to the client when it invokes a service. This future keeps track of the state of the service's concurrent computation and only provides a value to clients when the computation is complete.

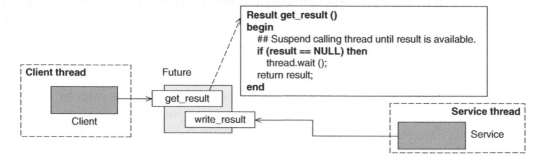

If the client accesses the service's result before it is available, the future suspends the client thread. After the result is available and stored in the future, the client's thread will be resumed automatically so that the client can continue executing and use the result of the service. A client can also poll a future through a non-blocking or timed accessor, as well as a completion query, which enables it to check whether the result is available without indefinitely suspending the client thread.

Using a FUTURE can enhance parallelism by allowing clients to synchronize with services that they invoked concurrently at the latest possible point in time. A FUTURE also enables method results to be processed in a different order than that in which the methods were invoked, which can enhance flexibility and performance.

To enhance parallelism, do not access the future immediately after receiving it, since this is an expensive way of achieving a synchronous two-way service call. Instead, let the client execute as many different operations or instructions as possible after the service invocation, and access the future only when the client cannot make any further progress without the service's result. The more time that passes between the service invocation and the access to the future, the less likely it is that the client will block, which increases concurrency and parallelism.

A FUTURE acts as a VIRTUAL PROXY (497) for data that is not yet computed. It may be implemented directly in terms of locking primitives that support GUARDED SUSPENSION (380), or it may be layered on top of an event-handling scheme expressed in terms of ASYNCHRONOUS COMPLETION TOKENS (268).

Thread-Safe Interface *

In a REQUESTOR (242), CLIENT REQUEST HANDLER (246), MESSAGE CHANNEL (224), MESSAGE ROUTER (231), SHARED REPOSITORY (202), EXPLICIT INTERFACE (281), PROXY (290), PAGE CONTROLLER (337), FRONT CONTROLLER (339), APPLICATION CONTROLLER (341), MONITOR OBJECT (368), OBJECT MANAGER (492), or BUILDER (527) arrangement . . .

. . . we must often ensure thread-safe access to components in a concurrent program.

♦♦♦

Components in a concurrent program must be thread-safe. Often their methods acquire locks to protect critical sections from concurrent access. Self-deadlock can occur, however, if an acquired lock is non-recursive and the method calls another method in the component that tries to acquire the same lock.

Although a re-entrant lock prevents self-deadlock, for some platforms it incurs unnecessary overhead when acquiring and releasing the lock multiple times across intra-component method calls. Ideally, a design that avoids self-deadlock, or does not take advantage of a lock's support for re-entrancy, should also incur minimal locking overhead. Assigning the responsibility for synchronizing the shared component with its clients is undesirable, however, because this design couples these clients tightly with the component. Such coupling increases both the complexity of usage and the probability of incorrect usage.

Therefore:

Split a component's methods into publicly accessible interface methods and corresponding private implementation methods. An interface method acquires a lock, calls its corresponding implementation method, and releases the lock. An implementation method assumes the necessary lock is held, does its work, and only invokes other implementation methods.

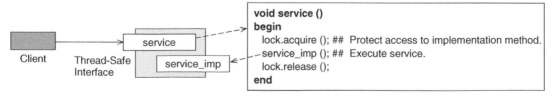

To ensure proper synchronization, clients of a component designed using THREAD-SAFE INTERFACE can only invoke its interface methods. Once an interface method obtains the necessary lock, it forwards control to the corresponding implementation method, which then processes the client's request. Self-deadlock and locking overhead are thus avoided, because the code in the implementation method does not acquire the component's lock, nor do any other implementation methods it may call on this component. When control returns from the implementation method to its interface method, the lock held by the interface method is released and any results are returned to the client that invoked the method.

A THREAD-SAFE INTERFACE ensures that self-deadlock does not occur as a result of intra-component method calls. In addition, locks are not acquired or released unnecessarily. Finally, a THREAD-SAFE INTERFACE separates locking and functionality issues, which helps to simplify both aspects.

Note, however, that the self-deadlock problem is not resolved if control leaves the component's scope temporarily and the underlying locking mechanism is strict. This situation can occur if an implementation method delegates control to a different component which then tries to re-enter the first component by calling one of its interface methods. In this case, the interface method will try to reacquire the locks the component already holds. A common way to resolve this problem is to realize a THREAD-SAFE INTERFACE using a re-entrant lock.

Often a component with a THREAD-SAFE INTERFACE is designed as a class with public synchronized interface methods and private non-synchronized implementation methods. Alternatively, a THREAD-SAFE INTERFACE arrangement can be designed as a TEMPLATE METHOD (453), with template methods corresponding to interface methods and hook methods corresponding to implementation methods. Components can use STRATEGIZED LOCKING (388) to vary their configuration with the optimal lock type.

Double-Checked Locking

When performing a LAZY ACQUISITION (507) in a concurrent environment . . .

. . . at times it may be necessary to perform thread-safe, one-time initialization in a method without paying the cost of synchronization for all subsequent calls of the method.

A common way of avoiding race conditions within a component shared between threads is to serialize access to its critical sections. A thread that wants to enter a critical section must first acquire a lock. This design, however, can incur excessive locking overhead if the object's critical section is entered frequently but is executed conditionally only once.

For example, consider an object whose representation is initialized by LAZY ACQUISITION. In a multi-threaded environment the just-in-time initialization code—the part that checks whether the representation already exists, creating it if it does not—is a critical section that runs just once during the object's lifetime. Guarding this code with a lock, however, incurs an overhead for *all* calls to the accessor method, not just the *one* call when initialization occurs. The lock is then acquired and released unnecessarily, because the object's existence check prevents control flow from executing the critical initialization code.

Therefore:

Provide the shared object with a 'hint' as to whether execution of a particular critical section is necessary. Check this hint *before* and *after* acquiring the lock that guards this critical section.

```
## Perform first-check to evaluate 'hint'.
if (first_time_in_flag is FALSE)
    acquire the lock
    ## Perform double-check to avoid race condition.
    if (first_time_in_flag is FALSE)
        execute the critical section
        set first_time_in_flag to TRUE
    fi
    release the lock
fi
```

If the critical code has already been executed, the hint's first check lets threads skip this code and its associated lock acquisition: no locking overhead is incurred. The hint's second check prevents race conditions if two or more threads passed the first check in parallel. Only one of these threads will successfully acquire the lock, pass the hint's second check, execute the critical section, and change the hint. Once the lock is released, any waiting threads will bypass the critical section, because the hint's second check indicates that it has already been executed.

Within an object, DOUBLE-CHECKED LOCKING ensures that locks are only acquired and released if a critical section guarded by a conditional statement must really be executed, which is often an 'exceptional' situation. The common case of not executing the critical situation requires no locking, and thus executes quickly and efficiently.

The hint used for DOUBLE-CHECKED LOCKING should initially indicate that the critical section has yet to be executed. If this hint also has an application-specific purpose, such as a pointer to an internal representation object, ensure that it has an atomic type. Guard the critical section by checking the hint, only letting threads enter if the critical section has yet to be executed. Inside the critical section acquire the lock, check the hint again, and—depending on its value—execute the critical section. Before releasing the lock, change the hint so that subsequent threads do not enter the critical section. STRATEGIZED LOCKING (388) supports configuration of the lock with a type appropriate for the application.

In the absence of a platform supporting a memory model that guarantees a coherent view of memory updates, CPU-specific instructions such as memory barriers are needed to access the hint safely. There is currently no portable memory model for C++, so platform-specific approaches must be adopted. Current versions of Java support an appropriate memory model, but older versions do not. As with any lock-free technique, the double-checked aspect of DOUBLE-CHECKED LOCKING can be remarkably subtle and error prone. Developers need to be keenly aware of its subtleties [MeAl04a] [MeAl04b]. If access to this level of mechanism is not possible, or is otherwise impractical, an alternative design should be considered, in particular one that avoids the need for any locking.

Strategized Locking **

When realizing a REQUESTOR (242), CLIENT REQUEST HANDLER (246), SHARED REPOSITORY (202), PAGE CONTROLLER (337), FRONT CONTROLLER (339), APPLICATION CONTROLLER (341), COMMAND PROCESSOR (343), THREAD-SAFE INTERFACE (384), or DOUBLE-CHECKED LOCKING (386) . . .

. . . a key issue in multi-threaded programming is the selection of the appropriate locking strategy for a particular environment.

♦♦♦

Components that are shared across threads in multi-threaded environments must protect their critical sections from concurrent access. However, different software configurations may require different locking strategies, such as mutexes, readers–writer locks, or semaphores.

Hard-coding the locking strategy into the components and adapting it to specific environments is a straightforward solution to this problem, but infeasible for most applications. Components would depend on their environment, and whenever that environment changes and suggests a different locking strategy, all components must be updated, with corresponding maintenance overhead. Providing different component versions for each environment is also infeasible—it causes similar maintenance overhead. Ideally, it should be possible to customize a component's locking strategy without making its implementation dependent on a specific environment.

Therefore:

Define locks in terms of 'pluggable' types, with each type objectifying a particular synchronization strategy. Provide all types with a common interface, so that a component can use all lock types uniformly without being dependent on their implementation.

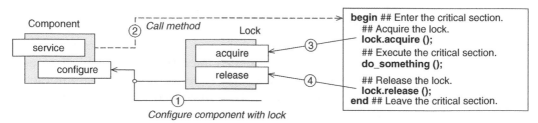

Configure component with lock

Configure the component with an instance of the appropriate lock type to use at its creation or declaration time, for example by passing a lock object to its constructor or parameterizing the component's class with a particular lock type. Use this lock instance to protect all critical sections within the component.

A STRATEGIZED LOCKING design offers several benefits. Rather than a separate implementation for each concurrency model, there is only one core implementation. Enhancements and bug fixes for a component therefore do not have to be duplicated. Configuring and customizing a component for specific concurrency models is simple and non-intrusive for the component, because the synchronization aspects of components are strategized. Conversely, STRATEGIZED LOCKING exposes a parameterization decision to the component user, which may be considered intrusive for common cases. Nevertheless, such an open and orthogonal approach allows the component to be used beyond its original context.

To make locks 'pluggable,' define a lock acquisition and release STRATEGY (455) interface that is implemented by all concrete lock types. Use the same lock type to configure related components within the same application. Where a variation in lock implementation is with respect to the platform rather than the locking policy, make concrete lock types WRAPPER FACADES (459) that encapsulate the details of a particular platform-specific locking mechanism. To optimize components for single-threaded environments where no locking is needed, provide a null lock type, which is a NULL OBJECT (457) whose lock acquisition and release methods are empty 'no-ops.'

SCOPED LOCKING (390) helps to simplify and automate safe acquisition and release of the lock within the component's implementation.

Scoped Locking **

When providing locks for a shared component in a concurrent program, either by hard-coding a particular lock type into the component or by implementing STRATEGIZED LOCKING (388) . . .

. . . a key issue in multi-threaded programming is to ensure that locks are acquired and released automatically when entering and leaving critical sections.

A critical section of code that should run sequentially is often protected by a lock, which is acquired and released whenever control enters and leaves the critical section. If programmers must acquire and release this lock explicitly, however, it can be hard to ensure that all paths through the code release the lock.

Control can leave a scope early due to an uncaught exception, or an explicit 'exit statement' such as `return`, `break`, or `goto`. The lock's release code may therefore be missed as a result of programmer oversight. The more complex and verbose code becomes, the more likely such oversights will occur. Code that tries to achieve exception-safety through the explicit use of statements like `try`, `catch`, and re-`throw` is error prone, losing both clarity and the intended safety.

Therefore:

Scope the critical section—if this has not already been done— and acquire the lock automatically when control enters the scope. Similarly, automate the release of the lock when control leaves the scope via any exit path.

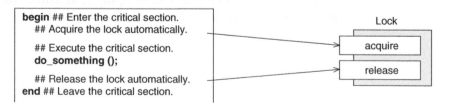

Entering a critical section becomes thread-safe, and leaving the critical section safely releases all acquired locks.

Scoped Locking increases the robustness of concurrent software by eliminating common programming errors related to synchronization and multi-threading. In addition, locks are acquired and released automatically when control enters and leaves critical sections, which are defined by programming language method and block scopes.

The implementation of Scoped Locking depends on the language used to program concurrent software. For example, Java provides a language feature, the `synchronized` block, that instructs Java compilers to generate a corresponding block of bytecode instructions in which a `monitorenter` and a `monitorexit` bracket the block. To ensure that the lock is always released, the compiler also generates an exception handler to catch all exceptions thrown in the synchronized block [Eng99]. If the locking scope covers the whole method, the method itself can be marked as `synchronized`. However, because marking the method is slightly simpler to write than a `synchronized` block, it is tempting to fall back on this briefer approach. Unfortunately, in many cases this means that the lock scope becomes larger than the critical section, leading to a loss of concurrency.

C++, by contrast, does not provide direct language support for Scoped Locking, but it can be implemented as a C++ idiom via an Execute-Around Object (451). Use this idiom to create a guard class whose constructor acquires a lock and whose destructor releases it. A guard object is thus declared as a local variable within the critical section's scope and before its first statement. When control enters the critical section, the guard's constructor is called and acquires the lock. When control leaves the critical section via any exit path, the guard's destructor is called automatically, due to C++ semantics, to release the lock. Designing the guard object as a Wrapper Facade (459) helps to encapsulate the details of a particular platform-specific locking mechanism behind a uniform interface.

Thread-Specific Storage

When working with code developed without threads or unanticipated integration in mind, or when designing a WRAPPER FACADE (459) that encapsulates an error-handling mechanism for concurrent C/C++ legacy systems running in a UNIX environment ...

... the use of state is often considered global within an application but, within a concurrent realization, its representation needs to be expressed as physically local to each thread.

♦♦♦

Access to an object that is tied to its environment makes it appear logically global. However, if the environment needs to appear specific to each thread, the object cannot simply be physically global with a single copy of state.

Locking each access to the object, and looking up the appropriate value based on the thread, can degrade system performance if the object is used frequently. Ideally, access to the object should be atomic without incurring *any* locking overhead. In addition, retrofitting its implementation to run in multiple threads it is often infeasible, as is the case for many legacy components written without concern for multi-threading that rely on specific objects being global in some way.

Therefore:

Introduce a common access point for the environmentally bound object, but maintain its physical object instances in storage that is local to each thread.

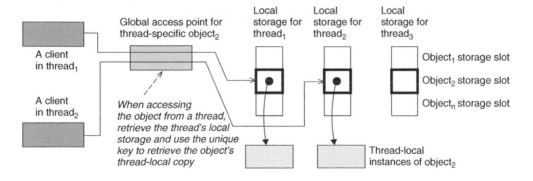

Ensure that every thread-local copy of an object can be retrieved from its corresponding thread-local storage via a globally unique key. Using this key, forward all method calls on the object's global access point to the particular copy of the thread-specific object that is maintained in the thread from which the access point is called. Thus no locking is required to access a thread-local object copy. Let client threads manipulate the thread-specific object only through its global access point, to preserve the object's logically global appearance.

A THREAD-SPECIFIC STORAGE design needs no locking to access thread-specific data. In addition, THREAD-SPECIFIC STORAGE is easy for software developers to use when dealing with legacy code that makes global assumptions about its objects, or that does not provide suitable parameters for distributing context information. However, this pattern is not without its liabilities, foremost of which is the encouragement such a facility may provide to developers to make 'global' objects that should be considered local and passed more explicitly as parameters.

Implement the global access point for the thread-specific object as a PROXY (290). At runtime, instantiate the global access point to the thread-specific object in every thread, but none of its thread-local instances. When a client thread calls a method on the access point, let a FACTORY METHOD (529) use LAZY ACQUISITION (507) to check first if a globally unique key exists that identifies the thread-specific object, and to create one if not. Finally, forward the original call on the access point to this thread-specific object and execute the request. Note that no locks are needed to protect the object's existence check, its creation, and also its use from concurrent access. Although clients invoke calls via a logically global access point, they actually operate on object state that is not shared between threads.

Multiple thread-specific components can be maintained in an indexed container whose index type is the key type, such as a map or an OBJECT MANAGER (492), of which a separate instance is provided per thread.

Copied Value **

When expressing a value in an application via a DOMAIN OBJECT (208), dispatching events to event handlers in a REACTOR (259) or PROACTOR (262), or when specifying a NULL OBJECT (457) . . .

. . . we must ensure that representations of values do not introduce thread-safety problems or efficiency bottlenecks if they must be known in different threads in a concurrent program.

◆◆◆

Value objects are commonly distributed and stored in fields. If value objects are shared between threads, however, state changes caused by one object to a value can have unexpected and unwanted side effects for any other object sharing the same value instance. In a multi-threaded environment shared state must be synchronized between threads, but this introduces costly overhead for frequent access.

Value objects form the principal type of representation and communication between many object types, such as entities and services. Identity is not significant for a value object, but its state is. Aliasing of these objects can often cause surprises, particularly where an object is used to represent the value of an attribute within an object. Between threads, the aliasing becomes more deeply problematic, with the possibility of race conditions for any state modification. Synchronizing methods addresses the question of valid individual modifications, but does nothing for the general problem of sharing, nor for the performance cost of synchronization of changes.

Therefore:

Define a value object type whose instances are copyable. When a value is used in communication with another thread, ensure that the value is copied.

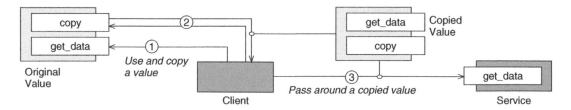

Each thread receives its own copy of a passed value, so value objects are not shared between threads.

The absence of any sharing means that there is no reason to synchronize. COPIED VALUES are disjoint across threads and incur no locking overhead. Value objects can support state-changing operations, but the effect of the state changes is localized.

C++'s language's object model is essentially based on value objects, and support for copying is provided easily and transparently to applications via copy constructors. Beyond ensuring appropriate copy construction behavior and declaring the appropriate call signatures for functions, therefore, developers do not need to make any extra arrangements to communicate values as COPIED VALUES. However, if the COPIED VALUES share representation, they are unsuitable if clients modify their state.

In C#, fine-grained objects that require no special construction can be expressed as `struct` objects, for which copying is an implicit operation. If a value requires complex construction, however, expressing them as COPIED VALUES might become infeasible due to copying overhead, and an alternative representation should be considered.

Java lacks an automatic mechanism for ensuring that objects are copied when communicated through methods between threads. The use of COPIED VALUES therefore requires more manual support, creating copies explicitly on call, and is therefore error-prone.

Immutable Value **

When expressing a fine-grained value via a DOMAIN OBJECT (208) or designing a CLIENT PROXY (240) ...

... we want to communicate values between different threads of an application efficiently and safely.

♦♦♦

References to value objects are commonly distributed and stored in fields. However, state changes to a value caused by one object can have unexpected and unwanted side-effects for any other object sharing the same value instance. Copying the value can reduce the synchronization overhead, but can also incur object creation overhead.

Copying can be used for modifiable value objects to minimize aliasing problems. Without proper language support, however, this practice is tedious and error-prone. It may also cause excessive creation of small objects, especially where values are frequently queried or passed between components. In principle, values are unchanging, so the creation of multiple instances of a value just to communicate it may be wasteful and incur excessive space and time overhead, depending on the underlying object creation model.

In a multi-threaded environment the problems of sharing and state change are multiplied. Synchronizing methods addresses the question of valid individual modifications, but does nothing for the general problem of sharing. Synchronization of change also incurs a performance cost.

Therefore:

Define a value object type whose instances are immutable. The internal state of a value object is set at construction and no subsequent modifications are allowed.

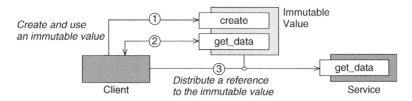

In an immutable value only query methods and constructors are provided: no modifier methods are defined. A change of value thus becomes a change in the value object referenced.

The absence of any possible state changes means there is no reason to synchronize. Not only does this make IMMUTABLE VALUES implicitly thread safe—the absence of locking means that their use in threaded environment is also efficient. Sharing of IMMUTABLE VALUES is also safe and transparent in other circumstances, so there is no need to copy an IMMUTABLE VALUE.

In Java, declaring the fields of an IMMUTABLE VALUE final ensures that no change promise is honoured. This guarantee also implies that either the class itself must be final, or that its subclasses must also be IMMUTABLE VALUES. In C++ a fully const-qualified object can play a similar role, distributed and shared by pointer. Restriction of further inheritance, however, must be communicated through convention rather than language mechanism.

If a value with different attributes is required, a new object is created or found with the desired value: references are changed, rather than attributes. There are complementary techniques for creating IMMUTABLE VALUES. A direct construction from a set of input values is supported by a complete and intuitive set of constructors, or by a number of class-level FACTORY METHODS (529). A MUTABLE COMPANION [Hen00b] helps in constructing IMMUTABLE VALUES as a result of an operation on another value object, such as calculating a value that is twice as large as another given value. A RESOURCE POOL (503) helps providing access to a set of pre-defined IMMUTABLE VALUES, and an OBJECT MANAGER (492) supports the construction of singleton IMMUTABLE VALUES.

Value objects do not represent resources, so managing finalization is not the issue that it might be with resource objects. AUTOMATED GARBAGE COLLECTION (519) can thus be used to reclaim the resources of IMMUTABLE VALUES that are no longer used. In contrast, sharing IMMUTABLE VALUES in a non-garbage collected environment needs to involve careful management: thread lifetimes must either be shorter than the lifetimes of the IMMUTABLE VALUES they share, or they should be referred to via COUNTING HANDLES (522).

17 Object Interaction

Kevlin and Frank at JAOO 2006, interacting about objects
© Mai Skou Nielsen

An application architecture's task is not always just a simple matter of calling methods on objects in other components. In many cases, an application defines a framework of some kind for use by others, whether for simple extension or for plugging in. A framework that encapsulates a model of interaction tends to have more sophisticated inter-object choreography than a component that offers simpler, more passive object types. This chapter presents a number of patterns that support interaction between objects that reside in different components of an application, framework, or product line.

Applications that are built on top of a component framework can take advantage of the framework's execution, resource, and relationship management features, in exchange for agreeing to abide by the terms of the framework's collaboration protocols. Collaboration between objects in such applications often involves much more than just calling synchronous methods and services on one another, passing parameters along with the calls, and collecting the results by way of immediate return. Although collaboration between component objects often follows this simple model, even in sequential programming it may not hold for an entire application.

The following issues arise when designing such interactions, some general, others specific to the context of distribution:

- *Decoupling.* In frameworks, product lines, and generally in large, long-lived systems, components are often loosely coupled to avoid unnecessary dependencies on one other, to support their independent evolution and reuse, as well as their composition within higher-level services. The aspect of loose coupling also extends to interactions between the components: explicit dependencies on specific collaboration protocols and policies, as well as on the data structures that are exchanged between the components, should be minimized. Another need for decoupling arises if the behavior offered by a component depends on the type of its caller. Solutions to this problem based on conditional statements within the code of components are possible, but to avoid structural complexity and to support maintenance and evolution, however, such dependencies should not be hard-coded.

- *Coherent coordination.* Components in a software system can act independently of one another, which is true especially for distributed and concurrent software systems. However, there may be a need to coordinate components in a coherent manner, for example to avoid inconsistencies in their internal states, or to orchestrate their execution according to specific higher-level collaboration or integration scenarios.

- *Communication overhead.* Communication between component objects across a distributed system can incur much higher latency and jitter overheads than in stand-alone systems. For example, the higher the current network load, the more time is needed to exchange messages between a client and a remote component object. A key goal in designing efficient and scalable distributed systems is therefore both to minimize and optimize network communication.

As a consequence of the above challenges, application designers must determine carefully how component objects *collaborate* with one another, not only if they develop distributed or concurrent software, but also when building frameworks or specifying product-line architectures. Eight patterns in our pattern language for distributed computing help to address these challenges, by enabling efficient yet flexible and cohesive object interactions:

The OBSERVER pattern (405) [GoF95] helps to synchronize the state of cooperating component objects by enabling one-way propagation of changes. Observers of a component object are notified by the object when its state changes.

The DOUBLE DISPATCH pattern (408) [Beck97] helps organize the communication between component objects where the behavior of the called object depends on the class of the calling object.

The MEDIATOR pattern (410) [GoF95] encapsulates the way in which a set of component objects interact. Mediator promotes loose coupling by keeping objects from referring to each other explicitly, and helps to vary their interaction independently.

The COMMAND pattern (412) [GoF95] encapsulates a request as a component object, thereby enabling the parameterization of clients with different requests, and support for undo-able objects.

The MEMENTO (414) [GoF95] pattern captures and externalizes the internal state of a component object without violating its encapsulation.

The CONTEXT OBJECT pattern (416) [ACM01] [Kel04] [KSS05] [Hen05] captures environmental services and information in component object form that can be passed to services or plug-in component objects that need to access their surrounding execution context.

The DATA TRANSFER OBJECT pattern (418) [ACM01] [Fow03a] reduces the number of update or query calls made to a remote component object by packaging groups of attributes into a simple object for passing or returning in single calls.

The MESSAGE pattern (420) [HoWo03] encapsulates the information that two application component objects can exchange into a data structure that can be transmitted across a network.

The eight object interaction patterns in this chapter fall into two groups: *collaboration* and *data exchange*.

The collaboration patterns, OBSERVER, DOUBLE DISPATCH, MEDIATOR, and COMMAND, help in coordinating or orchestrating the interaction between components and objects in an application. Each pattern addresses a specific aspect of this context, as outlined in their abstracts above. Consequently all four patterns are complementary to one another rather than alternatives.

The integration of the collaboration patterns into our pattern language is shown in the following diagram:

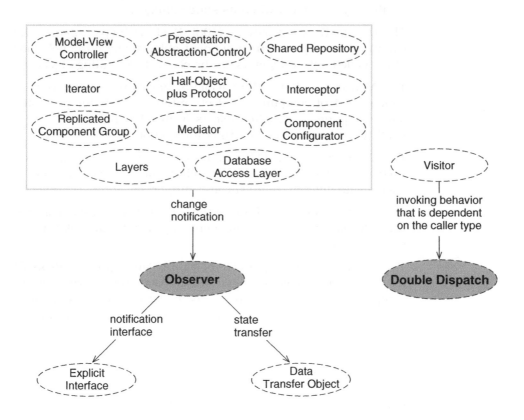

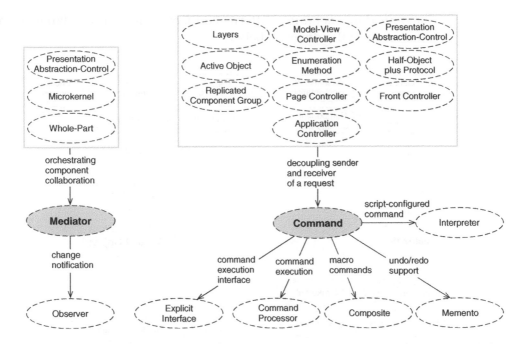

The four data exchange patterns, MEMENTO, CONTEXT OBJECT, DATA TRANSFER OBJECT, and MESSAGE, also address different aspects of object interaction. They are therefore often applied in conjunction when designing the interfaces of components. For example, clients can pass a CONTEXT OBJECT to a component when invoking a method and receive a DATA TRANSFER OBJECT in return, which encapsulates the results of the invocation, or a MEMENTO when the result is a snapshot of the component's internal state. A MESSAGE can represent instances of the three other patterns, as well as service requests and COMMANDS in a serialized form, which enables their transmission across a network in a specific on-the-wire protocol.

MEMENTO also covers flavors of CLIENT SESSION STATE, SERVER SESSION STATE, and DATABASE SESSION state [Fow03a], which specify different locations for storage of the state of a client session, which is encapsulated in a separate object. CONTEXT OBJECT, which has been described in a variety of sources, also address additional variations of the pattern that we do not cover in this book [ACM01] [Kel04] [KSS05] [Hen05].

The four data exchange patterns connect to our pattern language as illustrated in the diagram below.

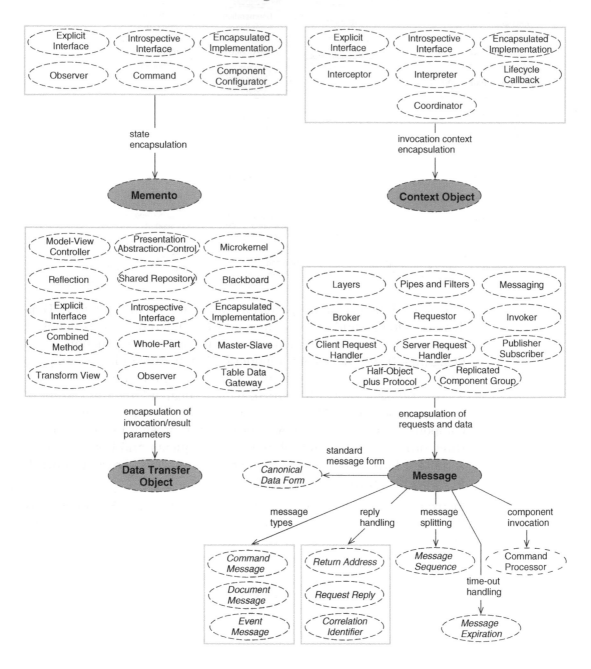

Observer **

In a LAYERS (185), MODEL-VIEW-CONTROLLER (188), PRESENTATION-ABSTRACTION-CONTROL (191), SHARED REPOSITORY (202), ITERATOR (298), HALF-OBJECT PLUS PROTOCOL (324), REPLICATED COMPONENT GROUP (326), INTERCEPTOR (444), MEDIATOR (410), COMPONENT CONFIGURATOR (490), or DATABASE ACCESS LAYER (538) arrangement ...

... we must provide a means to keep the state of a set of cooperating component objects consistent with each other.

◆◆◆

Consumer objects sometimes depend on the state of, or data maintained by, another provider object. If the state of the provider object changes without notice, however, the state of the dependent consumer objects can become inconsistent.

Common solutions to this problem are to hard-code connections from the provider object to all its dependent consumer objects, or to have the consumers poll the provider. These approaches are often impractical, however, since a consumer may not be dependent on the provider indefinitely, and new instances and types of consumers may emerge over an application's lifetime. Moreover, polling may either consume excessive resources, or may not detect changes quickly enough.

Therefore:

Define a change-propagation mechanism in which the provider—known as the 'subject'—notifies registered consumers—known as the 'observers'—whenever its state changes, so that the notified observers can perform whatever actions they deem necessary.

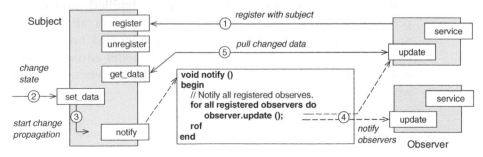

Observers must define a specific update interface that is notified by the subject when its state changes. This interface is the primary coupling between the subject and its observers. Observers can register and unregister from the subject dynamically. When the subject notifies its observes, it can either push the state to the observers along with the state change notification, or the observers can selectively pull the changed state from the subject at their discretional after being notified.

In an OBSERVER arrangement, the dynamic registration of observers with the change notification mechanism avoids hard-coding dependencies between the subject and its observers: they can join and leave at any time, and new types of observer that implement the update interface can be integrated without changing the subject. The active propagation of changes by the subject avoids polling and ensures that observers can update their own state immediately in response to state changes in the subject.

In a typical OBSERVER implementation, an EXPLICIT INTERFACE (281) defines the update interface to be supported by observers. Concrete observers implement this interface to define their specific update policy in response to notifications by the subject. The subject, in turn, offers an interface for observers to register with and unregister from, the change notification mechanism. Internally, the subject manages its registered observers within a collection, such as a hashed set or a linked list.

The OBSERVER change notification protocol can be implemented in several ways. The simplest option is based on a generic pull model: when the subject changes its state, it notifies *all* registered observers that a state change has occurred. The notified observers can then call back to the subject to retrieve more detailed information. This protocol works well if all observers depend on all state that the subject maintains. If different observers depend on different state in the subject, however, the generic pull model causes unnecessary updates, because the subject notifies all observers, not just those who depend on the state that has changed.

If subject and observer execute in different address spaces, the 'chattiness' of the generic pull model can consume network and processing resources unnecessarily. In this case, a categorized pull model can be used to allow observers to register with one or more different types of state changes in the subject. These observers are only notified if particular types of state change. The pull model therefore may still be inappropriate for remote communication, due to the overhead of having all the observers call back to the subject to obtain the state.

To minimize interactions between subject and observer, there are two other options for implementing the change notification protocol, both based on a push model rather than a pull model. In the generic push model, the subject pushes a snapshot of its attribute state to the observers along with each notification, using a DATA TRANSFER OBJECT (418) to communicate the attributes. This model is useful if all observers depend on the entire state being pushed, or when the cost of communicating all the state is less than the cost of having each observer call back for specific state.

A variant of the generic push model is the categorized push model, which is based on some type of filtering [GoF95]. If a change in the subject affects only a small portion of its entire state, this portion is pushed only to those observers who are interested in it. If these observers can also decide to not update themselves each time they are notified, however, even the categorized push model produces overhead, because many 'expensive' data pushes are unnecessary.

Choosing the best option for the change notification mechanisms in a specific OBSERVER configuration is also influenced by coupling issues. Pull models generally result in a looser coupling between the subject and the observers than push models, and the generic pull model decouples subject and observers better than the categorized pull model.

Double Dispatch **

When implementing a VISITOR (447) or when communicating between class hierarchies ...

... we must realize behavior that depends on the types of two objects.

♦♦♦

A method's behavior clearly depends on its argument's values. Sometimes, however, its behavior also depends on the type of an argument. In most object models, this 'multi-method dispatch' is not supported, and only single-dispatch is available.

Polymorphism is normally expressed in terms of single dispatch: the target of the method is the receiver of the call, and the selected method implementation depends on its class. Sometimes, however, behavior depends on both the type of the caller and the type of the called object, so the caller passes itself as argument. One solution to express such a configuration uses explicit selection, such as an `if...else` or `switch` statement, based on the argument's runtime type in each concrete class of the receiver's class hierarchy. This approach, however, is brittle and verbose. Another approach uses a map whose key is made up of a pairing of the receiver and the argument's runtime type, and whose mapped value is a method reference of some kind, such as a member function pointer in C++, or a delegate in C#. This approach can suffer from undue brittleness and runtime overhead.

Therefore:

Pass the caller object to the receiver object as an extra argument. Within the receiver, call back the caller object to run caller-class dependent logic, passing the receiver as an additional argument, so that the caller can behave appropriately.

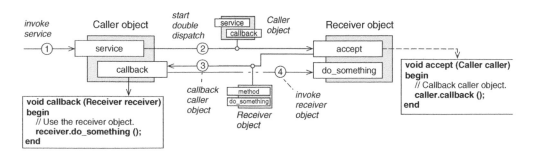

Behavior is now split across the caller and receiver objects. The caller object supports an interface that is based on the possible types of the receiver object: a set of methods—either overloaded or specifically named—each corresponding to a concrete receiver type. Each implementation of the caller object's interface defines the type-specific behavior in each receiver-matched method. The receiver is responsible for calling back on to the caller with itself as argument, selecting the method that corresponds to its type.

Double Dispatch avoids executing caller-class dependent behavior via large `if...else` or `switch` statements in the receiver object. Such solutions are hard to maintain and extend, even though they appear to centralize all programming logic in one place [Beck97]. Instead, both the caller and receiver objects are involved in the computation—hence the name Double Dispatch. This callback arrangement results in simpler and more cohesive code.

One liability with Double Dispatch, however, is that it incurs additional communication overhead between remote objects. Moreover, the maintainability of Double Dispatch relies on the stability of the receiver type's hierarchy. If new concrete classes are added to the receiver hierarchy, the argument's interface must be updated, as must all implementations of the argument interface. Depending on how widely this interface is distributed, such changes range from being tedious to impossible—organizational boundaries, widespread release in a published API, binary stability, and so on, all restrict the evolvability of an interface.

Mediator *

When implementing PRESENTATION-ABSTRACTION-CONTROL (191), a MICROKERNEL (194), or a WHOLE-PART (317) ...

... we must reduce the coupling between multiple cooperating objects.

Sometimes the relationships between a set of objects is complex: each object in the set cooperates with several other objects. Allowing each object to maintain all these cooperation relationships by itself, however, would overly couple the objects.

The resulting interdependencies would be hard to understand, test, and maintain in subsequent modifications of the collaborating classes, since introducing participants to the collaborating set of objects is subtle and error-prone. If the essence of the collaboration—but not the specific types involved—is needed elsewhere, such tight coupling can preclude effective reuse.

Therefore:

Decouple the objects via a separate mediator object that encapsulates the collective cooperative behavior of all objects in the set. Collaboration is achieved indirectly via mediation, rather than directly through point-to-point communication.

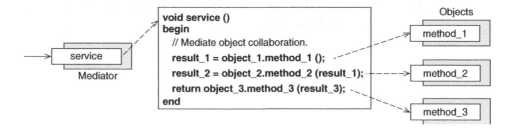

If an object wants to cooperate with another object, it does so by sending its request, message, or data to the mediator, which then routes the information anonymously to the appropriate receiver. Results can be returned accordingly.

A mediator preserves the self-containment and independence of multiple cooperating objects, which need not maintain explicit relationships with their peers. Instead, they delegate the routing of requests, messages, and data that they exchange with other objects to the mediator. The mediator is the orchestrator that connects the cooperating objects, maintains oversight of them, and controls their collaborations.

Although a mediator preserves the cohesiveness, encapsulation, and simplicity of individual collaborating objects, the centralization of control may make the mediator itself a potential maintenance problem. Similarly, a mediator can also be a potential performance bottleneck and a single point of failure in a distributed system.

There are two general approaches for implementing a mediator: either it can hard-code the relationships between the objects whose cooperation it coordinates, or it can act as a subject in an OBSERVER (405) design that provides requests, messages, and data to consuming objects. The latter option follows an implicit invocation style of execution that is very loosely coupled. This approach, however, makes the actual control model harder to see, and can require more development effort than a hard-coded design.

Command **

When implementing LAYERS (185), MODEL-VIEW-CONTROLLER (188), PRESENTATION-ABSTRACTION-CONTROL (191), ACTIVE OBJECT (365), ENUMERATION METHOD (300), HALF-OBJECT PLUS PROTOCOL (324), REPLICATED COMPONENT GROUP (326), PAGE CONTROLLER (337), FRONT CONTROLLER (339), or APPLICATION CONTROLLER (341) ...

... we must invoke actions on a component independently of selecting the actions to invoke.

♦♦♦

Accessing an object typically involves calling one of its methods. Sometimes, however, it is useful to decouple the sender of a request from its receiver. It may also be useful to decouple the selection of a request and receiver from the point of execution.

While explicit coupling is beneficial for many client/service relationships and deployments, it can introduce too much coupling if the request chosen by the client is more important than the identity of the receiver. Similarly, it is hard to invoke a method asynchronously in programming languages that use the conventional synchronous call/return model of method invocation. Moreover, housekeeping functionality, such as logging and undo, cannot be supported transparently. Ideally, clients ought be able to issue a request and the 'right' things should just happen.

Therefore:

Encapsulate requests to the receiving object in command objects, and provide these objects with a common interface to execute the requests they represent.

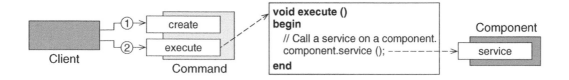

Clients that want to issue a particular request create the corresponding command object. When invoked, the command object initiates and controls the execution of the represented request with respect to any arguments it receives when executed.

COMMAND decouples the requestor of behavior from the recipient, as well as the selection of behavior from the point of execution. This loose coupling ensures that requestors do not depend on a specific receiver interface. Modifications to the receiver's interface therefore do not ripple through to its clients. In addition, the reification of requests into command objects allows the handling of requests as first-class entities within an application, which in turn enables the implementation of extra request-handling features such as undo and logging.

To realize a COMMAND structure, first specify an EXPLICIT INTERFACE (281) for uniform command execution. The interface will define one or more methods for execution, receiving arguments as necessary. Concrete commands implement this interface to reify particular requests. Each concrete command is initialized with whatever state is needed to support its execution, such as a receiver object or method arguments for later use. An INTERPRETER (442) is a special form of COMMAND in which a script from a simple language is transformed into an executable runtime structure.

Command objects can offer an undo mechanism by retaining the state necessary to roll back the behavior they execute. If the state is heavyweight or hard to restore, however, a MEMENTO (414) that snapshots the receiver's state before executing the command may provide a simpler, more lightweight option.

A COMPOSITE (319) structure supports the construction and execution of macro commands, aggregating multiple command objects uniformly behind a single interface, and executing or rolling them back in a particular order. A separate COMMAND PROCESSOR (343) that executes command objects on behalf of their sender can provide additional request-handling support, such as for multiple undo/redo, scheduling, and logging.

Memento **

When implementing an EXPLICIT INTERFACE (281), INTROSPECTIVE INTERFACE (286), or ENCAPSULATED IMPLEMENTATION (313), or when realizing an OBSERVER (405), COMMAND (412), or COMPONENT CONFIGURATOR (490) arrangement . . .

. . . we need to exchange state between participants without breaking encapsulation.

◆◆◆

It is often necessary to record the internal state of an object. Allowing other objects to access an object's state directly breaks encapsulation and introduces unnecessary complexity in dependent objects.

Storing and retrieving object state is common in distributed systems. For example, a persistence service may need to extract an object's state when it is passivated and hold this state so it is available the next time the object is run. If the internal state of an object is exposed for this purpose, however, it may lose control over which other objects access—and perhaps modify—its state. This lack of encapsulation can bind dependent objects to a particular state representation, which makes it hard to modify the software.

Therefore:

Snapshot and encapsulate the relevant state of the originating object within a separate memento object, and pass this memento to the object's clients instead of letting them access the object's internal state directly.

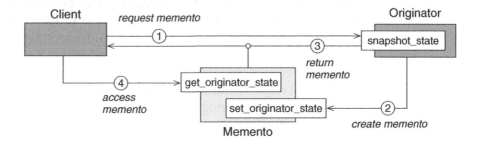

The originating object can recover and reactivate its previous state from the memento if and when it is passed back by a client or a state-recovery service.

A MEMENTO preserves the encapsulation of the originating object: dependent objects cannot access its state directly, but the originating object can. MEMENTO allows these dependent objects to receive the latest state, in wrapped form, from the publishing object on request, without being dependent on the representation of the state.

The internal representation stored in the MEMENTO is free to evolve over different versions of the software without any need for source-level changes in the dependent objects. In fact, binary compatibility may also be preserved across versions, depending on the programming language and class design techniques used.

Most MEMENTOS offer two interfaces. For the originating object they provide a wide interface, with setter and getter methods to initialize the MEMENTO and to access the state it maintains. Clients of the originating object, however, often see only a narrow interface that allows them to access the MEMENTO'S state, but not to modify its state. Some languages, such as Java and C#, support packaging structures that allow different visibility for class methods inside a package than outside it, which makes it easy to segregate the two interfaces. C++ supports these differences in visibility via `friend` or forward-declared classes, and source files as packages. Alternatively, separation of interfaces via inheritance can help to differentiate the wide and narrow interfaces.

Context Object **

When implementing an EXPLICIT INTERFACE (281), INTROSPECTIVE INTERFACE (286), ENCAPSULATED IMPLEMENTATION (313), INTERCEPTOR (444), INTERPRETER (442), LIFECYCLE CALLBACK (499), or TASK COORDINATOR (501) . . .

. . . we need to share information about the system or invocation context of a component without introducing global coupling.

Loose coupling is a key design goal in distributed systems. In a loosely coupled system, however, there may be a need to share common information that relates to the program's execution *context*, such as its externally configured values, client session state, and logging, across its disparate parts or layers.

Although the scope of a program's execution context is generally more global than the scope of its parts, global variables and SINGLETONS [GoF95] provide uncontrolled access from all parts of a program and introduce unnecessary coupling. Globals and SINGLETONS also do not provide late binding easily: the implementation and instance on which they are based is often hard-coded at design-time rather than configurable at runtime. Conversely, propagating many items of fine-grained information as individual variables, and services as individual operations, can yield unmanageable and unstable argument lists.

Therefore:

Represent the information and services in an object that encapsulates the required context. Provide this object to the operations, components, and layers that need the context.

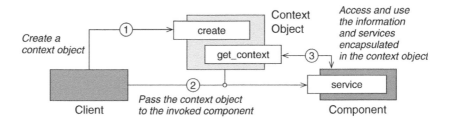

Clients that issue a request on a component create the context object, which can be passed explicitly or implicitly along with other parameters of the invocation. The receiving component uses the information and services in the context object to guide its own execution.

With a CONTEXT OBJECT, basic runtime substitutability can be supported *explicitly* via the standard argument passing mechanisms, or *implicitly* via THREAD-SPECIFIC STORAGE. It is possible to modify the execution context of a component without necessarily having to modify the configuration or code of other parts of a system. It is also possible to run with multiple, different contexts within the same program, perhaps in different threads. Over time, small changes to the information and services in the context are absorbed, since the unit of stability is the CONTEXT OBJECT, not its individual items of information and service operations.

If the dependency of a piece of code is simply on a passable value rather than a broader notion of execution context, the value itself should be passed rather than any kind of CONTEXT OBJECT, partitioned or not. In such cases a CONTEXT OBJECT would draw in more context, significance, and dependencies than were justified by the use of an isolated value. Although execution context represents a cross-cutting feature, this does not necessitate it being global, either as a global variable or as a universal type.

A CONTEXT OBJECT introduces an inversion of dependencies [Mar04] and responsibilities. It may also introduce an inversion of control flow, but this is not necessarily always the case: an informational context may be more passive, but a behavioral service context will generally result in a more obvious inversion of control flow.

Data Transfer Object **

When realizing a Model-View-Controller (188), Presentation-Abstraction-Control (191), Microkernel (194), Reflection (197), Shared Repository (202), Blackboard (205), Explicit Interface (281), Introspective Interface (286), Combined Method (296), Whole-Part (317), Master-Slave (321), Transform View (347), Observer (405), or Table Data Gateway (544) configuration ...

... we must make calls to query and update data in remote component objects.

♦♦♦

Many stateful component objects need an interface that supports querying and optionally updating of their attributes. Remote communication can incur significant overhead on each call, however, so individual methods for getting and setting each attribute are inefficient.

Accessing individual attributes of remote objects via correspondingly fine-grained calls is expensive. In addition, such an interface introduces coherence problems, because if a client needs to query more than a single attribute at a time, another client may change the state between the individual calls, even though each individual query was synchronized. Similarly, locking the remote object for the duration of a client's attribute queries is inefficient. A Combined Method (296) would make sense if only a single method were involved, but if the same data items appear in the argument lists of multiple methods, duplication and interface instability may occur if argument lists change. Moreover, not all languages support the concept of *out* parameters to support queries simply and directly.

Therefore:

Bundle all data items that might be needed into a single data transfer object used for querying or updating attributes together.

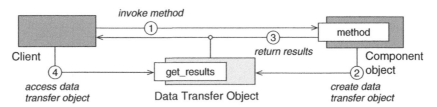

A DATA TRANSFER OBJECT has little behavior of its own, containing only the data corresponding to the attributes, queries to access them, and a way of initializing and optionally setting the data values.

The resulting DATA TRANSFER OBJECT is more network-friendly, since only a single remote call is needed to query or update a set of attributes. If the set of attributes changes, moreover, the call interface of the remote object remains stable, even though the data transfer object changes. DATA TRANSFER OBJECTS are also useful in non-distributed systems, where they help to avoid many fine-grained data access calls to component objects, and also dependencies of clients on concrete data representations used within component objects.

Even if not all the attributes are needed from a query, the cost of a single call to copy the transfer object across the network is still often lower than the repeated cost of querying each attribute individually. If only a few attributes need to be updated, the caller must either resupply the existing values—which could require an additional call to query them and the additional risk of overwriting another update—or indicate that some attributes are not updated. This can either be expressed in the data transfer object or in the method signature.

A data transfer object needs some way of indicating that a value has not been set, which for certain data types can be indicated using nulls. For primitive types, however, additional flags may be needed. Alternatively, a simple set of flags indicating which values have been set can be passed along with the data transfer object, though this solution can be brittle and awkward to use. A more loosely typed approach can use a data transfer object made up of name–value pairs.

Message **

When implementing a LAYERS (185) or PIPES AND FILTERS (200) architecture, or when realizing a MESSAGING (221), BROKER (237), REQUESTOR (242), INVOKER (244), CLIENT REQUEST HANDLER (246), SERVER REQUEST HANDLER (249), PUBLISHER-SUBSCRIBER (234), HALF-OBJECT PLUS PROTOCOL (324), or REPLICATED COMPONENT GROUP (326) configuration ...

... we must provide a means of exchanging pieces of information across the network without introducing dependencies on concrete component types and their interfaces.

◆◆◆

Distributed components collaborate like collocated components, invoking services on one another and exchanging data. However, on-the-wire protocols such as HTTP only support byte streams, the most basic form of data transmission, but not the notions of service invocations and data types.

We however need a means to transmit service requests, invocation parameters, service results, and other information such as errors across the network in a typed and structured manner. Otherwise, sending and receiving components have no clue about the semantics of the byte streams they receive.

Therefore:

Encapsulate method requests and data structures to be sent across the network into messages: byte streams that include a header specifying the type of information being transmitted, its origin, destination, size, and other structural information, and a payload that contains the actual information.

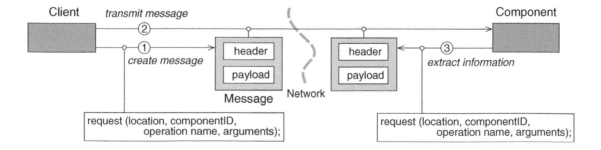

On the sender's side, method requests on remote components, or data exchanged with them, are marshaled into a message that is sent across the network. When arriving at the receiver's side, the message is unmarshaled into its original form.

The key benefit of a MESSAGE is that it allows the structure of the information it carries to be preserved in a 'flat' format, so that the structure can be recreated by the message receiver. In addition, MESSAGES support loose coupling: senders and can be independent of concrete receiver interfaces as long as both parties agree on a common message format.

Although all messages should follow a common CANONICAL DATA MODEL [HoWo03], a whole range of different message types can be distinguished. A COMMAND MESSAGE [HoWo03] represents a request for invoking a specific method or procedure on the message receiver, a DOCUMENT MESSAGE [HoWo03] allows a set of data to be passed to it, and an EVENT MESSAGE [HoWo03] supports notification of the message receiver about a change in the state of the message sender.

If the receiver component is expected to respond to a message it receives, the message header should contain a RETURN ADDRESS [HoWo03]. The specific response is also encapsulated in an appropriate message, which leads to a REQUEST-REPLY [HoWo03] scenario. A CORRELATION IDENTIFIER [HoWo03] in the message header—which is basically an ASYNCHRONOUS COMPLETION TOKEN (268)—indicates to the receiver of the reply message to which concrete request message the reply corresponds.

If the size of the information to transmit exceeds the maximum message length, break it into multiple smaller messages that are transmitted to the receiver as a MESSAGE SEQUENCE [HoWo03]. If the data encapsulated in a message is only useful or valid for a limited time, specify a corresponding MESSAGE EXPIRATION [HoWo03] in the message header.

A separate COMMAND PROCESSOR (343) helps to transform a specific message (sequence) into a concrete method invocation on the message receiver, and can provide additional request-handling support, such as for multiple undo/redo, scheduling, and logging.

18 Adaptation and Extension

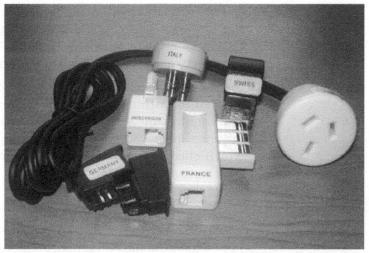

A set of pluggable adapters
© Frank Buschmann

The only constant in life is change! This wisdom from the 17th century French author François de la Rochefoucauld seems particularly true of software. Software is a 'living thing.' The ability of applications and components to adapt to specific environments, extend to meet customer-specific requirements, and evolve over their lifetime, can be a deciding factor for their long-term use and success. This chapter presents thirteen patterns that support developers in building software that is open to adaptation, extension, and evolution.

No single profile covers either the types of modern applications developed or the range of customers for which they are developed. Some applications are specifically developed for a single customer, whereas others are developed as products with a mass market in mind. Although some applications are targeted at a single customer, repeat business for the customer—or for similar applications sought by other customers—can motivate and justify the definition of a common base for the applications to built upon. Even if multiple customers can benefit from a particular software system or infrastructure, each often has unique and specific requirements not yet supported by default. For example:

- *Out-of-band extensions.* Customers sometimes request additional algorithms or services that should be interwoven into the control flow of the system and its components. Examples include the system's integration with existing applications, or with specific monitoring or security services. These out-of-band extensions, however, are often highly customer-specific.

- *Specialized algorithms.* Customers often demand specialized or tailored algorithms for key system services, even if all customers require the same set of services. For example, business information systems must consider relevant tax and accounting regulations, which often change over time. These regulations also vary depending on country or region, as well as on the legal status of companies using the system.

- *Service extensions and restrictions.* Customers often ask for particular extensions or restrictions to specific services of a system. For example, some customers could require specific pre-processing before executing the services of a particular component, or specific post-processing after their execution. Other customers may require restriction of the full services of a component to the strict subset that they need. By contrast, other customers may wish to extend some components with additional services.

- *Multi-platform support.* Different customers may want to run a system in different environments. The system's components should therefore be portable to different operating systems, libraries, networks, and hardware platforms. Components of distributed systems must also be prepared to run in a heterogeneous computing environment: the component may be deployed on multiple platforms across multiple network nodes.

It is hard to design a software system that supports customer-specific configuration, adaptation, and extension without also destroying its baseline architecture and fundamental design. To complicate matters, most requests for such changes are made when the system is in production, rather than during development or installation. An iterative, feedback-based development lifecycle can help to clarify requirements sooner rather than later, but this will not shift all such changes into the main development lifecycle: the greatest source of feedback comes once a system is used in production.

Instead of considering changing a normal part of the continued development process following initial installation, it is unfortunately still common practice to handle individual customer requirements and change requests via *ad hoc* system modifications. Such tactics are rarely sustainable in the long term. Instead, with every such adaptation and extension, developers often dilute and pollute the original architectural vision with localized fixes and workarounds that make the code base increasingly brittle, subtle, and costly. Since developers often do not have the opportunity to see adaptive changes in the context of the whole system, it becomes increasingly hard to focus on the quality of implementation and stability of the architecture. Instead, code that is general becomes mixed with case- or customer-specific code, and vice-versa. Over time, these *ad hoc* modifications wreck the system's architectural integrity, and can ultimately lead to product that cannot cope with new requirements or environments [BeLe76] [Par94].

To avoid a creeping death by a thousand cuts, a software system must be designed thoughtfully and consciously for its own configuration, adaptation, and evolution. Without appropriate constraints and sensibility, however, we can end up overdosing on 'speculative generality' and introducing unnecessary accidental complexity and bloat into our systems [FBBOR99]:

> Brian Foote suggested this name for a smell to which we are very sensitive. You get it when people say, 'Oh, I think we need the ability to do this kind of thing someday' and thus want all sorts of hooks and special cases to handle things that aren't required. The result is often harder to understand and maintain. If all this machinery were being used, it would be worth it. But if it isn't, it isn't. The machinery just gets in the way, so get rid of it.

In striving for the right balance between stability and adaptability, it is important to take into account the nature of the system that is being deployed and changed. In a closed architecture with limited deployment, for example, the criticality of decisions concerning change is far lower than the consequences of change in more widely deployed, open architectures. A wide range of techniques can be applied to converge on designs that are both sufficiently stable and suitably adaptable for their intended context. For example, analytical techniques such as *Open Implementation Analysis and Design* [KLLM95], *Commonality/Variability Analysis* [Cope98], or *Feature Modeling* [CzEi02] can help to identify and separate stable from changeable aspects. General design techniques, such as aggressive dependency management, can also help to isolate change within a code base. Development process approaches, such as iterative and incremental lifecycles, can help to replace purely speculative design with empirical feedback based on concrete user experience.

In all cases, the desired result is a set of stable design centers for the system under development, each being open to extension and adaptation where needed, but closed with respect to fundamental structural and behavioral aspects that should remain unchanged, thus following the open–closed principle [Mey97].

Our pattern language for distributed computing includes thirteen patterns that support the configuration, adaptation, extension, and evolution of software system components. Each pattern addresses a specific challenge from those outlined at the beginning of this section. In addition, their scope is not limited to distributed systems: all patterns apply to any software that has adaptation and extension requirements to fulfill, or that must be maintained and evolved over a long period of time:

The BRIDGE pattern (436) [GoF95] decouples an abstraction from its implementations so that the two can vary independently. It partitions an object into a handle, which represents the abstraction, and a body, which contains the implementation.

The OBJECT ADAPTER pattern (438) [GoF95] converts the interface of a class into another interface that clients expect. Adaptation lets classes work together that could not otherwise because of incompatible interfaces. The use of an object relationship to express wrapping ensures that the adaptation is encapsulated.

The CHAIN OF RESPONSIBILITY pattern (440) [GoF95] avoids coupling the sender of a request to its receiver by giving more than one object a chance to handle the request. The receiving objects are chained together and the request is passed along the chain until an object handles it.

The INTERPRETER pattern (442) [GoF95] defines an interpreter for a simple language by modeling the grammar in terms of objects, and making this grammar representation directly executable, parameterized by a context object that carries invocation state.

The INTERCEPTOR pattern (444) [POSA2] allows event-related processing to be plugged into a framework transparently and triggered automatically when specific events occur.

The VISITOR pattern (447) [GoF95] allows an operation to be performed on the elements of an object structure in which the objects can be of different types. The operation can be specialized for each type visited without actually needing to modify the types visited.

The DECORATOR pattern (449) [GoF95] supports dynamic attachment of additional behaviors to an object. Decorators provide a flexible alternative to subclassing for extending functionality.

The EXECUTE-AROUND OBJECT idiom for C++ (451) [Hen01a] defines a helper object that executes actions before and after a sequence of statements in its constructor(s) and destructor to ensure correctness and exception-safety, as well as reduce code duplication.

The TEMPLATE METHOD pattern (453) [GoF95] defines a skeleton of an algorithm for an operation, deferring some steps to subclasses. This pattern allows subclasses to redefine specific steps of an algorithm without changing the algorithm's structure.

The STRATEGY pattern (455) [GoF95] captures a family of operations that vary together. Each variant is encapsulated within an object that shares a common interface with other variations. The use of these pluggable behavior objects is independent of the implementation variant.

The NULL OBJECT pattern (457) [And96] [Woolf97] [Hen02a] encapsulates the absence of an object by providing a substitutable alternative that offers suitable default 'do-nothing' behavior.

The WRAPPER FACADE pattern (459) [POSA2] encapsulates the functions and data provided by existing non-object-oriented APIs within more concise, robust, portable, and cohesive object-oriented class interfaces.

The DECLARATIVE COMPONENT CONFIGURATION pattern (461) [VSW02] allows components to indicate how they want to be integrated into the container's component execution environment and into the container itself, so that the container can perform this integration automatically.

These patterns alone do not cover all aspects of system configuration, adaptation, and evolution. Their scope is largely limited to the internals of services. Protecting clients of a service from changes within its implementation is the subject of several patterns that we present in Chapter 12, *Interface Partitioning*. The act of creating a concrete service configuration and the runtime management of a particular system configuration is handled by several patterns that are described in Chapter 20, *Resource Management*.

While a common theme of all patterns in this chapter is decoupling a specific aspect of a component from its core implementation, they differ in the specific aspects that they decouple. Naturally, some patterns address related aspects and form alternatives to one another.

BRIDGE and OBJECT ADAPTER generally help with decoupling interfaces from implementation, and with mapping from interfaces that clients expect or require from a component to the interfaces the component actually provides. Such a decoupling ensures that the implementation of a component can vary independently of its interface and transparently for clients. The difference between the two patterns is in their scope. BRIDGE connects interface and implementation of the same component, while OBJECT ADAPTER helps plugging different components together.

The integration of BRIDGE and OBJECT ADAPTER into our pattern language for distributed computing is shown in the diagram below.

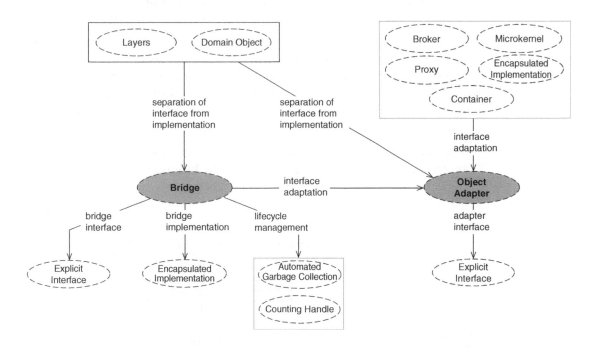

The ADAPTER pattern described in *Design Patterns* [GoF95] is too broad to be considered a single pattern at this level: it captures the general essence of a family of patterns concerned with adaptation, which also includes WRAPPER FACADE, but it does not categorically define a single group of forces and a corresponding solution. Two principal versions are documented, each with specific trade-offs and solution structures: CLASS ADAPTER and OBJECT ADAPTER. Other variations are defined that relate to plugability, but the principal forms are sufficient for most discussions. The former implements adaptation with respect to inheritance, a class relationship, whereas the latter implements adaptation with respect to aggregation, an object relationship. The latter is less problematic and more widely applied of the two patterns, and is the one we have found most effective within our language.

The next pattern, CHAIN OF RESPONSIBILITY, helps with decoupling the sender of a request from its receiver. The pattern chains all potential receiver objects of a request so that a sender can just issue a request to the first sender in the chain. The request is passed along the chain until it arrives at its intended receiver, where it is handled. CHAIN OF RESPONSIBILITY thus provides a very flexible approach for dispatching requests from clients to the object that executes the request.

INTERPRETER helps with realizing components whose behavior in response to a request is orchestrated by interpreting data or scripts. Such a design is helpful if a typical invocation scenario for the component involves many of its offered services, but common orderings of these services that could be coalesced to a COMBINED METHOD (296) on its interface cannot be identified, or are otherwise unfeasible.

The following diagram outlines how CHAIN OF RESPONSIBILITY and INTERPRETER connect to the patterns in our language.

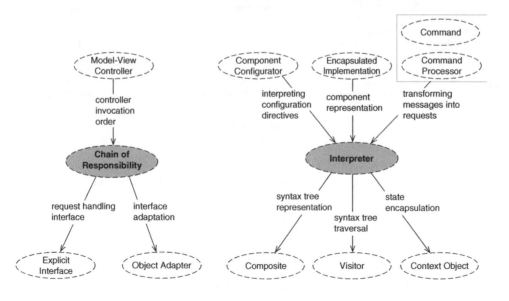

A further group of four patterns deal with extending component implementations with additional functionality. INTERCEPTOR supports the integration of out-of-band or extended control flow to the methods of a component, while VISITOR supports the addition of new functions to an entire group of interconnected components. DECORATOR supports the addition of new methods to a specific component, or to decorate any existing method with additional pre- and post-processing behavior, and EXECUTE-AROUND OBJECT the addition of pre- and post-processing behavior to the methods and code blocks of a C++ object.

DECORATOR and EXECUTE-AROUND OBJECT are similar in the sense that they wrap an object with pre- and post-processing behavior to be executed when specific methods are invoked, but they differ significantly in their granularity and scope. Most obviously, DECORATOR is a general-purpose pattern, whereas EXECUTE-AROUND OBJECT is a C++ idiom. The other difference is that DECORATOR can wrap only entire methods of a component with additional pre- and post-processing, whereas EXECUTE-AROUND OBJECT can also wrap specific code blocks within a method.

The diagrams below outline how the four patterns that provide functional extensions to components integrate with our pattern language for distributed computing.

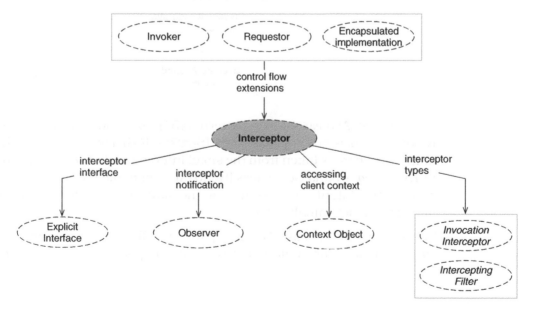

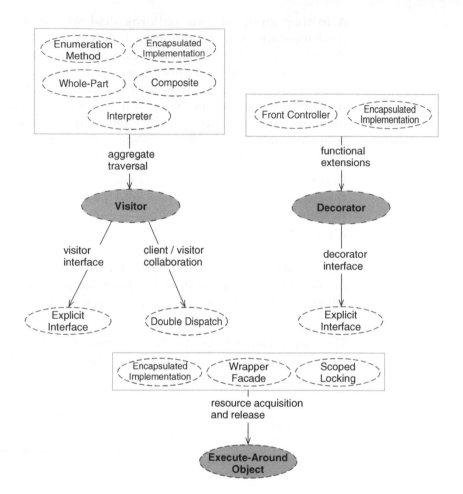

The EXECUTE-AROUND OBJECT pattern (451) is popularly known as
RESOURCE ACQUISITION IS INITIALIZATION [Str97]—RAII for short—but the
name used here is taken from the small interconnected set of patterns
in *Executing Around Sequences* [Hen01a]. The name more accurately
reflects the intent: the essence of the pattern is in deterministic
finalization, not initialization.

The TEMPLATE METHOD and STRATEGY patterns offer alternatives for realizing variant algorithmic behavior in a component. The difference

between the two patterns is in their underlying solution principles: TEMPLATE METHOD uses inheritance to address the problem, while STRATEGY uses delegation. In general, delegation is the more flexible option for realizing variant algorithmic behavior, so STRATEGY has a broader applicability than TEMPLATE METHOD. NULL OBJECT encapsulates a specific STRATEGY: doing nothing. NULL OBJECT thus addresses a specific flavor of variability in which an algorithm not only can vary, but actually is optional: in some configurations the algorithm must or should not be executed. Such a form of variability is commonly known as *negative variability* [Cope98].

TEMPLATE METHOD, STRATEGY, and NULL OBJECT connect with our pattern language as shown in the diagram below.

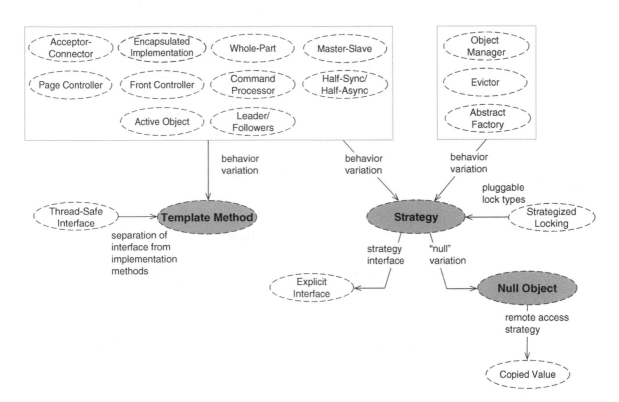

The WRAPPER FACADE pattern provides object-oriented and semantically meaningful access to a low-level API that offers a whole set of non-object oriented functions, such as an operating system or graphical user interface library. The goal of WRAPPER FACADE is to simplify access to a low-level API, thereby ensuring robust access and platform independence. In some ways WRAPPER FACADE is thus similar to OBJECT ADAPTER, but in addition to their different levels of scope, WRAPPER FACADE encapsulates the low-level API, whereas OBJECT ADAPTER still allows access to the adaptee's interface directly.

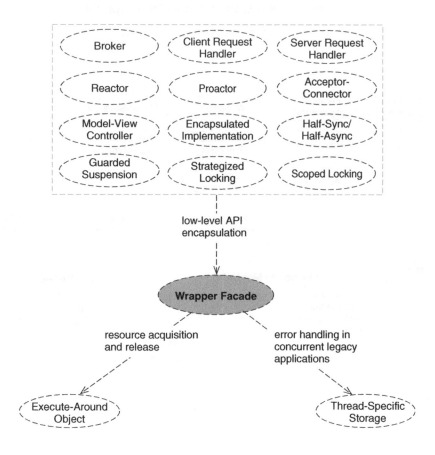

The last pattern in this chapter, DECLARATIVE COMPONENT CONFIGURATION, addresses how the resource and infrastructure needs of a component can be passed to its hosting infrastructure so that it can generate a specific binding for the component. DECLARATIVE COMPONENT CONFIGURATION thus avoids the need for such bindings to be hard-coded.

In its original source, *Server Component Patterns* [VSW02], the DECLARATIVE COMPONENT CONFIGURATION pattern is called ANNOTATIONS. The name used in our language is intentionally more specific, because 'annotations' can be more broadly interpreted as related to any form of code-specified metadata, as is implied by the standard Java feature of the same name.

The diagram below shows how DECLARATIVE COMPONENT CONFIGURATION connects to our patterns language.

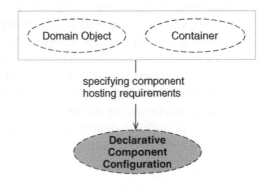

Bridge **

When specifying a LAYERS (185) design or a DOMAIN OBJECT (208) ...

... we must consider that the implementation of objects can vary independently of their interfaces.

♦♦♦

An object may have one of several different implementations. The difference between these implementations could be platform-specific, or a runtime decision. Using inheritance to separate interface and implementation, however, can expose the client of the object to decisions about its implementation.

Inheritance is a typical approach to separating interface and implementation: an interface declares the object's visible functionality, and an implementation realizes the methods declared in the interface. If accessed via the concrete class, however, there is a coupling that becomes a liability when striving for a stable design: client code now depends on the underlying implementation type. If accessed consistently through the interface, object users will be unaffected by changes in the underlying implementation class, but they are *not* free of all dependencies on the implementation: at the point of creation, a client must make a decision concerning the underlying type, which can clutter and overcomplicate client code.

Therefore:

Split the object into two parts: a handle abstraction that provides its interface, and a separate implementor hierarchy that provides the various implementations for the body.

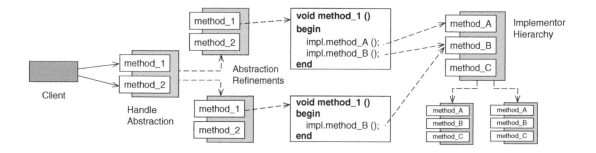

Clients only communicate with the handle object, which in turn is configured with a body that is an instance of the required implementor class. Method calls on the handle are forwarded to the associated body to perform the implementation. The handle may also be responsible for managing the lifecycle of the body.

Using a BRIDGE makes clients of an object depend directly only on an interface: the implementation decision and detail is encapsulated. Consequently, clients are unaffected by implementation changes. Similarly, changes in an object's interface do not ripple through to its implementation if the new handle interface can be mapped onto the existing body, for example with an OBJECT ADAPTER (438). This strict separation of concerns can incur a performance overhead, however, due to the additional level of indirection introduced by using BRIDGE. The shorter the execution time of the body, the higher this performance penalty becomes.

Either side of a BRIDGE structure can be concrete, or based on a class hierarchy. In the latter case, it is often based on two EXPLICIT INTERFACES (281): one for the abstraction hierarchy, one for the implementor hierarchy. Concrete implementations of the body hierarchy are often realized as ENCAPSULATED IMPLEMENTATIONS (313). The handle must choose a suitable, specific concrete implementation for the body, which may be linked dynamically at runtime.

Normally the body instance is exclusive to a given handle, but if it is immutable it can be shared. Sharing is sometimes also used as a space optimization when the cost of modifying the body can be deferred. AUTOMATED GARBAGE COLLECTION (519) helps to prevent the accidental destruction of a body by multiple handle instances. If garbage collection is not supported, the handle can be implemented as a COUNTING HANDLE (522) to keep track of the number of handles using the body.

Object Adapter **

When realizing Layers (185), Domain Object (208), Broker (237), Microkernel (194), Proxy (290) Encapsulated Implementation (313), Bridge (436), Chain of Responsibility (440), or Container (488) ...

... we may need to address the mismatch between the provided interface of an existing component and the interface required by clients.

Applications can benefit from reusing existing code. An existing class, however, does not always provide the interface that its clients expect, but instead might provide too much, too little, or in the wrong style.

Using the original class interface directly may be simple, but is often problematic because clients are coupled tightly to a particular implementation and interface. Interface changes can affect all clients, which is an unnecessary side-effect arising from reuse. In addition, the original interface may not reflect the intended usage scenarios of the application, which requires either extra glue code or bending the usage code towards the existing interface. The former option would pollute the clients with (duplicated) infrastructure code, which is tedious and error-prone to maintain, and also does not contribute to realizing their main responsibilities. The latter option could result in client domain models that are suboptimal from the perspective of the application using the component. Since reusing existing code should ideally be a means to an end and not an end in itself, reused code should offer an interface that allows clients to use it in new contexts on their own terms.

Therefore:

Introduce a separate adapter between the component and its clients that converts the provided interface of the component into the interface that the clients expect, and vice versa.

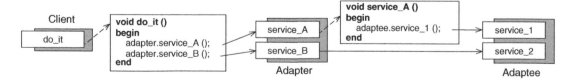

Calling a method on the adapter maps the request onto the adaptee—the instance of the class being reused. Result data structures returned by the component are transformed into the result data structures expected by the calling client.

An OBJECT ADAPTER shields clients from a specific decision to use an existing implementation in a new context, while still integrating with a uniform client interface. If the adaptee interface changes, corresponding modifications in the application are localized in the adapter. These interface changes are transparent to the adapter's clients.

The adapter class itself may be based on an EXPLICIT INTERFACE (281) that its clients expect or require. The implementation of the adapter normally relies on composition. During construction, either the adapter initializes an instance of the adaptee directly or, in the case of a looser relationship, it receives an instance of the adaptee. Pluggable adapters can be defined either with respect to an adaptee instance passed in on construction, or with respect to a parameterized type. Regardless of which construction variant is used, calls on the adapter are forwarded to the adaptee.

An OBJECT ADAPTER may introduce an additional level of indirection and an additional object creation. This cost is not necessarily incurred if the adaptee's representation is embedded within that of the adapter. For C++, a data member of the adaptee type is contained in this way, and the adapter method calls can be inlined to minimize overhead. For C#, the adaptee would have to be a struct type. In other cases, such as accessing via a pointer, or in other languages such as Java, the indirection and extra creation cost will always be incurred.

The more complex the mapping between the interface required by clients and the interface provided by the adaptee becomes, the more expensive the mapping can become, in terms of runtime resources, performance, and development effort. If the application cannot afford this overhead, consider not using the adaptee at all, or refactor the code to allow simpler adaptation.

Chain of Responsibility *

When passing user input from the view to the controller in a MODEL-VIEW-CONTROLLER (188) architecture ...

... we want to reduce the coupling between the sender of requests and the objects that can handle these requests.

♦♦♦

Sometimes more than one object in an application could handle a particular client request, such as user input received from an input device. However, clients are often not interested in knowing which specific objects are handling their requests—they only want the application to execute requests appropriately.

Clients may also not be interested in the dispatching logic that decides which application object should process a specific request, so that any changes in the object structure or the request dispatching-logic do not change the clients. Factoring out the request dispatching logic to a separate infrastructure object is not always practical, however. If only a few application objects can handle a specific client request, or if the request dispatching logic is fairly simple, the complexity of developing a general request dispatching infrastructure can outweigh its benefits. Nevertheless, we need a mechanism for dispatching a client request to its receiver object, and this mechanism should be simple and efficient.

Therefore:

Chain the objects that can handle the requests and let each object decide whether or not it can execute a particular request. If it can, the object executes the request, if it cannot, the object forwards the request to the next object in the chain.

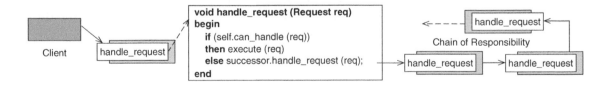

Clients initially issue their requests to the first object in the 'chain of responsibility.' As the request passes through the chain, each object checks whether or not it can execute the request. If it can, the object performs its processing and returns any results. If it cannot, the object forwards the request to the request handling interface of its successor in the chain, if there is one, otherwise it returns an error.

A CHAIN OF RESPONSIBILITY frees clients from knowing the 'right' object that will process each request they issue. This flexibility allows dynamic composition of arbitrary request-dispatching chains without modifications in either the clients or existing objects in the chain. The longer a CHAIN OF RESPONSIBILITY becomes, however, the more overhead is incurred due to the increased number of hops that requests make before an object processes them. In addition—and perhaps more significantly—clients have no assurance that the chain contains an object that handles the requests they issue.

To specify a CHAIN OF RESPONSIBILITY, provide all objects with a reference to a potential successor object and a common EXPLICIT INTERFACE (281) to receive client requests. This interface is invoked on each object until one of the them decides it is qualified to process the request and return the results. If the objects do not have a common EXPLICIT INTERFACE, use an OBJECT ADAPTER (438) to bring them into conformance.

Interpreter

When designing a COMMAND PROCESSOR (343) that receives request messages, or a COMMAND (412) or COMPONENT CONFIGURATOR (490) that receives script-based configuration parameters, or—more generally— a parameterizable ENCAPSULATED IMPLEMENTATION (313) . . .

. . . a mechanism is needed to interpret the data or scripts and execute the right services on the component.

Some problems are often resolved via interpretation rather than by precompiled algorithms. For example, searching for strings that match a particular pattern can be resolved by interpreting regular expressions. Interpreting an input stream or a data model in a little domain-specific language, however, requires grammar representation and an implementation of execution semantics.

Automated code-generation language processing tools, such as lex, yacc, Boost.Spirit, and ANTLR support parsing the source of a language, but they do not necessarily address representation of the abstract syntax tree or the execution of the code. For little languages [Ben86], such as a shell based on single-line commands, intermediate representation is not necessary, and direct execution is possible, even bypassing the need for a more formal parsing stage. Languages with control structures or context-free grammars cannot be run so easily or directly off the back of a stream of lexing or parsing events.

Therefore:

Introduce an interpreter that represents the grammar of the language and its execution. The interpreter is a whole-part hierarchy of classes, typically with one class per grammar rule.

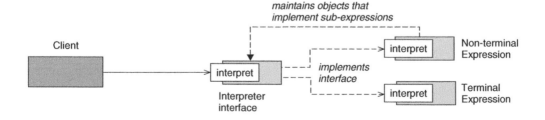

The concrete dependencies between the expressions of the language form the basis of its abstract syntax tree. Clients need to address lexical analysis and parsing, and the tree structure forms the basis of the INTERPRETER model. Leaves define the terminal expressions in the grammar, non-leaves the non-terminal expressions, which consist of multiple sub-expressions. Sub-expressions can be either non-terminal or terminal.

The root of the tree represents the most general non-terminal expression of the language and thus defines its entry point for execution. After all sub-expressions are interpreted, the root assembles the final interpretation of the received sentence and returns it to the caller of the interpreter.

An INTERPRETER design defines a direct and convenient way to represent and interpret grammars for little languages, such as structured messages and scripts, and thus avoids the complexities of more sophisticated representation models. The more complex is the grammar to be represented, however, the less practical an INTERPRETER arrangement becomes, because for each rule in the grammar there is a separate class to implement and maintain. Other approaches that separate the concerns of interpretation from those of grammar, such as automated code-generation language processing tools, may therefore become simpler in practice.

Typically, the syntax tree of the represented language is realized as a COMPOSITE (319), to provide an infrastructure for managing the structure of—and the interactions within—recursive whole-part hierarchies of objects of similar type. Functionality that operates on the entire object hierarchy of the interpreter, such as syntax checking, type checking, and generation of output, can be localized within a VISITOR (447), to avoid it being scattered across the interpreter's construct classes.

The INTERPRETER structure is stateless with respect to any given execution: execution state is expressed in a CONTEXT OBJECT (416) that is passed into the methods of an INTERPRETER arrangement.

Interceptor **

When implementing the Requestor (242) or Invoker (244) parts of communication middleware, a Command Processor (343), or—more generally—an Encapsulated Implementation (313) ...

... it may be necessary to add out-of-band service extensions to a component or framework.

◆◆◆

It can be hard to anticipate how the behavior of a framework may need to be tailored for different environments or applications. Features and attributes of an otherwise stable core set of services may need adaptation or extension. However, some behavioral modifications might be cross-cutting and associated with certain uses for all objects rather than just a few specific objects.

For example, communication middleware must provide remote IPC services, but not every user requires load-balanced communication or the same security policy. A gradual integration of such service extensions into a middleware framework may not be practical, as it will bloat both functionality and code over time, and all users (and developers) will incur the overhead of many rarely used extensions. Moreover, the original developers or maintainers of a middleware framework may not have made the most appropriate choice when implementing certain extensions. Yet some applications will need to integrate out-of-band service extensions into a middleware framework to meet their particular requirements.

Therefore:

Allow users to tailor a software framework by registering out-of-band service extensions via predefined callback interfaces, known as 'interceptors,' then let the framework trigger these extensions automatically when specific events occur.

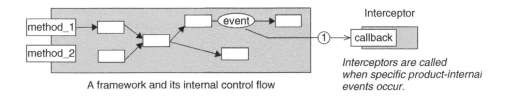

A framework and its internal control flow

Interceptors are called when specific product-internal events occur.

The interceptors realize predefined callback interfaces to implement service extensions that process occurrences of the events in a (user-) specific manner. Interceptors must register with the framework so that it will notify them when events of interest occur. When an interceptor is notified by the framework, it executes its out-of-band functionality. Control flow returns to the framework after the interceptor finishes its execution.

An INTERCEPTOR infrastructure supports the configuration of a framework, or components within a framework, with new and unanticipated features that only a few applications need, without incurring significant overhead for applications who do not use these features. The framework thus stays lean, offering only the core functionality needed by all users, thereby improving its usability and commonality. The strict separation of framework and interceptors also allows independent variation and evolution of core functionality and service extensions.

The high degree of flexibility supported by an INTERCEPTOR design can also incur some costs, however. For example, the infrastructure for notifying interceptors is always executed when relevant events occur, even if no concrete interceptor is registered with the framework. This may incur excessive time and space overhead if there are many interception points and many events. In addition, the framework has no direct control over registered interceptors and is unaware of their operational qualities. It is therefore hard to specify a precise contract for the framework with regard to its performance and behavior in the event of errors or security holes caused by interceptors.

To realize an INTERCEPTOR arrangement, first select all events internal to the product on whose occurrence users are likely want to perform out-of-band service extensions. For example, in an Object Request Broker (ORB) clients often require transaction or security support before and after marshaling and demarshaling service requests. Partition the selected events into two sets: a reader set and a writer set. When events from the reader set occur, users are only allowed to obtain information about the event. Intervention of the product's control flow is prohibited, which supports product stability. When events from the writer set occur, users are also allowed to modify the state of the product: this supports sophisticated service extensions, but can corrupt state in the product or cause misbehavior. Group related events into disjoint interception groups, for example events that deal with request sending in an ORB, because it is likely that users want to execute the same out-of-band behavior in response these events.

For each interception group, define an interceptor callback interface, an Explicit Interface (281) that specifies one method for each of the group's events. Concrete interceptors derive from these interfaces to implement specific out-of-band service extensions. Ideally interceptors should catch and handle all internal failures before they return, but a robust Interceptor implementation should not assume this and should assume the worse, or risk failure rather than resilience in the face of faulty interception.

When an interceptable event occurs in the framework, notify the corresponding interceptors via a dispatcher. The necessary notification chain can be implemented via two Observer (405) arrangements. The framework is a publisher to which dispatchers subscribe, to be notified about the occurrence of particular events. Each dispatcher is also a publisher to which interceptors subscribe, to be called back when events of interest occur so that they can execute their functionality. Within the dispatchers, implement an appropriate interceptor callback policy, such as the order in which interceptors register, or interceptor priorities. The main benefit of introducing a dispatcher rather than letting the framework notify interceptors directly is that it keeps the product's design and implementation independent of interceptor callback interfaces, as well as of the interceptor registration and notification infrastructure.

When a framework calls back to a interceptor it can pass along a Context Object (416) containing information about the event that occurred. This design allows the interceptor to adapt its behavior depending on the current execution context of the framework.

Two specific types of Interceptor are Intercepting Filters [ACM01] and Invocation Interceptors [VKZ04]. An Intercepting Filter allows service requests on a component to be intercepted and manipulated before they are executed. An Invocation Interceptor supports the injection of optional infrastructure functionality into interprocess communication, such as for load balancing and security.

Visitor **

When implementing an ENUMERATION METHOD (300), an ENCAPSULATED IMPLEMENTATION (313), a WHOLE-PART (317) or COMPOSITE (319) assembly, or an INTERPRETER (442) . . .

. . . at times we want to implement services that operate on an aggregate object structure.

♦♦♦

Some services operate on complex, often heterogeneous object structures, for example state summarization and queries in a topological tree. Scattering the service implementation across the classes that define the object structure, however, creates a design that is hard to understand, maintain, and evolve.

These problems arise from a lack of modularity. A single functionality is split across multiple parts, one for every object type on which it operates, and its implementation cross-cuts the classes of all objects in the structure. The more scattered the service, the harder it becomes to see the big picture, since there is no single place that contains the service implementation. Lack of modularity also bloats the classes of the object structure with functionality that is not their prime responsibility and whose boundary is not limited to the implementing class. The alternative of collocating all behavior in a single method that implements type-specific behavior through runtime-type identification and a cascaded if else structure is not much better.

Therefore:

Implement the service in terms of a separate visitor class that expresses the type-specific behavior associated with each class in the object structure. Extend the classes that define the object structure with a method that accepts a visitor, and selects and calls back the correct corresponding method to execute.

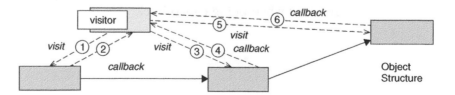

The visitor class defines a method for each class on whose instances it operates. Each method implements that portion of the service that operates on the instances of the corresponding class. Pass the visitor to the object structure to be visited, and let each object in this structure call back that method of the visitor that corresponds to the object's class. The called method then executes the respective part of the service.

The visitor modularizes services whose code would otherwise be scattered across many application classes, thereby improving the understandability and maintainability of service algorithms and code by centralizing everything in one location: the visitor. The visitor infrastructure also protects a stable design center [Gam97] from uncontrolled changes: it is possible to attach new services to an object structure without touching its design and implementation. Stability is a two-way contract, however, so the object structure must be stable for VISITOR to be effective. Adding to the set of classes that define the object structure will ripple through the whole visitor hierarchy, requiring the addition of a new method to every visitor class.

VISITOR is commonly implemented using DOUBLE DISPATCH (408). An EXPLICIT INTERFACE (281) declares the required set of visit methods, each taking an instance of their corresponding object structure class as a parameter. Concrete visitors realize this interface to implement a particular service. Each visit method of a concrete visitor implements the portion of behavior that operates on the object structure class with which it is associated.

All classes whose instances participate in the object structure should have an accept method that takes an abstract visitor as an argument and calls back the corresponding visit method on the received visitor, passing the object to be visited along as a parameter—that is, the object on which the accept method was invoked. Each visit method then executes its service on the particular object that it receives when being called back.

Decorator

When realizing an adaptable and flexible Encapsulated Implementation (313) or Front Controller (339) . . .

. . . at times we want to add responsibilities to an individual object, but not to the methods of its corresponding class.

♦♦♦

It is sometimes necessary to extend the methods of an object dynamically with additional pre- and post-processing behavior, such as data compression, logging, or security checks. Such extensions, however, should not affect other instances of the same class if they do not need these extensions.

Integrating the additional behavior into the class directly, and allowing it to be switched on or off depending on the needs of an object's clients, is at best a short-term solution to this problem. Over time the class becomes polluted with a 'shopping list' of optional behavior that only few clients need and use, but for which all clients (and developers) must pay in terms of resource consumption, performance overhead, and complexity. Separating the add-on behavior avoids such bloat, but introduces a challenge: clients generally do not wish to distinguish between accessing and using the 'core' object versus a new object augmented with additional behavior.

Therefore:

Wrap the original object in a decorator object whose interface conforms to the original object. Implement the optional, extra functionality within the decorator object, and forward requests on its interface to the original object after or before its add-on functionality is executed.

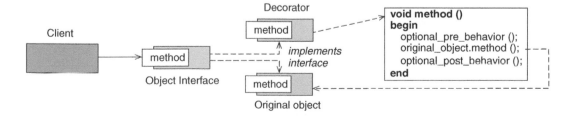

If a client invokes a method on a decorator, the optional behavior is executed in addition to the original object's core behavior: if a client invokes a method on the original object, only its core behavior is executed.

Decorating an object keeps its core implementation clean and lean, but extensible. In addition, extensions are transparent to the object's clients. Hiding extensions from clients, however, can introduce hidden costs, because clients are unaware of whether they access the original object or its decorator.

To apply DECORATOR, organize both the original object and its decorators within a single class hierarchy. The root of this hierarchy is an EXPLICIT INTERFACE (281) that defines the visible behavior of the object that can be decorated. Two types of class realize this interface: the first class represents the original object whose behavior can be extended by decorators, and the second class forms the base for all concrete decorators. This class maintains a reference to an object conforming to the explicit interface of the hierarchy, which enables a concrete decorator to 'decorate' either the original object or another decorator. This design allows addition of nested decorators to the original object, forming a chain in which each decorator extends the original object's methods with additional behavior. Concrete decorators inherit from the decorator base and implement a particular additional pre- and post-processing for some the original object's methods.

Clients program only to the explicit interface of the class hierarchy. Via polymorphism it is then possible to (dynamically) configure the clients transparently with either the original object or a (nested) decorator. When a client invokes a method on the outermost decorator, it and all of the associated decorators in the chain are run, terminating at the original object.

Execute-Around Object **

When implementing an adaptable and extensible ENCAPSULATED IMPLEMENTATION (313), a SCOPED LOCKING (390) arrangement, or a WRAPPER FACADE (459) that encapsulates a resource ...

... we need to execute a pair of related actions around a sequence of C++ statements.

♦♦♦

In C++, paired actions—in which a function is called before some statement sequence and a corresponding function afterwards—are commonly associated with resource acquisition and release. Pre- and post-sequence actions are a common feature of block-scoped resource management, for example to allocate memory, use it, and deallocate it. Programming such action pairs explicitly for each such sequence in an application, however, is error-prone, not exception-safe, and leads to repetitive code.

Practice shows that it is easy to forget the action following the sequence. First, developers must make sure that the action is executed in every return path out of the sequence, whether unlocking a lock, releasing a resource, deleting an object. Second, when exceptions are thrown, they can bypass the post-sequence action, further complicating matters.

Therefore:

Provide a helper class whose constructor implements the pre-sequence action and whose destructor the post-sequence action. Define an object of this class on the stack before the sequence of statements, and provide its constructor with the necessary arguments to perform the pre- and post-sequence actions.

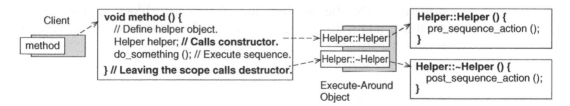

In C++, a constructor is called on creation of an object for the sole purpose of initializing it; that is, the constructor describes the 'boot sequence' for an object. Conversely, a destructor is called automatically at the end of an object's life to 'shut it down' in an orderly fashion. The calling of the destructor is deterministic: for stack variables lifetime is tied to the enclosing scope, even if exceptions are thrown.

It is this determinism that allows constructor and destructor to straddle a sequence. A helper object can take advantage of this: executing the pre-sequence action in the constructor and the post-sequence action in the destructor. Where the helper object must make calls on another object, the object and any additional state must be passed to the constructor.

An EXECUTE-AROUND OBJECT addresses both exception safety and control-flow abstraction, which results in less repetitive and less error-prone code. Destructors are called for stack objects as the stack is unwound upon leaving a scope. Stack unwinding occurs as a result of either normal control flow out of the scope, or exceptional flow from a thrown exception. Clean-up actions therefore occur independently of how control flow leaves a sequence of statements.

If the post-sequence action depends on whether or not an exception has been thrown, the `std::uncaught_exception` function can be used to determine the reason the destructor is being called. The result of `std::uncaught_exception` is worthless, however, if the stack was already unwinding when the helper object was created.

EXECUTE-AROUND OBJECT relies on two key language features, the combination of which is specific to C++: the deterministic and scope-bound destruction of objects created locally, and the ability to execute code automatically within an object just before its destruction. Other forms of execution wrapping behavior are possible in other languages. For example, in C# the combination of a `using` block and an object that implements the `IDisposable` interface comes close to realizing EXECUTE-AROUND OBJECT.

Template Method *

When implementing an ACCEPTOR-CONNECTOR (265), ENCAPSULATED IMPLEMENTATION (313), WHOLE-PART (317), MASTER-SLAVE (321), PAGE CONTROLLER (337), FRONT CONTROLLER (339), COMMAND PROCESSOR (343), HALF-SYNC/HALF-ASYNC (359), LEADER/FOLLOWERS (362), ACTIVE OBJECT (365), or THREAD-SAFE INTERFACE (384) arrangement . . .

. . . we often need to express objects that share a common structural and behavioral core, but vary in particular behavioral aspects.

♦♦♦

Some objects have a common structural and behavioral core, but differ in specific behavioral aspects. Providing full, separate classes for each behavioral variant, however, can duplicate code and complicate maintenance of the object's invariant core.

Although stable, the common behavioral core may evolve. Whenever it does so, each separate class must be updated—which is not only tedious, but also error-prone, since version skew can result if updates are done inconsistently. Separating the object's invariant core from its variant aspects by delegating to another object would avoid version skew, but is not necessarily self-contained, since it involves creating and managing two separate objects.

Therefore:

Create a superclass for the behavioral variants that provides a template method that expresses the common behavioral core. Within the template method, delegate execution of variant actions to separate hook methods that are overridden by each subclass that implements the variant behavior.

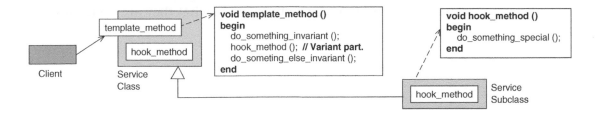

Clients using this pattern thus depend on only a single class and a single object. Calling the template method executes the common core inherited from its superclass, which in turn calls and executes the hook method versions implemented in the subclass.

A TEMPLATE METHOD design allows all object variants to share a single implementation of its structural and behavioral core, which avoids code duplication and maintenance overhead for the object's invariant parts. In addition, the clear separation of a service's variant parts from its invariant parts supports independent modification and evolution of the two aspects. The use of inheritance to separate the two allows variant and invariant parts of the object to share the same data structures directly.

TEMPLATE METHOD can also *increase* code duplication and maintenance costs, however, if multiple service subclasses share implementations of specific hook methods, and the problems this design is intended to avoid for the object's invariant core are reintroduced at the level of its variant parts. TEMPLATE METHOD is a class-level rather than an object-level decision, so there is a strong coupling of variants to the superclass. The *fragile base class problem* [Szy02] is therefore a potential liability unless the superclass is a strong design center. TEMPLATE METHOD is also not appropriate if a component needs to export only interfaces for its plug-in behaviors, because it relies on a partially implemented class.

One way to ensure the invariance of the common behavioral core when implementing TEMPLATE METHOD is to make the public template method non-polymorphic. It is also common to implement default behaviors for private hook methods [Pree94]. If the default is more complicated than a do-nothing implementation, however, this can make the design less stable and overriding more subtle, since subclass developers must be more aware of what they are overriding.

Strategy **

In an ACCEPTOR-CONNECTOR (265), ENCAPSULATED IMPLEMENTATION (313), WHOLE-PART (317), MASTER-SLAVE (321), PAGE CONTROLLER (337), FRONT CONTROLLER (339), COMMAND PROCESSOR (343), HALF-SYNC/HALF-ASYNC (359), LEADER/FOLLOWERS (362), ACTIVE OBJECT (365), STRATEGIZED LOCKING (388), OBJECT MANAGER (492), EVICTOR (515), or ABSTRACT FACTORY (525) arrangement . . .

. . . we often need to realize objects that share a common structural and behavioral core, but vary in multiple behavioral aspects.

◆◆◆

Some objects need to implement behavior across one or more methods that differ on a case-by-case basis. To identify the case with a flag, so that distinct behavior can be implemented by explicit selection, is however a brittle and closed solution that scales poorly.

The problems with flag-based approaches are that methods are coupled to the flag, and each flag-dependent method duplicates the same `switch` selection structure. This approach suffers all the usual problems arising from duplication: adding new cases leads to repetition of case structure, or, worse, the change is made incorrectly. Such methods are typically long and get longer with time. Not only does this approach scale poorly, it is also a closed solution that requires modification of source code every time a new option is added.

Therefore:

Capture the varying behavioral aspects of the object separately from its defining service class in a set of strategy classes. Plug in an appropriate strategy instance, and delegate the execution of the variant behavior to the appropriate strategy within the implementation of the service class.

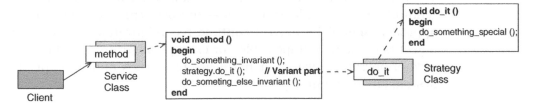

STRATEGY allows parameterization of the variant part of code that needs to have a stable behavioral core.

In a given STRATEGY design, a service class defines the usage code, such as a common behavioral core, and a separate strategy interface with one or more hook methods expresses the variant aspects. The strategy interface is an EXPLICIT INTERFACE (281) that the implementation of the service class uses to delegate the execution of the variant service behavior to a separate object. Concrete strategy classes implement the strategy interface, to implement the variant behavior for a specific service variant. The clear separation of variant parts from invariant parts supports independent modification and evolution. If a strategy class needs to perform an action that depends on some or all of the state of the service object itself, the service object needs to pass a reference to itself or to a CONTEXT OBJECT (416).

STRATEGY is useful for implementing behavioral *extensions* to an object's services. The STRATEGY service class interface defines these extension points, and pluggable extensions implement extended behavior as appropriate. For this reason, the STRATEGY pattern is also known as PLUGGABLE BEHAVIOR [Beck97]. If no behavior is needed, a NULL OBJECT (457) offers a simpler and more consistent approach than introducing null checks throughout the code.

There are two basic options for implementing STRATEGY: runtime polymorphism, based on instance methods, and parametric polymorphism, based on generic mechanisms such as templates in C++ or generics in Java. In the runtime approach, strategy classes often implement the strategy interface to implement the behavioral variants. Instances are used to parameterize behavior at runtime. The templated approach, also known as POLICY [Ale01], fixes the parameterization decision at compile time, which reduces object creation and indirection costs, and offers opportunities for compiler inlining. The flexibility trade-off, where available, is in terms of type intrusion, binding time—compile or runtime—and performance. The templated approach should be used if runtime reconfiguration of the context object is unlikely or impossible, for example if strategies take advantage of operating system or hardware properties and APIs, or other system environment aspects.

Wrapper Facade **

When realizing a BROKER (237), CLIENT REQUEST HANDLER (246), SERVER REQUEST HANDLER (249), REACTOR (259), PROACTOR (262), ACCEPTOR-CONNECTOR (265), MODEL-VIEW-CONTROLLER (188), ENCAPSULATED IMPLEMENTATION (313), HALF-SYNC/HALF-ASYNC (359), FUTURE (382), STRATEGIZED LOCKING (388), or SCOPED LOCKING (390) arrangement . . .

. . . we want to access low-level, function-based APIs in a convenient, robust, and portable manner.

Applications often have some code that needs to use services provided by low-level, non-object-oriented APIs. Programming applications with these APIs directly, however, makes the code hard to understand during development. It is also a poor choice for testability, portability, and the long-term stability of the code, since today's choice of platforms may not be tomorrow's.

When using low-level, function-based APIs—typically C—the code is often repetitive, focused on API minutiae, and error-prone. It can also be non-portable, even across different versions of the *same* platform. It is often unclear how different functions in the same API are related. Programming against such APIs scatters common code across an application, making it hard to 'plug in' alternative solutions.

Therefore:

Avoid accessing low-level function-based APIs directly. Instead, wrap each related group of functions and data within such an API in a separate, cohesive wrapper facade class.

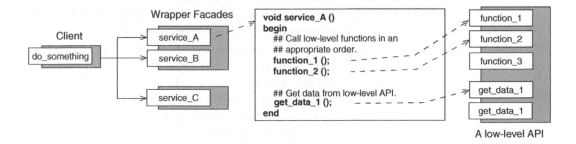

Calling a method on a wrapper facade maps the client request to a corresponding API function, or executes a sequence of API functions in a specific, predefined order.

Wrapper Facade provides a concise and robust set of classes for accessing functions of system APIs, such as those of operating systems and GUI libraries. The code for accessing low-level APIs is encapsulated, so the access code need not be repeated. Wrapper Facade also improves application portability, since the wrapper interfaces can remain stable even if underlying APIs change. A Wrapper Facade is a class, thus it can be used as the basis for pluggable components in a generative programming model [CzEi02].

Within the API to be encapsulated, identify existing abstractions and their relationships, which may be different than the ones documented in the original API. Cluster each group of cohesive functions and data structures into a separate wrapper facade. Errors signaled by the API should be handled in the style appropriate for the target language—which may not be the style of the API. For example, C APIs typically signal failure via return values, whereas object-oriented languages use exceptions. In C/C++ legacy systems running on UNIX, Thread-Specific Storage (415) allows for the safe retention and handling of errors on a per-thread basis. To support the robustness of a wrapper facade, automate resource acquisition and return where possible. In C++, for example, provide an Execute-Around Object (451).

A Wrapper Facade arrangement should make the common use of low-level APIs simple and easy, but also allow more complex usage scenarios. The interface of a wrapper facade may therefore need an 'escape hatch' that allows more direct access to the wrapped low-level APIs. Although this design is a compromise, it avoids the need to modify the wrapper facade for every special case, which would yield a bloated, hard-to-use interface. C APIs are perhaps the most common for low-level access. C++ allows simple, in-language wrapping, but the Wrapper Facade pattern is more general than this specific scenario. The same advice applies where a more sharply defined language barrier exists, such as in Java or Ruby using C. In these situations, a Wrapper Facade offers a more appropriate and cohesive design than simply rewrapping the underlying API directly by exporting handles as integers and functions as class `static` methods.

Declarative Component Configuration *

When realizing a DOMAIN OBJECT (208) or a CONTAINER (488) . . .

. . . we must tell the hosting environment of an application how to handle the technical requirements of a specific component, such as its transaction and security needs.

A runtime environment provides system resources and services such as threads, network connections, security, and transactions to components of an application. These resources and services allow components to execute as specified. A runtime environment, however, cannot always anticipate the specific resources and technical services each component requires, and how each component wants to use these resources and services.

The runtime environment still needs this information to manage its resources and components appropriately. Hard-coding the resource and technical service requirements in the component's implementation is an impractical solution, however: functional aspects would be mixed with technical aspects, although the two areas are generally independent of one another. Changing either independently is awkward, and adapting the component implementation to handle different aspects is manual and costly. Each adaptation would also create a new component version, which must be maintained and managed explicitly.

Therefore:

Specify a separate declarative component configuration for each component that indicates to the runtime environment the system resources and services it needs to execute correctly, as well as how it will use these resources and services.

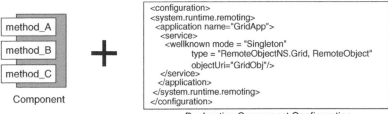

Declarative Component Configuration

Pass the declarative component configuration to the runtime environment during component deployment. The runtime environment can use the specifications in the declarative component configuration to configure itself so that each component can be managed accordingly.

A DECLARATIVE COMPONENT CONFIGURATION tells an application's runtime environment how to manage the components it hosts, so the runtime environment can thus respond to the individual environmental requirements of each component. This pattern supports flexibility because components can shape the environment in which they are located, rather than being forced to use a single 'one-size-fits-all' environment, or have application developers handcraft the environment for each component. Keeping the DECLARATIVE COMPONENT CONFIGURATION separate from the component interface and implementation simplifies changing the specification of component system resources and service requirements without modifying the components themselves.

A DECLARATIVE COMPONENT CONFIGURATION often includes the component's name, its resource requirements, dependencies to other component interfaces, the security and transaction support it needs, its threading model, and various quality of service parameters [VSW02]. Typically it is provided in form of configuration scripts, for example as XML files [OMG02] [MaHa99] [Ram02].

19 Modal Behavior

Display for a pedestrian crossing in Bristol
© Kevlin Henney

Some objects in a system are inherently state-driven: entire methods, or significant portions of them, behave differently depending on their current state. Such object lifecycles are often best implemented in terms of state machines, which allow explicit modeling of—and control over—their modal behavior. This chapter presents three patterns that support the implementation of state machines, considering trade-offs such as solution complexity, performance, memory usage, and internal versus external control of state change.

There are many ways to implement state-driven lifecycles for an object. Sometimes simple flags and conditional statements within the object's method control flow are enough. Sometimes, however, many or all of an object's methods can behave entirely differently in different object states. Such a lifecycle is often modeled as a state machine, but in implementation a developer faces many choices, and some design paths lead to unnecessarily complex implementations. The following issues influence the choice and shape of the solution:

- *Minimizing conditionals.* Gigantic `switch` statements and long `if else if` cascades are often inappropriate for capturing stateful lifecycle behavior because of the accidental complexity they introduce. Anything more than a few conditional cases becomes hard to manage and results in duplication of the conditional structure across multiple methods. Such repeated control coupling of methods on a particular piece of state scales poorly.

- *Inter-mode dependencies.* In some objects states are completely independent of one another: methods do not operate on common data structures, and transition from one state to another requires little or no transfer of context information between the states. In other objects the situation is the opposite: states share and operate on a whole set of common data and context information. The design of the object's state machine should reflect the interdependencies between its modes. Coupling independent states too tightly reduces their independence, while coupling dependent states too loosely can decrease performance and increase resource-management overhead.

- *Mode visibility.* In many situations clients do not care about the current state of an object, they just want it to behave appropriately in any state on any method call. Management of states and state changes should ideally be transparent to such clients, and therefore be the responsibility of the object. In other scenarios, it is the object's clients that view its behavior as being state-dependent, and the object itself is the one that should be independent of these state models.

Each of the three patterns in this chapter addresses a specific configuration of the forces outlined above, spawning a solution space for developing objects with strong modal behavior:

> The OBJECTS FOR STATES pattern (467) [GoF95] [DyAn98] divides an object in two, separating the mode-dependent behavior of an object from the representation of the normal instance data. The main data-holding object forwards method calls to a mode object, which is an instance from a class hierarchy in which each class represents the behavior in a particular state.

> The METHODS FOR STATES pattern (469)[Hen02c] realizes all the behavior of an object as internal methods within a single class, rather than across multiple classes. Groups of method references are used to define the object's behavior in a particular mode.

> The COLLECTIONS FOR STATES pattern (471) [Hen99] externalizes the state of an object by associating each state of interest with a separate collection that refers to all objects in that state. State transitions become transfers between collections.

The OBJECTS FOR STATES pattern is commonly known as STATE [GoF95], but is listed here using its synonym for reasons of clarity and similarity. The name OBJECTS FOR STATES emphasizes the solution structure rather than the problem, which is the common reading of STATE. The common naming style emphasizes similarity of intent but difference in structure with both METHODS FOR STATES and COLLECTIONS FOR STATES.

The following considerations influence which of the three patterns is most appropriate when realizing modal behavior:

- *Mode visibility.* OBJECTS FOR STATES and METHODS FOR STATES implement the state machine *within* the modal object—the machine is transparent to clients. Clients 'just' invoke a method, and the object does the 'right thing' [Hearsay02], dependent on its state. OBJECTS FOR STATES and METHODS FOR STATES are thus most suitable for realizing objects that encapsulate a specific workflow. COLLECTIONS FOR STATES, in contrast, implements the state machine *externally* to the modal objects within their clients: the objects themselves are unaware of their state. Such a view is not as uncommon as it may appear at a first glance. For example, a garbage collector distinguishes between objects that are referenced by other objects, and thus cannot be deleted, and unreferenced objects, which it can delete. The objects themselves are not aware of these states, as obviously they should not be. Similarly, a mechanism that supports multiple undo/redo distinguishes request objects that are executed and can be undone, and request objects whose actions were undone, but can be redone. Again, the request objects themselves are generally uninterested in the state-dependent view that their clients have of them, so COLLECTIONS FOR STATE is the right implementation choice.

- *Mode independence.* Sometimes the state machine of an object consists of states that are completely independent of one another, not sharing behavior or data structures. The individual states in such a state machine should therefore be strictly decoupled to avoid accidental structural and logical complexity in the state machine implementation. OBJECTS FOR STATES addresses requirement by encapsulating each state inside a separate state object. Similarly, COLLECTIONS FOR STATES introduces a separate collection for each state of a state machine. If, on the other hand, many states share behavior and data, encapsulating each state would introduce space and performance overhead due to duplicated code and transfer of shared data between states. METHODS FOR STATES addresses this problem by providing a set of shared methods and data structures from which the behavior of a specific state can be composed.

The following diagram outlines how the three patterns for modal behavior tie into our pattern language for distributed computing.

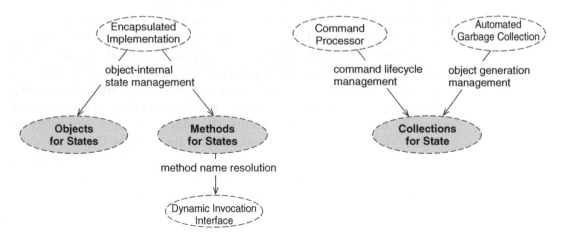

Objects for States *

When realizing an ENCAPSULATED IMPLEMENTATION (313) ...

... we sometimes need to support object behavior that alters significantly whenever an object changes its internal state.

The behavior of an object may be modal, where the mode depends on its current state. Hard-wiring the corresponding multi-part conditional code within the object's implementation, however, can frustrate its comprehensibility and future development.

For example, an object that represents a controller for a user interface needs to respond to common events in a way that is appropriate to the current state of the view. The view may have many different modes, depending on options and validation. Hard-coding a state machine directly via `switch` and `if` statements does not scale effectively, and is effective only for a small number of states that affect only a small number of methods. Different state machine aspects cannot evolve independently, such as code that represents the behavior of a specific state, the transition logic that connects the states, or the integration of new states.

Therefore:

Encapsulate the state-dependent behavior of the object into a hierarchy of state classes, with one class per different modal state. Use an instance of the appropriate class to handle the state-dependent behavior of the object, forwarding method calls.

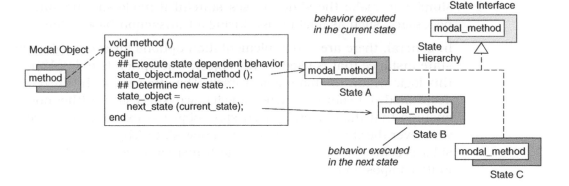

Whenever a client calls a method on the modal object whose behavior is state-dependent, the object delegates the execution of the method to an instance of the corresponding state class. Upon creation, the modal object is associated with an instance of the state class that implements the behavior to apply in its initial state. When the modal object changes its state, the state object it uses is exchanged so that it behaves correctly in the new state.

The encapsulation and organization of state-dependent behavior in a class hierarchy allows the modal object to be configured dynamically with instances of arbitrary state classes. An extension of the hierarchy with new state classes is also simplified, as well as the modification of an existing state class.

An OBJECTS FOR STATES design, however, distributes responsibility across multiple classes, which can make it appear unnecessarily complex when there are few states and few state-dependent methods. This design can also be hard to manage if there are many states, where the corresponding class explosion becomes the key cause of complexity. Class nesting, or localizing state classes within packages or files, can help to contain such complexity.

Implementations of the state classes are—somewhat ironically— normally stateless. Each state object receives the main object, or a reference to its instance data, as an argument in each of its methods. This statelessness allows modal objects to share the same instances of the state objects, which can be accessed as `static` data. This style of programming, however, may seem more indirect than necessary for such a closely coupled system of classes. Conversely, it may be simpler to make the state classes stateful if mode-specific state is necessary, such as might exist during a transaction-based state.

In general, there are two implementation options for exchanging the state instance that is used by the object. One option is to implement this logic within the main object itself. The other is for the currently associated state object to determine its own 'successor.' Either option ensures that the currently used state object is exchanged correctly whenever the object transitions into a new state. The trade-off to consider is central control over the state-transition logic versus flexibility in its composition.

Methods for States *

When realizing an ENCAPSULATED IMPLEMENTATION (313) . . .

. . . we sometimes need to support object behavior that changes significantly whenever an object alters its internal state.

♦♦♦

The behavior of an object may be modal, where the mode depends on its current state. Hard-wiring the modal behavior within the object's methods, however, can make future development unnecessarily awkward. Yet delegating the behavior to one of a community of objects can also complicate the coordination of, and data sharing between, different modes.

For example, an object that represents a network connection must react differently if its methods are called before a connection is established, when it is connected to a remote peer, or after the connection is closed.

Conditional statements within an object's methods are one way to express such behavior, but the more complex the state machine becomes, the more complicated the object's evolution. Encapsulating each mode's behavior in a separate object untangles the modal functionality, but can yield overly complex state machines if different modes depend on the same data or require data-driven coordination.

Therefore:

Implement state-dependent behavior as internal methods of the object, and use data structures to reference the methods that represent the behavior of a specific state.

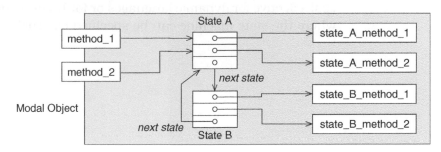

Whenever a client calls a method on the modal object whose behavior is state-dependent, the object delegates the request to the internal method referenced by the data structure that represents the current state. Upon creation, the modal object should be associated with the data structure that represents its initial state. When the modal object changes its state, the data structure it uses is exchanged so that it behaves correctly in the new state.

The encapsulation of state-dependent behavior in internal methods allows the modal object to share data and context information among different modes with maximal performance and minimal resource use. The use of data structures to reference the state-specific methods simplifies the configuration and evolution of the object's state machine.

The data structure holding the method references can be a record-like data structure with named fields, such as a C++ struct. Alternatively, a dictionary object can be used to locate the private method reference that corresponds to each history-sensitive public method. In effect, this configuration emulates the normal polymorphic method lookup mechanism, such as a C++ *vtable*, with a little added customization, evolution, and intelligence. Where only a single public method is state-dependent, no intermediate data structure is needed to represent the mode: a single method reference will suffice. Global, module, or class-wide variables can hold the single instance of the data structure or method reference required for each mode.

The method references may be actual method references, such as member function pointers in C++ or delegates in C#, or they may be symbolic method names that are resolved using reflection, executed by calling a Dynamic Invocation Interface (288). This latter option is only cost-effective for dynamic languages or for highly configurable objects where the state machine can be specified externally to the class.

Collections for States **

When managing service request objects in a COMMAND PROCESSOR (343), AUTOMATED GARBAGE COLLECTION (519), or a similar collection-managing arrangement ...

... we often need to handle the lifecycle of objects or operate on them collectively with respect to their current state.

◆◆◆

Objects whose behavior depends on their current state may be modeled as individual state machines. Sometimes, however, their clients view the behavior of these objects as modal, whereas the objects themselves are independent of any client-specific state model.

For example, a garbage collector distinguishes between referenced and unreferenced objects, but the objects themselves are, and should be, unaware of this view. Making objects aware of their state and allowing them to manage this state themselves would couple their implementation too closely with the way their clients are using them. Whenever a client changes its state model, all objects are affected, which complicates their maintenance and evolution. This situation is even worse if different clients have different state-dependent views onto the objects. Additional resource and performance penalties can occur if clients treat objects in the same state collectively, for example all objects waiting for deletion by a garbage collector.

Therefore:

Within the client, represent each state of interest by a separate collection that refers to all objects in that state.

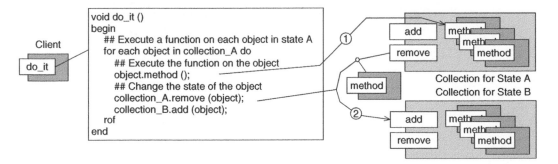

Whenever an object changes its state, it is moved from the collection that represents the source state to the collection that represents the target state. The client can invoke only those methods on objects referenced by a specific collection that are allowed to execute in the state represented by that collection.

The current collection that references the object implicitly determines its state, so there is no need to represent the state internally within the object. Extrinsic representation of state may also be used, in addition to intrinsic representation, as a speed optimization for selection of objects in a particular state.

All objects of a particular state can be managed collectively, which can yield a smaller object footprint and allow clients to execute actions efficiently on them as a group. Client-specific state models can be implemented without affecting the class of the objects, which reduces the structural complexity of the application and supports the independence and evolution of the objects and their class.

Within each client, there are at least as many collections as there are states of interest: the simplest approach is to represent each state exclusively from other states. It is also possible to add inclusive collections, such as a collection that holds all the objects, in addition to the inclusive ones that model a particular state.

With a growing number of states, therefore, COLLECTIONS FOR STATES becomes less applicable, as the collections—as well as the object management functionality across all collections—introduce resource management and performance overhead. Similarly, if the rate of state changes is high, COLLECTIONS FOR STATES can become impractical, due to the overhead of transferring objects between collections.

20 Resource Management

Tram depot in Amsterdam
© Kevlin Henney

The term *resource* covers a broad range of programmatic assets and entities, including database sessions, synchronization primitives, security tokens, file handles, network connections, and even distributed services and components. A resource can range from a heavyweight entity, such as an application server component process, to a fine-grained lightweight entity such as a memory buffer. This chapter describes twenty-one patterns that manage the lifecycle and availability of resources to clients. These activities include assuring that resources are created or acquired when needed and that they are deleted or released in a timely manner.

Managing resources is hard, and managing them efficiently in distributed systems is even harder. The quality properties of an application, such as its performance, scalability, flexibility, stability, predictability, reliability, and security, often depend heavily on appropriate resource management policies and mechanisms. What makes resource management particularly hard is balancing the trade-offs among requirements, because addressing one of them often affects the others. For example, flexibility often reduces performance, while robustness can reduce predictability due to the use of checkpointing and restore mechanisms. Similarly, optimizing for specific use cases, such as minimizing service initialization time, can increase complexity and latency for general use cases.

To implement efficient resource management for applications in distributed systems, therefore, the following challenges should be addressed to strike the right balance among these requirements:

- *Performance.* An application with performance-critical timelines must fulfill many properties, including low latency, minimum delay between an action and its reaction, and high throughput in terms of the number of actions performed per unit time. Since each action may involve many resources, it is important to minimize resource creation, initialization, acquisition, release, disposal, and access activities that incur processing overhead and delay.

- *Scalability.* Large and complex server applications usually require multiple resources to perform their functionality. They often also have many clients that access their resources multiple times. In many cases, servers are designed for specific usage profiles, such as the peak and average number of users expected. These usage profiles can expand over time as new requirements are added. For example, a new requirement could require a server to handle twice as many users and ten times more transfers without affecting system performance. A server application whose resource management strategies can fulfill these requirements is *scalable*.

- *Reliability.* A reliable service can satisfy its clients without interruption or inconsistency. To achieve reliability, applications must manage their resources carefully. For example, if multiple resources are involved in a transaction, their final states must be consistent and durable. When performance or scalability optimizations are applied, moreover, these optimizations must not diminish service reliability.

- *Flexibility.* A common requirement among applications is ease of configurability, which implies that application properties can be selected at compile time, initialization time, or runtime. Highly flexible applications leave this degree of freedom to their users. The mechanics of resource management must also therefore be flexible, while still meeting performance, reliability, and scalability requirements.

- *Updates.* Long-lived applications are likely to evolve throughout their lifetimes. Ideally this evolution will proceed smoothly and reliably, even when incorporating new resources. Shutting an entire application down to perform updates often cannot be tolerated, however, particularly for applications with stringent availability requirements.

- *Transparent lifecycle control.* Clients of a resource generally want to use the services the resource offers when they want to use them, and are uninterested in the details of its lifecycle management, such as when and how the resource is created or disposed of, or whether or not it is temporarily deactivated or evicted. Conversely, effective management of resources may require the deactivation of expensive resources that are sparsely used to allow the acquisition of new resources. It is hard to support resource lifecycle control that is both transparent to clients and supports the needs of resource provisioning environment effectively.

Since the challenges above are often interwoven, it is hard to tackle one without influencing others. This complicates resource management, and motivates the use of time-proven patterns to address these challenges. The following twenty-one patterns in our pattern language for distributed computing provide guidance for implementing efficient resource management, balancing conflicting challenges to help meet the needs and requirements of distributed and concurrent applications:

> The CONTAINER pattern (488) [VSW02] provides a runtime environment for components, together with infrastructure services that components need to execute properly.

The COMPONENT CONFIGURATOR pattern (490) [POSA2] allows an application to load and unload its component implementations at runtime without having to modify, recompile, or statically relink the application. It also supports the reconfiguration of components into different application processes without shutting down and restarting running processes.

The OBJECT MANAGER pattern (492) [POSA3] separates object usage from object management, to support explicit, centralized, and efficient handling of components, objects, and resources.

The LOOKUP pattern (495) [POSA3] helps to find and retrieve initial references to distributed objects and services.

The VIRTUAL PROXY pattern (497) [GoF95] loads or creates an expensive component on demand, and may delete it from memory after use.

The LIFECYCLE CALLBACK pattern (499) [VSW02] enables explicit control of a component's lifecycle.

The TASK COORDINATOR pattern (501) [POSA3] maintains system consistency by coordinating the completion of tasks that involve multiple participants. It presents a solution for tasks involving multiple participants in which either all work done by the participants is completed, or none is, which ensures consistency of system state.

The RESOURCE POOL pattern (503) [POSA3] avoids expensive acquisition and release of resources by recycling resources that are no longer being used.

The RESOURCE CACHE pattern (505) [POSA3] avoids expensive reacquisition of resources by not releasing resources immediately after their use. Instead, resources are kept in memory and reused to avoid having to recreate them.

The LAZY ACQUISITION pattern (507) [POSA3] defers resource acquisition to the latest possible point during system execution, to optimize resource usage.

The EAGER ACQUISITION pattern (509) [POSA3] makes runtime acquisition of resources predictable and fast by acquiring and initializing resources before their actual use.

The PARTIAL ACQUISITION pattern (511) [POSA3] optimizes resource management by decomposing the acquisition of a resource into multiple stages. Each stage acquires part of the resource based on system constraints such as available memory, as well as the availability of other resources.

The ACTIVATOR pattern (513) [StSc05] automates scalable on-demand activation and deactivation of services accessed by many clients, so that resources are not consumed unnecessarily.

The EVICTOR pattern (515) [HV99] [POSA3] specifies how and when to release resources such as memory and file handles, to optimize resource usage.

The LEASING pattern (517) [POSA3] simplifies resource management by specifying how resource users can obtain access to a resource from a resource provider for a pre-defined time.

The AUTOMATED GARBAGE COLLECTION pattern (519) provides a safe and simple mechanism for reclaiming memory used by objects that are no longer needed.

The COUNTING HANDLE pattern (522) [Hen01b] simplifies the life-time management of a shared object by introducing handle objects that act as references to the shared object, and which track the number of references to the shared object.

The ABSTRACT FACTORY pattern (525) [GoF95] provides an interface for creating and deleting families of related or dependent components without coupling clients with concrete classes.

The BUILDER pattern (527) [GoF95] separates the construction and destruction of a complex component from its representation, so that the same construction and destruction processes can create and delete different representations.

The FACTORY METHOD pattern (529) [GoF95] encapsulates the concrete details of component creation by providing a method for component creation, rather than letting clients instantiate the concrete class themselves.

The DISPOSAL METHOD pattern (531) [Hen02b] encapsulates the details of component disposal by providing a method for destroying components, instead of having clients destroy the components themselves, or leaving them to a garbage collector.

The patterns outlined above can be partitioned into several groups, each addressing a specific resource management theme.

The first group of patterns, OBJECT MANAGER, CONTAINER, and COMPONENT CONFIGURATOR, specify entire resource management infrastructures. Since each pattern addresses a different set of forces, they are often used in conjunction:

- OBJECT MANAGER separates objects and resource usage from lifecycle management and access control.

- CONTAINER provides a whole life-support system for component objects, which offers lifecycle management, infrastructure services, and resources to components, including security, transactions, and persistence. A CONTAINER often builds on one or more OBJECT MANAGERS.

- COMPONENT CONFIGURATOR complements the other two patterns by allowing replacement and redeployment of component implementations throughout an application's lifecycle, even when it is executing.

The following diagrams outline the integration of these three patterns into our pattern language for distributed computing:

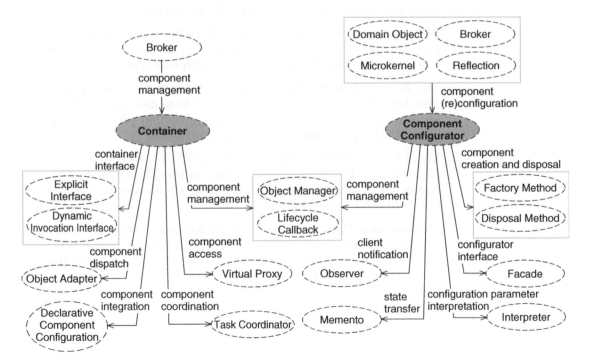

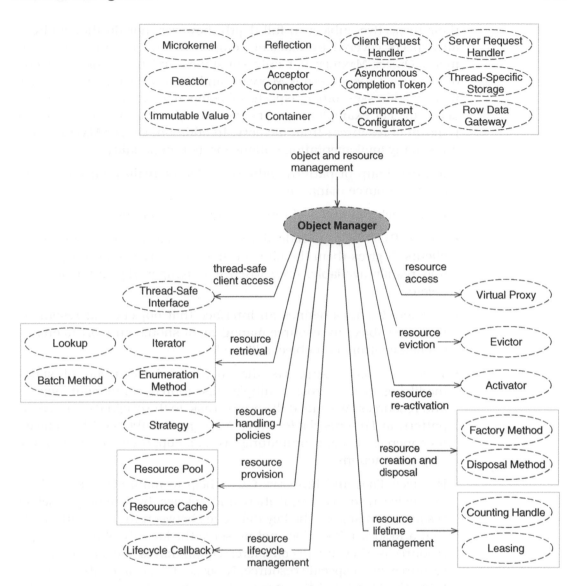

Through OBJECT MANAGER we offer a different perspective on three overlapping patterns in the documented pattern space: MANAGER [Som97], OBJECT LIFETIME MANAGER [LGS00], and RESOURCE LIFECYCLE MANAGER [POSA3]. All three patterns address important aspects of component and resource management, such as obtaining access to resources and controlling their lifetime. None of the patterns cover their respective subject in full depth, however, nor do they address all aspects covered by efficient component and resource management. OBJECT MANAGER not only subsumes and broadens the focus of MANAGER, OBJECT LIFETIME MANAGER, and RESOURCE LIFECYCLE MANAGER, it also addresses other aspects of component and resource management. For example, it covers resource sharing and the temporal removal of resources from memory. In addition, OBJECT MANAGER outlines many implementation options for its functionality.

The next group of patterns address different realization aspects of effective resource management:

- LOOKUP helps to find and retrieve concrete resources.

- VIRTUAL PROXY helps to hide all resource management activities from clients. It gives them the illusion that a resource is always present and readily available, even when it is temporarily deactivated or deleted.

- LIFECYCLE CALLBACK defines an interface that objects and resources that are subject to resource management should support to enable explicit control of an object's lifecycle.

- TASK COORDINATOR supports the coordinated execution of state-modifying tasks across multiple, distributed component objects and resources. We added the prefix 'Task' to the original COORDINATOR pattern in *Patterns for Resource Management* [POSA3] to indicate its concrete scope: coordinating tasks, as opposed to coordinating only transactions.

- RESOURCE POOL and RESOURCE CACHE help to minimize the need for expensive resource acquisition and release by keeping a set of resources 'in stock.' The key difference between the two patterns is that a RESOURCE POOL does not preserve the identity of the managed resources—they are all considered equal, that is, a client receives *a* resource, not a specific resource. RESOURCE CACHE, in contrast, maintains the identity of the managed resources: a request to a cache fails if it does not contain the specific resource requested, even if other resources of identical properties are available. RESOURCE POOL thus helps to optimize access to stateless resources such as memory, threads, or stateless application services, whereas RESOURCE CACHE optimizes access to stateful resources.

- RESOURCE POOL and RESOURCE CACHE correspond to the POOLING and CACHING patterns in *Patterns for Resource Management* [POSA3]. Since all pattern names in POSA4 are noun-phrased names, however, we decided to rename the two patterns. The new names also reflect the specific role of the two patterns in our pattern language for distributed computing.

Since the issues addressed by the six patterns above are fundamental to effective resource management, they are used in most practical realizations of the OBJECT MANAGER, CONTAINER, and COMPONENT CONFIGURATOR resource management infrastructures outlined earlier.

The following diagrams show how the patterns described above connect with our pattern language:

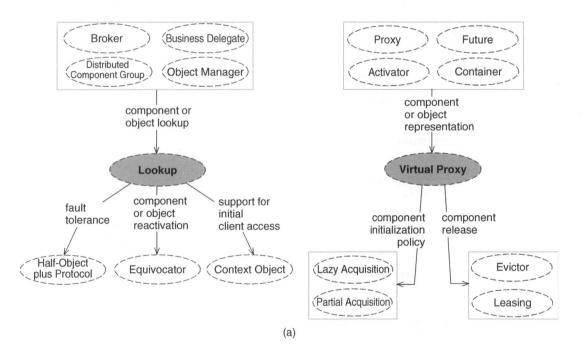

(a)

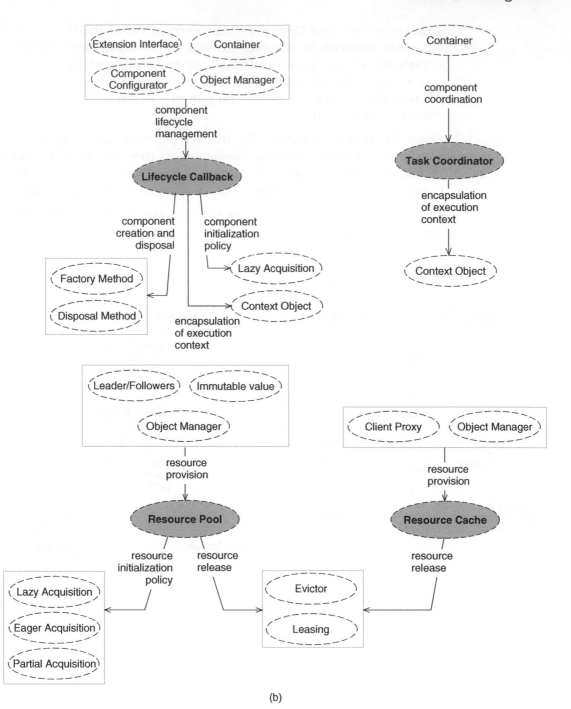

(b)

The third group of patterns address three different resource acquisition strategies: EAGER ACQUISITION provides an up-front acquisition strategy, LAZY ACQUISITION provides an on-demand acquisition strategy, and PARTIAL ACQUISITION is a mixture of the two other strategies in which core parts of a resource are acquired eagerly, whereas supplementary parts are acquired on demand. The trade-off to consider when choosing a particular acquisition strategy is performance and availability versus resource consumption, such as memory footprint. Although EAGER ACQUISITION ensures that resources are available when needed, this strategy can increase memory footprint, which may be unacceptable if resources are only used sparsely or not used at all. LAZY ACQUISITION ensures that memory is consumed only when a specific resource is actually needed, but incurs performance and availability penalties on first access. PARTIAL ACQUISITION strives to balance trade-offs between performance and availability on one hand and memory footprint on the other.

The following diagram outlines how LAZY ACQUISITION, EAGER ACQUISITION, and PARTIAL ACQUISITION relate to one another and to other patterns in our pattern language for distributed computing:

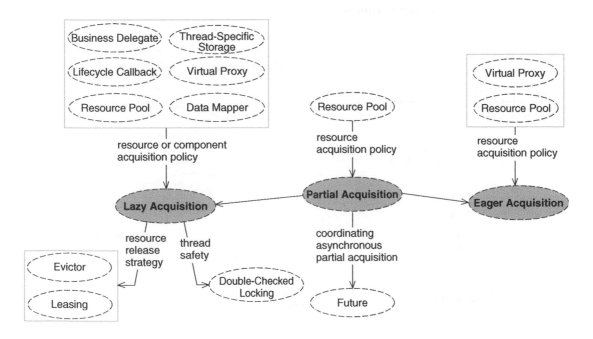

EVICTOR and ACTIVATOR are a pair of complementary patterns that support centralized (re)activation and release of resources. EVICTOR addresses the wholesale release of resources at defined points in time, such as releasing cached resources that have not been used recently. If resources, such as component objects in a container, could still be referenced and used by clients, however, the ACTIVATOR can reactivate them on the next client access.

ACTIVATOR can thus be seen as a concrete example of LAZY ACQUISITION: it defers the acquisition of resources until late in the system lifecycle, for example at installation or runtime. Although the two patterns are similar, they address different problem contexts at different levels of abstraction. LAZY ACQUISITION defines a broad strategy for allocating resources, from shared, passive entities like memory or connections, to active entities such as services. ACTIVATOR, in contrast, is a more focused pattern that addresses the activation and deactivation of services in resource-constrained distributed computing environments. ACTIVATOR, however, also shares many of LAZY ACQUISITION's pros and cons, such as less predictable performance.

The following diagram shows how ACTIVATOR and EVICTOR integrate into our pattern language:

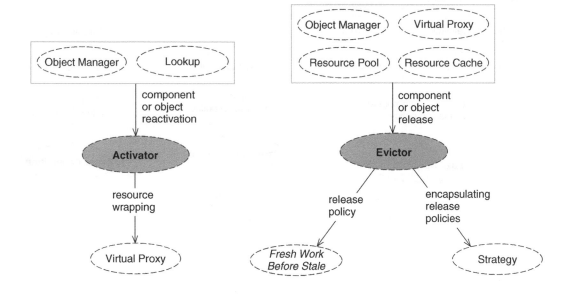

The next group of three patterns address release strategies for objects and resources shared by multiple clients:

- LEASING specifies a predefined period during which a resource is available. After all granted leases have expired, the resource can be reclaimed safely by the resource management environment.

- AUTOMATED GARBAGE COLLECTION defines an 'acquire and forget' strategy for resource release. A garbage collector periodically monitors all active resources in an application and releases resources that are no longer referenced by clients.

- COUNTING HANDLE implements reference counting. As long as multiple clients reference a shared object or resource, it cannot be released on client initiation. The resource is released only when the last client using the resource initiates its disposal.

The trade-offs to consider when choosing one of these three patterns include aspects such as:

- *What initiates the release of the resource?* Choices include the resource itself, as in LEASING, the resource users, as in COUNTING HANDLE, or something else, as in AUTOMATED GARBAGE COLLECTION.

- *When is the resource released?* Choices include when no client is using it, such as in COUNTING HANDLE, or at a later point in time, as in LEASING and AUTOMATED GARBAGE COLLECTION.

All three patterns share the property that resource release is transparent to clients—they need not care.

Note that we have substituted the COUNTING HANDLE pattern (546) from the *Reference Accounting* pattern language [Hen01b] for the COUNTED POINTER idiom from *A System of Patterns* [POSA1]. There were two reasons for this replacement:

- COUNTING HANDLE is more accurate than COUNTED POINTER and is the entry point into a rich pattern language.

- This replacement allows us to describe reference accounting in more depth and generality than we could do with COUNTED POINTER.

The following diagram shows how the three patterns described above connect into our pattern language for distributed computing:

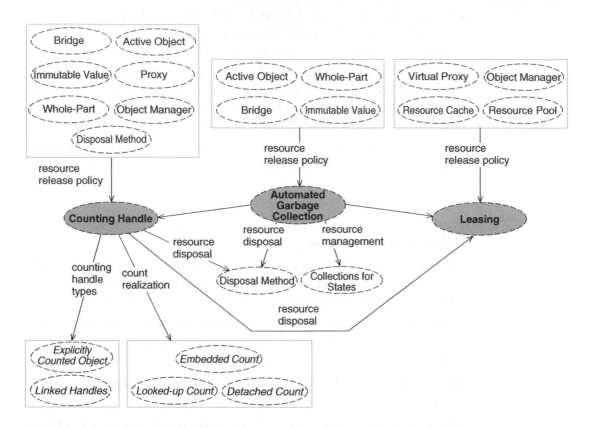

The final four patterns in this chapter address different aspects of object creation and destruction:

- ABSTRACT FACTORY supports the consistent creation and disposal of sets of related objects.

- BUILDER addresses the flexible creation and disposal of complex objects that consist of multiple parts.

- FACTORY METHOD and DISPOSAL METHOD are two complementary patterns that hide the details of object creation and disposal behind a simple and easy-to-use interface.

The following diagram shows how the four pattern described above are used in our pattern language for distributed computing:

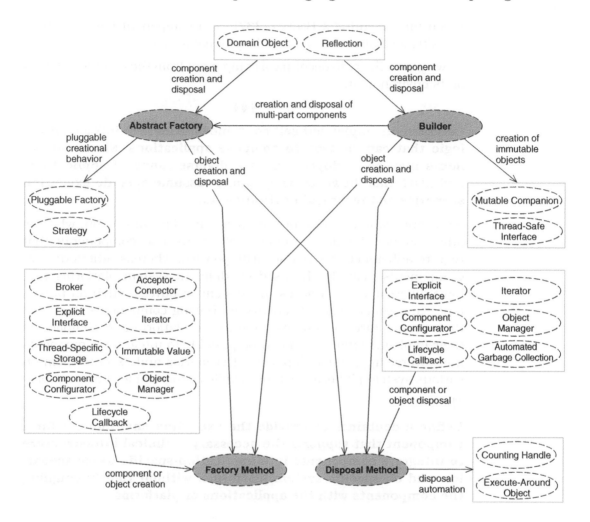

Readers familiar with the Gang-of-Four book may notice the omission of two object-creational patterns from this chapter: SINGLETON and PROTOTYPE [GoF95]. SINGLETON is not included because it introduces more problems—such as deletion, thread-safety, and configurability—than it resolves. We simply did not find a use for PROTOTYPE in the context of our pattern language, although this pattern is used in other domains, such as user interface frameworks.

Container *

When implementing a BROKER (237) for a component-based system, or using a component within a distributed system ...

... we generally try to decouple a component from the technical details of its environment.

♦♦♦

Components implement self-contained business or infrastructure logic that can be used to compose applications. Since components may be deployed across a diverse range of applications and platforms, however, they cannot assume specific execution scenarios and technical environments.

Some applications use components as part of a transaction, whereas other do not. Similarly, some applications use components that require adherence to strict security policies, whereas others do not. Components may also be used on different system platforms that have different ways of accessing system resources, such as persistence and concurrency mechanisms. Having components deal with these issues directly couples them to the platform and complicates their implementation. It should be possible to integrate components into diverse application deployment scenarios and execute them on various system platforms without explicit programmer intervention.

Therefore:

Define a container to provide the execution environment for a component that supports the necessary technical infrastructure to integrate components into application-specific usage scenarios, and on specific system platforms, without tightly coupling the components with the applications or platforms.

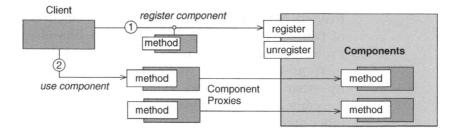

Use the container to initialize and provide the runtime context for the components it manages. Define operations that enable component objects to access their connections to ports of other components, as well as to access common middleware services such as persistence, event notification, transactions, replication, load balancing, and security. Provide a means to integrate a component with its container automatically from a declarative specification, rather than programmatically with imperative code.

CONTAINER separates component usage from the integration of a component into a particular application or platform environment. The container allows developers to focus on providing the core logic of their components and applications, rather than handling the environmental aspects manually. In essence, a container provides a 'life-support system' for components.

A component can integrate with a container by registering itself along with a DECLARATIVE COMPONENT CONFIGURATION (461) that specifies which infrastructural services and resources it requires and how it wants to use them. The container interprets this configuration to generate the concrete integration of the component automatically. To benefit from the container's life-support system, components can either access their container directly via an EXPLICIT INTERFACE (281), or be notified of service details via LIFECYCLE CALLBACKS (499).

The container plays the role of an OBJECT MANAGER (492) to manage its registered components. Similarly, the container uses one or more object managers to manage the middleware services and resources it offers to them. VIRTUAL PROXY (497) instances give clients the illusion that their component objects are always alive. To access component objects that do not provide such a proxy, the container can offer a DYNAMIC INVOCATION INTERFACE (288).

A TASK COORDINATOR (501) helps to control state-modifying tasks performed across multiple component objects by ensuring that either all participating component objects complete successfully, or the entire task is not executed at all. A container uses OBJECT ADAPTERS (438) to transform component invocations received via its dynamic invocation interface, or an underlying middleware, from their general format to the specific interface method of the invoked component.

Component Configurator *

When realizing DOMAIN OBJECTS (208), a BROKER (237) middleware, or a REFLECTION (197) or MICROKERNEL (194) architecture . . .

. . . we need to support flexible component configuration at runtime.

◆◆◆

Prematurely committing an application to a particular set of component implementations can be inflexible and near-sighted. Some decisions cannot be made until late in the lifecycle, even after deployment, and it is undesirable to force applications either to carry the overhead of components they do not use, or be unable to take advantage of better or newer components.

Components have their own lifecycle: they evolve and mature. For example, new versions provide better algorithms or fix bugs. Applications using these components should therefore benefit from such improvements. Similarly, components whose implementations depend on specific software or hardware environments must be replaced when these environments change. Applications with high availability requirements, however, cannot tolerate downtime, so updates must have minimal affect on a running system.

Therefore:

Decouple component interfaces from their implementations and provide a mechanism to (re)configure components in an application dynamically without having to shut down and restart it.

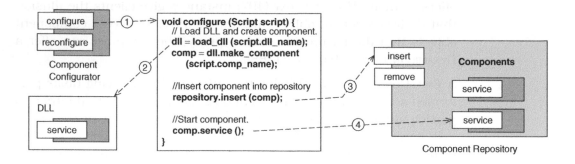

Organize components into suitable units of deployment so that they are loadable dynamically, and provide a framework that supports component (re)configuration under the explicit control of running applications. Manage configured components centrally via a component repository, and offer an API or use some form of scripting to (re)configure designated sets of components at runtime.

A COMPONENT CONFIGURATOR enhances flexibility by allowing replacement and redeployment of component implementations throughout an application's lifecycle, even when it is executing. Similarly, applications only pay for the time and space overhead of components they actually use, in contrast to unnecessary components linked into an application statically.

To support effective component (re)configuration, all components should define a common administrative LIFECYCLE CALLBACK (499) interface that includes operations to initialize a component and start its execution, shut down a component and clean up its resources, suspend and resume a component's execution, and access information about a component's current execution status. The component configurator framework uses this interface to (re)configure each component. This administrative interface may also provide a protocol, such as OBSERVER (405), to notify clients when a component terminates, as well as to transfer state to a new version. State and relationships to other components can be passed to a new version via a MEMENTO (414) that is cached by the component repository during the replacement. Organize components into dynamically linked libraries (DLLs) that can be (un)loaded dynamically, and provide each DLL with FACTORY METHODS (529) to create component objects and DISPOSAL METHODS (531) to destroy these objects when they are no longer needed.

Internally, a component configurator consists of a component repository, which is an OBJECT MANAGER (492) that manages the configured components. The interface of the component configurator is often a FACADE (294) that shields clients from its internal structure and delegates requests to its appropriate participants. It may also contain an INTERPRETER (442) to process configuration directives if these are in a simple scripting language.

Object Manager **

When implementing a CLIENT REQUEST HANDLER (246), SERVER REQUEST HANDLER (249), REACTOR (259), ACCEPTOR-CONNECTOR (265), ASYNCHRONOUS COMPLETION TOKEN (268), MICROKERNEL (194), REFLECTION (197), THREAD-SPECIFIC STORAGE (392), IMMUTABLE VALUES (396), CONTAINER (488), COMPONENT CONFIGURATOR (490), or ROW DATA GATEWAY (542) arrangement . . .

. . . we must often manage the access to and lifetime of specific types of objects, and their resources and relationships.

◆◆◆

Some objects within an application, such as resource or server-side component objects, require careful access control and life-cycle management to maintain and use them efficiently and correctly. Implementing this functionality within the objects themselves, however, burdens them with complex responsibilities and makes them hard to use and evolve.

Similarly, clients are not responsible for the actual management of such objects, since that would couple them to the concrete type of the objects, their access constraints, and the lifecycle policy. This situation would also make discovery of objects harder, such as finding an object via a key. Ultimately, these dependencies increase coupling and complexity within an application. Ideally, therefore, a client should depend only on an object's usage interfaces, not its house-keeping obligations.

Therefore:

Separate object usage from object lifecycle and access control. Introduce a separate object manager whose responsibility is to manage and maintain a set of objects.

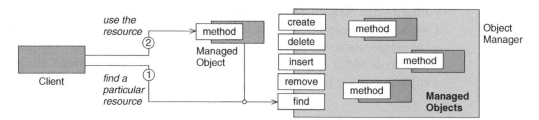

Clients can use the object manager to access objects with specific capabilities. If a requested object does not yet exist, the object manager can create it on demand. Clients may also request creation of objects explicitly via the object manager. In some situations the client may already have created the objects, and may hand custody of them to a manager. The manager can also control the disposal of its objects, either transparently or in response to client requests.

An OBJECT MANAGER frees managed objects and their clients from detailed lifecycle-management and retrieval activities. It concentrates and localizes object management for a particular kind of object into a well-defined, easy to find, and encapsulated object type.

Some applications provide only one object manager for each type of managed object. For example, one object manager could handle threads, another could handle connections. Alternatively, an application can provide multiple object managers for different purposes and different contexts. An example might be one object manager per group of objects that are managed according to a specific set of policies. If an object manager is shared between multiple threads, it should offer a THREAD-SAFE INTERFACE (384). On the other hand, if objects are only ever used within the thread that initiated their creation, an object manager per thread would offer a simpler and more efficient design.

Clients use the object manager retrieval services to request access to objects. LOOKUP (495) services allow a client to search for a specific object, for example based on object names, object properties, or other types of key. An ITERATOR (298), ENUMERATION METHOD (300), or BATCH METHOD (302) supports traversal of multiple objects without revealing the internal structure of an object manager.

An object manager has several options for maintaining managed objects. For widespread and diverse deployments, it may be appropriate to parameterize these options and policies with STRATEGY (455) objects or types. In the typical case, however, a simple method interface for setting options is sufficient.

A RESOURCE POOL (503) can be used to keep a fixed number of objects of equal type and identity constantly available, which is useful for managing critical computing resources that are used continuously, such as processes, threads, and connections. A RESOURCE CACHE (505), in contrast, keeps specific objects available only for a certain amount of time. To avoid degrading an application's quality of service, the cache can dispose of unused objects and release their resources for other objects to use. An EVICTOR (515) supports *controlled* removal of infrequently used objects from a cache. Evicted objects may still be referenced and accessed by clients, however, in which case they can be reactivated by an ACTIVATOR (513). Alternatively, clients access the objects via a VIRTUAL PROXY (497), and the proxy is responsible for reactivation.

To prevent premature release of actively referenced objects, an object manager can use various object removal policies. LEASING (517) enables an object manager to specify the time for which references to objects are valid, and offers clients the opportunity to renew their leases. After a lease has expired, the object manager can destroy the objects safely. COUNTING HANDLES (522), in contrast, initiate the removal of an object as soon as it is known to be no longer referenced.

Objects maintained by an object manager must be created internally or provided by clients. Registration functionality allows clients to transfer custody of externally created objects to an object manager, whereas FACTORY METHODS (529) support encapsulated and explicit object creation. Objects can also be created for clients transparently, without their explicit intervention. Although client creation of objects offers a certain flexibility, it also weakens design cohesion, reduces the opportunities for resource-management optimization by the manager, and increases the likelihood of custody-related errors.

Objects maintained by an object manager must be destroyed at some point. Deregistration functionality allows clients to assume responsibility for objects from the object manager. DISPOSAL METHODS (531) request the deletion of objects explicitly. When shutting down an application, the object manager often disposes of all remaining managed objects before terminating, thereby ensuring proper release of the resources used by the objects.

A set of LIFECYCLE CALLBACKS (499) common to all objects allows an object manager uniform control over their lifecycle, including their initial creation, eviction, reactivation, and final disposal.

Lookup **

When implementing a Broker (237), a Business Delegate (292), a Replicated Component Group (326), or an Object Manager (492) ...

... we typically need to discover and retrieve references to resources, objects, and services that are held either locally or remotely.

In a distributed system, a server may offer many services to clients. A client does not necessarily know which services are initially on offer when it is started. Similarly, services can be added or removed over time. If clients do not know which services are available, however, they cannot use them.

One way for clients to discover services in a distributed system is to hard-code the addresses of the services into the client software. This approach is clearly inflexible, however. Ideally, a server should be able to publish services—and clients to find these services—efficiently and scalably. However, a broadcast approach can be costly in its use of bandwidth and processing time.

Therefore:

Provide a lookup service that allows services in a distributed system to register their references when they become available, and deregister their references when they become unavailable.

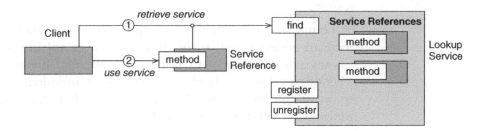

Clients in the system can use the lookup service to retrieve the references of registered services.

LOOKUP is a 'clearing house' between clients and servers, allowing clients to access server services without having clients hard-code the location or references to the servers or the services they offer. Equally, servers do not need to know the location of the clients that want to access their services.

There are essentially two styles for organizing a LOOKUP service:

- *Centralized*, in which information about services resides in a single location. The lookup service stores this information persistently to ensure proper recover in case of system failures. This approach is relatively straightforward to implement, but scales poorly and can be a single point of failure.

- *Distributed*, in which a group of lookup services periodically publish the availability of their registered services. Some form of group communication protocol may be used to multicast this information between the federated lookup services. Typically, a distributed lookup service is realized as a HALF-OBJECT PLUS PROTOCOL (324). Although a distributed lookup service is harder to implement, it scales better and avoids a single point of failure.

The reference of a service can be associated with properties that describe the service and the interfaces it offers. The lookup service maintains this information internally to allow clients to select one or more services based on queries. An ACTIVATOR (513) can (re)start a lookup service when clients need to locate services, to minimize the number of services that actively consume resources in a distributed system.

To communicate with the lookup service, the clients and servers need an access point. If the access point is not known, clients and servers use a protocol to find it, which may involve contacting a preconfigured set of bootstrap servers or broadcasting a message. An available lookup service responds with a message containing information about its access point.

The lookup service is the one resource that clients need to be able to access simply, typically as part of its initial context, and by a well-known name or via a CONTEXT OBJECT (416).

Virtual Proxy **

When implementing a PROXY-based (290) interface, or a FUTURE (382), OBJECT MANAGER (492), CONTAINER (488), or ACTIVATOR (513) arrangement using potentially expensive objects ...

... we may need to reduce the cost of acquisition for optionally or infrequently accessed resources.

Creating an object can be expensive in terms of memory or time. This expense is particularly wasteful if the object is never used, or is not used soon after creation. When it is needed, however, the object must be present.

The cost of loading all objects that correspond to the rows in a large database is costly and unnecessary, especially if only a few of the objects are actually used. Similarly, a large collection of server objects managed by a container could consume excessive memory and space in the table of active objects. If these objects are used infrequently, resources are needlessly overcommitted. Ideally, a resource user should not have to incur overhead for resources they do not use, or do not use for long periods. Managing a resource's lifecycle should also not encumber resource users.

Therefore:

Introduce a proxy for an object that does not currently exist in memory. The proxy may be able to handle simple requests, such as a query of the intended target object's identifying key, but when more complete object behavior is needed, the actual target object is created and initialized as needed.

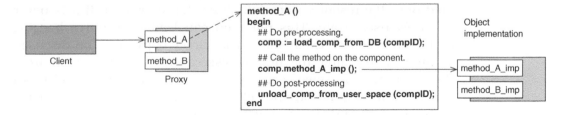

The proxy offers the same interface as the intended target object. Each method is executed, either in terms of state that is stored in advance of creating the actual target object, or in terms of on-demand creation followed by forwarding. In the latter case, the existence of the target is checked, the target is created if it does not already exist, and the method invoked on the proxy is called in turn on the target object.

VIRTUAL PROXY introduces a level of indirection to resource access, using the offset in structure to support an offset in time: the time at which the target object is created and committed is delayed until the first point of use. There is always some cost associated with adding an additional object to introduce a level of indirection, and this cost must be balanced against the benefit and likelihood of optimization under the expected application load.

The common implementation of VIRTUAL PROXY is simply in terms of LAZY ACQUISITION (507) or a collocated ACTIVATOR (513). For objects that can be decomposed into separately acquirable parts each of which is associated with a different load cost, however, PARTIAL ACQUISITION (535) offers an alternative that can spread the acquisition load more evenly in some applications.

The cost of object creation is not eliminated in VIRTUAL PROXY, it is simply deferred. Similarly, the likelihood that the late initialization fails is also deferred. So instead of dealing with just the application errors that might arise from using the resource, a client may also have to deal with more fundamental resource errors, which affects the transparency of the optimization.

The cost of first access is deferred when the option of consuming a resource is exercised. A proxy to an infrequently accessed object will hold onto the resource once initialized, however, even if it is never or rarely used again. This retention can lead to resource hogging and even resource exhaustion. The target object can be disposed of immediately after the first access, as a follow-on action from the forwarding. In some cases, however, this will simply lead to an expensive (re)acquisition and release cycle. Alternatively an EVICTOR (515) or LEASING (517) can be used to release the resource at a later time so that is readily available for immediate subsequent use.

Lifecycle Callback **

When implementing an EXTENSION INTERFACE (284), OBJECT MANAGER (492), CONTAINER (488), or COMPONENT CONFIGURATOR (490) that is responsible for managing the lifecycle of framework objects ...

... we need to ensure that framework objects are able to respond to lifecycle-related events initiated by the framework.

The lifecycle of some objects is simple: their clients create them before they are used, they stay alive as long as they are used, and they are disposed of by their clients when no longer used. However, some objects have a much more complex lifecycle, driven by the needs and events of their component environment and constrained by additional resource-managing techniques, such as pooling and passivation.

Rather than *ad hoc* creation and disposal by their clients, the lifecycle of the latter type of object is often controlled by frameworks according to application-specific policies and architectural needs. An object may also be passivated during its lifetime, for example to save memory and other resources, and reactivated when it is accessed again. In addition, the knowledge of how to perform these operations is specific to the object, not the application. Yet it should be possible for the application to control the lifecycle of these objects explicitly.

Therefore:

Define key lifecycle events as callbacks in an interface that is supported by framework objects. The framework uses the callbacks to control the objects' lifecycle explicitly.

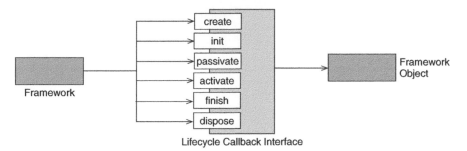

Typically the set of callbacks includes operations for initializing and finalizing the object, for passivating and activating it, and for passing its state to and from persistent storage.

LIFECYCLE CALLBACKS enable a framework to control the lifecycle of components explicitly, but without any knowledge of their internal structure: the framework calls through an interface with appropriate methods, and the object types implement this interface according to their own structure and needs. All object types for a framework often share the same LIFECYCLE CALLBACK interface, which allows the framework to treat them uniformly.

It is one thing to create an object, but quite another to start using it. A LIFECYCLE CALLBACK interface, therefore, often separates these two phases explicitly: a FACTORY METHOD (529) is responsible for object creation, and a separate initialization callback for the LAZY ACQUISITION (507) of the resources used by the object. This two-phase construction is often mirrored by two-phase destruction, in which a lifecycle callback for finalization is responsible for resource release, and a DISPOSAL METHOD (531) for the actual object destruction.

Where the object is likely to need access to component environment details or framework services, a CONTEXT OBJECT (416) can be passed through to each callback.

OBJECT MANAGERS and CONTAINERS typically use lifecycle callbacks to activate, passivate, and remove component objects that they manage.

Task Coordinator *

When implementing a CONTAINER (488) ...

... we need to ensure that partial failure of a task divided across multiple, cooperating participants does not make the state of the system inconsistent.

◆◆◆

Partial failure of computers, networks, and software components is a common problem in large-scale systems. If a portion of system fails, however, it may leave applications in an inconsistent state, which may be worse that total failure. This problem is exacerbated when a task has been distributed across multiple components.

Many applications execute tasks that involve more than one participant, where participants may include resource provides and resource users. Each participant executes part of the task in a sequence: for the task to succeed as a whole, the work performed by each participant must succeed. If a task is successful, the changes made should keep the system in a consistent state. If the work performed by one participant fails, however, the work of other participants may have modified the application state, but the participant that failed would not have made the necessary changes. As a consequence, the application could produce incorrect results.

Therefore:

Introduce a coordinator that supervises the execution and completion of a task by all participants. The coordinator ensures that either all contributing participants complete successfully or, in the event of even a single participating task failing, it appears that the entire task did not execute at all.

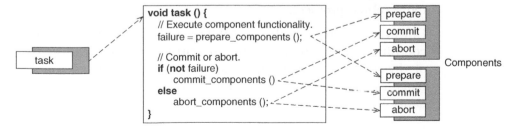

A two-phase model is the simplest model of coordination that keeps communication to a minimum, maximizes opportunities for distribution and parallelism, and keeps tasks separate from one another. On completion of the task, successful or otherwise, all resources involved in the task are released automatically.

A COORDINATOR ensures that a task involving multiple participants appears to be atomic to clients that initiate the task. This coordination in turn maintains the consistency of the entire application by ensuring that multi-step state transitions are controlled and fail-safe.

To implement a coordinator with a two-phase approach, split the work performed by each of the participants as follows:

- *Prepare.* In this phase, the coordinator asks each participant to check whether the execution of its part of the task could fail. If a participant indicates a potential failure, the coordinator stops the execution sequence of the entire task and asks all participants that successfully completed their prepare phase to roll back by aborting and restoring their original state. Since none of the participants made any persistent changes, the system state remains consistent.

- *Commit.* If all participants pass the prepare phase, the coordinator initiates the commit phase in which all participants do their actual work. As each participant has indicated in the prepare phase that its work would succeed, the commit phase should also succeed, leading to the overall success of the task.

The resulting task execution is transactional: it appears *atomic*, and the resulting state of the system is *consistent*. During the transaction, state changes are *isolated* from one another: successful state change is *durable* beyond the transaction. These are the so-called 'ACID' properties of a transaction. Failure is still a possibility during the commit phase, and three-phase commit is sometimes considered a more robust protocol.

However, in spite of the scalability and integrity offered by such coordination, use of a coordinator introduces overhead in the form of division and management of the task, as well as the need to pass transactional context to the participants, typically via a CONTEXT OBJECT (416).

Resource Pool **

When implementing a LEADER/FOLLOWERS (362) concurrency model, IMMUTABLE VALUES (396), or an OBJECT MANAGER (492) configuration in which there is a high turnover of resources ...

... we may need to support rapid acquisition and release for a limited set of stateless resources.

Acquiring and releasing system resources, such as network connections, threads, or memory, can incur performance overhead that may vary for each acquisition and release. Applications with a need for performance and scalability, however, require efficient and predictable access to these resources.

Any given access strategy to resources must scale: it must be fast and predictable even as the number of resources used, and the number of resource users, increases. Moreover, to ensure predictable performance, acquisition and release time for resources of the same type should not vary significantly. For example, consider a server on which each request is handled by a separate thread. For frequent short requests the repeated cost of creating, preparing, and destroying each thread can dominate the actual time taken to handle the request.

Therefore:

Keep a certain number of resources available in an in-memory resource pool. Rather than repeatedly creating resources from scratch, retrieve the resources from the pool quickly and predictably. When the application no longer needs a resource, it must be returned to the pool so it becomes available for subsequent acquisition.

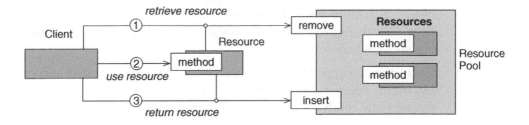

A resource pool encapsulates the knowledge of resource acquisition, access, and management. To acquire a resource, a resource user must know the appropriate pool. Depending on the nature of the resource and how it is managed by the pool, the resource user may or may not need to return the resource to the pool explicitly. Resources are released either when the pool is disposed of or by explicit request—assuming that the pool supports such an interface.

RESOURCE POOL avoids performance penalties due to the repeated overhead of creating and destroying resources on demand from scratch. By storing the resources in a pool, the time to access them is shorter and more predictable. All resources in a pool that have the same properties are considered equivalent, that is, a client gets *a* resource on request, not a particular resource.

The number of resources in a pool may be fixed at creation, or it may be grown dynamically according to some policy, such as exponential or fixed increment, with growth either bounded or unbounded. For resource pools that are to be used in different application environments, the policy may be configurable, either through a simple set of methods that can be used to set policy parameters, or via a STRATEGY. For pools that grow, it may make sense to allow shrinkage, either explicitly or transparently. A pool that tracks its resources can easily resize itself. Alternatively, a more complex approach based on EVICTOR (515) or LEASING (517) can be employed to manage resource retirement from the pool.

Pooled resources are often created during the initialization of the OBJECT MANAGER, using either EAGER ACQUISITION (509), PARTIAL ACQUISITION (511), or LAZY ACQUISITION (507). LAZY ACQUISITION defers the creation of an object until the first time it is accessed. Conversely, EAGER ACQUISITION creates an object completely before it is accessed, so the object is usable immediately after creation. If creation takes a long time, PARTIAL ACQUISITION can be used to reduce the initial creation time via stepwise object assembly.

Resources returned to the pool are reinitialized before they are reused by other clients. Reinitialization ensures that resources are in a defined and ready-to-use state, or that security requirements are met.

Resource Cache **

When realizing a CLIENT PROXY (240) or an OBJECT MANAGER (492) ...

... we need to optimize the cost of repeated access to the same set of resources.

Repeated creation and disposal of resources for a few resources users can incur unnecessary performance overhead. For applications in which this overhead makes it hard to meet performance requirements, there is a need to minimize the cost of initialization and disposal of frequently used resources.

An application that frequently uses and disposes of a particular kind of resource, such as memory buffers or threads, may benefit from a pooling arrangement. However, although a pool may offer a policy that is good for an application as a whole, it may not necessarily benefit a more local context such as a specific component or subsystem. An appropriate optimization needs to be localized, simple to implement, and low in execution cost.

Therefore:

Rather than destroying a resource after use, store it in an in-memory cache. When the resource is needed again, fetch it from the cache and return it, instead of creating it anew.

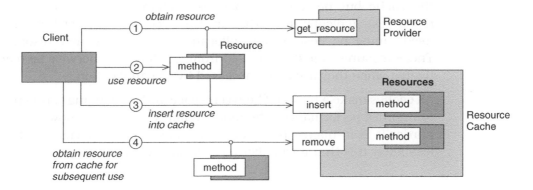

A resource cache stores a resource or small set of resources temporarily for fast retrieval. To acquire a specific resource, a resource user looks in the cache first. If the cache does not contain the requested resource, it then looks to the resource provider for the resource. The presence of a cache allows rapid, localized recycling of a resource. Resources are released either when the cache is disposed of or is full, or by explicit request—assuming that the cache supports such an interface.

By storing frequently accessed resources instead of destroying them, a RESOURCE CACHE minimizes the cost of (re)acquiring and releasing resources. Ideally, resources are created only once, either before or when they are accessed for the first time. Similarly, they are destroyed only once, when they are no longer needed, or when the application terminates.

All resources in a cache are considered different, even if they have the same properties. If a specific resource requested by a client is not in the cache, the request fails, even if resources with identical properties are available.

Clearing a cache to release its resources can be an explicit activity executed by an EVICTOR (515), or an implicit operation through LEASING (517). Some overhead can occur, however, when a resource must be evicted from the cache even though an application has not explicitly released it. For example, if a new resource is inserted into the cache but not enough space is available for it, other cached resources—typically those that are least-recently or least-frequently used—must be destroyed to allocate space for the new resource. These resources must be created from scratch, or otherwise be reactivated when they are again accessed by the application.

All caches make a trade-off between space and time, using extra space to improve performance. The more complex a cache is, however, the harder it is to maintain from a development point of view, and the less likely it is that it will offer a performance advantage.

Lazy Acquisition **

When realizing BUSINESS DELEGATE (292), THREAD-SPECIFIC STORAGE (392), LIFECYCLE CALLBACK (499), VIRTUAL PROXY (497), RESOURCE POOL (503), PARTIAL ACQUISITION (511), DATA MAPPER (540), or any potentially costly or optional initialization . . .

. . . we may need to ensure that object creation and resource acquisition satisfy high throughput and availability demands.

Applications that access many resources, but which must also satisfy high availability requirements, need a way to reduce the initial cost of acquiring the resources they need or the resource usage footprint that they have at any point in time.

In particular, acquiring all resources during system or subsystem initialization can make start-up unnecessarily or even unacceptably slow. Moreover, many resources may be acquired over-optimistically, making the initial acquisition wasteful if they are not consumed during the lifetime of the application. Over-acquisition can lead to resource exhaustion and prevent resource recycling. Applications that use many resources, however, need to access them when needed, ideally without paying for the space overhead or early start-up cost associated with early acquisition.

Therefore:

Acquire resources at the latest possible point in time. The resource is not acquired until it is actually about to be used. At the point at which a resource user is about to use a resource, it is acquired and returned to the resource user.

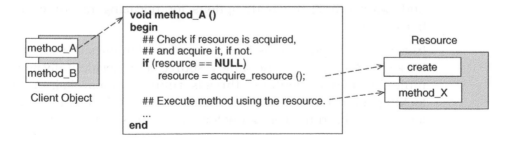

Lazy acquisition is an optimistic optimization that defers, but does not eliminate, the cost of resource acquisition. Its use should be fully encapsulated by the resource provider, shielding the resource user from the policy and mechanism details.

Lazy Acquisition follows a 'mañana, mañana' philosophy for resource acquisition: never do today what you can put off until tomorrow. Perhaps more positively, it can be seen to exercise the lean principle 'decide as late as possible,' deferring actual acquisition to 'the last responsible moment' [PP03].

Lazy Acquisition ensures that each resource is acquired 'just in time,' that is, when the need for it is concrete and it is about to be used. Lazy Acquisition therefore does not incur any resource acquisition costs early in an application, component, or subsystem's lifecycle. Further more, it does not waste time or space acquiring resources that are never used.

However, there is normally some space overhead associated with Lazy Acquisition, resulting from either introducing intermediate objects, such as a Virtual Proxy, or holding some additional state, such as a status flag to indicate the state of the acquisition or attributes to be used in acquiring the resource.

The cost of acquisition is moved rather than eliminated, so any code that relies on an object that uses Lazy Acquisition will be slower to execute the first time than subsequently. This deferral reduces the predictability of execution. Another predictability-related risk is introduced by the lateness of acquisition: failure. There is no guarantee that when the resource is needed, it will be available.

Because the actual acquisition is transparent, it may not be obvious when, if, or how a resource should be released. Evictor (515) and Leasing (517) are both options for releasing resources in the background.

In concurrent applications Lazy Acquisition often uses Double Checked Locking (386) to prevent the same resource being accidentally acquired multiple times by multiple threads running in parallel. A simple locking approach may be thread-safe, but it can be costly, incurring locking overhead unnecessarily for every access but the first.

Eager Acquisition **

When implementing PARTIAL ACQUISITION (511), RESOURCE POOL (503), or any potentially costly initialization ...

... we may need to ensure that object creation and resource acquisition satisfy high predictability and performance requirements.

Every application needs to access certain resources, such as memory, threads, network connections, and file handles. Applications with stringent predictability and performance requirements, however, often cannot afford the overhead of acquiring such resources on demand at runtime.

Resource acquisition can be a costly business, and an application may not be able to afford the time taken to acquire a resource dynamically to fulfill a task. The time needed to acquire a specific resource is often unpredictable, especially in general-purpose operating environments. As a result, applications may not be able to meet their predictability requirements. In a layered system, in which primitive resources from one layer are wrapped up by the next, lazy acquisition of primitive resources in one layer can reduce predictability of acquisition in the next higher layer. Furthermore, handling resource exhaustion may complicate the implementation of the task. Exhaustion may even be unacceptable from an operational perspective, so the possibility should be minimized.

Therefore:

Eagerly acquire the resources before they are used. The resource is then available to a resource user when immediately it requests it.

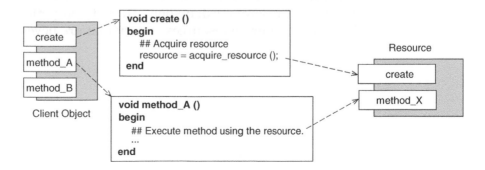

The point in time at which resources should be acquired can depend on several factors, including the time it takes to create them, when they are needed, the number of resources to create, and their dependencies to other resources. These factors should be considered in the context of any application using EAGER ACQUISITION.

EAGER ACQUISITION is an optimization that applies Isabella Beeton's kitchen-management maxim that 'there is no work like early work' to resources.

In considering when to acquire resources, one option is to acquire resources at system initialization. Such an immediate acquisition allows an application to ensure that there is no dynamic resource acquisition during the runtime of the application. Another option is to acquire them at some later designated point in time after system initialization but before their first use by applications. For example, at component load-time for dynamically loaded components, or on creation of a RESOURCE POOL or other responsible object. Regardless of which strategy is applied, however, EAGER ACQUISITION ensures that resources are properly acquired *and* are readily available before they are actually used. The resource user is guaranteed that the resources are available and at no (or minimal fixed) cost of access.

However, in applying EAGER ACQUISITION, a developer must be aware that the optimization involves a trade-off rather than unconditional benefits. The cost of resource acquisition is not eliminated, it is simply moved to an earlier point in an application's lifecycle. If many resources are managed in this fashion, an application's, component's, or subsystem's start-up will be noticeably slowed, which is not acceptable for applications that need rapid start-up. EAGER ACQUISITION also carries with it the risk of over-acquisition, tying up resources unnecessarily and, in conflict with one of the design objectives, incurring the risk of resource exhaustion. There is no performance or space benefit to acquiring resources eagerly that are never used.

Partial Acquisition *

When implementing RESOURCE POOL (503), VIRTUAL PROXY (497), or any potentially costly or complex initialization ...

... we may need to ensure that object creation and resource acquisition satisfy throughput and predictability demands.

◆◆◆

Some applications with stringent performance, scalability, and robustness requirements must access resources whose size is large or unknown. Acquiring these resources eagerly during system initialization may therefore introduce excessive start-up overhead. However, acquiring them on demand can incur an untimely cost.

If memory or processing time is not available for acquiring all required resources during system initialization, an application's overall quality of service can suffer. Indeed, some of the resources may not be readily available at start-up. Similarly, acquiring these resources 'just in time' when they are actually used may incur unpredictable performance overheads that also cannot be tolerated within an application's operational constraints. For example, acquiring remote resources is expensive, whenever it is done.

Therefore:

Split the acquisition of each resource into multiple stages. In each stage, acquire only a part of the resource, so that its acquisition gradually completes over time, in accordance with overall application quality of service needs.

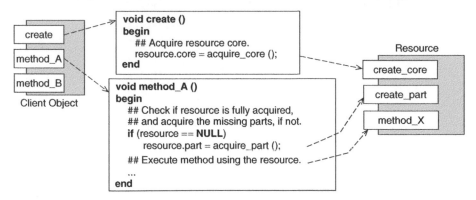

Divide up the resource acquisition with respect to the cost, the availability, the space overhead of holding or managing deferral of acquisition, the perceived value or debt of holding a resource that is not used, and any natural division of a resource's acquisition into stages. For example, a remote resource may have separate instance creation and initialization steps, which would map cleanly onto two stages of partial acquisition.

PARTIAL ACQUISITION ensures that resource acquisition does not create too much overhead and that each resource acquisition stage does not incur excessive performance penalties. The original forces of large resource size and long resource acquisition time are not completely resolved, but instead are balanced against other demands.

The number of stages for a resource acquisition, the amount of resource to acquire at each stage, and the timing of each stage depend on various factors, such as available memory, required response time, the availability of dependent resources, and the lifecycle of resources. It is possible that some resources can be acquired asynchronously, so that at an initial stage they are requested and at a later stage they are committed. Managing such asynchronicity can be simplified, for example by using a FUTURE (382).

After it has partially acquired a resource, an application can use the resource as if it were fully acquired and initialized. PARTIAL ACQUISITION strategies often build on LAZY ACQUISITION (507) and EAGER ACQUISITION (509). However, PARTIAL ACQUISITION tends to be more complex in implementation than both LAZY ACQUISITION and EAGER ACQUISITION, and is subject to a combination of the liabilities of each of these two approaches.

Activator **

When implementing an Object Manager (492) or a Lookup (495) service that releases resources that could still be used by clients ...

... we need to offer simple access to temporarily released resources.

◆◆◆

Some types of services in a distributed system should only consume resources when they are accessed actively by clients. Clients should be shielded as much as possible from where services are located, how they are deployed on hosts in a network, and how their lifecycle is managed.

Unconstrained use of resources such as communication channels, threads, or memory can degrade the overall quality of service of an application. Applications may periodically evict less frequently used resources from memory to make space for other resources needed by an application. If an evicted resource is re-accessed by its clients, however, it must be re-activated, which can involve recreating the resource, reloading its state, restarting it on its server, and reacquiring any resources that it in turn uses. Such resource reactivation should be transparent to clients, however, so that it appears as if the accessed resources are always available. It should not be part of the client's responsibility to manage such reactivation.

Therefore:

Minimize resource consumption by activating services on demand and deactivating services when they are no longer accessed by clients. Use proxies to decouple client access transparently from service behavior and lifecycle management.

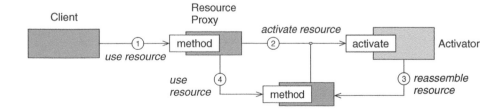

Introduce an activator that initiates and supervises the reactivation of previously deactivated resources. Whenever a resource is evicted, the activator receives information about the resource, such as its identity, its location in the network, the location of its persistent state, and its required computing resources. Whenever the client re-accesses the de-activated resource, the activator reactivates it according to a given policy using the information it maintains about the resource.

An ACTIVATOR frees clients from the responsibility of reactivating the resources they use: it appears to them as if all resources were always available. An ACTIVATOR also ensures that reactivating a resource incurs minimal overhead, because it maintains information about how to optimize this process. For example, the ACTIVATOR could reload the resource's persistent state and reacquire the necessary computing resources in parallel, thereby speeding resource initialization.

To make the use of an activator transparent, the resource must be wrapped, such as with a VIRTUAL PROXY (497). There is normally some space overhead associated with activation, however, resulting from either introducing intermediate objects, such as a VIRTUAL PROXY, or holding some or all attributes used when acquiring the resource. In addition, the cost of acquisition is moved rather than eliminated, so any code that relies on an object that needs reactivation will be slower to execute the first time than subsequently. This deferral reduces the predictability of execution.

Evictor **

When implementing an OBJECT MANAGER (492), Virtual Proxy (497), RESOURCE POOL (503), or RESOURCE CACHE (505) for resource-constrained applications . . .

. . . we need to ensure that infrequently used resources are released in a timely manner.

The simplest model of resources is that a resource client acquires a resource, uses it once, and then releases it. However, for clients that need a resource more than once, albeit infrequently, a repeating (re)acquire—use—release cycle incurs overhead. But a resource provider may not be able to afford unlimited use of its resources.

The frequency of use, time of use, or some other quality of usage, should influence the lifecycle of a resource. The lifecycle should be constrained by system environment, not just by explicit actions by resource clients, such as resource release. Ideally, the solution should be as transparent as possible to the resource client, otherwise this pushes the complexity of resource management detail back out to the client.

Therefore:

Introduce an evictor to monitor the use of resources and control their lifetime. Resources that are not accessed after a specific period of time are removed to free up space for other resources.

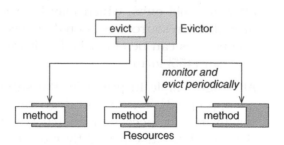

Add a marker such as a flag, counter, or timestamp to each resource, which indicates when the resource is used. Initialize the marker to indicate that the resource is unused, then update it when the resource is used. Periodically or on demand, evict unmarked or uncommonly accessed resources, but keep resources that are marked because they are currently, recently, or frequently in use. Other criteria for eviction are possible, including ones based on resource footprint rather than frequency of use.

EVICTOR prevents frequently or recently used resources from being destroyed, thereby avoiding reacquisition costs when these resources are re-accessed. Similarly, applications can control when less frequently used resources are released. This increases their predictability and performance, because resource housekeeping activities do not interfere with critical application operations. If the application re-accesses an evicted resource, however, it must be created from scratch or otherwise be reactivated, thereby incurring performance overhead.

Common eviction policies are *Least Recently Used* (LRU) and *Least Frequently Used* (LFU). Application-specific *policies* are also possible. For example, the size of resources in memory-constrained applications could be used to determine which resources to evict, so a large resource could be evicted even if it was used recently. Similarly, it is possible to use domain-specific knowledge. For example, if an application knows that a resource is scheduled for use soon, it may not be evicted even if it has not been accessed recently. For overloaded reactive systems, a policy of FRESH WORK BEFORE STALE [Mes96] results in new tasks or requests—as opposed to resources—being given priority over old ones, which may be evicted. In all policies the state of stateful resources is stored persistently before releasing them. The policies can be either be hardwired or expressed in a pluggable STRATEGY (455) form.

Although simple in principle, the subtlety of EVICTOR lies in finding an appropriate eviction strategy and dealing with the question of reactivation or access of evicted resources. The need for reactivation can introduce a slightly more complex lifecycle for resources, involving two additional lifecycle events: (*re*)*activate* and *passivate* (or *deactivate*).

Leasing **

When realizing an OBJECT MANAGER (492), RESOURCE POOL (503), RESOURCE CACHE (505), LAZY ACQUISITION (507), LEASING (517), AUTOMATED GARBAGE COLLECTION (519), or COUNTING HANDLE (522) structure in which resource allocation crosses distribution boundaries . . .

. . . we need to ensure that resource-constrained applications always release resources in a timely manner.

♦♦♦

Applications working with a constrained set of resources need to ensure that resources are returned after use. Unless resource clients explicitly terminate their relationship with resource providers and releases the resources, they may retain unused resources needlessly. However, a crashed client is unable to release resources, and a rogue client may be unwilling to do so.

In a typical scenario, a client asks a provider for one or more resources. Assuming the provider grants the resources, the client can then start using them. Either the client or the provider may crash, or the provider may no longer offer some of its resources, or a client may have a defect that prevents correct return of a resource. However, unless resource providers are explicitly informed that resources are no longer used, the resource will leak, which could lead to resource exhaustion. And unless clients are explicitly informed that the resources are no longer available, they may continue to hold invalid resources.

Therefore:

Have the provider create a lease for each resource held by clients. Include a time duration in the lease that specifies how long a client can use the resource. After the time duration expires, release the reference to the resource in the client and the resource in the provider.

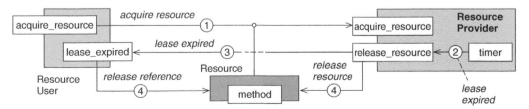

While a lease is active, the client can cancel the lease, in which case the corresponding resource is freed in the provider. Before a lease expires, the client can try to renew the lease from the lease provider. As long as the lease is renewed, the corresponding resource will continue to be available.

LEASING simplifies resource usage and management for both clients and providers. Clients are freed from the responsibility of releasing resources explicitly. They also know that the resource is available and valid for the granted time. Providers can control resource usage more efficiently: by bounding resource usage to a time-based lease, unused resources are not wasted and are released as soon as possible so that they can be granted to new clients.

The concept behind LEASING is simple, and the result is efficient, stable, and scalable. Alternative schemes, such as requiring resource clients and providers to emit a heartbeat or to ping one another, tend to be more complex and less efficient than LEASING. Overall, resource management is simple for both resource provider and resource consumer, but both parties need to be timer-aware. It is possible for a lease to be lost if a client or network is overloaded, so that the resource provider does not receive the lease renewal in time. In such cases, the client will find itself working with a stale resource and will have to handle this runtime error, for example by acquiring a new resource.

The duration of a lease depends very much on the kind of application, and is often also a configurable parameter. In support of distributed objects, as used in Java RMI and. NET Remoting, the default lease period is of the order of minutes [VKZ04]. For IP addresses issued by DHCP the default is of the order of days. For software licenses the period is normally of the order of months.

Automated Garbage Collection **

When realizing a WHOLE-PART (317), ACTIVE OBJECT (365), IMMUTABLE VALUE (396), or BRIDGE (436) configuration, or when providing runtime support for objects allocated dynamically on the heap . . .

. . . we often need a safe and simple mechanism to reclaim memory from objects that are no longer needed.

◆◆◆

Heap memory is a finite resource managed by the runtime environment and consumed by any dynamically created object in an application. Failure to return memory to the heap when it is no longer needed can exhaust memory, or lower performance due to thrashing virtual memory pages. Similarly, errors in manual management can yield memory leaks and memory corruption.

It is relatively easy to manage objects that are created and used only within other objects or within a single method. For example, stack-based value objects in C++ or C# are scope-bound, and EXECUTE-AROUND OBJECTS can automatically reclaim heap objects in C++. Objects that are shared or involved in complex object relationships, however, are more likely to invite programmer error or complex designs aimed at taming manual memory management. Object relationship graphs may also include cycles, in which one object refers to another which directly or indirectly points back to the first.

Therefore:

Define a garbage collector that identifies which objects are no longer referenced by live objects in the application, and reclaims their memory. The garbage collector performs the identification and reclamation automatically and transparently.

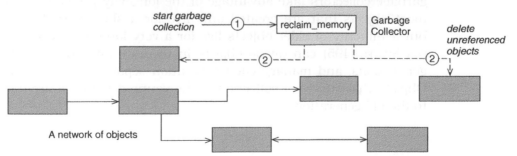

The set of unreferenced objects is determined by finding the set of objects the running system uses and subtracting it from the set of all allocated objects. The root set of references defines objects that are known directly to be used by the system: objects referenced by global (or static) variables and objects referenced by the stack in each thread of control. From the root set it is possible to follow the references from each object to determine which other objects are in use, and so on.

AUTOMATED GARBAGE COLLECTION lives up to its name in the sense that it classifies unreferenced objects as garbage and collects their memory without direct application intervention. The greatest benefit of garbage collection is that it is simple to work with for many programs, programmers, and types of object, notably those that—with the exception of memory—are not resource consumers. Garbage collection is hard to implement deterministically, however, so quality of service may vary, and it is hard to ensure that resource-based objects will be released in a timely manner, if at all. Where such control is needed, programmers are often required to resort to a more manual scheme, such as calling DISPOSAL METHODS (531) explicitly, or employing COUNTING HANDLES (522).

Garbage collectors can run synchronously and completely, or asynchronously and incrementally. The simplest model is the synchronous mark-and-sweep approach: all objects reachable from the root set are marked in one pass, then a second pass through all the objects in memory collects the unmarked ones. Although simple to implement, mark-and-sweep algorithms can have a 'stop-the-world' effect on an application, which is inconvenient for user interfaces and intolerable for high-performance servers or real-time systems. Generational garbage collectors take advantage of the longevity profile of objects: most objects that are created only live for a short period of time, but a minority of older objects live for a very long time. COLLECTIONS FOR STATES (495) can divide objects in memory into young and old generations, and manage each generation separately for collection. Objects that survive a collection of the young generation are moved to the old generation.

Garbage collectors can be configured in terms of the various parameters that govern their operation, such as maximum generation size for generational collectors. Garbage collection APIs also normally allow explicit execution of the garbage collector and, for some collectors, explicit disabling and enabling of the collector. Explicit control of the collector is particularly important for applications that must meet real-time constraints, in which an inappropriate garbage collection cycle could mean the difference between meeting a hard deadline or missing it, causing a catastrophic application failure.

In a distributed environment, collection strategies based on traversing the set of all objects would perform and scale poorly. The process of garbage collection would flood the network with many fine-grained book-keeping messages and would introduce blocking behavior across the network. Local garbage collection within the same address space can be efficient, but to scale to a distributed system a complementary strategy such as Leasing (529) is required.

A form of memory leakage often occurs in garbage-collected systems in which an object that should be collected is not because some type of lookup table retains a reference to it. These tables are often intended to show available objects, rather than to use them directly and keep them alive. By referring to them, however, that is just what they end up doing. To resolve this problem, ordinary object references can be complemented with 'weak references' that are not counted when looking for reachable objects. If an object is collected, any corresponding weak references will yield null when they are checked.

It is still possible to employ garbage collection in runtime environments in which manual memory management is the native model, such as in C and C++. A more conservative approach is needed, however, to collect object pointers expressed in terms of raw memory addresses rather than as special handles. Raw memory is untyped, so any pointer-sized piece of memory that matches the address of an allocated object, or points into such an object, is considered a pointer. These faulty matches can not only leak memory, but can also be fooled by addresses that have been encoded in some way, such as in terms of offset values rather than actual pointers.

Counting Handle **

In a PROXY (290), WHOLE-PART (317), ACTIVE OBJECT (365), IMMUTABLE VALUE (396), BRIDGE (436), OBJECT MANAGER (492), AUTOMATED GARBAGE COLLECTION (519), or DISPOSAL METHOD (531) arrangement ...

... we often need to arrange for guaranteed and deterministic disposal of shared objects and their resources.

An object created dynamically on the heap must be destroyed following its use to avoid leaking memory and other resources. However, some languages, such as C++, manage heap object lifetime manually. Errors in management lead to memory leaks and memory corruption. Even in garbage-collected environments, issues can arise with resource reclamation, because garbage collection is not deterministic.

Instead, we must ensure that the shared object created on the heap is disposed of reliably, safely, and in a timely fashion. The sooner it is disposed of, the less perception there will be of any resource leakage or starvation. If this is done too soon, however, there will be dangling references to the object. As long as at least one client is referencing the object, it must not be reclaimed: as soon as no client is using the object, it is a candidate for disposal. Implementing this logic within the object's clients is not practical, since it pollutes clients with additional housekeeping code and couples them tightly to the object.

Therefore:

Introduce or nominate a handle object as the only means of accessing the shared object. Let this handle object encapsulate the responsibility for tracking references to the shared object and, consequently, for its disposal if it is no longer referenced.

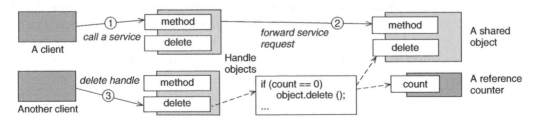

The handle object ensures, transparently, that the shared object is disposed of on behalf of its clients without producing either dangling references or memory leaks.

The handle object's lifecycle methods are responsible for tracking the number of references to, and managing the lifetime of, the shared object. When there are no more references, when a handle itself is about to be destroyed or re-bound to another object, is when the (no longer) shared object can be disposed of. In C++ the operations in question are the constructors, destructor, and assignment operator for the handle.

There are two basic options for implementing handle objects. An EXPLICITLY COUNTED OBJECT [Hen01b] tracks the references to the shared object via reference counting, so that there is an explicit, physical count. By contrast, LINKED HANDLES [Hen01b] introduces bidirectional links between the handle objects, so that they are aware of both the shared object and other handle objects referring to the shared object. However, LINKED HANDLES cannot be made thread-safe with any kind of reasonable efficiency, so they are not applicable for objects shared between threads.

An explicit count avoids the penalties of linking COUNTING HANDLES and makes the task of checking sharing against a specific limit such as zero simple and explicitly visible. It is easy to determine when a COUNTING HANDLE is the last one to point to the shared object and it must delete it upon its own deletion.

There are three placement options for the reference count for an EXPLICITLY COUNTED OBJECT. An EMBEDDED COUNT places the counter within the shared object itself [Hen01b]. This option is efficient time-wise and space-wise, requiring only a single heap allocation not much larger than the allocation of an uncounted version of the shared object. If it is impossible, hard, or inappropriate to add an EMBEDDED COUNT to the shared object, for example if there is no access to its source code, we can introduce a DETACHED COUNT, which is a separate object that holds the reference count for the shared object [Hen01b]. A DETACHED COUNT does not affect the type of the shared object, and is managed exclusively by the COUNTING HANDLES. The DETACHED COUNT is created when the shared object is first introduced to a COUNTING HANDLE—only then does it become an EXPLICITLY COUNTED OBJECT. When the last COUNTING HANDLE disposes of the shared object, it also disposes of the corresponding DETACHED COUNT.

A third placement option is a LOOKED-UP COUNT. This centralizes the management of shared objects and their counts collectively in a separate object, using some identity of the shared objects as the key for its direct access from their COUNTING HANDLE [Hen01b]. A LOOKED-UP COUNT can introduce an additional time overhead for the lookup, but it can also provide the opportunity for collective operations on all the shared objects if that is needed.

In multi-threaded applications any reference count implementation must be thread-safe, to avoid corrupting its state due to race conditions caused by concurrent access from multiple COUNTING HANDLES. Unless incrementing and decrementing the count are infrequent operations, lock-based solutions are not time- or resource-efficient enough to be practical. The lock-free increment and decrement operations offered by modern operating systems are the preferred approach, but note that although these may be lock free, they are not cost free: they still incur an overhead, especially on multiprocessor systems and multi-core processors.

In a distributed environment, synchronous reference counting is insufficient as a practical or scalable scheme when the lifetime of a shared object in one address space is managed by handles in remote address spaces. Increments and decrements can make for a great deal of idle chatter on the network, and all it takes is for a client to crash, or a rogue client to not adhere to the reference-counting protocol, for the scheme to unravel. If COUNTING HANDLES are introduced in such an environment, they need to be supplemented with other lifetime management schemes such as LEASING (517). Similarly, COUNTING HANDLES fail for object relationships that have cycles. In cyclic relationships the reference counts are never zero, so they leak.

Abstract Factory **

When implementing a DOMAIN OBJECT (208), a REFLECTION (197) archi-tecture, or a BUILDER (527) ...

... we often need to separate details of related implementation classes from their client interfaces to keep a system loosely coupled.

Clients—particularly clients in a framework—are generally not interested in how families of related objects they use are created, configured, represented, and disposed of. Instead they are only interested in the services that these objects offer, as well as knowing that the objects in the families are semantically compatible.

Frameworks, for example, such as graphical user interface toolkits and object request brokers, as well as applications designed for flexibility, often create families of objects that encapsulate variants in the software such as control-flow extensions, algorithms, and data representations. Creating each object individually and separately can create a configuration nightmare if the created objects are not semantically compatible with one another.

Therefore:

Define a factory interface for the creation and, optionally, the disposal of families of related objects. Fulfill this interface with specialized factories that actually carry out the creation work on behalf of their clients.

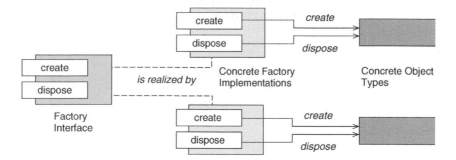

An abstract factory specifies a uniform object creation and disposal interface for all related object types. Concrete factory classes derive from this abstract factory to control the creation and disposal of particular object types, and to ensure that the objects created are semantically compatible.

In general, factories separate object lifetime concerns from object usage, so that clients do not depend on how the objects they use are created and destroyed. Neither do they depend on structural details of the objects that are relevant for proper creation and destruction.

An abstract factory interface contains two kinds of methods: one or more FACTORY METHODS (529) create objects and, optionally, the corresponding DISPOSAL METHODS (531) dispose of the objects. Abstract factories are typically expressed in terms of their own class rather than by adding new responsibilities to an existing class, because most objects created are not related to each other via inheritance.

The variability sometimes needed for object creation can often be accommodated by configuring the factory with objects that specify the actual creation logic for the factory's creation methods. Such a PLUGGABLE FACTORY [Vlis98b] [Vlis99] is essentially a framework into which other parts are plugged and offers a simpler, more flexible, and less repetitive alternative to creating many different concrete factories. Pluggable creational behavior can be expressed through STRATEGY (455) objects or types. Alternatively, prototypical instances can be provided for each type created by the factory. A *homomorphic* FACTORY METHOD—a specialized form of FACTORY METHOD in which the resulting product type is the same as the creating type—can express polymorphic copying.

Builder *

When implementing a DOMAIN OBJECT (208) or a REFLECTION (197) architecture ...

... we often need to create objects that are complex or the cumulative result of many steps.

Some objects are complex enough to prevent them being created in a single 'atomic' step. Instead they must be created step-wise, in which each step of the builder creates a portion of the complex object. Alternatively, even if the object being created is simple in representation, its state may be the outcome of complex or ongoing calculations. The execution order of the steps may differ for each object created.

Clients are generally not interested in the complexity and variability of an object's creation. The details of the process should not result in the creation of many temporary objects or the complication of application logic. Clients just want a 'product' that is created correctly and reliably so that they can access its functionality. Similarly, what holds for an object's creation often also holds for its disposal.

Therefore:

Introduce a builder that provides separate methods for constructing and disposing of each different part of a complex object, or for combining cumulative changes in the construction of whole objects. Let a separate director implement the algorithms for creating and disposing of the object by using the builder interface.

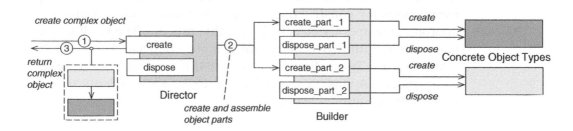

A builder encapsulates the knowledge of how to construct an appropriate product, whether it is encapsulation of process that can be used to work on the product, or the encapsulation of assembly structure. The builder offers a method for retrieving the resulting product object. A director uses the builder to construct an appropriate product object. Object disposal can optionally also be supported.

The separation into builder and director roles supports flexible variation of an object's creation and, optionally, disposal process. The builder provides and encapsulates the basic *mechanisms* for the creation and deletion of the object's different parts via corresponding FACTORY METHODS (529) and DISPOSAL METHODS (531). The director is either an *ad hoc* client, or a factory such as an ABSTRACT FACTORY (525), that implements the *policy* for assembling and disassembling the object in a particular way, which may depend on client input or global application. Both parts can vary independently: changes to the builder implementation need not affect the director, and vice versa, as long as the builder interface remains stable.

Hierarchically related objects can be created and deleted by introducing a builder hierarchy. An abstract builder declares the build and disposal interface for elements of the object hierarchy, and concrete builders that derive from this abstract base implement the build and disposal steps for a particular object. Clients can retrieve the created object from the builder directly, via the director, or pass the object to the director for correct disposal.

A simple form of BUILDER, MUTABLE COMPANION [Hen00b], supports the creation of IMMUTABLE VALUES (396) with less overhead and in more ways than ordinary constructors, for example, the use of a `StringBuffer` or `StringBuilder` in Java to construct a `String` by concatenation. In particular, a value builder eliminates the need for complex expressions for constructing immutable values, and minimizes the creation of temporary objects during this process. The modifier methods enable cumulative or complex state changes. These methods should have a THREAD-SAFE INTERFACE (384) if used in a multi-threaded environment. A single FACTORY METHOD (529) allows clients to access the resulting immutable object.

Factory Method **

When implementing a BROKER (237), ACCEPTOR-CONNECTOR (265), EXPLICIT INTERFACE (281), ITERATOR (298), THREAD-SPECIFIC STORAGE (392), IMMUTABLE VALUE (396), OBJECT MANAGER (492), COMPONENT CONFIGURATOR (490), LIFECYCLE CALLBACK (499), ABSTRACT FACTORY (525), or BUILDER (527) configuration ...

... we often need to encapsulate the details of object creation to preserve looseness of coupling and stability of use.

◆◆◆

Object creation is often a simple matter of using a new expression, with respect to a class, that allocates memory and initiates a constructor. However, not all objects can be constructed so easily. For example, the type of the objects may depend on the type of another object, or some initialization steps may need to be handled outside the constructor.

Direct object creation may inadvertently obfuscate and reduce the independence of the calling code if any of the necessary ingredients for correct object creation are not readily available. The concrete class, the full set of constructor arguments, or the enforcement of other constraints may not be known at the point of call. To require them would increase the complexity of the calling code and reduce its stability, making changes in creation detail harder to introduce.

Therefore:

Encapsulate the concrete details of object creation inside a factory method, rather than letting clients create the object themselves.

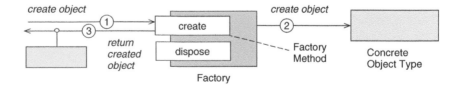

Clients call through the factory method to obtain a new object.

◆◆◆

FACTORY METHOD frees clients from creating any complex objects that they use, thereby making the clients easier to understand and maintain. This pattern also simplifies the instantiation of objects whose constructor cannot easily contain their creation logic, for example if external validation or object relationships must be established that is beyond the scope of the object's immediate responsibility.

There are three main variants of FACTORY METHOD that address different creational needs:

- *Simple.* A method on an object of concrete class type that simply encapsulates the logic of creation and the policies that may surround it.

- *Polymorphic.* Where the possible types of the product object are drawn from a class hierarchy, and the type to be created depends on an existing object, a polymorphic factory method on the existing object encapsulates the knowledge of the concrete class used.

- *Class.* Considered as a meta-object, a class creates its instances. It is possible to provide class-level factory methods—expressed as `static` methods in many languages—to play the role of constructors.

These variants can be combined and refined to produce an appropriate design solution, depending on specific goals and context.

Note that unless created specifically for the purpose, including the role of factory in an interface can sometimes be considered an addition that weakens its cohesiveness a little. The solution is certainly more encapsulated than the alternatives, but the cohesion can be considered less than in a design in which such creation was never needed.

Disposal Method **

When realizing an Explicit Interface (281), Iterator (298), Object Manager (492), Component Configurator (490), Lifecycle Callback (499), Automated Garbage Collection (519), Abstract Factory (525), or Builder (527) structure ...

... we need to preserve the encapsulation of object creation and resource acquisition when discarding an object.

◆◆◆

Disposing of an object is not always as simple as destroying it explicitly or leaving it to the mercy of a garbage collector. Objects whose creation was encapsulated may have more to them than can be addressed by simple collection of memory. Reliance on manual deletion can introduce too much coupling, whereas garbage collection lacks deterministic execution.

For manual memory management, as found in C++, and even with Counting Handles, it is too much to assume that an object whose creation was encapsulated is a suitable candidate for deletion. Its allocation may have been optimized in a way that is incompatible with deletion, or it may need to be recycled instead of deleted because its creation is expensive. Making applications responsible for this housekeeping functionality would make their code more complex than necessary due to coupling to encapsulated lifecycle concerns.

Therefore:

Encapsulate the concrete details of object disposal within a dedicated method, instead of letting clients delete or discard objects themselves.

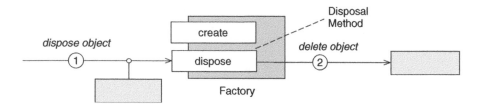

When a client has finished using an object, it—or a helper mechanism—calls the disposal method to ensure that the object is cleaned up in an appropriate manner. This may be outright deletion, careful dismantling, or recycling.

DISPOSAL METHOD frees clients from deleting or dismantling any complex objects that they use, thereby making the clients easier to understand and maintain. In addition, DISPOSAL METHOD simplifies the destruction of objects whose deletion logic cannot be implemented easily in their destructor or by the garbage collector, for example because the object or its parts should be recycled or made available to other clients. DISPOSAL METHOD makes these variations in the way an object is deleted transparent to its clients.

There are two basic options for placing a DISPOSAL METHOD. One option, a factory DISPOSAL METHOD, places the disposal method on the factory or object responsible for originally creating the object. This explicit arrangement makes the intended lifecycle of the created objects clearer in the interface of the factory. However, it means that the object user must be aware of the object's origins in order to return the object when it is done. The other option, self-DISPOSAL METHOD, provides a method on the object to be disposed of. The lifecycle relationship is not as obvious in this design and, if the disposal action involves return to a pool, the object may also require a back reference to the factory so that it can, so to speak, 'return home.'

Because manual use of a disposal method can be error-prone, its use can be wrapped by an EXECUTE-AROUND METHOD [Hen01a] or a COUNTING HANDLE. (522). In C#, the `IDisposable` interface provides a general purpose self-disposal interface that can be used with the `using` control-flow construct.

21 Database Access

Frank and some of his books
© Frank Buschmann

Many business systems need to persist some or all of the data they use. Distributed systems are no exception. There is a mismatch, however, between the relational model, the dominant persistence paradigm, and the object-oriented model, the favored paradigm for distributed application development. This chapter presents five patterns that help to bridge these two models, to support mapping between object-oriented applications and relational databases.

Many software systems use databases to store their persistent data. In most of these systems the databases follow the relational model for the following reasons, mainly due to economic factors:

- *Existing legacy data and IT infrastructures.* Databases are a common and long-standing feature of many IT organizations. As a result, the cost of transferring data to a different database model, or even to a different relational database, often outweigh the benefits of such a change, even if another database is technically superior.

- *Customer support.* Due to the maturity of relational databases and the ecosystem that supports them, users typically receive competent and timely customer support world-wide. This level of service is not necessarily available for other database models.

- *Experience.* Developers, administrators, and users of databases are often most familiar with the relational database model, having gained significant experience in designing and provisioning applications that use relational databases, designing relational database schemas, and tuning such databases. Achieving this proficiency with other database models is expensive and time consuming.

Nevertheless, there are also two technical reasons that advocate the use of relational databases:

- *Performance.* Over time, a great deal of effort has been invested in optimizing relational databases. As a result, they provide good performance for most applications that need to persist data.

- *Data usage scenarios.* The profile of application data and its use fits best with the kind of collective and query-based relational model supported by relational databases. From a bird's-eye perspective, most applications deal with data records that they use and modify, and collections of data records on which they perform typical operations for collections, regardless of how data is represented in the applications. This conceptual view of data is well-supported by relational databases.

Although the relational model remains the dominant database paradigm, the technologies used to design and implement applications have changed considerably over time. Two decades ago, procedural programming was common, whereas most new applications are now object-oriented. This trend, however, often causes an impedance mismatch, since applications that use object features such as inheritance, polymorphism, and navigational inter-object relationships cannot map easily and efficiently to a relational database schema.

There are dozens of patterns and pattern languages [BW95] [KC97] [Kel99] [Fow03a] that describe how to combine relational and object-oriented models effectively. Exploring them in detail, however, is beyond the scope of our pattern language, which centers on building distributed systems. However, because of the important role that relational databases play in many distributed systems, we describe the following key patterns that help to bridge the chasm [BW95] between the object and the relational models:

> The DATABASE ACCESS LAYER pattern (538) [KC97] separates an object-oriented application design from a relational database by introducing a mapping layer between the two.

> The DATA MAPPER pattern (540) [Fow03a] acts as a mediator that transfers data between an application and a database, to decouple an object model from a relational database schema so that the two can evolve independently.

> The ROW DATA GATEWAY pattern (542) [Fow03a] introduces objects that act as gateways to individual records in a database table, but can be accessed using object-oriented programming mechanisms.

> The TABLE DATA GATEWAY pattern (544) [Fow03a] introduces an object that acts as a gateway to an entire database table, but can be accessed using object-oriented programming mechanisms.

> The ACTIVE RECORD architectural pattern (546) [Fow03a] specifies an object that wraps a record data structure in an external resource, such as a row in a database table, and provides additional domain logic for that object.

The DATABASE ACCESS LAYER pattern was published originally by Wolfgang Keller and Jens Coldewey [KC97]. The four other patterns are found in Martin Fowler's *Patterns of Enterprise Application Architecture* [Fow03a]. Some patterns outlined above also appear in the J2EE patterns literature [ACM01]: DATABASE ACCESS LAYER corresponds to DOMAIN STORE, and TABLE DATA GATEWAY to DATA ACCESS OBJECT.

All of these patterns connect to other, finer-grained and detailed patterns for database access, which are also included in our pattern language. For reasons of brevity, however, we refer only to their original sources and do not describe them in detail. These other patterns are documented in *Patterns of Enterprise Application Architecture*, but most were also published earlier [BW95] [KC97] [Kel99].

DATABASE ACCESS LAYER can be considered the root pattern for dealing with database access, whereas the other four patterns describe approaches for the refinement of a database access layer.

- DATA MAPPER provides complete decoupling of an application's data model from the table format in which it is persisted. The pattern is the most complex refinement option for a DATABASE ACCESS LAYER access layer. It should therefore only be considered when the mapping between the data model and the table formats is not straightforward, for instance because the data model includes cycles, or the information stored in data objects is spread across multiple tables.

- ROW DATA GATEWAY and TABLE DATA GATEWAY also decouple the data model of an application from database table formats. The two patterns are most applicable if the application data model consists of collections of homogeneous application data objects that can be mapped directly onto corresponding database tables. If the application's programming platform offers support for record sets, such as ADO.NET and JDBC 2.0, TABLE DATA GATEWAY is the best choice, because record sets already provide an object-oriented encapsulation for tabular data. Otherwise ROW DATA GATEWAY is the better option: it provides explicit mapping between individual data objects and data stored in a specific table row.

- ACTIVE RECORD relaxes the decoupling between the object-oriented data model of the application and the table formats of the database. The pattern simply wraps a specific table row within a database table or view, and adds domain logic to that data. Due to this tight coupling, ACTIVE RECORD should only be preferred if the data object's domain logic is simple, its data representation maps directly to a single database table, and the database design—or even the underlying database itself—does not change often during the application's lifetime.

The following diagram illustrates how the five patterns for accessing relational databases connect to our pattern language and to other database access patterns and idioms.

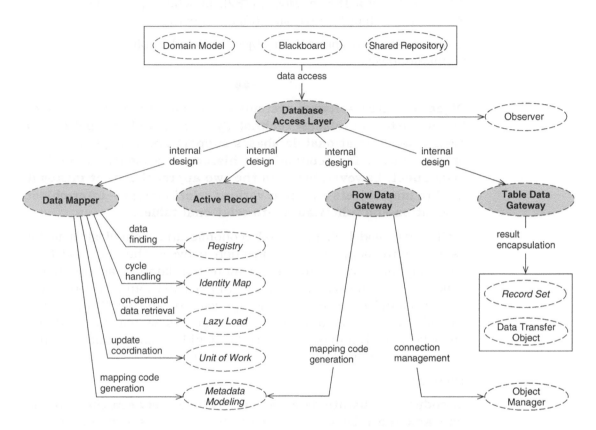

Database Access Layer **

When realizing a DOMAIN MODEL (182), or when specifying a SHARED REPOSITORY (202) or BLACKBOARD (205) architecture ...

... we must often connect an object-oriented application to a relational database.

Object-oriented software systems often use relational databases for persistence: object technology can simplify application design, while relational databases support efficient persistence, or are chosen for economic or historical reasons. There is a disconnect, however, between the two approaches that makes it hard to map objects and their various relationships—inter-object navigation and inheritance—to relational tables.

While each model offers a good economic and technological fit for its respective domain, the connection between the two models is not straightforward. Neither applications nor database access should suffer from the mismatch, however. In particular, an object-oriented design should be usable for the application, and application code should not be littered with database access statements and API housekeeping. Database access code should similarly make best use of mechanisms provided by the relational model.

Therefore:

Introduce a separate database access layer between the application and the relational database that provides a stable object-oriented data-access interface for application use, backed by an implementation that is database-centric.

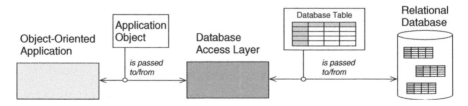

Applications can store and retrieve their persistent data by calling an appropriate method on the database access layer, or by asking the data to persist itself, depending on the design. The database access layer is responsible for mapping between the data structures used by the applications and the format required by the database tables.

DATABASE ACCESS LAYER decouples an object-oriented application from the details of the database. All concrete mappings of objects to tables are encapsulated within this layer, so that it appears to the application as if it were storing and retrieving 'its own' objects rather than table entries. DATABASE ACCESS LAYER thus offers a suitable bridge to the underlying persistence technology. In addition, modifications to the DATABASE ACCESS LAYER do not affect application components directly.

Many options exist for designing a DATABASE ACCESS LAYER. A DATA MAPPER (540) shields objects from knowing even that there is a database present, which is useful when the application design and the database schema should evolve independently. A ROW DATA GATEWAY (542) specifies objects that look exactly like a record in a record structure, but which can be accessed with ordinary object-oriented methods. This is useful if application data structures map directly onto database records and instances of the records are accessed individually, rather than in record sets. A TABLE DATA GATEWAY (544), in contrast, provides an interface with several *find* methods to retrieve sets of data records from the database, with corresponding *update*, *insert*, and *delete* methods. This is useful if application data structures map directly to database records, and the records are usually accessed in entire record sets rather than individually. ACTIVE RECORDS (546) uses the most obvious approach, and puts all data access logic into application objects. This is useful when the object model of an application maps directly onto the database schema and its domain logic is not too complex—for example, if it is centered around operations such as *create*, *read*, *update*, and *delete*.

The database access layer is also responsible for notifying the application if values in the database change because another application accesses them. Typically the notification mechanism is realized via some form of OBSERVER (405) arrangement, with the database notifying the database access layer, and the database access layer notifying the application. Without such a mechanism, the view the application has of the database is stale, which could lead to incorrect application behavior.

Data Mapper **

When designing a DATABASE ACCESS LAYER (538) ...

... we must shield applications from the way in which data is represented in persistent storage.

Object-oriented applications and relational databases use different mechanisms for structuring data. While it is still necessary to transfer data between the two, if the object-oriented domain model knows about the relational database schema, and vice versa, changes in one tend to ripple to the other.

Mapping between an object-oriented and a relational database schema introduces accidental complexity into an application. For example, collections and inheritance are not present in relational databases, while relational constructs such as SQL queries are not behavioral primitives in conventional object-oriented languages. It is easy to add database access code to an application object, but this makes the object's implementation unnecessarily complex and brittle if the schema or database changes. A direct transliteration of classes to tables, however, may not yield the most appropriate database schema design either. A solution is needed that is loosely coupled and stable.

Therefore:

Introduce a data mapper for each type of persistent application object whose responsibility is to transfer data from the object to the relational database, and vice versa.

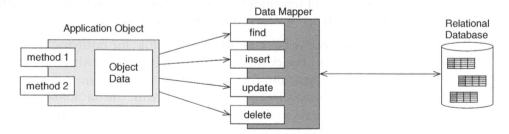

A data mapper is a mediator between an object-oriented domain model and a relational database. A client can use the data mapper to retrieve an application object from the database, or ask it to store an application object in it. The data mapper performs all necessary data transformations and ensures consistency between the two representations.

Using a DATA MAPPER, in-memory objects need not know that a database is present. Moreover, they require no SQL interface code and have no knowledge of the database schema. DATA MAPPER allows the relational database schema and the object-oriented domain model to evolve independently. This design also simplifies unit testing, allowing mappers to real databases to be replaced by mock objects that support in-memory test fixtures.

If an application's domain model is simple and corresponds largely to its physical representation in the database, the data mapper can just map a database table to an equivalent application object on a field-to-field basis. If the domain model is more complex, however, several patterns can be used to support the implementation of a data mapper. A REGISTRY [Fow03a] helps to find data belonging to a specific application object. An IDENTITY MAP [Fow03a] ensures that data is loaded only once if complex and cyclic dependencies exist between application objects. If an application object contains a large data set, a LAZY LOAD [Fow03a] enables the data mapper to load a subset of key data during object creation, and defer loading less important or infrequently used data when it is first accessed. In general, LAZY LOAD combines PARTIAL ACQUISITION (511) and LAZY ACQUISITION (507) to control and optimize the process of loading data from the database. When inserting and updating data into the database, a UNIT of WORK [Fow03a] helps the data mapper understand which objects have been changed, created, or destroyed.

A data mapper that supports the handling of data from multiple types of application objects can employ a METADATA MAPPING [Fow03a] to avoid hard-coding different mapping schemes.

DATA MAPPER simplifies application objects both programmatically and in terms of their dependencies. It offers a degree of isolation and stability, protecting both application objects and schemas from changes in the other. DATA MAPPER is not without its own complexity, however, and changes in either the application object model or the database schema may require changes to a data mapper.

Row Data Gateway **

When designing a DATABASE ACCESS LAYER (538) . . .

. . . we need a means to access and manipulate a single data record.

In-process data structures in some applications map directly to relational database schemas, so there is a one-to-one correspondence between rows and objects. Having each object access its corresponding row directly, however, tightly couples and dilutes application code with infrastructural code.

When application data structure types correspond to tables, instances of each structure to rows, and data fields of the structures to columns in the tables, it is tempting to access and use the relational data directly within the application code, since memory footprint is small and code is direct. The drawbacks to this design, however, are that application code and database-access code can become tightly coupled, and the cohesion of the application code suffers. If the schema changes, mapping code must be added to the application wherever the data is used. As more such changes occur, the complexity of both application and mapping code increases. Similarly, if the application supports multiple databases with different SQL dialects, the application code must handle these variations explicitly, so the original advantage of a small footprint and direct access becomes a disadvantage.

Therefore:

Wrap the data structures and their database access code within row data gateways whose internal structure looks exactly like a database record, but which offer a representation-independent data access interface to clients.

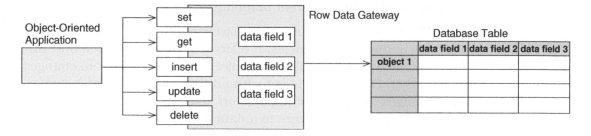

There is one row data gateway instance per row in the table. Clients can use the gateways as if they were 'ordinary' application objects. When the client creates a new gateway instance, its data is inserted into a new row of the corresponding database table. When a client commits changes to the row data gateway, the corresponding fields in the database table are updated. Disposal of the gateway object triggers the deletion of the content of the corresponding table row.

A ROW DATA GATEWAY is most useful if database records are accessed, manipulated, and stored explicitly and separately from other database records. Each row data gateway instance acts as an object that mimics a single record, such as one row of a particular database table, but hides all details of access to the database behind its interface. Changes to the table representation of the data structures are thus transparent to clients, as well as changes of the database access code if the row data gateway is ported to another database that uses a different SQL dialect.

The row data gateway is responsible for any type conversion from the data source types to the in-memory types. This type conversion is often straightforward, since each column in the database table typically corresponds to a field in the row data gateway—which suggests that the mapping code be generated via METADATA MAPPING [Fow03a].

A row data gateway has a simple interface: *set* and *get* methods to access and modify the in-memory data structure, and *update*, *insert*, and *delete* methods to execute the appropriate SQL for the action and data against the database. A row data gateway does not implement application logic that operates on the encapsulated data structure, which keeps the two concerns independent.

Each row data gateway object must be associated with a network connection of some kind. To keep this management code simple and self-contained, use an OBJECT MANAGER (492) to create new records. This also addresses the potential problem of creating more than a single row data gateway instance for a particular row. Also consider supporting row deletion via the manager rather than via the gateway object. OBJECT MANAGER can also offer finder capabilities that search the appropriate table in the database.

Table Data Gateway **

When designing a DATABASE ACCESS LAYER (538) ...

... we must provide measures to manipulate whole collections of data.

In-process data structures in some applications map directly to a relational database schema. Directly manipulating collections of data within the application's business logic via SQL, however, tightly couples the application model and the database schema.

When application data structure types correspond to tables, it is tempting to access and use relational data directly within application code, since memory footprint is small and the code is direct. The resulting coupling creates development friction, however, if the schema evolves or the database technology changes. Moreover, applications are burdened with non-cohesive infrastructure code. Although Row DATA GATEWAYS offer a simple solution to these problems, they introduce other problems, such as row management, and can yield a proliferation of objects. While these problems may not arise for small tables or when only a few tables are accessed during a session, they may significantly complicate large applications. Row DATA GATEWAYS also do not handle collections of objects, as they manipulate individual objects directly, rather than sets.

Therefore:

Wrap the database access code for a specific database table within a specialized table data gateway, and provide it with an interface that allows applications to work on domain-specific data collections.

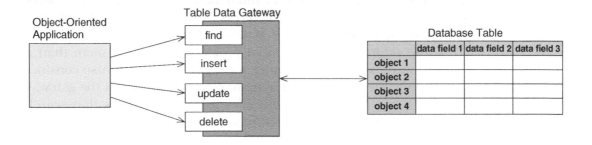

There is one table data gateway instance per table in the database. Clients can use the gateway to manipulate collections of data of the same type. When a client adds a new object to the collection, its data is stored as a new row in the table accessed by the gateway. Modification and deletion of rows in the table are negotiated via the gateway.

TABLE DATA GATEWAY is most useful if database records are accessed, modified, and stored in sets, rather than individually. Each table data gateway encapsulates the details of access to the database, as well as the transformation of that data into collections of domain-specific objects and vice versa. Changes to the table representation of domain-specific objects become largely transparent to clients, as well as changes to database access code when porting the table data gateway to another database that uses a different SQL dialect. Significant changes to the schema that change the normalization of rows and partitioning of tables, however, are not as well supported.

A table data gateway has a simple interface consisting of several *find* methods to get data from the database, together with corresponding *update*, *insert*, and *delete* methods. Each method maps the input parameters and action into SQL and executes it against a database connection. The table data gateway is usually stateless with respect to domain data, because its role is to push data back and forth. One constraint on the interface, however, is that update and deletion actions may not be available when a table data gateway corresponds to a view.

Many alternatives exist for returning the results of queries to clients, which may contain multiple database records. One is to return a simple data structure such as a map or a DATA TRANSFER OBJECT (418). Some environments, such as ADO.NET and JDBC 2.0, can return a RECORD SET [Fow03a], which is an in-memory representation of tabular data. Since RECORD SET mirrors a table structure directly in application code, however, it can tightly couple that code to database-specific aspects. TABLE DATA GATEWAY can also act as a factory and manager and return the appropriate domain-specific objects.

Active Record

When designing a DATABASE ACCESS LAYER (538) ...

... we may want to avoid complex data mapping for self-contained data records that offer only simple data manipulation methods.

In most object-oriented applications, some parts of the domain logic are bound to the data on which they operate. If the data is actually in the database, however, direct manipulation is not possible. For data structures with only simple associated behaviors, a multi-layered solution may be too complex.

Raw use of a database API in the main parts of an application can yield code that is non-cohesive and brittle in the face of changes such as schema evolution or database technology migration. Database access code and application code should therefore not be mixed too freely in such cases. Introducing too much separation between application objects and database access, however, may be too cumbersome when the associated object behavior for each record is simple, such as attribute queries, or queries based on simple calculations over the attributes.

Therefore:

Encapsulate the data, the corresponding database access code, and the data-centered domain behavior in active record objects that offer a domain-specific interface to clients.

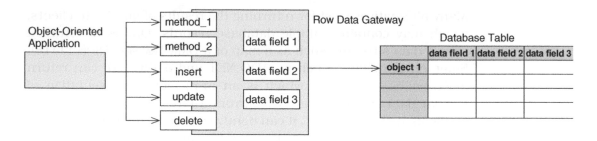

Clients can use active record objects via their domain-specific interfaces as if they were ordinary application objects. Any change in the encapsulated data values' results can lead to a change in the row data via an additional *update* method. If a client creates a new active record, a new row in the corresponding database table is created. If a client disposes of an active record, the corresponding table row is deleted.

ACTIVE RECORD can be an appropriate choice when the domain logic of an application is relatively simple, for example if it is centered around *create*, *read*, *update*, and *delete* operations, attribute manipulation, and simple calculated values based on attributes. In such cases, changes to the table representation of the data structures have only a local and limited affect on application-specific code, as well as changes to the database access code due to porting the active object to another database that uses a different SQL dialect. If a domain object type is more complex, for example if it uses inheritance, inter-object relationships, and collections, an ACTIVE RECORD may be less suitable.

An ACTIVE RECORD class typically offers methods for constructing instances from database domain objects. These can include SQL result sets, `static` finder methods that wrap commonly used SQL queries, methods to update the database and to insert the data encapsulated within the active record into the database, `get` and `set` methods for the active record data fields, and domain-related methods that implement some data-centric pieces of the application's business logic. The implementation can suffer, however, if it mixes problem domain concepts with infrastructural concepts, which results in tight coupling between application and database parts.

22 A Departing Thought

Nach dem Spiel ist vor dem Spiel
German football wisdom

The German football adage above can be taken literally for this book: 'after the match is before the match.' In our departing thoughts we reflect briefly on our pattern language for distributed computing, and outline the upcoming steps and activities involved in continuing and completing the vision of *Pattern-Oriented Software Architecture*.

The pattern language we present in this book distills our own experience, and the experience of many experts around the world, in building distributed systems. We have seen the language behind the documented patterns applied to guide the development of many production distributed systems, ranging from industrial automation, telecommunication, and medical imaging, over Web-based e-commerce systems, to component and communication middleware. The intent of our language was twofold:

- To provide an overview about, introduction to, guide through, and communication vehicle for the best practices and state-of-the-art in key areas of the construction of distributed software systems.

- To connect many stand-alone patterns, pattern collections, and pattern languages from the existing body of literature that relate to, or are useful for, distributed computing, to form a single language that provides a consistent and coherent holistic view of the craft of building distributed systems.

Our language is still a work in progress, despite its length and broad coverage of relevant topics, and will probably never be finished completely. As our collective experience of building distributed systems grows, and with the hindsight of applying the language, further patterns from the body of the literature should be integrated, new patterns must be written, and existing patterns will need refactoring for their content and relationships to other patterns in the language. Such a Herculean task cannot be mastered by ourselves alone, however, otherwise we would probably never finish with the language or keep our day jobs! We therefore hope that you, a reader of this book, will work together with other members of the software pattern community to help us evolve the language towards its next state. The goal is to keep improving its practical value for architects and developers of distributed systems.

The second area that suggests future work is the conceptual framework on which this and other pattern languages build. Chapter 1, *On Patterns and Pattern Languages*, briefly introduced the relevant concepts, such as patterns, pattern sequences, and pattern languages, but there is much more to explore than we can present and discuss in the context of this book. Examples of remaining topics to explore include what the concepts are about, which other detailed properties should be explored, and—most interestingly—how all the concepts relate to one another to form a consistent and coherent view onto patterns.

We leave the answers to these questions to the next POSA volume, *On Patterns and Pattern Languages*, which will form the closure of the *Pattern-Oriented Software Architecture* series. Watch out for it!

Glossary

This glossary defines key terms that we use frequently throughout the book. All the terms are related to various aspects of distributed computing software and systems. When a definition refers to other terms in the glossary, we italicize these terms.

We have omitted many terms that we only use in one context, such as enterprise resource planning (ERP). When we felt that such terms needed an explanation, we gave it in context rather than including them in the Glossary.

For completeness, we have also included common terms such as *pattern*, *software architecture*, and *idiom* that were explained in depth in various sections of [POSA1].

Abstract Class A *class* that does not implement all the methods defined in its *interface*. An abstract class defines a common abstraction for its *subclasses*.

Abstract Component A *component* that specifies one or more *interfaces* for other components. An abstract component can either be explicit, such as an *abstract class*, or implicit, such as a class *parameter* of a C++ *template* function. Abstract components form the basis for exploiting *polymorphism* and implementing flexible *systems*. This term is used in the same way as abstract class, to avoid restricting *patterns* to *object-oriented languages*.

Abstract Method The declaration of an operation of an *abstract class* that must be defined by a *subclass*.

Active Connection Establishment The connection role played by a peer application that initiates a connection to a remote peer. (Compare with *Passive Connection Establishment*.)

Active Object An *object* that executes its *methods* in a different *thread* than the *clients* that invoke its methods. (Compare with *passive object*.)

API   Application programming *interface*. The external interfaces of a reusable software *platform*, such as an *operating system*, that is used by *systems* or *applications* built on top of it.

Application A program or collection of programs that fulfills a customer or user's requirements.

Application Framework An integrated set of *components* that collaborate to provide a reusable *software architecture* for a family of related *applications*. In an object-oriented environment, an application framework consists of *abstract* and *concrete classes*, and inversion of control. *Instantiation* of such a framework consists of composing and *subclassing* from existing classes.

Architectural Pattern An architectural *pattern* expresses a fundamental structural organization schema for software *systems*. It provides a set of predefined *subsystems*, specifies their responsibilities, and includes rules and guidelines for organizing the *relationships* between them.

Associative Array An array indexed via arbitrary key values such as strings, rather than by integers. Hash tables and binary search trees are a common way to implement associative arrays.

Asynchronous I/O A mechanism for sending or receiving data in which an I/O operation is initiated, but the caller does not block waiting for the operation to complete.

Backus Naur Form (BNF) A standard technique for describing the syntax of a language.

Bandwidth The capacity of a communication medium, such as a *network* or *bus*.

Broadcast A special form of *multicast* in which messages are transmitted to all *servers* in a particular *domain*.

Bus A high-speed communication channel that links computing *devices*, such as *CPUs*, disks, and *network interfaces*.

Busy Wait A technique used by a *thread* to wait for a *lock* by executing a tight loop and polling to see if the lock is available on each iteration, in contrast to waiting for the lock to be released by sleeping and allowing other threads to run.

Cache Affinity A *thread scheduling* optimization that gives preference to dispatching a thread on the *CPU* on which it most recently ran, to maximize the probability of its state being present in the CPU's *instruction and data caches*.

Callback   A *function* or *object* that specifies the action that should occur whenever a particular *event* happens.

Class   A fundamental building block in object-oriented languages. A class specifies an *interface* and encapsulates its internal data structure as well as the functionality of its *instances* or *objects*. A class can extend one or more other *superclasses* via *inheritance*, in which case it is also known as a *subclass*.

Client   In our descriptions *client* denotes a *role*, *component*, or *subsystem* that invokes or uses the functionality offered by other components.

Closure   See *Method Closure*.

Collaborator   A *component* that cooperates with another component. An element of a *CRC card*.

Collocation Optimization   A technique used in middleware to remove unnecessary overhead of (de)marshaling data or transmitting requests/replies when the sender and receiver are collocated, that is, when communication occurs in the same process or on the same computer. (Compare with *Distribution*.)

Completion Event   A *event* containing response information related to a *request event* initiated by a *client*.

Component   A self-contained, deployable, and executable part of a software *system* that implements a specific *service* or set of services to other components or *clients*. A component has one or more *interfaces* that provide access to its services. Components serve as building blocks for structuring a system. Although a component is self-contained, it can be composed of, or have dependencies on, other components. At the programming language level, components may be represented as *modules*, *classes*, or a set of related *functions*.

Component Object   An *object* whose *class* definition is encapsulated within a deployed *component*. The *interface* a component object implements is made up of *methods* and exposes no implementation. A component object's class is encapsulated within a component.

Concrete Class   A *class* from which objects can be *instantiated*. In contrast to *abstract classes*, all methods are implemented in a concrete class. The term is used to distinguish concrete *subclasses* from their abstract *superclass*.

Concrete Component   A *component* that implements all elements defined in its *interfaces*. Used to distinguish components from the *abstract component* that defines their interface, in the same way that a *concrete class* is distinguished from an *abstract class*.

Concurrency The ability of an *object*, *component*, or *system* to execute operations that are 'logically simultaneous.' (Compare with *parallelism.*)

Condition Variable A condition variable is a *synchronization* mechanism used by collaborating *threads* to suspend themselves temporarily until condition predicates involving data shared between the threads attain desired states [IEEE96]. A condition variable is always used in conjunction with a *mutex*, which the thread must acquire before evaluating the condition predicate. If the condition predicate is false the thread atomically suspends itself on the condition variable and releases the mutex, so that other threads can change the shared data. When a cooperating thread changes this data, it can notify the condition variable, which atomically resumes a thread that had previously suspended on the condition variable, and acquires its mutex again.

Connection A *full association* that is used by *peers* to exchange data between *endpoints* of a networked *application*.

Container A common name for data structures that hold a collection of elements. Examples of containers are lists, sets, and *associative arrays*. In addition, *component* models, such as Enterprise JavaBeans, ActiveX Controls, and the CORBA Component Model, define containers that provide a runtime environment that shields components from the details of their underlying infrastructure, such as an *operating system.*

CORBA The Common *Object Request Broker* Architecture, a distributed object computing *middleware* standard defined by the Object Management Group (OMG).

CPU Central processing unit. A hardware component that executes binary program instructions.

CRC Card Class-Responsibility-Collaborator card. A design tool and notation for describing the *responsibilities* and collaborators of *classes* in a *software architecture.*

Critical Section Code that should not execute *concurrently* in an *object* or *subsystem* can be *synchronized* by a critical section. A critical section is a sequence of instructions that obeys the following *invariant*: while one *thread* or *process* is executing in the critical section, no other thread or process can execute in the critical section. (Compare with *Read-side and Write-side Critical Section.*)

Data Caches Special high-speed memory collocated with a *CPU* that can improve overall system performance. A cache holds a copy of a specific portion of the main memory which then gives an *application* the illusion of access to the main memory.

Data-Mode Socket See *Socket.*

Deadlock A deadlock is a *concurrency* hazard that occurs when multiple *threads* attempt to acquire multiple *locks* and become blocked indefinitely in a circular wait state.

Demarshaling The conversion of a *marshaled message* from a *system-* and *application*-independent format into a system- and application-specific format.

Demultiplexing A mechanism that routes incoming *events* from an input *port* to its intended receivers. There is a 1:N relationship between input port and receivers. Demultiplexing is commonly applied to incoming events and data streams. The reverse operation is known as 'multiplexing.'

Design The activities performed by software developers that result in the *software architecture* of a *system.* The term is also used as a name for the result of these activities.

Design Pattern A design *pattern* provides a scheme for refining elements of a software *system* or the relationships between them. It describes a commonly recurring structure of interacting *roles* that solves a general design problem within a particular context.

Developmental Property A *non-functional property* that addresses requirements related to developing and evolving a software *system,* such as maintainability, extensibility, adaptability, and reusability. Developmental qualities are typically not visible for a system user, and customers tend not to be interested in them. It is mainly the software development organization that is interested in, and affected by, the developmental qualities of a software system. (Compare with *Operational Quality.*)

Device A hardware *component* that provides a service in a computing and/or communication *system.*

Device Driver A software *component* in an *operating system kernel* that is responsible for controlling a hardware *device* attached to the computer, or a software device, such as a RAM disk.

Distribution   The activities associated with placing an *object* into a different *process* or *host* than the *clients* that access it. Distribution is often applied to improve fault tolerance or to access remote resources. (Compare with *Collocation.*)

Distributed System   A distributed system is a computing system in which a number of components cooperate by communicating over a network. The explosive growth of the *Internet* and the World Wide Web in the mid-1990s moved distributed systems beyond their traditional application areas such as industrial automation, defense, and telecommunications, into nearly all domains, including e-commerce, financial services, health care, government, and entertainment.

Domain   Denotes concepts, knowledge and other items that are related to a particular problem area. Often used in 'application domain' to denote the problem area addressed by an *application*. On the *Internet, a domain is a logical addressing entity, such as* uci.edu *or* siemens.de.

Domain Analysis   An inductive, feedback-driven process that examines an application *domain* systematically to identify its core challenges and *design* dimensions in order to map them to effective solution techniques.

Dynamic Binding   A mechanism that defers the association of an operation name (a *message*) to the corresponding code (a *method*) until runtime. Used to implement *polymorphism* in object-oriented languages.

Dynamically Linked Library (DLL)   A library that can be shared by multiple *processes* and linked into and out of a *process' address space* dynamically, to improve application flexibility and extensibility at runtime.

Endpoint   The termination point of a *connection*.

Event   A message that conveys the occurrence of a significant activity, together with any data associated with the activity.

Event Handler   An *object* whose interface consists of one or more *methods* that can process *application*-specific *events*.

Exception-Safe   A unit of code is exception-safe if an exception raised in the code, or propagated from other code called by the unit of code, does not cause resource leaks or an unstable state.

Factory   A *method* or *function* that creates and assembles the resources needed to instantiate and initialize an *object* or *component* instance.

Flow Control   A communication *protocol* mechanism that prevents a fast sender from overrunning the buffering and computing resources of a slow receiver.

Framework	See *Application Framework*.
Full Association	The five-tuple in the *Internet* protocol domain that identifies a *TCP connection*. It consists of the protocol type, the local address and *port number*, and the remote address and port number.
Function	A closed subroutine that is passed zero or more *parameters* and which may return a value to its caller. Functions are typically 'stand-alone,' as opposed to *methods*, which are associated with a *class*.
Functional Property	A particular aspect of a *system*'s functionality, usually related to a specified functional requirement. A functional property may be either made directly visible to users of an *application* by means of a particular *function*, or it may represent aspects of its implementation, such as the algorithm used to compute the function.
Future	A future allows a *client* to obtain the result of a *method* at any point in time after its invocation. The future reserves space for the invoked method to store its result. When a client wants to obtain the result, it can rendezvous with the future, either blocking or polling until the result is computed and stored in the future.
Gateway	A gateway decouples cooperating components in a *network* and allows them to interact without having direct dependencies between each other.
GUI	Graphical user *interface*.
Handle	A handle identifies resources that are managed by an *operating system kernel*. These resources commonly include network *connections*, open files, timers, and *synchronization* objects.
Hardwiring	Writing inflexible programs, for example by using a literal number or string instead of a variable. Such literals are also known as 'magic numbers,' because the number itself provides no clue to understanding its origin or purpose. Another form of hardwiring is to make code dependent on concrete types.
Host	An addressable computer attached to a *network*.
HTTP	The HyperText Transfer Protocol, which is a simple *protocol layered* on top of *TCP* and used by *clients* to download content from a Web *server* via `GET` requests.
Idempotent Initialization	*Object* initialization is idempotent if an object can be reinitialized multiple times without harmful side-effects.

Idiom   An idiom is a *pattern* specific to a programming language or programming environment. An idiom describes how to implement particular behavior or structures in code using the features of the given language or environment. The term is also used more generally to refer to common practices associated with a programming language or environment, without necessarily being patterns.

Indication Event   A *event* containing request information sent from a *client* to a *service* provider.

Inheritance   A feature of object-oriented languages that allows new *classes* to be derived from existing ones. Inheritance defines implementation reuse, a subtype relationship, or both. Depending on the programming language, *single* or *multiple inheritance* is possible.

Inlining   Code expansion that inserts the code of a *function* or *method* body instead of the code used to call the function or method. Inlining long function/method bodies can lead to code 'bloat,' with negative effects on storage consumption and paging effects.

Instance   An *object* originated from a *concrete class*. Often used as a synonym for 'object' in an object-oriented environment. This term may also be used in other contexts (see *Instantiation*).

Instantiation   A mechanism that creates a new *instance* from a template. The term is used in several contexts. *Objects* are instantiated from *classes*. C++ *templates* are instantiated to create new classes or *functions*. An *application framework* is instantiated to create an *application*. The phrase 'instantiating a pattern' is sometimes used to refer to taking the *pattern* as described and filling in the necessary details to implement it in the context of a specific application.

Intercession   The addition to, or modification of, the structure, behavior or state of a *system* by the system itself.

Interface   A publicly accessible portion of a *class*, *component*, *subsystem*, or *application*. The term *interface* is also commonly used to refer to a programming construct that is conceptually equivalent to a fully *abstract class*.

Internet   A world-wide 'network of networks' that is based on the *Internet Protocol* (IP). Widely considered to be the most important human invention since fire and MTV.

Internet Protocol (IP)   A *network layer protocol* that performs segmentation, reassembly, and routing of *packets*.

Intranet A *network* of computers within a company or other organization. Such a network may be secured from outside access and provide a *platform* for company-wide information exchange, co-operative work, and work flow, using *Internet* technologies for communication.

Interprocess Communication (IPC) Communication between processes located in separate address spaces. Examples of IPC mechanisms include *shared memory*, UNIX pipes, message queues, and *socket* communication.

Introspection The examination of selected aspects of the structure, behavior, or state of a *system* by the system itself.

Invariant A property of the state of an *object*, *component*, or *module* that always holds at a specific point in time or space. For example: 'the invariant `a < b` holds whenever control passes line 50 of method `foo`.'

Jitter The standard deviation of the *latency* for a series of operations. Jitter decreases the predictability of an *application* and is thus undesirable for some application types, such as AV streaming or real-time applications.

Late Binding Synonym for *Dynamic Binding*.

Latency The delay experienced by operations.

Layer A level of abstraction that defines a particular set of *services* in a hierarchy. Layer$_n$ is a consumer of services at layer$_{n-1}$ and a supplier of services to layer$_{n+1}$.

Load Balancing A technique used to distribute *client* workloads among various *processes* and *hosts* in a *network*.

Lock A mechanism used to implement some type of a *critical section*. A lock that can be acquired and released serially, such as a static *mutex*, may be added to a *class*. If multiple *threads* attempt to acquire the lock simultaneously, only one thread will succeed and the others will block until the lock is available. Other locking mechanisms, such as *semaphores* or *readers/writer* locks, define different *synchronization* semantics.

Marshaling The conversion of an unmarshaled *message* from a *host*-specific format into a host-independent format.

Message Messages are used to communicate between *objects*, *threads*, or *processes*. In an object-oriented *system* the term message is used to describe the selection and activation of an operation or the *method* of an object. This type of message is synchronous, which means that the sender waits until the receiver finishes the activated operation.

Threads and processes often communicate asynchronously, in which the sender continues its execution without waiting for the receiver to reply. Remote procedure calls (RPC) are a means of synchronous *IPC* over a *network*. While messages in IPC communication *protocols* consist of a protocol-defined structure and are generally not visible to higher *layers*, message queueing systems, such as IBM MQSeries or Microsoft MSMQ messages, define a user-defined body with which higher layers can implicitly transmit user data.

Message Passing An *IPC* mechanism that exchanges *messages* between *threads* or *processes*. (Compare with *shared memory*.)

Method An operation implemented by an *object*. A method is specified within a *class*. The term is also used in 'software development method,' which consists of a set of rules, guidelines, and notations to be used by engineers during the process of developing software.

Method Closure An *object* that contains the context of a *method*, which can include the method's parameters, a binding to the servant or completion handler that will process the method, and potentially a *future* for the method's result.

Middleware A set of *layers* and *components* that provides reusable common *services* and *network* programming mechanisms. Middleware sits on top of an *operating system* and its *protocol stacks*, but below the structure and functionality of any particular *application*.

Module A syntactical or conceptual entity of a software *system* that is often used synonymously for *component* or *subsystem*. Sometimes *modules* also denotes compilation units or files. We use the term in its former sense. Other writers use the term as an equivalent to 'package' when referring to a code body with its own name space.

Monitor A monitor encapsulates *functions* and their internal variables into *thread*-safe *modules*. To prevent *race conditions*, a monitor contains a *lock* that allows only one thread at a time to be active within the monitor. Threads that want to leave the monitor temporarily can block on a *condition variable*.

Moore's Law A surprisingly accurate heuristic that states that the pace of change in microchip technology is such that the component density of microchips doubles regularly. When preparing a lecture in 1965, Gordon Moore noticed that up to that time microchip capacity seemed to double each year. As the pace of change has slowed a little over the past few years, the definition has changed—with Gordon Moore's approval—to reflect the fact that the doubling occurs only every eighteen months to two years.

Multicast A communication *protocol* that allows a *client* to transmit *messages* to multiple servers.

Multiple Inheritance *Inheritance* in which a *class* can have more than one *superclass*.

Mutex A mutex is a 'mutual exclusion' *locking* mechanism that ensures only one *thread* at a time is active *concurrently* within a *critical section* in order to prevent *race conditions*.

Network A communication medium that enables *hosts* and other *device*s to exchange *messages*.

Network Interface A hardware *device* that connects a *network* with a *host*.

Non-functional Property A feature of a *system* not covered by its *functional* description. A non-functional property addresses either a *developmental property* of a system, such as adaptability, extensibility, or maintainability, or an *operational property*, such as ease of use, performance, reliability, and scalability. (See also *Developmental Property* and *Operational Property*.)

Object An identifiable entity in an object-oriented *system*. Objects respond to *messages* by performing a *method* (operation). An object may contain data values and references to other objects, which together define the state of the object. An object is therefore characterized in terms of state, behavior, and identity.

Object-Oriented Language A programming language typically characterized by its support for *inheritance*, static and dynamic *polymorphism*, and exception handling.

Object Request Broker (ORB) A *middleware layer* that allows *clients* to invoke *methods* on distributed *objects* without concern for object location, programming language, *operating system platform*, communication *protocols*, or hardware.

On-the-wire Protocol An 'on-the-wire *protocol*' defines how higher-level communication *middleware*, such as DCE, *CORBA*, or Java *RMI*, or other communication protocols, such as *HTTP*, transform *messages* or *objects* into buffers that can be passed 'across the wire' (*network*). The term 'wire' encompasses a range of transmission media, such as microwave, fiber-optics, and radio.

One-way Method Invocation	A call to a *method* that passes *parameters* to a *server object* but does not receive any result, error values, or other information from the server. (Compare with *Two-way Method Invocation*.)
Operating System	A collection of *services* and *APIs* that manage hardware and software resources on behalf of *applications* and end users.
Operating System Kernel	A collection of core *operating system services*, such as *process* and *thread* management, *virtual memory*, and *interprocess communication (IPC)*.
Operational Property	A *non-functional property* that addresses requirements related to the productive use of a software *system*, such as stability, performance, scalability, availability, and security. Operational properties directly impact the usability and acceptance of a software system. Consequently it is mainly the customers and users of a software system that are interested in, and affected by, the operational properties of a software system. Compare with *Developmental Quality*.
Out-of-Band	A *protocol* or mechanism that occurs outside the normal 'in-band' processing sequence, or data that is needed only for one specific system installation or client.
Packet	A *message* used to convey header and data information in the *TCP/IP protocols*.
Parallelism	The ability of an *object*, *component*, or *system* to execute operations that are 'physically simultaneous.' (Compare with *Concurrency*.)
Parameter	An instance of a data type or *object* passed to a *function*, *method*, or *parameterized type*.
Parameterized Type	A programming language feature that allows *classes* to be parameterized by various other types. Support for different type of parameterization mechanisms exists in many languages, including Java and C++. (Compare with *Template*.)
Passive-Mode Socket	See *Socket*.
Passive Connection Establishment	The connection role played by a peer application that accepts a connection from a remote peer. (Compare with *Active Connection Establishment*.)
Passive Object	An *object* that borrows the *thread* of its caller to execute its methods. (Compare with *Active Object*.)

Pattern	A pattern describes a particular recurring design problem that arises in specific design contexts and presents a well-proven solution for the problem. The solution is specified by describing the *roles* of its constituent participants, their *responsibilities* and *relationships*, and the ways in which they collaborate.
Pattern Compound	A *pattern* that is made up of a community of patterns. A commonly recurring subcommunity of patterns that can be identified as a distinct pattern in its own right. Pattern compounds are also known as 'compound patterns' and 'composite patterns.'
Pattern Language	A network of interrelated *patterns* that define a process for resolving software development problems systematically.
Pattern Sequence	A sequence of *patterns* applied to create a particular architecture or design in response to a specific situation. From the point of view of a *pattern language*, a pattern sequence represents a particular path through the language.
Pattern Story	A narrative that captures a *pattern sequence* and specific design issues involved in constructing a concrete system or creating a particular design example.
Peer-to-Peer	In a distributed *system* peers are processes that communicate with each other. In contrast to *components* in client-server architectures, peers may act as *clients*, as *servers*, or as both, and may change these *roles* dynamically.
Platform	The combination of hardware and/or software that a *system* uses for its implementation. Software platforms include *operating systems*, libraries, and *frameworks*. A platform implements a *virtual machine* with *applications* running on top of it.
Polymorphism	A concept in which a single name may denote different things. For example, a *function* name may be bound over time to several different operations, or a variable may be bound to objects of different types. This concept makes it possible to implement flexible *systems* based on abstractions. In object-oriented languages polymorphism is implemented by the *dynamic binding* mechanism of operations. This implies that a fixed portion of code may behave differently depending on its collaborating objects.
Port	An *endpoint* of communication.
Port Number	A 16-bit number used to identify an *endpoint* of communication in the *TCP protocol*.

Priority Inversion	A *scheduling* hazard that occurs when a lower-priority thread or request blocks the execution of a higher-priority thread or request.
Process	A process provides specific resources, such as *virtual memory*, and protection capabilities, such as user/group identifiers and a hardware-protected address space, that can be used by one or more *threads* in the process. Compared with a *thread*, however, a process maintains more state information, requires more overhead to spawn, *synchronize*, and *schedule*, and often communicates with other processes via *message passing* or *shared memory*.
Product Family	See *Product Line*.
Product Line	A group of products that share a common, managed set of *services* that satisfy specific needs of a selected market or mission area, and that are developed from a common set of core assets in a prescribed way. Products in a product line share much of their *software architecture* and implementation, often because every system is derived from the same *framework*. When a single product evolves over time, its delivered releases also build a product line.
Product-Line Architecture	An *architecture* that describes the structural properties for building a group of related *systems* (a *product line*), typically the components and their interrelationships. The inherent guidelines about the use of *components* must capture the means for handling required variability among the systems.
Protocol	A set of rules that describe how *messages* are exchanged between communicating *peers*, as well as the syntax and semantics of the messages.
Protocol Stack	A group of hierarchically layered *protocols*.
Proxy	A software *component*, *service*, or *object* that stands in for another component, service, or object offering the same usage *interface*, while adding some intelligence of access. For example, a remote proxy stands in for a remote object, offering the same method interface but implementing a *remote method invocation* instead of implementing the requested behavior itself. An *HTTP* proxy can add security and caching to improve performance.
Quality of Service	The probability that a system will deliver particular levels of measurable computational and communication properties, such as availability, *bandwidth*, *latency*, and *jitter*. Policies and mechanisms are

typically designed to control and improve the quality of service of a system.

Race Condition A race condition is a *concurrency* hazard that can occur when multiple *threads* execute simultaneously within a *critical section* that is not properly *serialized*.

Read-side Critical Section A set of sequences of instructions that obeys the following *invariant*: while one or more *threads* or *processes* are executing in the read-side *critical section*, no thread or process can execute in a corresponding write-side critical section. (Compare with *Write-side Critical Section*.)

Readers/Writer Lock A *lock* that allows multiple *threads* to access a resource *concurrently*, but allows only one thread at a time to modify the resource, and further prevents concurrent access and modifications.

Reification The act of creating a concrete *instance* of an abstraction. For example, a concrete reactor implementation is a reification of the REACTOR *pattern* (275). Similarly, an *object* reifies a *class*.

Request Event An *event* sent by a *client* to a service provider asking it to perform some processing on the client's behalf.

Response Event An *event* sent by a *service* provider containing the reply to a *client*'s *request event*.

Recursive Mutex A *lock* that can be re-acquired by the *thread* that owns the *mutex* without incurring self-*deadlock* on the thread.

Refactoring An incremental activity that improves the internal structure of *components* and *frameworks*.

Relationship An association between *components*. A relationship may be static or dynamic. Static relationships show directly in source code, and deal with the placement of components within an architecture. Dynamic relationships deal with the interaction between components, and may not be easily visible from source code or diagrams.

Remote Method Invocation (RMI) The object equivalent of *remote procedure calls*, in which a client on one computer invokes a method on a proxy, to cause a method on a remote object running a server computer to be executed. The term is also used to refer specifically to Java's RMI mechanism.

Remote Procedure Call (RPC) A protocol that allows a computer program running on a client computer to cause a procedure on a server computer to be executed without the programmer explicitly coding the details for the interaction.

Responsibility The functionality of an *object* or a *component* in a specific context. A responsibility typically is specified by a set of semantically related operations. The responsibility section is an element of a *CRC card*.

Role The *responsibility* of a design element within a context of related elements. For example, an object-oriented *class* defines a single role that all its instances support. Another example is an *interface* that defines a role that all implementations support. If an element supports a given role, it must provide an implementation of the interface that defines the role. Elements expose different roles by implementing different interfaces. Different elements may expose the same role by implementing the same interface, which allows *clients* to treat them polymorphicaly with respect to that particular role. An implemented element may take different roles, even within a single *pattern.*

Scheduler A mechanism that determines the order in which *threads* or *request events* are executed.

Self-Describing Message A *message* that contains both metadata that describes the message schema, and the values corresponding to the schema.

Semaphore A *locking* mechanism that maintains a count. As long as the count is greater than zero, a *thread* can acquire the semaphore without blocking. After the count becomes zero, however, threads block on the semaphore until its count become greater than zero as a result of another thread releasing the semaphore, which increments the count.

SEP Somebody Else's Problem, Software Engineering Process, or Software Engineering with Patterns, whichever you prefer.

Serialization A mechanism for ensuring that only one *thread* at a time executes within a *critical section* in order to prevent *race conditions*. The term is also used to refer to the persistent storage of an object in a linear format, such as a byte sequence or XML.

Servant A *component* triggered by *client* requests. When a client request arrives the servant attempts to fulfill it, either by itself or by delegating subtasks to other components.

Server Servers denote *applications* that provide *services* such as *middleware* functionality, database access, or Web page access, to *clients*. In distributed object computing middleware such services are typically implemented by *servants* that represent distributed *objects*.

Service A set of functionality offered by a service provider or *server* to its *clients*. A service typically is implemented in terms of one or more *components*.

Service-Oriented Architecture A style of information systems architecture that enables the creation of applications that are built by combining loosely coupled and interoperable *services*. These services inter-operate based on an *interface* definition that is independent of the underlying platform and programming language.

Shared Memory An *operating system* mechanism that allows multiple *processes* on a computer to share a common memory segment. (Compare with *message passing*).

Single Inheritance *Inheritance* in which a *class* can have at most one direct *superclass*.

Socket A family of terms related to network programming. A socket is an *endpoint* of communication that identifies a particular network address and *port number*. The Socket API is a set of *function* calls supported by most *operating systems* and used by *network applications* to establish *connections* and communicate via socket endpoints. A *data-mode socket* can be used to exchange data between connected *peers*. A *passive-mode socket* is a *factory* that returns a *handle* to a connected data-mode socket.

Software Architecture A software architecture is a description of the *subsystems* and *components* of a software system and the *relationships* between them. Subsystems and components are often specified via different *views* to show the relevant *functional* and *non-functional properties* of a software system. The software architecture of a system is an artifact that results from software *design* activities.

Starvation A *scheduling* hazard that occurs when one or more *threads* are continually pre-empted by higher-priority threads and never execute.

Subclass A *class* that inherits from a *superclass*.

Subsystem A set of collaborating *components* that perform a given *service or* services. A subsystem is considered a separate entity within a *software architecture*. It performs its designated service(s) by interacting with other subsystems and components.

Superclass A *class* from which another class inherits.

Synchronization A *locking* mechanism that coordinates the order in which *threads* execute.

Synchronous I/O A mechanism for sending or receiving data in which an I/O operation is initiated and the caller blocks waiting for the operation to complete.

System A collection of software and/or hardware performing one or several *services*. A system can be a *platform*, an *application*, or both.

System Family See *Product Line*.

Template A C++ programming language feature that enables *classes* and *functions* to be parameterized by various types, constants, or pointers to functions. A template is often called a generic or *parameterized type*.

Thread An independent sequence of instructions that executes within the address space of a program that can be shared with other threads. Each thread has its own runtime stack and registers, which enables it to perform synchronous I/O without blocking other threads that are executing concurrently. Compared to *processes*, threads maintain minimal state information, require relatively little overhead to spawn, *synchronize* and *schedule*, and usually communicate with other threads via objects in global memory rather than *shared memory*.

Thread-per-Connection A *concurrency* model that associates a separate *thread* for each *network connection*. This model handles each *client* that connects with a *server* in a separate thread for the duration of the *connection*. It is useful for servers that must support long-duration sessions with multiple clients. It is not useful for clients, such as *HTTP* 1.0 Web browsers, that associate a single request with each connection, which is effectively a *thread-per-request* model.

Thread-per-Request A *concurrency* model that spawns a new *thread* for each request. This model is useful for *servers* that must handle long-duration *request events* from multiple *clients*, such as database queries. It is less useful for short-duration requests, due to the overhead of creating a new thread for each request. It can also consume a large number of *operating system* resources if many clients send requests simultaneously.

Thread Pool A *concurrency* model that allocates a pool of *threads* that can execute *request events* simultaneously. This model is a variant of *thread-per-request* that amortizes thread creation costs by pre-spawning a pool of threads. It is useful for *servers* that want to bound the number of *operating system* resources they consume. *Client* requests can be executed concurrently until the number of simultaneous requests exceeds the number of threads in the pool. At this point, additional requests must be queued until a thread becomes available. However, if the actual number of threads used by an *application* is significantly smaller than the number of pre-allocated threads at all points in time during its execution, a thread pool wastes threads and the operating system resources that they use.

Transmission Control Protocol (TCP)
A *connection*-oriented transport *protocol* that reliably exchanges byte-streams of data in order and unduplicated between a local and remote *process*.

Transport Endpoint
An *endpoint* that connects *peer applications* at the *transport layer*.

Transport Layer
The *layer* in a *protocol stack* that is responsible for end-to-end data transfer and *connection* management.

Transport Layer Interface (TLI)
TLI is a set of *function* calls provided in System V UNIX and used by *network applications* to establish *connections* and communicate via connected *transport endpoints*.

Two-way Method Invocation
A call to a *method* that passes *parameters* to a *server object* and receives results back from the server. (Compare with *One-way Method Invocation*.)

Type-Safety
A property enforced by a programming language's type system to ensure that only valid operations can be invoked on instances of types.

Unicode
A standard for character representation using wide-character coding. Unicode includes characters for most written languages, as well as representations for punctuation, mathematical notations, and other symbols.

Unmarshaling
See *Demarshaling*.

Upcall
A *callback* that is invoked from a lower *layer* of a *software architecture* to a higher layer.

User Datagram Protocol (UDP)
An unreliable, connectionless transport *protocol* that exchanges datagram *messages* between local and remote *processes*.

View
A view presents a partial aspect of a *software architecture* that emphasizes specific properties of a software system.

Virtual Machine
An abstraction *layer* that offers a set of *services* to higher-level *applications* or other virtual machines.

Virtual Memory
An *operating system* mechanism that permits developers to program *applications* whose address space is larger than the amount of physical memory on the computer.

Write-side Critical Section   A set of sequences of instructions that obeys the following *invariant*: at most one *thread* or *process* may be executing in the write-side *critical section*, and while a thread or process is executing in this write-site critical section, no thread or process can execute in a corresponding read-side critical section. (Compare with *Read-side Critical Section*.)

References

[ACM01]   D. Alur, J. Crupi, D. Malks: *Core J2EE Patterns, Best Practices and Design Strategies*, Second edition, Prentice Hall, 2005

[AIS77]   C. Alexander, S. Ishikawa, M. Silverstein with M. Jacobson, I. Fiksdahl-King, S. Angel: *A Pattern Language—Towns · Buildings · Construction*, Oxford University Press, 1977

[Ale79]   C. Alexander: *The Timeless Way of Building*, Oxford University Press, 1979

[Ale01]   A. Alexandrescu: *Modern C++ Design: Generic Programming and Design Patterns Applied*, Addison-Wesley 2001

[And96]   B. Anderson: *Null Object*, presented at the First European Conference on Pattern Languages of Programming, EuroPLoP 1996, 1996

[Apache06]   Apache Software Foundation: *Web Service Invocation Framework*, http:// ws.apache.org/wsif/

[BEA06]   BEA Systems: *BEA MessageQ Product Overview*, http://www.bea.com/ framework.jsp?CNT=overview.htm&FP=/content/products/more/ messageq/, BEA Systems, 2006

[Beck97]   K. Beck: *Smalltalk Best Practices*, Prentice Hall, 1996

[BeCu87]   K. Beck, W. Cunningham: *Using Pattern Languages for Object-Oriented Programs*, submission to the OOPSLA '87 workshop on Specification and Design for Object-Oriented Programming, October 1987

[BeLe76]   L. A. Belady, M. M. Lehman: *A Model of Large Program Development*, IBM Systems Journal, Volume 15(3), pp. 225–252, 1976

[Bell06]   A. E. Bell: *Software Development Amidst the Whiz of Silver Bullets...*, ACM Queue Volume 4, No. 5, June 2006

[Ben86]   J. Bentley: *Little Languages*, Communications of the ACM, 29(8), pp. 711–721, August 1986

[BGB00]   G. Bollella, J. Gosling, B. Brosgol, P. Dibble, S. Furr, D. Hardin, M. Turnbull: *The Real-Time Specification for Java*, Addison-Wesley, 2000

[Bir05]   K. Birman: *Reliable Distributed Systems: Technologies, Web Services, and Applications*, Springer, 2005

[Bosch00]   J. Bosch: *Design and Use of Software Architectures—Adapting and Evolving a Product-Line Approach*, Addison-Wesley, 2000

[Box97]   D. Box: *Essential COM*, Addison-Wesley, 1997

[Bus03]   F. Buschmann: *Notes on The Forgotten Art of Building Good Software Architectures*, Tutorial at the Eighth Conference on Java and Object-Oriented Technology, JAOO 2003, Aarhus, Denmark, 2003

[BW95]   K. Brown, B. Whitenack: *Crossing Chasms: A Pattern Language for Object-RDBMS Integration*, in [PLoPD2], 1995

[Celtix06]   Celtix Enterprise Service Bus: *User Guides*, http://celtix.objectweb.org/, 2006

[CLF93]   D. de Champeaux, D. Lea, P. Faure: *Object-Oriented System Development*, Addison-Wesley, 1993

[ClNo01]   P. Clements, L. Northrop: *Software Product Lines: Practices and Patterns*, Addison-Wesley, 2001

[CMH83]   K. M. Chandy, J. Misra, and L. M. Haas: *Distributed Deadlock Detection*, ACM Transactions on Computer Systems, 1(2), 143–156, May 1983.

[Cope92]   J. O. Coplien: *Advanced C++ Programming Styles and Idioms*, Addison- Wesley, 1991

[Cope96]   J. O. Coplien: *Software Patterns*, SIGS Books, New York, New York, 1996. See also http://users.rcn.com/jcoplien/Patterns/WhitePaper/.

[Cope98]   J. O. Coplien: *Multi-Paradigm Design for C++*, Addison-Wesley, 1998

[CSKO+02]   A. Corsaro, D. C. Schmidt, R. Klefstad, Carlos O'Ryan: *Virtual Component: A Design Pattern for Memory-Constrained Embedded Applications*, Proceedings of the Ninth Annual Conference on the Pattern Languages of Programs, Monticello, Illinois, September 2002

[CzEi02]   C. Czarnecki, U. Eisenecker: *Generative Programming, Methods, Tools and Applications*, Addison-Wesley, 2000

References 575

[DBOSG05]   G. Deng, J. Balasubramanian, W. Otte, D. C. Schmidt, A. Gokhale: *DAnCE: A QoS-Enabled Component Deployment and Configuration Engine*, Proceedings of the Third Working Conference on Component Deployment, Grenoble, France, November, 2005

[DeGe04]   J. Dean, S. Ghemawat: *MapReduce: Simplified Data Processing on Large Clusters,* OSDI '04—Sixth Symposium on Operating System Design and Implementation, San Francisco, CA, December, 2004.

[DOC]   The DOC group open-source software, Institute for Software Integrated Systems, Vanderbilt University, www.dre.vanderbilt.edu

[DWT04]   A. Dennis, B. Haley Wixom, D. Tegarden: *Systems Analysis and Design with UML Version 2.0: An Object-Oriented Approach*, John Wiley & Sons, 2004

[DyAn98]   P. Dyson, B. Anderson: *State Patterns*, in [PLoPD3], 1997

[Eng99]   J. Engel: *Programming for the Java Virtual Machine*, Addison-Wesley, 1999

[EPL02]   R. Elfwing, U. Paulsson, L. Lundberg: *Performance of SOAP in Web Service Environment Compared to CORBA*, Proceedings of the Ninth Asia–Pacific Software Engineering Conference, December 2002, Gold Coast, Australia

[Evans03]   E. Evans: *Domain-Driven Design*, Addison-Wesley, 2003

[FBBOR99]   M. Fowler, K. Beck, J. Brant, W. Opdyke, D. Roberts: *Refactoring: Improving the Design of Existing Code*, Addison-Wesley, 1999

[FeMac02]   A. Ferrara, M. MacDonald: *Programming .NET Web Services*, O'Reilly, 2002

[FGMFB97]   R. Fielding, J. Gettys, J. Mogul, H. Frystyk, T. Berners-Lee: *Hypertext Transfer Protocol—HTTP/1.1*, Network Working Group, RFC 2068, January 1997

[FJS99a]   M. Fayad, R. Johnson, D. C. Schmidt (eds.): *Implementing Application Frameworks: Object-Oriented Frameworks at Work*, John Wiley & Sons, New York, NY, 1999

[FJS99b]   M. Fayad, R. Johnson, D. C. Schmidt (eds.): *Building Application Frameworks: Object-Oriented Foundations of Framework Design*, John Wiley & Sons, New York, NY, 1999

[Fow97]   M. Fowler: *Analysis Patterns*, Addison-Wesley, 1997

[Fow03a]   M. Fowler: *Patterns of Enterprise Application Architecture*, Addison-Wesley, 2002

[Fow03b]   M. Fowler: *UML Distilled: A Brief Guide to the Standard Object Modeling Language*, Third edition, Addison-Wesley, 2003

[Fow06]   M. Fowler: *The Model-View-Presenter Pattern*, http://www.martinfowler.com/eaaDev/ModelViewPresenter.html, 2006

[FoYo99]   B. Foote, J. Yoder: *Big Ball of Mud*, in [PLoPD4], 1999

[Fri06]   T. L. Friedman: *The World is Flat: A Brief History of the Twenty-First Century*, expanded and updated version, Farrar, Straus and Giroux, 2006

[Gar05]   J. J. Garrett: *Ajax: A New Approach to Web Applications*, February 2005, http://adaptivepath.com/publications/essays/archives/000385.php

[Gam92]   E. Gamma: *Objektorientierte Software-Entwicklung am Beispiel von ET++: Design-Muster*, Klassenbibliotheken, Werkzeuge, Springer, 1992

[Gam97]   E. Gamma: personal communication, 1997

[GoF95]   E. Gamma, R. Helm, R. Johnson, J. Vlissides: *Design Patterns: Elements of Reusable Object-Oriented Software*, Addison-Wesley, 1995

[GS97a]   A. Gokhale, D. C. Schmidt: *Design Principles and Optimizations for High-Performance ORBs*, OOPSLA '97 Poster Session, Atlanta, GA, ACM, 1997

[GS97b]   A. Gokhale, D. C. Schmidt: *Evaluating the Performance of Demultiplexing Strategies for Real-Time CORBA*, Proceedings of GLOBECOM '97, Phoenix, AZ, 1EEE, 1997

[GS98]   A. Gokhale, D. C. Schmidt: *Optimizing A CORBA IIOP Protocol Engine for Minimal Footprint Multimedia Systems*, submitted to *IEEE Journal on Selected Areas in Communications*, special issue on Service Enabling Platforms for Networked Multimedia Systems, 1998

[HBS+02]   M. Hapner, R. Burridge, R. Sharma, J. Fialli, K. Haase: *Java Message Service API Tutorial and Reference: Messaging for the J2EE Platform*, Addison-Wesley, 2002

[Hearsay02]   Kloster Hearsay (the daily EuroPLoP newspaper), Issue 02/2002, Joe Bergin: *Do the Right Thing*, Irsee, Germany, 2002

[Hen99]   K. Henney: *Collections for States*, Proceedings of the Fourth European Conference on Pattern Languages of Programming, EuroPLoP 1999, Irsee, Universitätsverlag Konstanz, July 2001

[Hen00a]   K. Henney: *Patterns of Value, Java Report* 5(2), February 2000

[Hen00b]   K. Henney: *Value Added, Java Report* 5(4), April 2000

[Hen00c]   K. Henney: *A Tale of Two Patterns, Java Report*, SIGS Publications, December 2000

[Hen01a]   K. Henney: *C++ Patterns—Executing Around Sequences*, Proceedings of the Fifth European Conference on Pattern Languages of Programming, EuroPLoP 2000, Irsee, Universitätsverlag Konstanz, July 2001

[Hen01b]   K. Henney: *C++ Patterns—Reference Accounting*, Proceedings of the Sixth European Conference on Pattern Languages of Programming, EuroPLoP 2001, Irsee, Universitätsverlag Konstanz, July 2002

[Hen01c]   K. Henney: *A Tale of Three Patterns, Java Report*, SIGS Publications, October 2001

[Hen02a]   K. Henney: *Null Object*, Proceedings of the Seventh European Conference on Pattern Languages of Programming, EuroPLoP 2002, Irsee, Universitätsverlag Konstanz, July 2003

[Hen02b]   K. Henney: *Patterns in Java: The Importance of Symmetry*, JavaSpektrum, Issue 6, 2002, SIGS–DATACOM GmbH, Germany

[Hen02c]   K. Henney: *Methods for States*, Proceedings of the First Nordic Conference on Pattern Languages of Programming, VikingPLoP 2002, Helsingør, Denmark Universitätsverlag Konstanz, July 2003

[Hen05]   K. Henney: *Context Encapsulation—Three Stories, A Language, and Some Sequences*, Proceedings of the Tenth European Conference on Pattern Languages of Programming, EuroPLoP 2005, Irsee, Universitätsverlag Konstanz, July 2006

[HMS97]   J. Hu, S. Mungee, D. C. Schmidt: *Principles for Developing and Measuring High-Performance Web Servers over ATM*, Proceedings of INFOCOM '98, March/April 1998

[HoWo03]   G. Hohpe, B. Woolf: *Enterprise Integration Patterns—Designing, Building, and Deploying Messaging Solutions*, Addison-Wesley, 2003

[HPS97]   J. Hu, I. Pyarali, D. C. Schmidt: *Measuring the Impact of Event Dispatching and Concurrency Models on Web Server Performance Over High-Speed Networks*, Proceedings of the 2nd Global Internet Conference, IEEE, 1997

[HV99]   M. Henning, S. Vinoski: *Advanced CORBA Programming with C++*, Addison-Wesley, 1999

[IBM99]   IBM Corporation: *MQSeries Version 5.1 Administration and Programming Examples*, IBM Redbooks, 1999

[IBM06]   IBM Corporation: *Cell Broadband Engine Programming Handbook*, pp. 603, April 2006

[IEEE96]   IEEE: *Threads Extension for Portable Operating Systems*, (Draft 10), February 1996

[John97]   R. Johnson: *Frameworks = Patterns + Components*, Communications of the ACM, M. Fayad, D.C. Schmidt (eds.), Volume 40, No. 10, October 1997

[Kaye03]   D. Kaye: *Loosely Coupled, The Missing Pieces of Web Services*, Rds Associates, 2003

[KC97]   W. Keller, J. Coldewey: *Accessing Relational Databases*, in [PLoPD3], 1997

[Kel04]   A. Kelly: *Encapsulated Context*, Proceedings of the Eighth European Conference on Pattern Languages of Programming, EuroPLoP 2003, Irsee, Universitätsverlag Konstanz, July 2004

[Kel99]   W. Keller: *Object/Relational Access Layer*, in Proceedings of the Third European Conference on Pattern Languages of Programming, EuroPLoP 1998, Irsee, Universitätsverlag Konstanz, July 1999

[KGS+05]   A. S. Krishna, A. Gokhale, D. C. Schmidt, V. P. Ranganath, J. Hatcliff: *Model-Driven Middleware Specialization Techniques for Software Product-Line Architectures in Distributed Real-Time and Embedded Systems*, Proceedings of the MODELS 2005 workshop on MDD for Software Product-Lines, Half Moon Bay, Jamaica, October 2005

[KLLM95]   G. Kiczales, R. DeLine, A. Lee, C. Maeda: *Open Implementation—Analysis and Design™ of Substrate Software*, Tutorial #21 of OOPSLA '95, October 1995

[Kof04]   T. Kofler: *Robust Iterators for ET++, Structured Programming*, Volume 14, Number 2, pp. 62–85, 1993

[KSK04]   A. S. Krishna, D. C. Schmidt, R. Klefstad: *Enhancing Real-Time CORBA via Real-Time Java Features*, Proceedings of the Twenty-Fourth IEEE International Conference on Distributed Computing Systems (ICDCS), Tokyo, Japan, May 2004

[KSS05]   A. Krishna, D. C. Schmidt, M. Stal: *Context Object: A Design Pattern for Efficient Middleware Request Processing*, Proceedings of the Twelfth Pattern Language of Programming Conference, Allerton Park, Illinois, September 2005

[Lak95]   J. Lakos: *Large-Scale C++ Software Design*, Addison-Wesley, 1995

[Lea02]   D. Lea: personal communication, May 2002

[Lea99]   D. Lea: *Concurrent Programming in Java: Design Principles and Patterns*, Second edition, Addison-Wesley, 2000

[Lee06]   E. A. Lee: *The Problem with Threads*, IEEE Computer, May 2006

[Lew95]   B. Lewis, D. J Berg: *Threads Primer: A Guide to Multithreaded Programming*, Prentice Hall, 1995

[LGS00]   D. L. Levine, C. D. Gill, D. C. Schmidt: *Object Lifetime Manager—A Complementary Pattern for Controlling Object Creation and Destruction*, in *Design Patterns in Communications*, L. Rising (ed.), Cambridge University Press, 2001

[Lin03]   D. Linthicum: *Next Generation Application Integration: From Simple Information to Web Services*, Addison-Wesley, 2003

[LY99]   T. Lindholm, F. Yellin: *The Java Virtual Machine Specification*, Second edition, Addison-Wesley, 1999

[Maf96]   S. Maffeis: *The Object Group Design Pattern*, Proceedings of the 1996 USENIX Conference on Object-Oriented Technologies, USENIX, Toronto, Canada, June 1996

[MaHa99]   V. Matena, M Hapner: *Enterprise JavaBeans*, Version 1.1, Sun Microsystems Inc., 1999

[Mar04]   R. Martin: *The Dependency Inversion Principle*, C++ Report, Volume 8, No 6, May 1996

[McK96]   P. E. McKenney: *Selecting Locking Designs for Parallel Programs*, in [PLoPD2], 1996

[MeAl04a]   S. Meyers, A. Alexandrescu: *C++ and the Perils of Double-Checked Locking: Part I*, Dr. Dobb's Journal, June 2004

[MeAl04b]   S. Meyers, A. Alexandrescu: *C++ and the Perils of Double-Checked Locking: Part II*, Dr. Dobb's Journal, June 2004

[Mes95]   G. Meszaros: *Half-Object plus Protocol*, in [PLoPD1], 1995

[Mes96]   G. Meszaros: *A Pattern Language for Improving the Capacity of Reactive Systems*, in [PLoPD2], 1996

[Mey97] B. Meyer: *Object-Oriented Software Construction*, Second edition, Prentice Hall, 1997

[MMW06] C. McMurtry, M. Mercuri, N. Watling: *Microsoft Windows Communication Foundation: Hands-On!*, Sams, 2006

[MPY+04] A. Memon, A. Porter, C. Yilmaz, A. Nagarajan, D. C. Schmidt, B. Natarajan: *Skoll: Distributed Continuous Quality Assurance*, Proceedings of the 26th IEEE/ACM International Conference on Software Engineering, Edinburgh, Scotland, May 2004

[MS03] Microsoft Corporation: *Enterprise Solution Patterns Using Microsoft .NET Version 2.0*, Microsoft Press, 2003

[MSS00] S. Mungee, N. Surendran, D. C. Schmidt: *The Design and Performance of a CORBA Audio/Video Streaming Service*, in *Design and Management of Multimedia Information Systems: Opportunities and Challenges*, M. Syed (ed.), Idea Group Publishing, Hershey, PA, 2000

[Mule06] Mule Enterprise Service Bus: user documentation, `http://mule.codehaus.org/`, 2006

[OASIS06a] Organization for the Advancement of Structured Information Standards: *Reference Model for Service-Oriented Architecture*, Version 1.0, Committee Specification, July 2006, `http://docs.oasis-open.org/soa-rm/v1.0/soa-rm.pdf`

Organization for the Advancement of Structured Information Standards: *Web Services Base Notification*, Version 1.3, Committee Specification, July 2006

[OG94] The Open Group: *DCE: Remote Procedure Call*, available at `http://www.opengroup.org/bookstore/catalog/c309.htm`, 1994

[OKS+00] C. O'Ryan, F. Kuhns, D. C. Schmidt, O. Othman, J. Parsons: *The Design and Performance of a Pluggable Protocols Framework for Real-Time Distributed Object Computing Middleware*, Proceedings of the ACM/IFIP Middleware 2000 Conference, Pallisades, New York, April 2000

[OMG02] Object Management Group: *CORBA Component Model*, Version 3.0, June 2002

[OMG03a] Object Management Group: *Real-Time CORBA Specification (static scheduling)*, Version 1.2, January 2005 `http://www.omg.org/cgi-bin/doc?formal/05-01-04`

[OMG03b] Object Management Group: *Specification for Deployment and Configuration of Component-based Distributed Applications*, adopted submission, OMG document ptc/03-07-08, 2003

[OMG04a] Object Management Group: *Common Object Request Broker Architecture*, Version 3.0.3, March 2004

[OMG04b] Object Management Group: *Lightweight CORBA Component Model*, draft adopted specification, May 2004 `http://www.omg.org/cgi-bin/doc?realtime/2003-05-05`

[OMG04c] Object Management Group: *Notification Service Specification*, Version 1.1, October 2004

[OMG05a] Object Management Group: *Real-Time CORBA Specification (dynamic scheduling)*, Version 1.2, January 2005

[OMG05b] Object Management Group: *Real-Time Data Distribution Service*, Version 1.1, December 2005

[Pal05] D. Pallmann: *Programming INDIGO*, Microsoft Press, 2005

[Par94] D. L. Parnas: *Software Aging*, Proceedings of the Sixteenth International Conference on Software Engineering (ICSE–16), Sorrento, Italy, May 1994

[PHS96] I. Pyarali, T. H. Harrison, D. C. Schmidt: *Design and Performance of an Object-Oriented Framework for High-Performance Electronic Medical Imaging*, *USENIX Computing Systems*, Volume 9, November/December 1996

[PLoPD1] J. O. Coplien, D. C. Schmidt (eds.): *Pattern Languages of Program Design*, Addison-Wesley, 1995 (a book publishing the reviewed Proceedings of the First International Conference on Pattern Languages of Programming, Monticello, Illinois, 1994)

[PLoPD2] J. O. Coplien, N. Kerth, J. Vlissides (eds.): *Pattern Languages of Program Design 2*, Addison-Wesley, 1996 (a book publishing the reviewed Proceedings of the Second International Conference on Pattern Languages of Programming, Monticello, Illinois, 1995)

[PLoPD3]   F. Buschmann, R. C. Martin, D. Riehle (eds.): *Pattern Languages of Program Design 3*, Addison-Wesley, 1997 (a book publishing selected papers from the Third International Conference on Pattern Languages of Programming, Monticello, Illinois, USA, 1996, the First European Conference on Pattern Languages of Programming, Irsee, Bavaria, Germany, 1996, and the Telecommunication Pattern Workshop at OOPSLA '96, San Jose, California, USA, 1996)

[PLoPD4]   B. Foote, N. B. Harrison, H. Rohnert (eds.): *Pattern Languages of Program Design 4*, Addison-Wesley, 1999 (a book publishing selected papers from the Fourth and Fifth International Conference on Pattern Languages of Programming, Monticello, Illinois, USA, 1997 and 1998, and the Second and Third European Conference on Pattern Languages of Programming, Irsee, Bavaria, Germany, 1997 and 1998)

[PLoPD5]   D. Manolescu, J. Noble, M. Völter (eds.): *Pattern Languages of Program Design 5*, Addison-Wesley, 2006 (a book publishing selected papers from the Pattern Languages of Programming conference series from 1999–2004)

[POSA1]   F. Buschmann, R. Meunier, H. Rohnert, P. Sommerlad, M. Stal: *Pattern-Oriented Software Architecture, Volume 1: A System of Patterns*, John Wiley & Sons, 1996

[POSA2]   D. C. Schmidt, M. Stal, H. Rohnert, F. Buschmann: *Pattern-Oriented Software Architecture, Volume 2: Patterns for Concurrent and Networked Objects*, John Wiley & Sons, 2000

[POSA3]   P. Jain, M. Kircher: *Pattern-Oriented Software Architecture, Volume 3: Patterns for Resource Management*, John Wiley & Sons, 2004

[POSA5]   F. Buschmann, K. Henney, D. C. Schmidt: *Pattern-Oriented Software Architecture, Volume 5: On Patterns and Pattern Languages*, John Wiley & Sons, 2007

[POSIX95]   *Information Technology—Portable Operating System Interface (POSIX)—Part 1: System Application: Program Interface (API) [C Language]*, 1995

[PP03]   M. Poppendieck, T. Poppendieck: *Lean Software Development: An Agile Toolkit for Software Development Managers*, Addison-Wesley, 2003

[PPR]   *The Portland Pattern Repository*, http://www.c2.com

[Pree94]   W. Pree: *Design Patterns for Object-Oriented Software Development*, Addison-Wesley, 1994

[PRS+00]   I. Pyarali, C. O'Ryan, D. C. Schmidt, N. Wang, V. Kachroo, A. Gokhale: *Using Principle Patterns to Optimize Real-Time ORBs*, IEEE Concurrency Magazine, Volume 8, Number 1, January/March 2000

[PSC+01]   I. Pyarali, M. Spivak, R. K. Cytron, D. C. Schmidt: *Optimizing Threadpool Strategies for Real-Time CORBA*, Proceedings of the ACM Workshop on Optimization of Middleware and Distributed Systems, pp. 214–222, June, 2001, Snowbird, Utah

[Rago93]   S. Rago: *UNIX System V Network Programming*, Addison-Wesley, 1993

[Ram02]   I. Rammer: *Advanced .NET Remoting*, APress, 2002

[Ris01]   L. Rising: *Design Patterns in Communications Software*, Cambridge University Press, 2001

[RKF92]   W. Rosenberry, D. Kenney, G. Fischer: *Understanding DCE*, O'Reilly and Associates, Inc. 1992

[SC99]   D. C. Schmidt, C. Cleeland: *Applying Patterns to Develop Extensible ORB Middleware*, IEEE Communications Magazine, special issue on Design Patterns, April 1999

[SCA05]   Service Component Architecture: *Assembly Model Specification*, Version 0.9, November 2005

[Sch00]   D. C. Schmidt: *Applying a Pattern Language to Develop Application-Level Gateways*, in *Design Patterns in Communications*, ed. Linda Rising, Cambridge University Press, 2000

[ScSc01]   R. E. Schantz, D. C. Schmidt: *Middleware for Distributed Systems: Evolving the Common Structure for Network-Centric Applications*, in *Encyclopedia of Software Engineering*, J. Marciniak, G. Telecki (eds.), John Wiley & Sons, New York, 2001

[ScVi99]   D. C. Schmidt, S. Vinoski: *Collocation Optimizations for CORBA*, C++ Report, SIGS, Volume 11, Number 10, pp. 47–52, November/December 1999

[SDL05]   A. Prinz, J. Reed, R. Reed (eds.): *SDL 2005: Model Driven*, Proceedings of the 12th International SDL Forum, Grimstad, Norway, June 20–23, 2005, Springer, 2005

[SFHBS06]   M. Schumacher, E. Fernandez-Buglioni, D. Hybertson, F. Buschmann, P. Sommerlad: *Security Patterns: Integrating Security and Systems Engineering*, John Wiley & Sons, 2006

[SGS01]   V. Subramonian, C. Gill, D. Sharp: *Towards a Pattern Language for Networked Embedded Software Technology Middleware*, ACM OOPSLA Workshop on Towards Patterns and Pattern Languages for OO Distributed Real-Time and Embedded Systems, Tampa Bay, Florida, October 2001

[SH02]   D. C. Schmidt, S. D. Huston: *C++ Network Programming, Volume 1: Mastering Complexity with ACE and Patterns*, Addison-Wesley, 2002

[SH03]   D. C. Schmidt, S. D. Huston: *C++ Network Programming, Volume 2: Systematic Reuse with ACE and Frameworks*, Addison-Wesley, 2003

[SMFG00]   D. C. Schmidt, S. Mungee, S. Flores-Gaitan, A. Gokhale: *Software Architectures for Reducing Priority Inversion and Non-Determinism in Real-Time Object Request Brokers*, Journal of Real-Time Systems, special issue on Real-Time Computing in the Age of the Web and the Internet, ed. A. Stoyen, Kluwer, 2000

[SN96]   R. W. Schulte, Y. V. Natis: *Service Oriented Architectures*, Part 1, SSA Research Note SPA–401–068, Gartner, 12 April 1996

[SNG+02]   D. C. Schmidt, B. Natarajan, A. Gokhale, N. Wang, C. Gill, *TAO: A Pattern-Oriented Object Request Broker for Distributed Real-Time and Embedded Systems, IEEE Distributed Systems Online*, Volume 3, Number 2, February, 2002

[Sol98]   D. A. Solomon: *Inside Windows NT*, Second edition, Microsoft Press, 1998

[Som97]   P. Sommerlad: *Manager*, in [PLoPD3], 1997

[Ste93]   W. R. Stevens: *TCP/IP Illustrated, Volume 1*, Addison-Wesley, 1993

[Ste98]   W. R. Stevens: *Unix Network Programming, Volume 1: Networking APIs: Sockets and XTI*, Second edition, Prentice Hall, 1998

[Str97]   B. Stroustrup: *The C++ Programming Language*, Third edition, Addison-Wesley 1997

[StRa05]   W. R. Stevens, S. A. Rago: *Advanced Programming in the UNIX environment*, Second edition, Addison-Wesley, 2005

[StSc05]   M. Stal, D. C. Schmidt: *Activator*, Proceedings of the Twelfth Pattern Language of Programming Conference, Allerton Park, Illinois, September 2005

[Sun88]   Sun Microsystems: *Remote Procedure Call Protocol Specification*, Sun Microsystems Inc., RFC–1057, June 1988

[Sun03]   Sun Microsystems: *Enterprise JavaBeans Specification*, Version 2.1, Sun Microsystems Inc., November 2003

[Sun04a]   Sun Microsystems: *Enterprise JavaBeans Specification*, Version 3.0, early draft, Sun Microsystems Inc., June 2004

[Sun04b]   Sun Microsystems: *Java Message Service (JMS)*, Version 3.0, early draft, Sun Microsystems Inc., June 2004

[Sun04c]   Sun Microsystems: *Java Remote Method Invocations (RMI)*, Sun Microsystems Inc., 2004

[Sut05a]   H. Sutter: *The Free Lunch Is Over: A Fundamental Turn Toward Concurrency in Software*, Dr. Dobb's Journal, 30(3), March 2005

[Sut05b]   H. Sutter: *Software and the Concurrency Revolution*, *InStat Fall Processor Forum*, October 2005

[Szy02]   C. Szyperski: *Component Software: Beyond Object-Oriented Programming*, Second edition, Addison-Wesley, 2002

[Tan92]   A. S. Tanenbaum: *Modern Operating Systems*, Prentice Hall, 1992

[Tan95]   A. S. Tanenbaum: *Distributed Operating Systems*, Prentice Hall, 1995

[TaSte02]   A. S. Tanenbaum, M. van Steen: *Distributed Systems: Principles and Paradigms*, First edition, Prentice Hall, 2002

[Thai99]   T. L. Thai: *Learning DCOM*, O'Reilly, 1999

[Vin03]   S. Vinoski: *Toward Integration: Integration with Web Services*, IEEE Internet Computing, November/December 2003, pp. 75–77, 2003

[Vin04a]   S. Vinoski: *An Overview of Middleware*, Ninth International Conference on Reliable Software Technologies Ada-Europe 2004, Palma de Mallorca, 14–18 June 2004

[Vin04b]   S. Vinoski: *WS-Nonexistent Standards*, IEEE Internet Computing, November/December 2004, IEEE, 2004

[Vlis98a]   J. Vlissides: *Pattern Hatching: Design Patterns Applied*, Addison-Wesley, 1998

[Vlis98b]   J. Vlissides: *Pluggable Factory*, Part I, *C++ Report*, November/December 1998

[Vlis99]   J. Vlissides: *Pluggable Factory*, Part II, *C++ Report*, February 1999

[VKZ04]   M. Völter, M. Kircher, U. Zdun: *Remoting Patterns: Foundations of Enterprise, Internet and Realtime Distributed Object Middleware*, John Wiley & Sons, 2004

[VSW02]   M. Völter, A. Schmid, E. Wolff: *Server Component Patterns—Component Infrastructures Illustrated with EJB*, John Wiley & Sons, 2002

[W3C03]   World Wide Web Consortium: *SOAP Version 1.2*, June 2003

[W3C06a]   World Wide Web Consortium: *Web Services Description Language (WSDL) Version 2.0*, June 2006

[W3C06b]   World Wide Web Consortium: *Extensible Markup Language (XML) 1.1*, September 2006

[WK01]   J. Weigmann, G. Kilian: *Decentralization with PROFIBUS-DP: Architecture and Fundamentals, Configuration and Use with Step 7*, John Wiley & Sons, 2001

[Woolf97]   B. Woolf: *Null Object*, in [PLoPD3], 1997

[WRW96]   A. Wollrath, R. Riggs, J. Waldo: *A Distributed Object Model for the Java System, USENIX Computing Systems*, ed. Douglas C. Schmidt, Volume 9, Number 4, MIT Press, November/December 1996

[WSG+03]   N. Wang, D. C. Schmidt, A. Gokhale, C. Rodrigues, B. Natarajan, J. P. Loyall, R. E. Schantz, C. D. Gill: *QoS-Enabled Middleware*, in *Middleware for Communications*, pp. 131–162, John Wiley and Sons, New York, 2003

[WWWK96]   S. C. Kendall, J. Waldo, A. Wollrath, G. Wyant (eds.): *A Note On Distributed Computing, Technical Reports and Essay Series*, Sun Microsystems Inc., 1996, http://research.sun.com/techrep/1994/abstract-29.html

Index of Patterns

Page numbers in bold are for main pattern descriptions

Index of Names

Subject Index

Printed and bound by CPI Group (UK) Ltd, Croydon, CR0 4YY

27/10/2024

14580374-0002